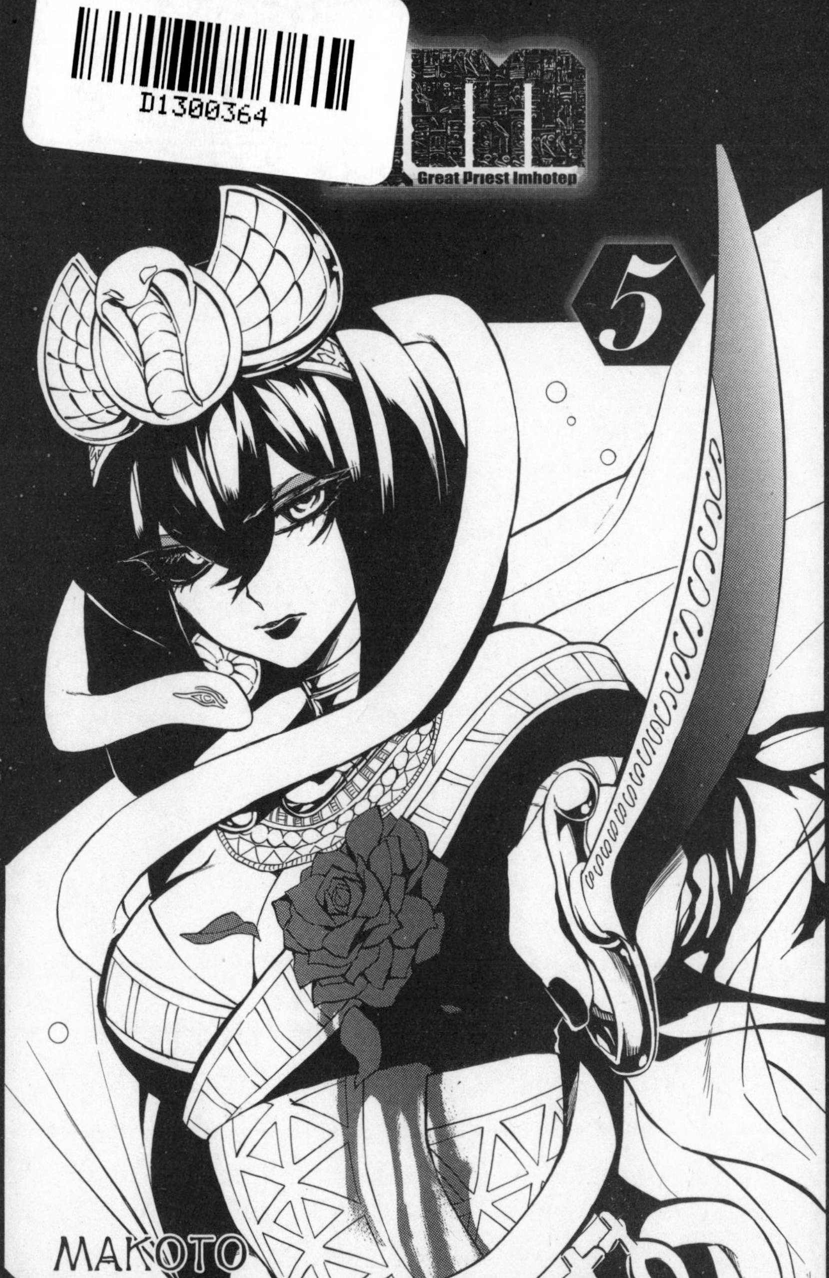
Great Priest Imhotep
5
MAKOTO
MORISHITA

Im

Great Priest Imhotep

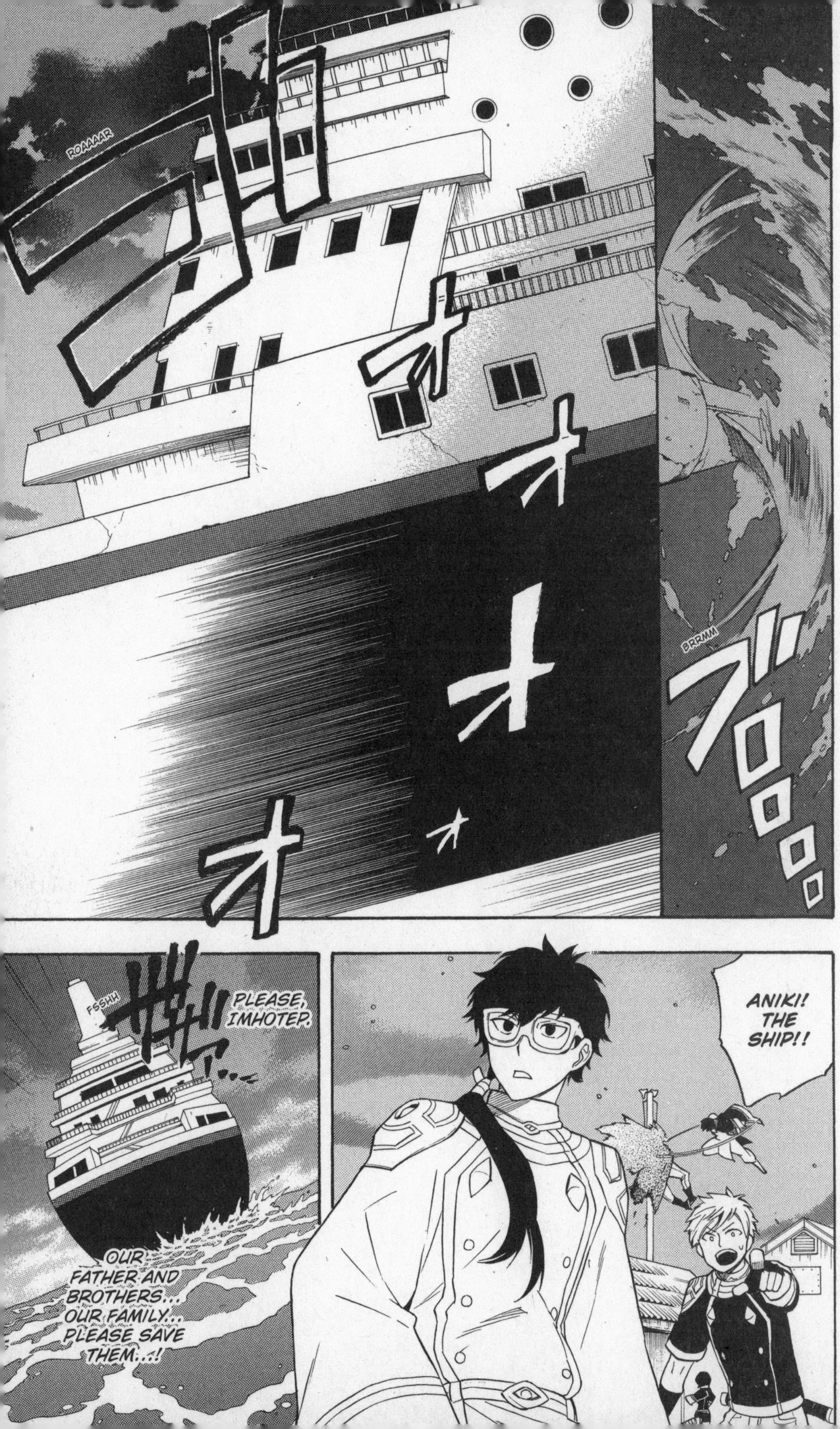
BRRMM
ROAAAR
ANIKI! THE SHIP!!
FSSHH
PLEASE, IMHOTEP.
OUR FATHER AND BROTHERS... OUR FAMILY... PLEASE SAVE THEM...!

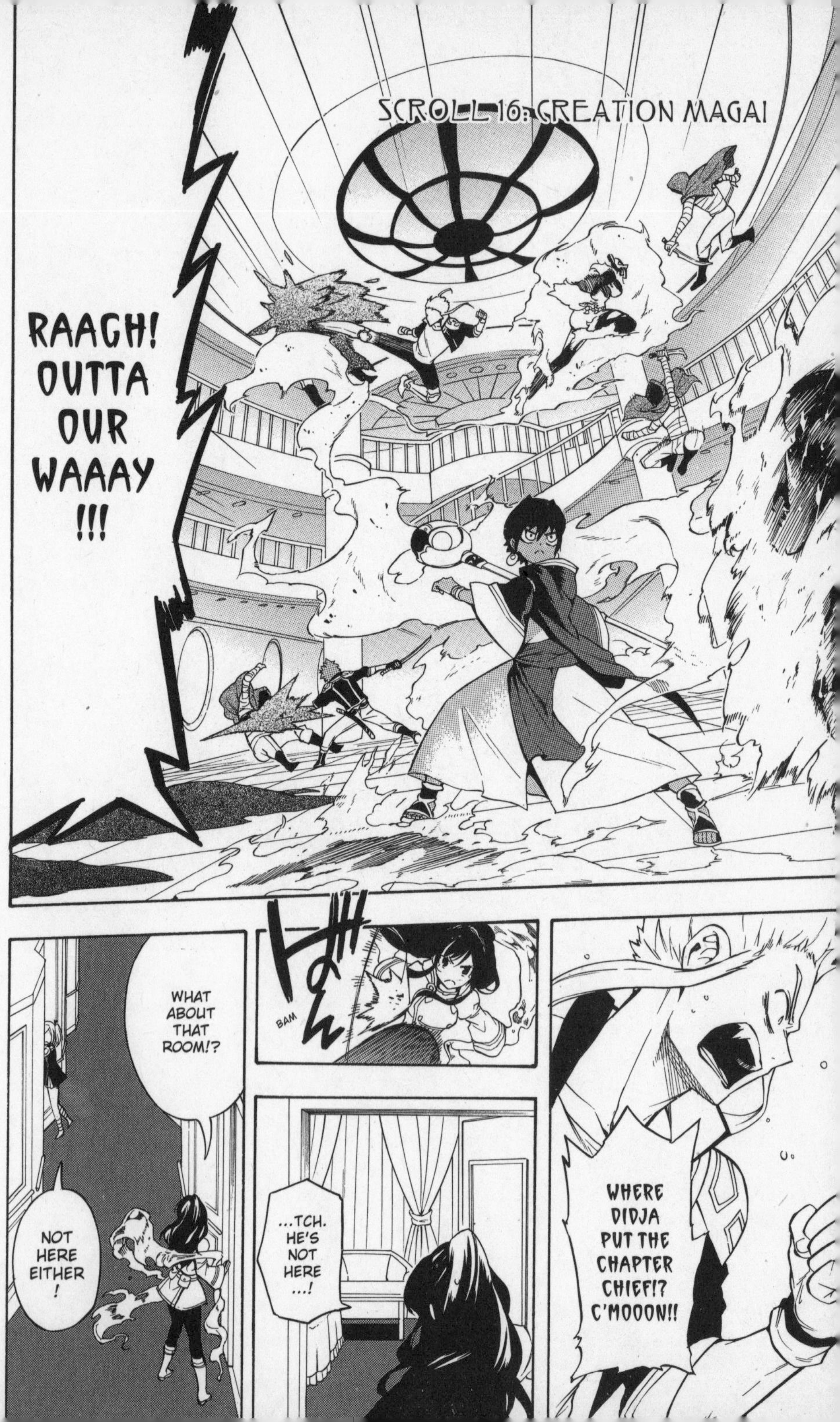
SCROLL 16: CREATION MAGAI
RAAGH! OUTTA OUR WAAAY!!!
WHERE DIDJA PUT THE CHAPTER CHIEF!? C'MOOON!!
BAM
...TCH. HE'S NOT HERE...!
WHAT ABOUT THAT ROOM!?
NOT HERE EITHER!

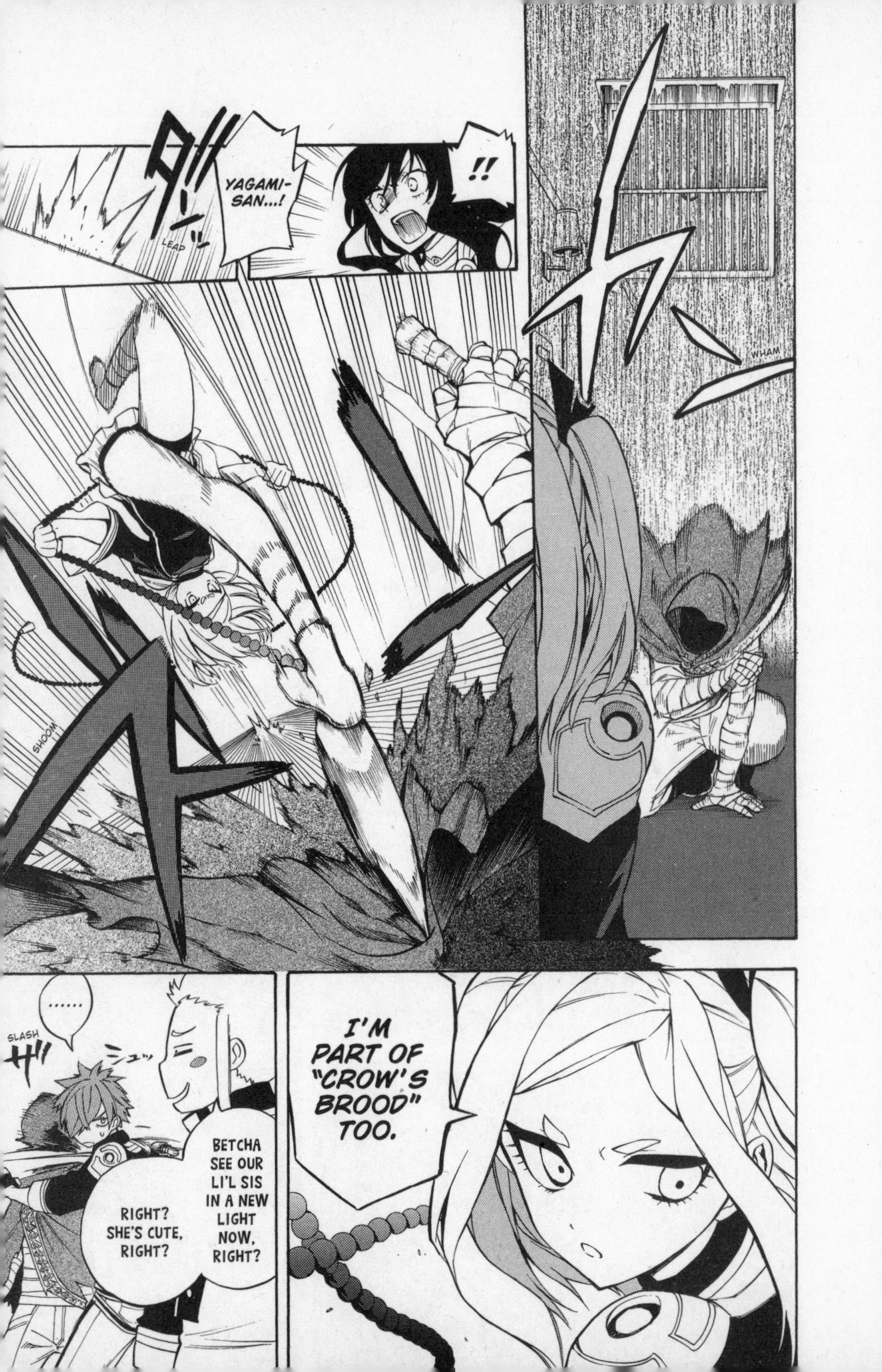

WHAM
!!
YAGAMI-SAN...!
LEAP
SHOOM
I'M PART OF "CROW'S BROOD" TOO.
......
SLASH
ザッ
シュッ
BETCHA SEE OUR LI'L SIS IN A NEW LIGHT NOW, RIGHT?
RIGHT? SHE'S CUTE, RIGHT?

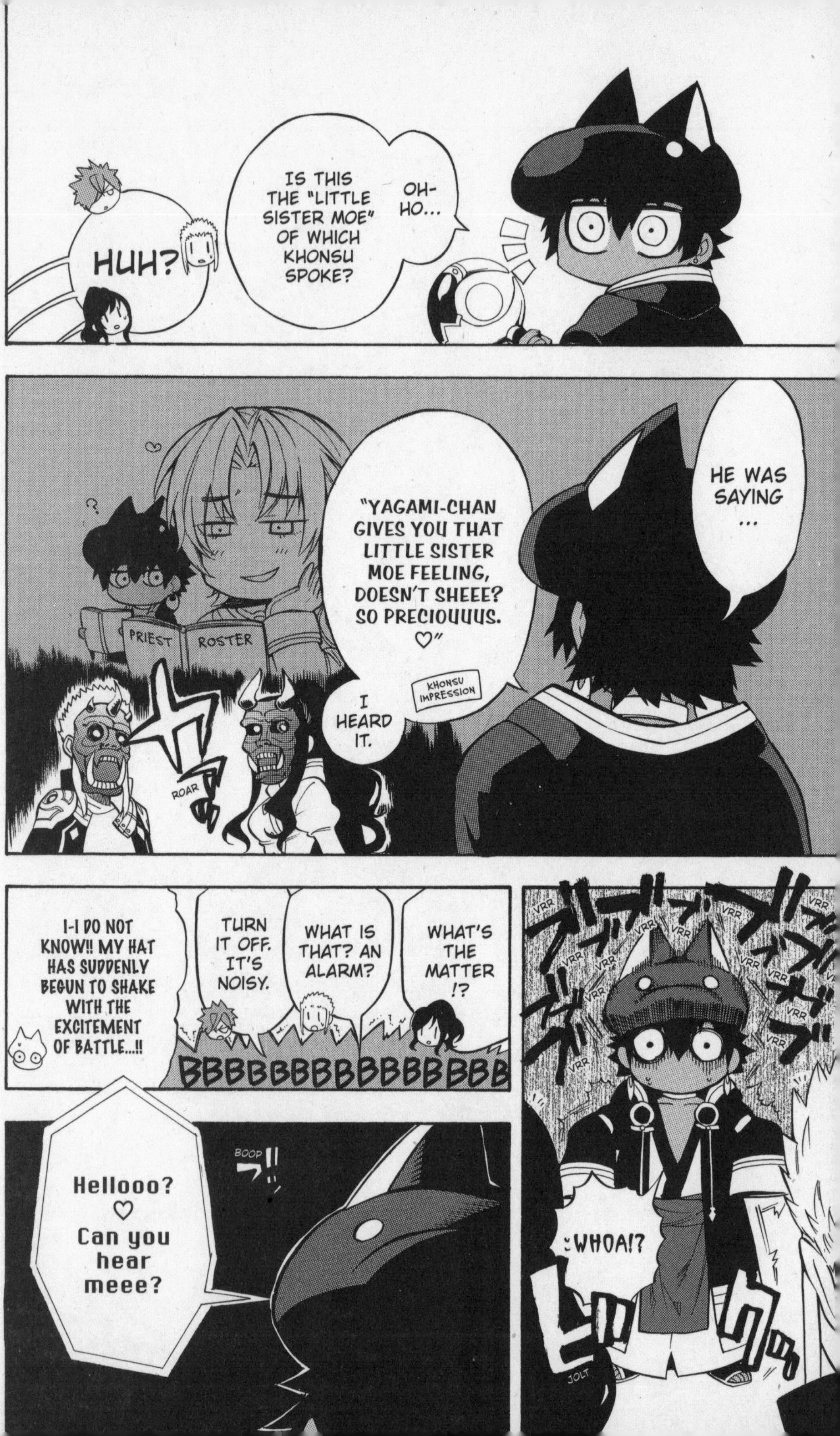
OH-HO… IS THIS THE "LITTLE SISTER MOE" OF WHICH KHONSU SPOKE?
HUH?
HE WAS SAYING…
"YAGAMI-CHAN GIVES YOU THAT LITTLE SISTER MOE FEELING, DOESN'T SHEEE? SO PRECIOUUUS. ♡"
KHONSU IMPRESSION
I HEARD IT.
PRIEST ROSTER
ROAR
VRR
WHOA!?
JOLT
WHAT'S THE MATTER!?
WHAT IS THAT? AN ALARM?
TURN IT OFF. IT'S NOISY.
I-I DO NOT KNOW!! MY HAT HAS SUDDENLY BEGUN TO SHAKE WITH THE EXCITEMENT OF BATTLE…!!
BBBBBBBBBBBBBBBB
BOOP
Hellooo? ♡ Can you hear meee?

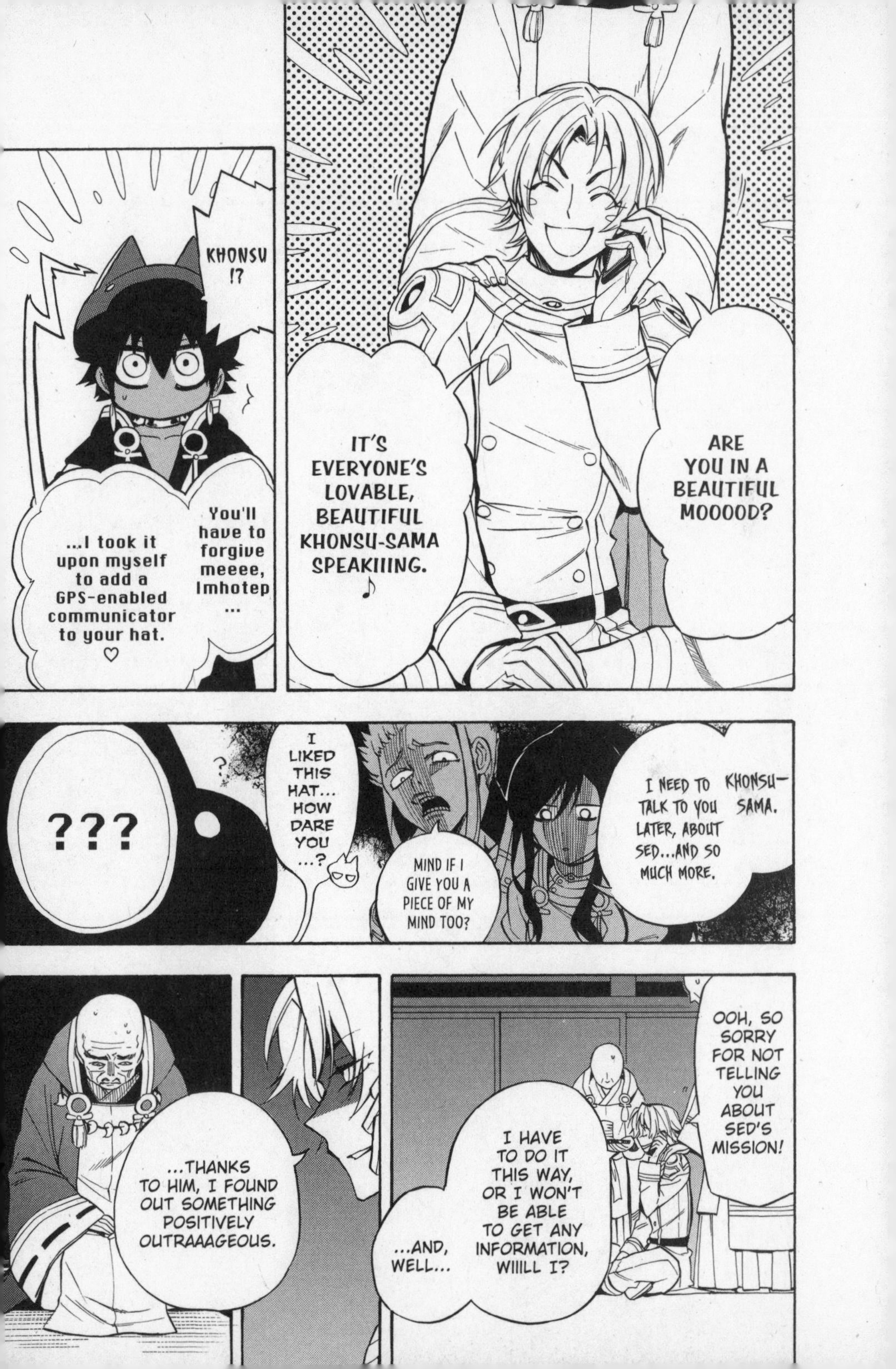
ARE YOU IN A BEAUTIFUL MOOOOD?
IT'S EVERYONE'S LOVABLE, BEAUTIFUL KHONSU-SAMA SPEAKIIING. ♪
KHONSU !?
You'll have to forgive meeee, Imhotep ...
...I took it upon myself to add a GPS-enabled communicator to your hat. ♡
KHONSU-SAMA.
I NEED TO TALK TO YOU LATER, ABOUT SED...AND SO MUCH MORE.
MIND IF I GIVE YOU A PIECE OF MY MIND TOO?
I LIKED THIS HAT... HOW DARE YOU ...?
???
OOH, SO SORRY FOR NOT TELLING YOU ABOUT SED'S MISSION!
I HAVE TO DO IT THIS WAY, OR I WON'T BE ABLE TO GET ANY INFORMATION, WIIILL I?
...AND, WELL...
...THANKS TO HIM, I FOUND OUT SOMETHING POSITIVELY OUTRAAAGEOUS.

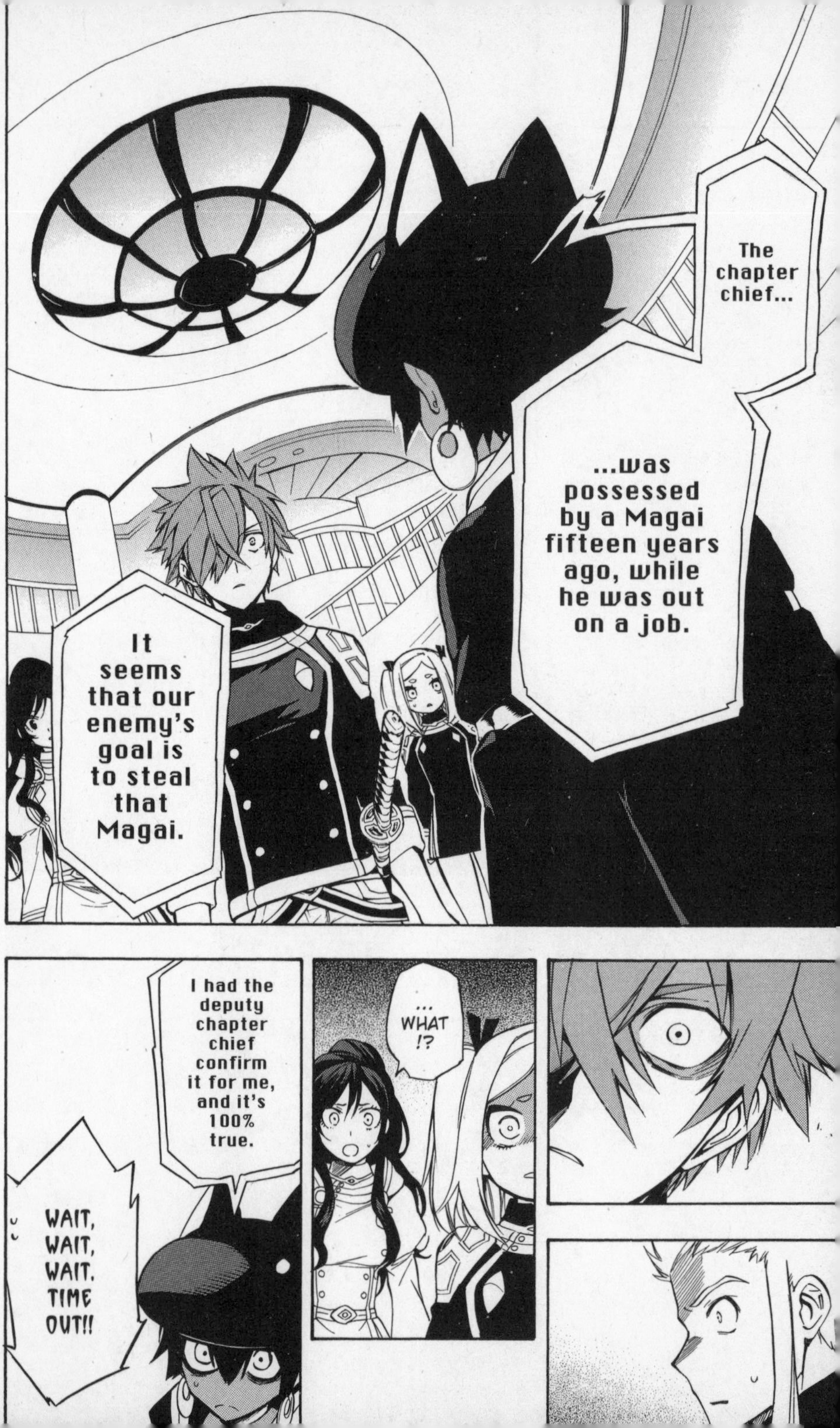
The chapter chief...
...was possessed by a Magai fifteen years ago, while he was out on a job.
It seems that our enemy's goal is to steal that Magai.
...WHAT!?
I had the deputy chapter chief confirm it for me, and it's 100% true.
WAIT, WAIT, WAIT. TIME OUT!!

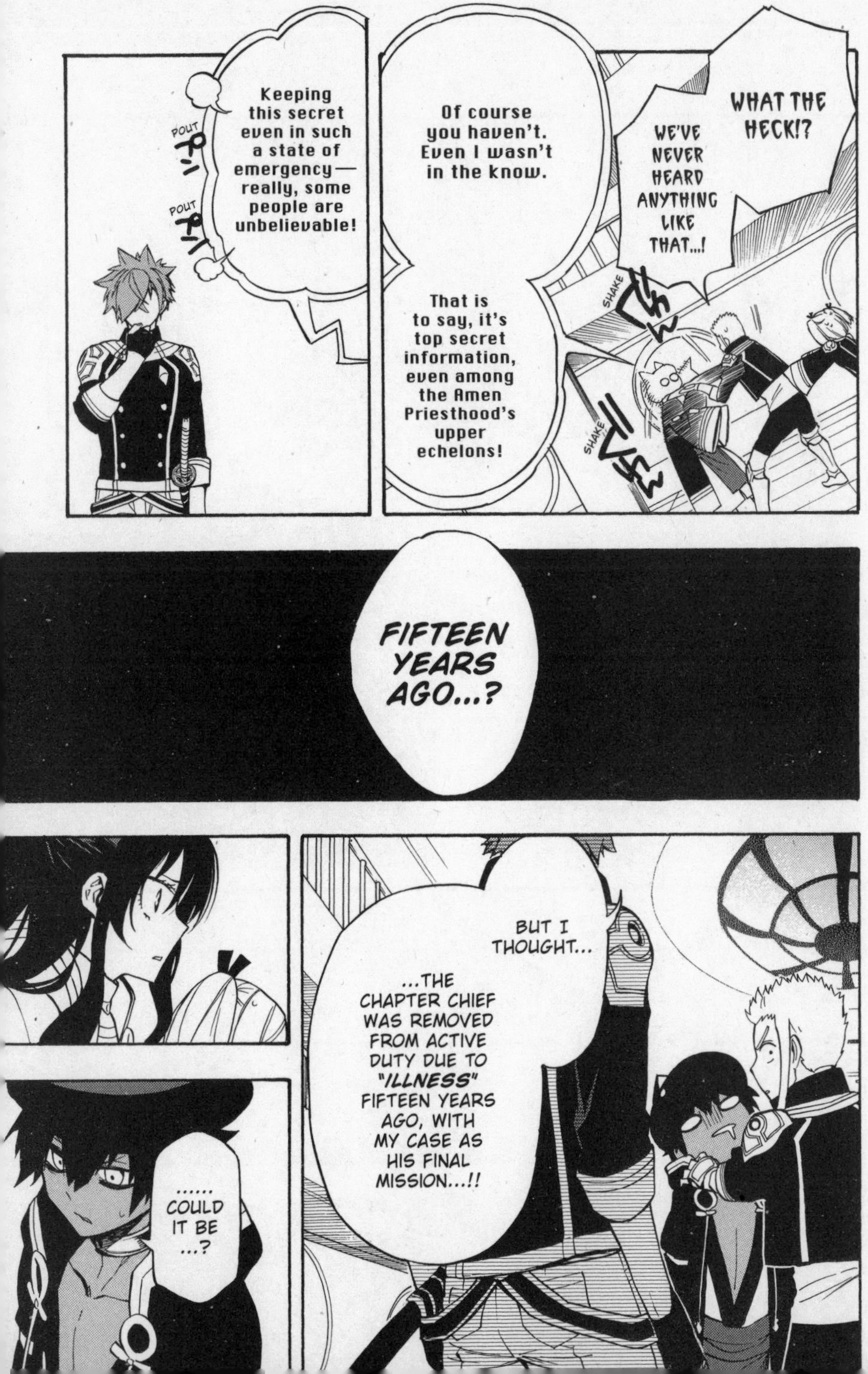
WHAT THE HECK!?
WE'VE NEVER HEARD ANYTHING LIKE THAT...!
SHAKE
SHAKE
Of course you haven't. Even I wasn't in the know.
That is to say, it's top secret information, even among the Amen Priesthood's upper echelons!
Keeping this secret even in such a state of emergency—really, some people are unbelievable!
POUT
POUT
FIFTEEN YEARS AGO...?
BUT I THOUGHT...
...THE CHAPTER CHIEF WAS REMOVED FROM ACTIVE DUTY DUE TO "ILLNESS" FIFTEEN YEARS AGO, WITH MY CASE AS HIS FINAL MISSION...!!
......COULD IT BE ...?

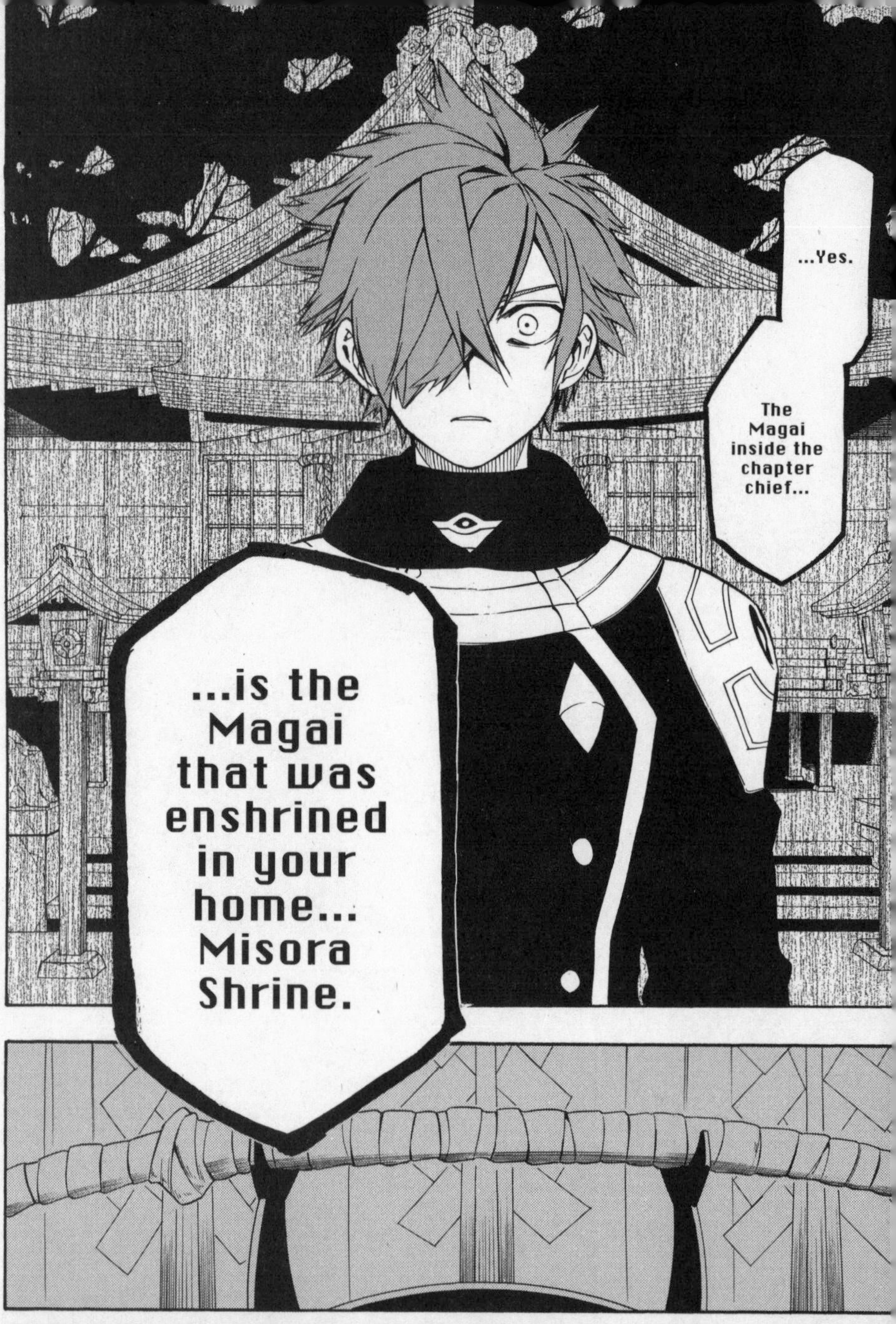
...Yes.
The Magai inside the chapter chief...
...is the Magai that was enshrined in your home... Misora Shrine.

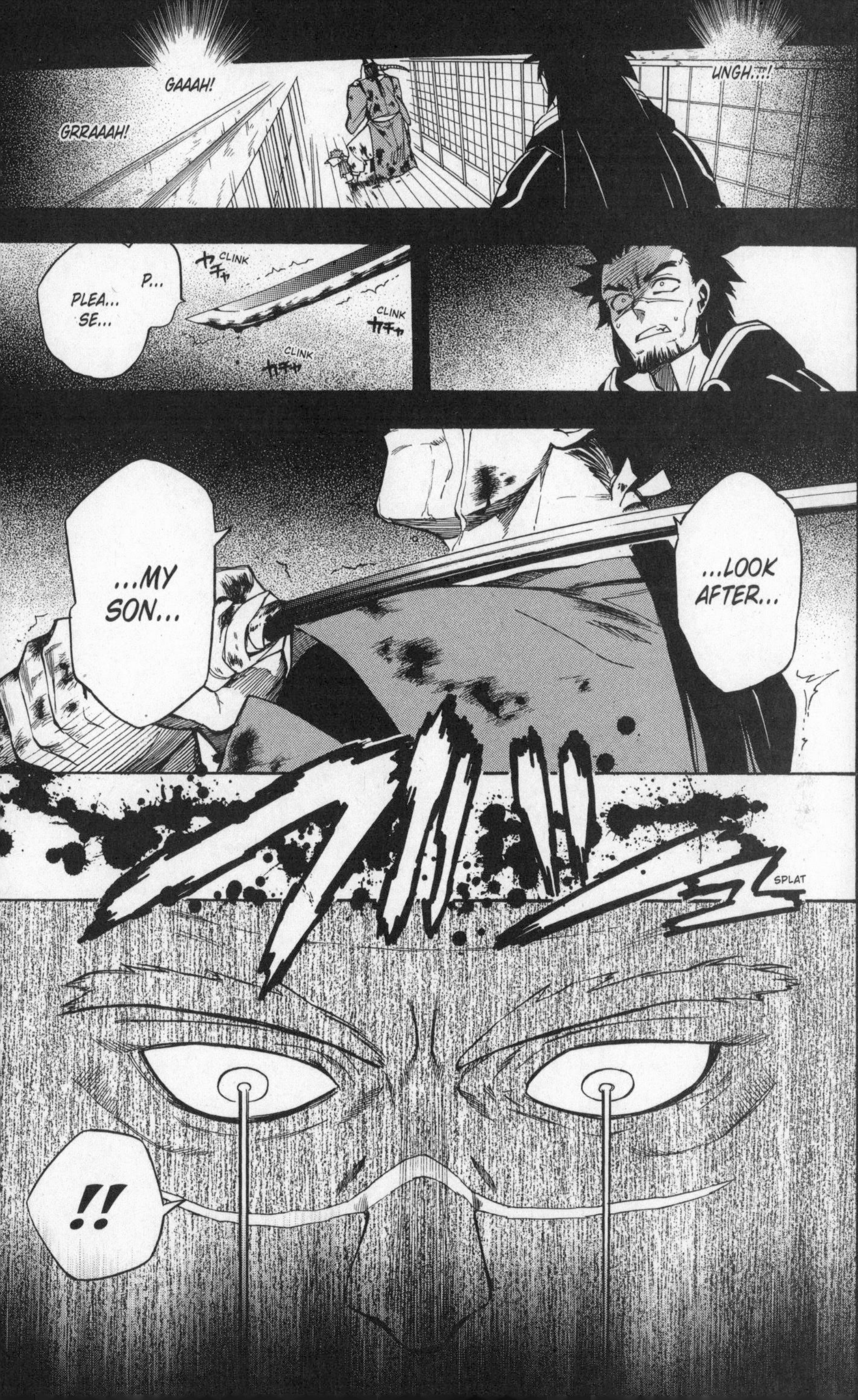
UNGH...!
GAAAH!
GRRAAAH!
P...
PLEA... SE...
CLINK
CLINK
CLINK
...LOOK AFTER...
...MY SON...
SPLAT
!!

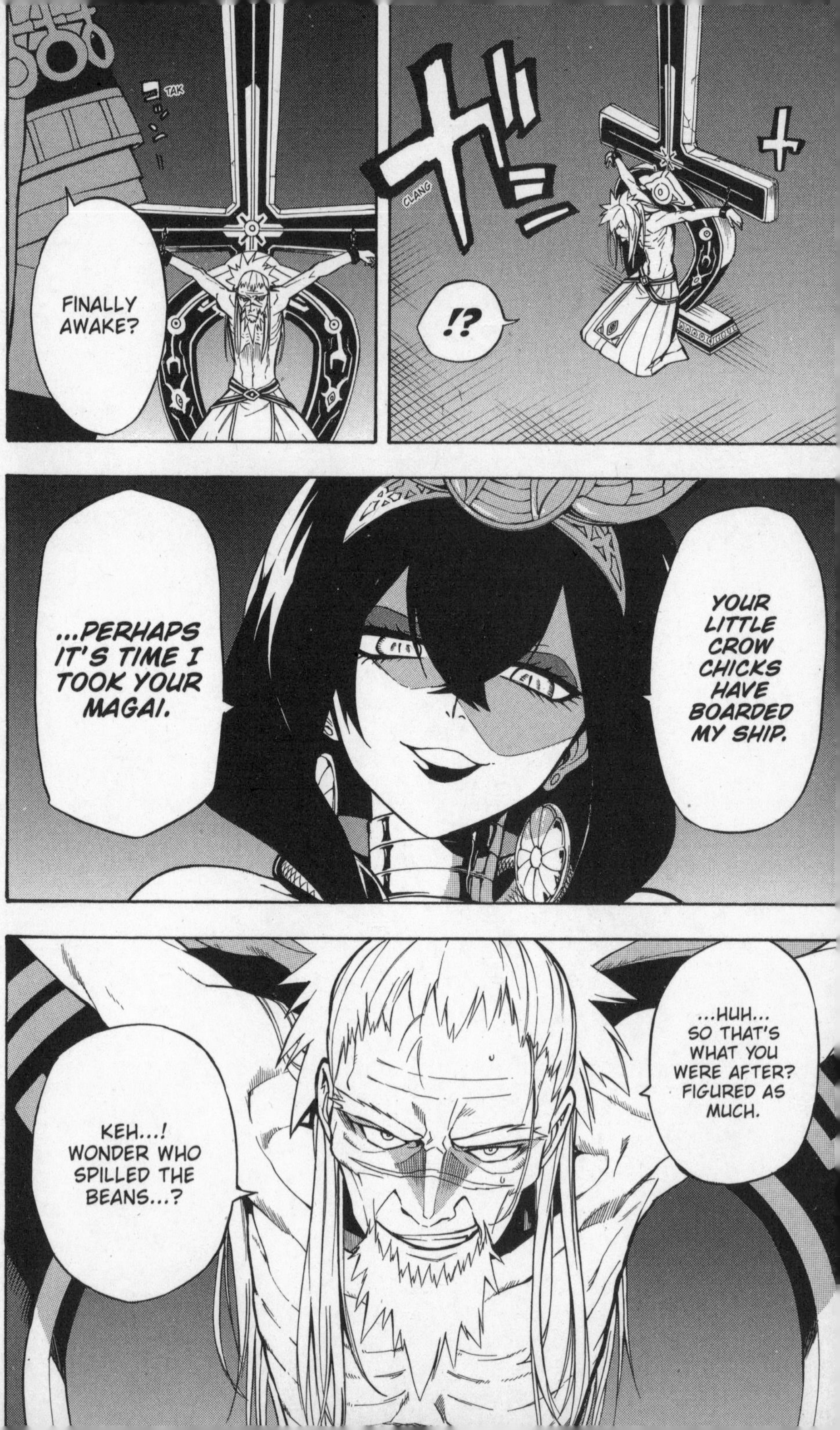
CLANG
!?
TAK
FINALLY AWAKE?
YOUR LITTLE CROW CHICKS HAVE BOARDED MY SHIP.
...PERHAPS IT'S TIME I TOOK YOUR MAGAI.
...HUH... SO THAT'S WHAT YOU WERE AFTER? FIGURED AS MUCH.
KEH...! WONDER WHO SPILLED THE BEANS...?

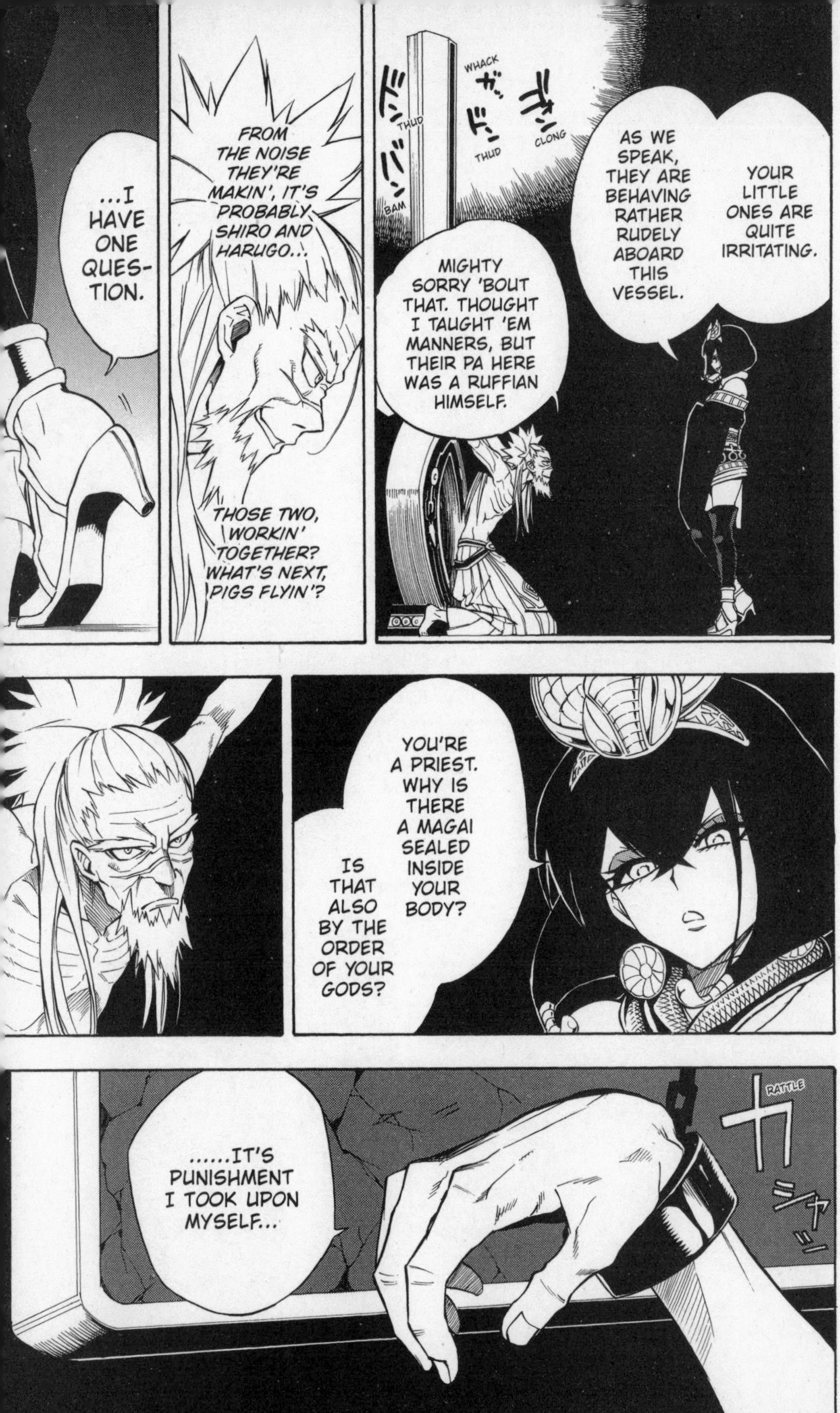
WHACK
CLONG
THUD
THUD
BAM
YOUR LITTLE ONES ARE QUITE IRRITATING.
AS WE SPEAK, THEY ARE BEHAVING RATHER RUDELY ABOARD THIS VESSEL.
MIGHTY SORRY 'BOUT THAT. THOUGHT I TAUGHT 'EM MANNERS, BUT THEIR PA HERE WAS A RUFFIAN HIMSELF.
FROM THE NOISE THEY'RE MAKIN', IT'S PROBABLY SHIRO AND HARUGO...
THOSE TWO, WORKIN' TOGETHER? WHAT'S NEXT, PIGS FLYIN'?
...I HAVE ONE QUESTION.
YOU'RE A PRIEST. WHY IS THERE A MAGAI SEALED INSIDE YOUR BODY?
IS THAT ALSO BY THE ORDER OF YOUR GODS?
RATTLE
......IT'S PUNISHMENT I TOOK UPON MYSELF...

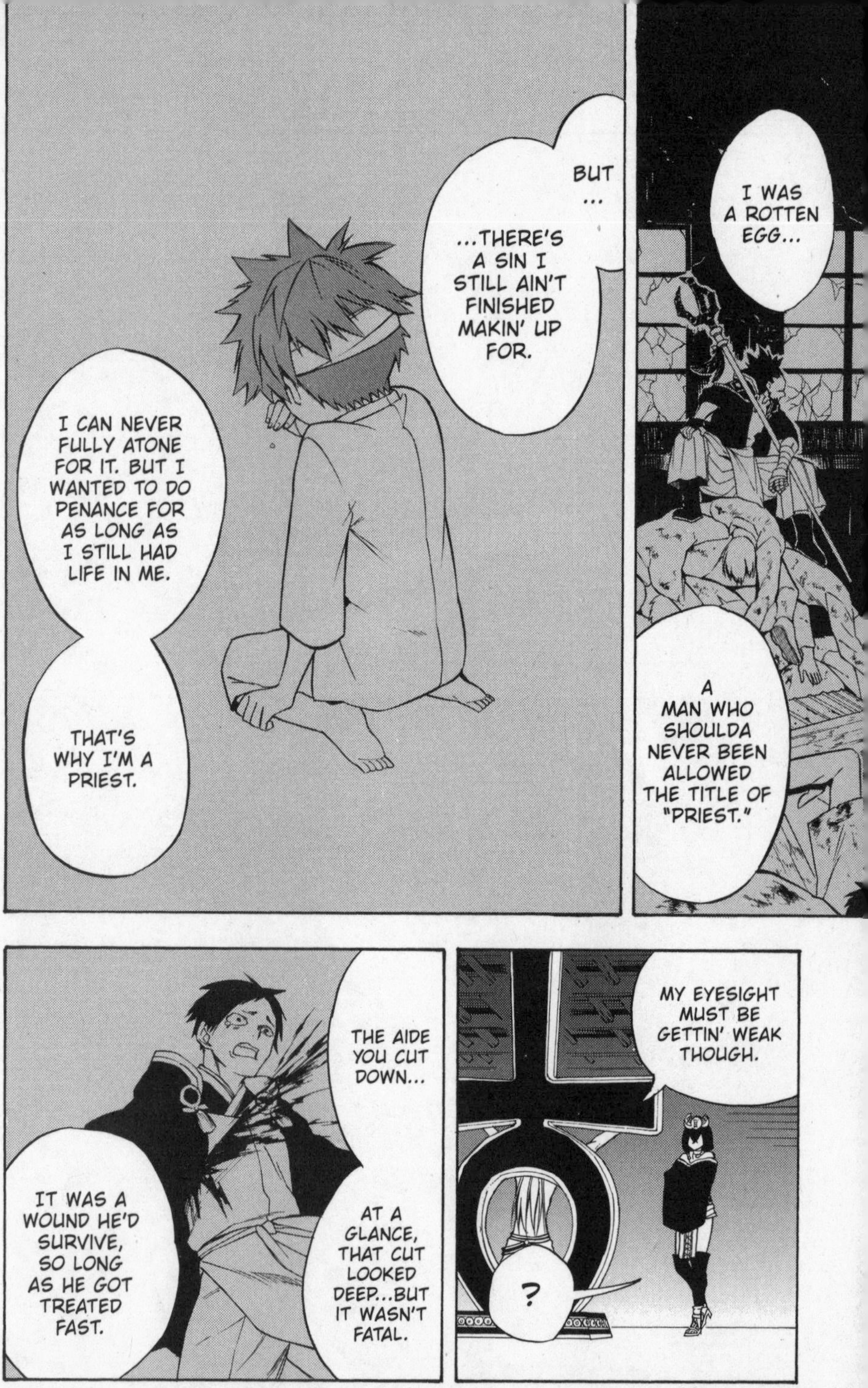
I WAS A ROTTEN EGG...
A MAN WHO SHOULDA NEVER BEEN ALLOWED THE TITLE OF "PRIEST."
BUT...
...THERE'S A SIN I STILL AIN'T FINISHED MAKIN' UP FOR.
I CAN NEVER FULLY ATONE FOR IT. BUT I WANTED TO DO PENANCE FOR AS LONG AS I STILL HAD LIFE IN ME.
THAT'S WHY I'M A PRIEST.
MY EYESIGHT MUST BE GETTIN' WEAK THOUGH.
?
THE AIDE YOU CUT DOWN...
AT A GLANCE, THAT CUT LOOKED DEEP...BUT IT WASN'T FATAL.
IT WAS A WOUND HE'D SURVIVE, SO LONG AS HE GOT TREATED FAST.

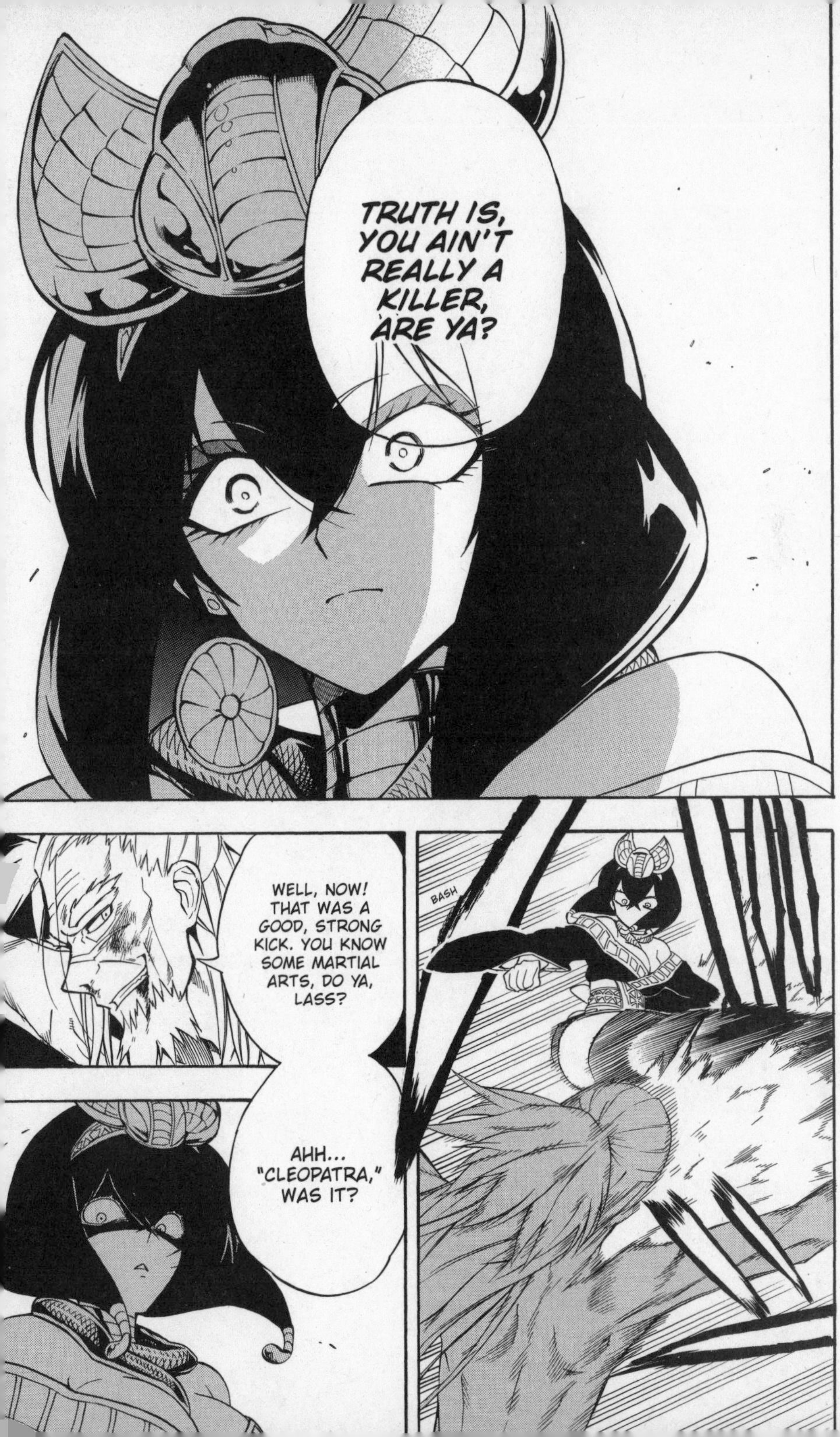
TRUTH IS, YOU AIN'T REALLY A KILLER, ARE YA?
BASH
WELL, NOW! THAT WAS A GOOD, STRONG KICK. YOU KNOW SOME MARTIAL ARTS, DO YA, LASS?
AHH... "CLEOPATRA," WAS IT?

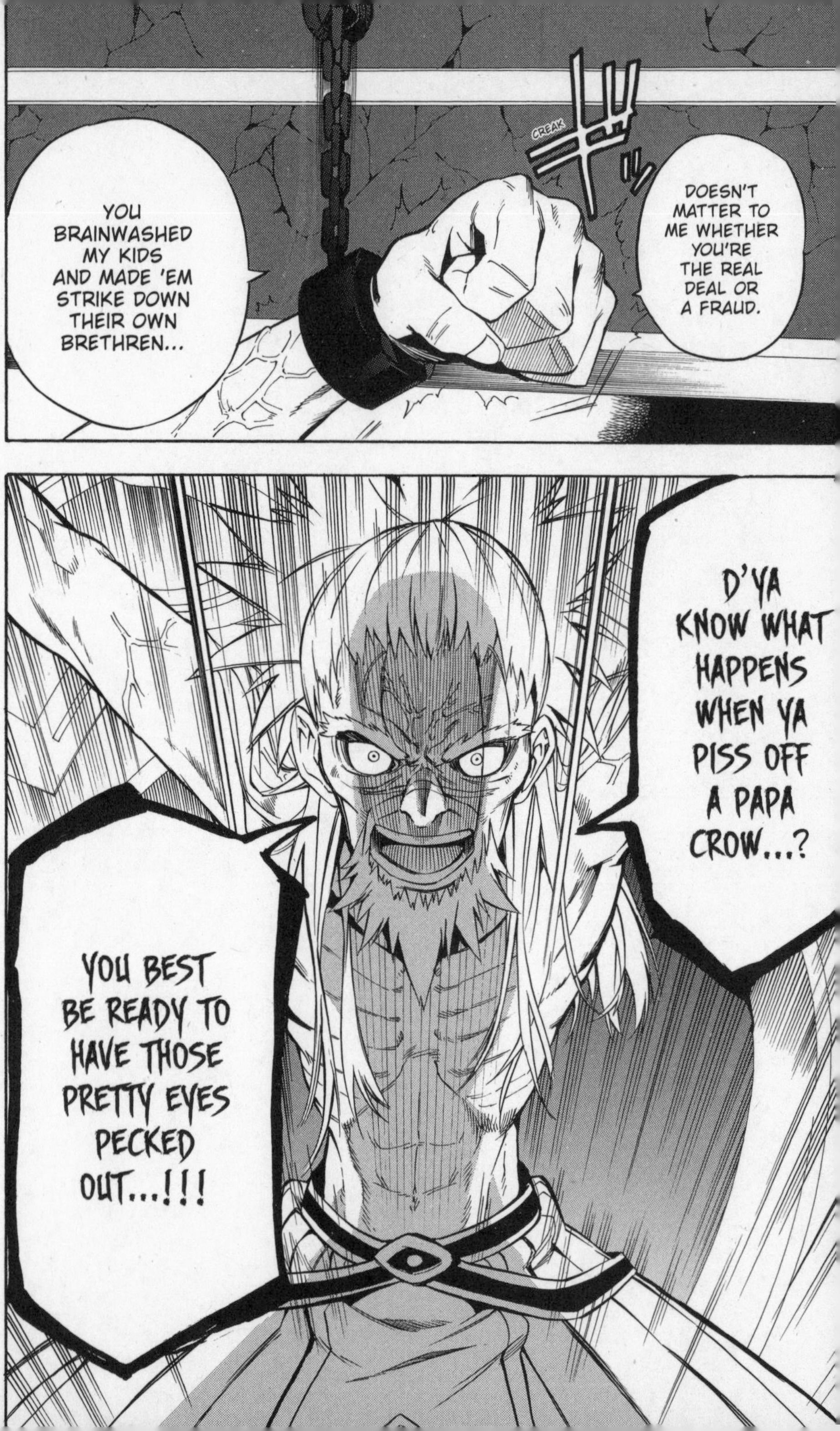
CREAK
DOESN'T MATTER TO ME WHETHER YOU'RE THE REAL DEAL OR A FRAUD.
YOU BRAINWASHED MY KIDS AND MADE 'EM STRIKE DOWN THEIR OWN BRETHREN...
D'YA KNOW WHAT HAPPENS WHEN YA PISS OFF A PAPA CROW...?
YOU BEST BE READY TO HAVE THOSE PRETTY EYES PECKED OUT...!!!

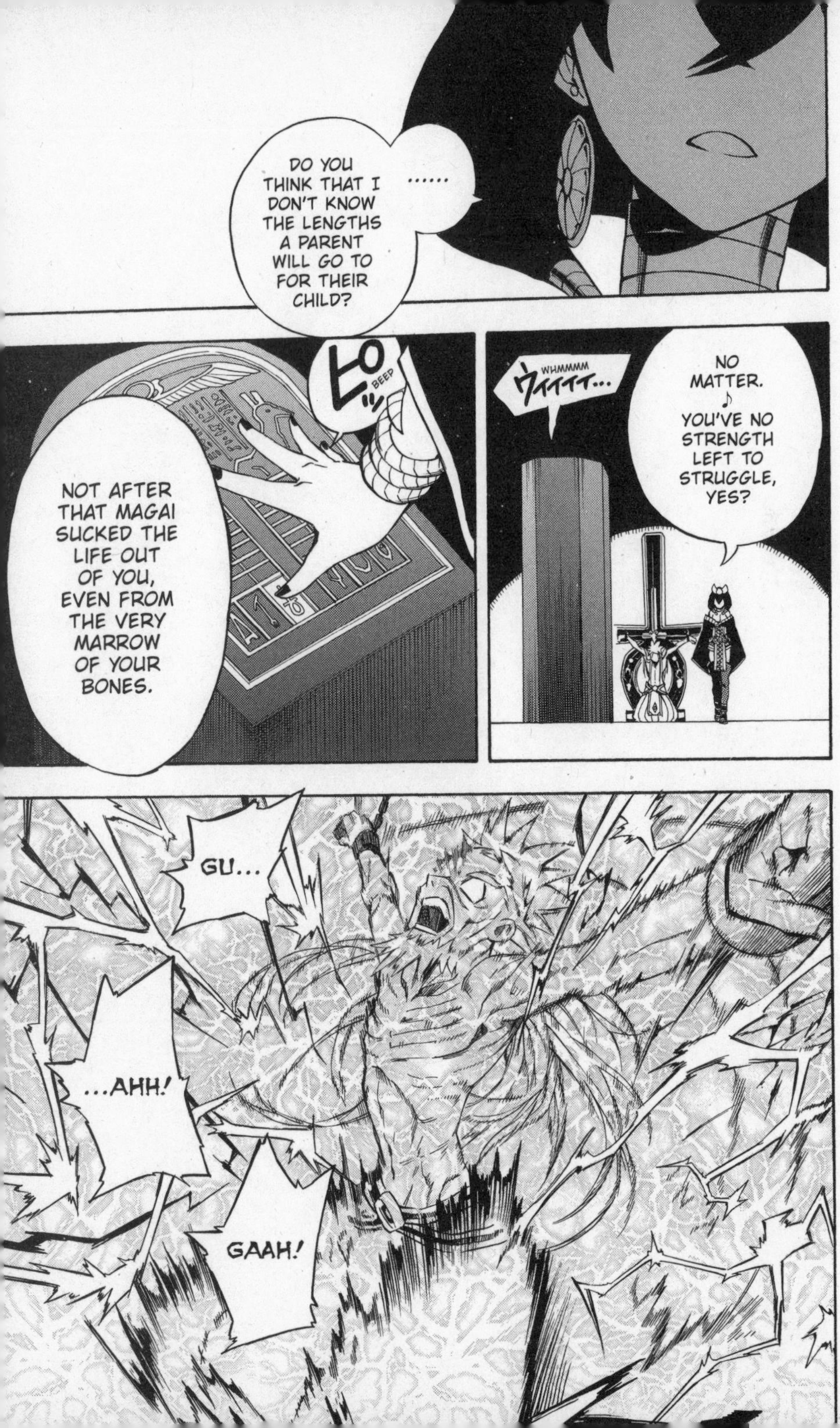
......
DO YOU THINK THAT I DON'T KNOW THE LENGTHS A PARENT WILL GO TO FOR THEIR CHILD?
NO MATTER. ♪ YOU'VE NO STRENGTH LEFT TO STRUGGLE, YES?
ウイイイイ... WHMMMM
ピッ BEEP
NOT AFTER THAT MAGAI SUCKED THE LIFE OUT OF YOU, EVEN FROM THE VERY MARROW OF YOUR BONES.
GU...
...AHH!
GAAH!

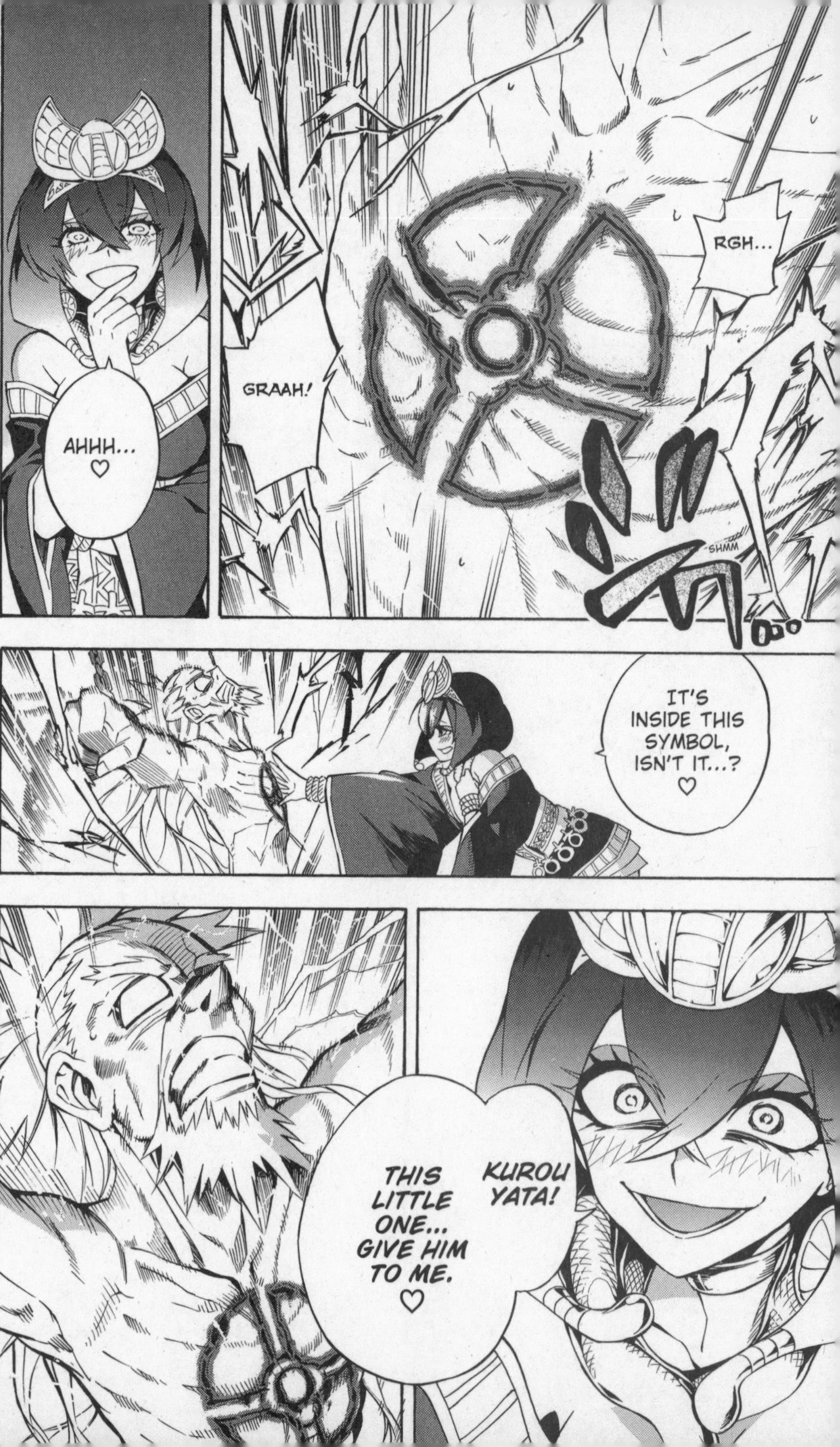
RGH...
GRAAH!
SHMM
AHHH... ♡
IT'S INSIDE THIS SYMBOL, ISN'T IT...? ♡
KUROU YATA!
THIS LITTLE ONE... GIVE HIM TO ME. ♡

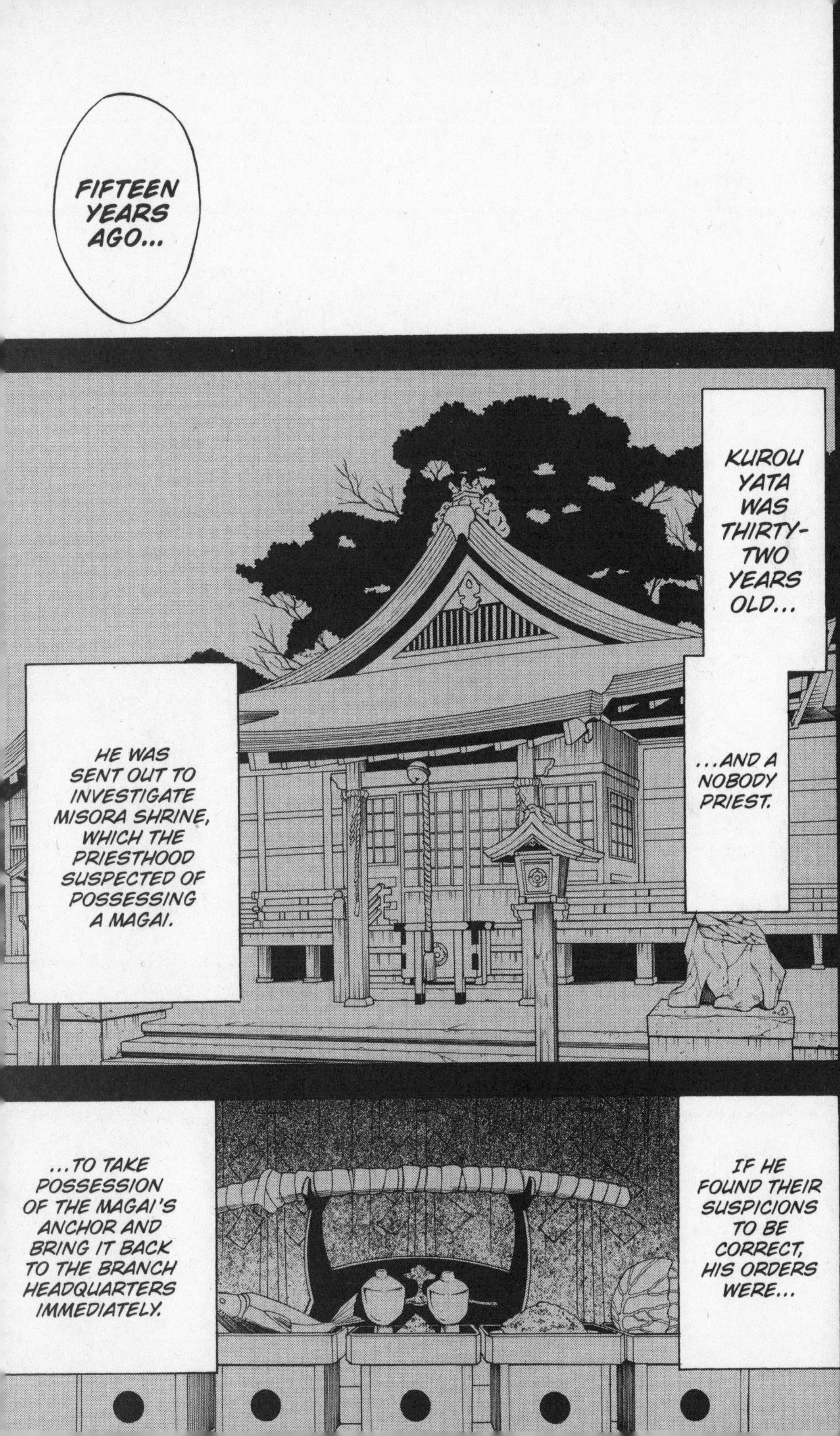
FIFTEEN YEARS AGO...
KUROU YATA WAS THIRTY-TWO YEARS OLD...
...AND A NOBODY PRIEST.
HE WAS SENT OUT TO INVESTIGATE MISORA SHRINE, WHICH THE PRIESTHOOD SUSPECTED OF POSSESSING A MAGAI.
IF HE FOUND THEIR SUSPICIONS TO BE CORRECT, HIS ORDERS WERE...
...TO TAKE POSSESSION OF THE MAGAI'S ANCHOR AND BRING IT BACK TO THE BRANCH HEADQUARTERS IMMEDIATELY.

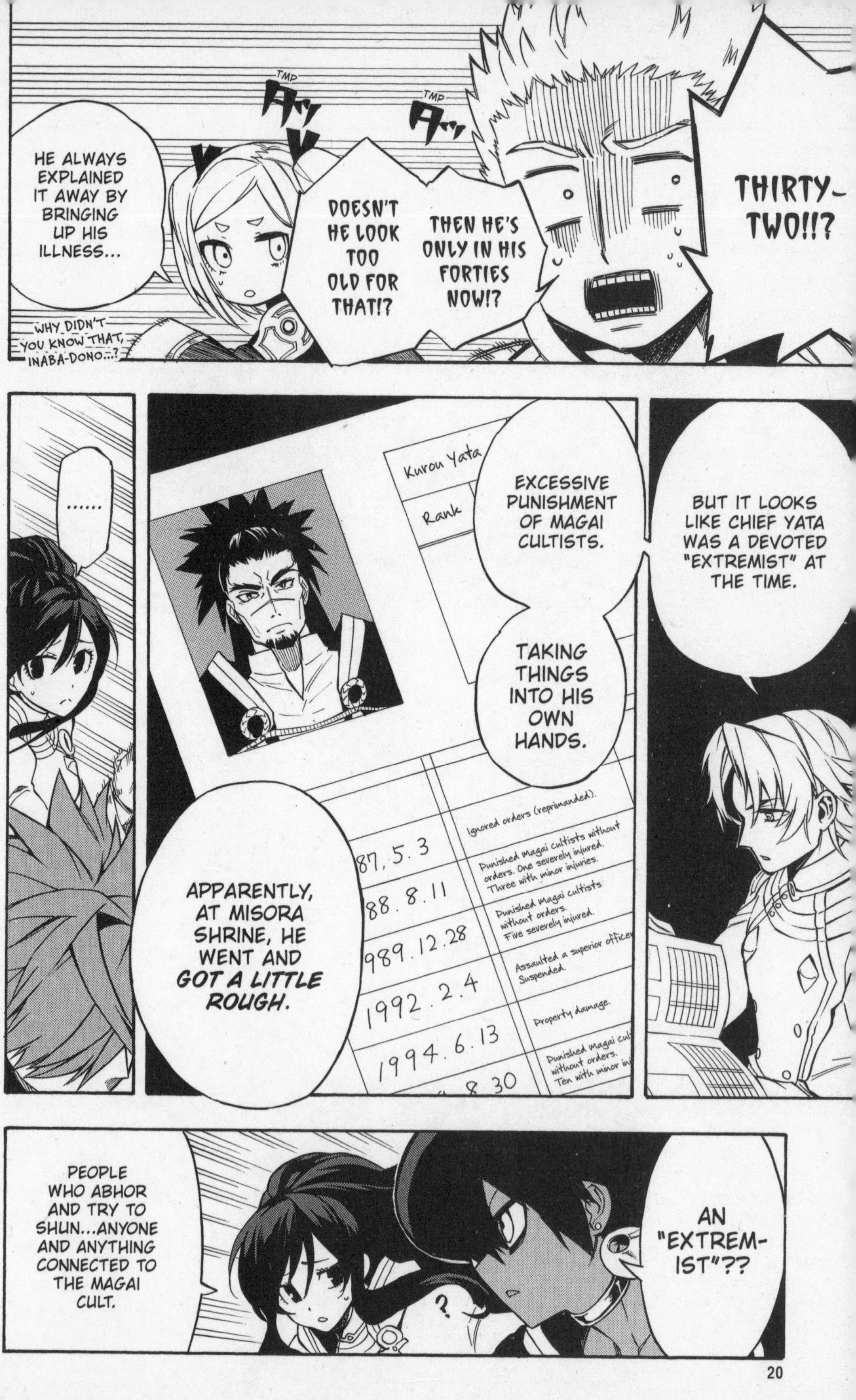
TMP
TMP
THIRTY-TWO!!?
THEN HE'S ONLY IN HIS FORTIES NOW!?
DOESN'T HE LOOK TOO OLD FOR THAT!?
HE ALWAYS EXPLAINED IT AWAY BY BRINGING UP HIS ILLNESS...
WHY DIDN'T YOU KNOW THAT, INABA-DONO...?
BUT IT LOOKS LIKE CHIEF YATA WAS A DEVOTED "EXTREMIST" AT THE TIME.
EXCESSIVE PUNISHMENT OF MAGAI CULTISTS.
TAKING THINGS INTO HIS OWN HANDS.
Kurou Yata
Rank
Ignored orders (reprimanded).
87. 5. 3
Punished Magai cultists without orders. One severely injured. Three with minor injuries.
88. 8. 11
Punished Magai cultists without orders. Five severely injured.
989. 12. 28
Assaulted a superior office
Suspended.
1992. 2. 4
Property damage.
1994. 6. 13
Punished Magai cul
without orders.
Ten with minor in
8. 30
APPARENTLY, AT MISORA SHRINE, HE WENT AND *GOT A LITTLE ROUGH*.
......
AN "EXTREM-IST"??
?
PEOPLE WHO ABHOR AND TRY TO SHUN...ANYONE AND ANYTHING CONNECTED TO THE MAGAI CULT.

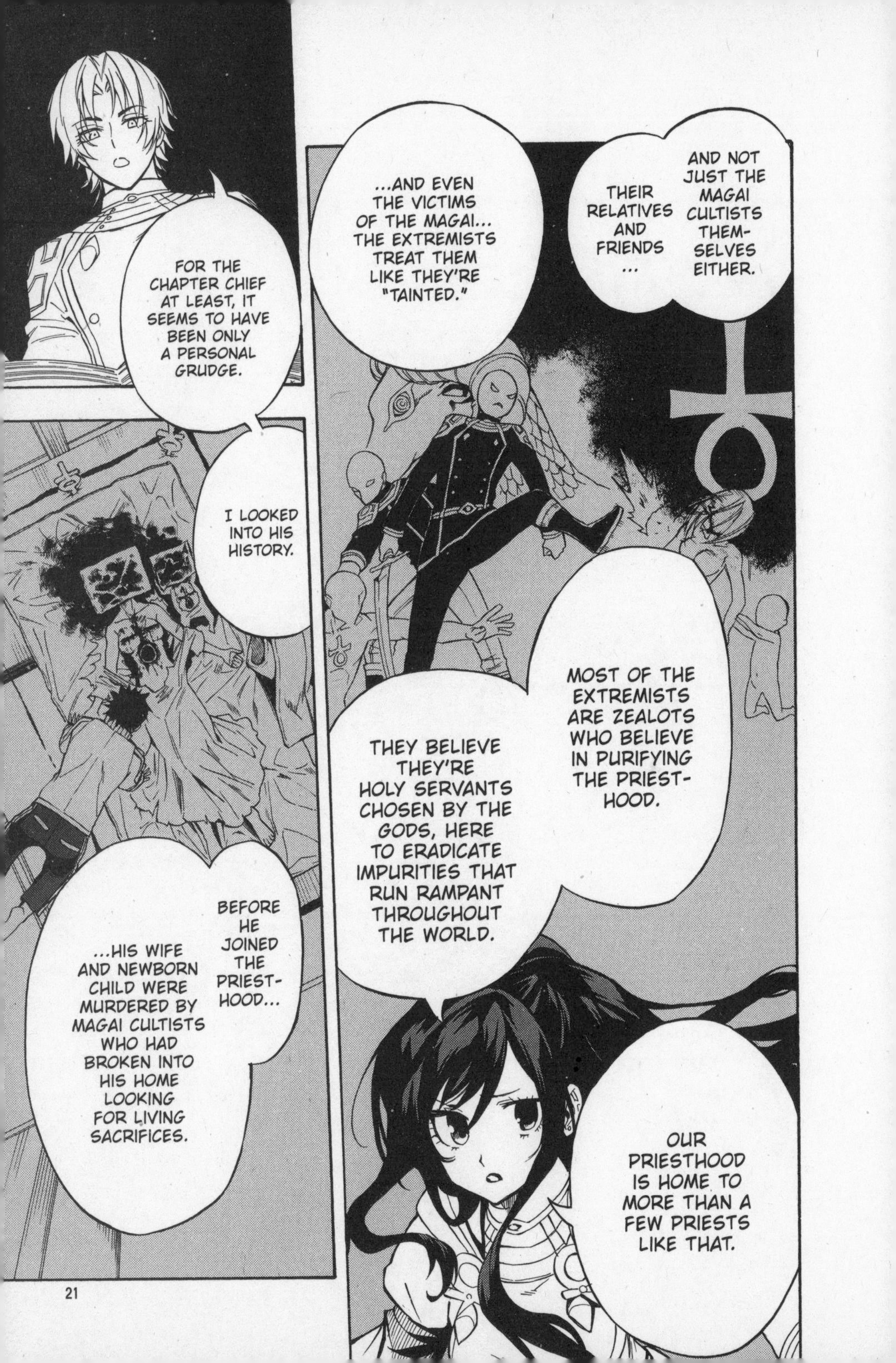
AND NOT JUST THE MAGAI CULTISTS THEM-SELVES EITHER.
THEIR RELATIVES AND FRIENDS ...
...AND EVEN THE VICTIMS OF THE MAGAI... THE EXTREMISTS TREAT THEM LIKE THEY'RE "TAINTED."
MOST OF THE EXTREMISTS ARE ZEALOTS WHO BELIEVE IN PURIFYING THE PRIEST-HOOD.
THEY BELIEVE THEY'RE HOLY SERVANTS CHOSEN BY THE GODS, HERE TO ERADICATE IMPURITIES THAT RUN RAMPANT THROUGHOUT THE WORLD.
OUR PRIESTHOOD IS HOME TO MORE THAN A FEW PRIESTS LIKE THAT.
FOR THE CHAPTER CHIEF AT LEAST, IT SEEMS TO HAVE BEEN ONLY A PERSONAL GRUDGE.
I LOOKED INTO HIS HISTORY.
BEFORE HE JOINED THE PRIEST-HOOD...
...HIS WIFE AND NEWBORN CHILD WERE MURDERED BY MAGAI CULTISTS WHO HAD BROKEN INTO HIS HOME LOOKING FOR LIVING SACRIFICES.

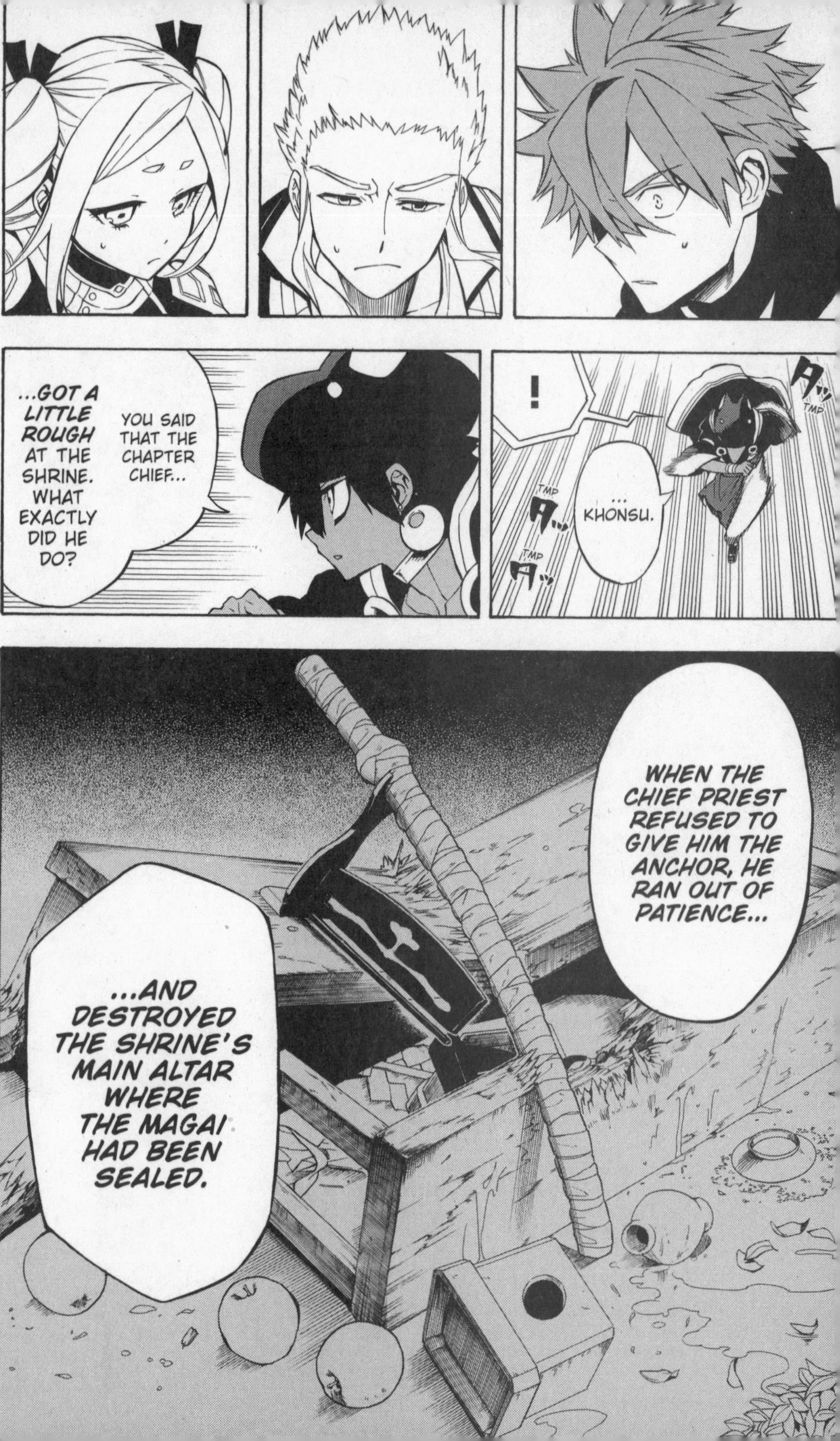
TMP
!
...KHONSU.
TMP
TMP
YOU SAID THAT THE CHAPTER CHIEF...
...GOT A LITTLE ROUGH AT THE SHRINE. WHAT EXACTLY DID HE DO?
WHEN THE CHIEF PRIEST REFUSED TO GIVE HIM THE ANCHOR, HE RAN OUT OF PATIENCE...
...AND DESTROYED THE SHRINE'S MAIN ALTAR WHERE THE MAGAI HAD BEEN SEALED.

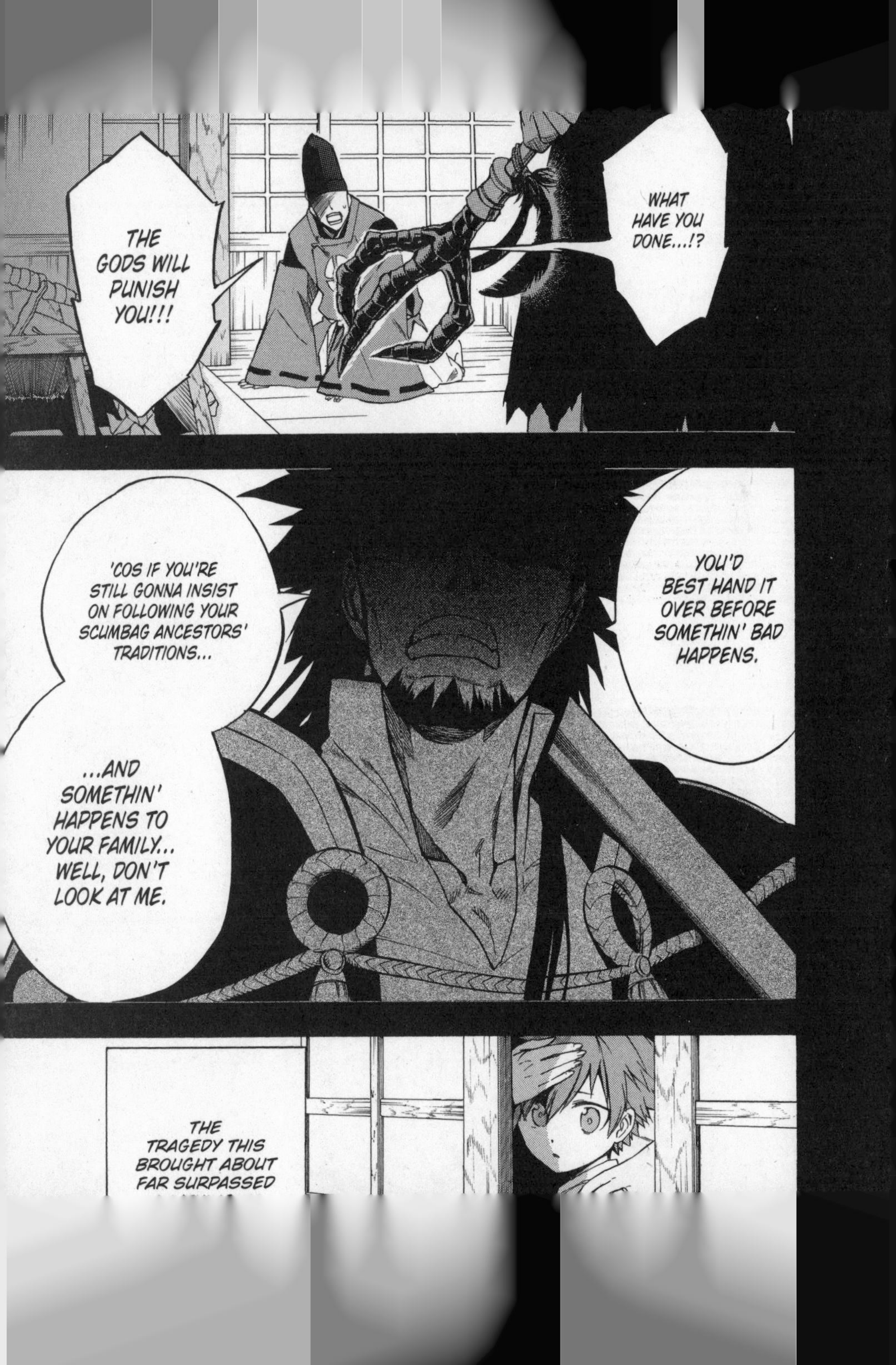
WHAT HAVE YOU DONE...!?
THE GODS WILL PUNISH YOU!!!
YOU'D BEST HAND IT OVER BEFORE SOMETHIN' BAD HAPPENS.
'COS IF YOU'RE STILL GONNA INSIST ON FOLLOWING YOUR SCUMBAG ANCESTORS' TRADITIONS...
...AND SOMETHIN' HAPPENS TO YOUR FAMILY... WELL, DON'T LOOK AT ME.
THE TRAGEDY THIS BROUGHT ABOUT FAR SURPASSED

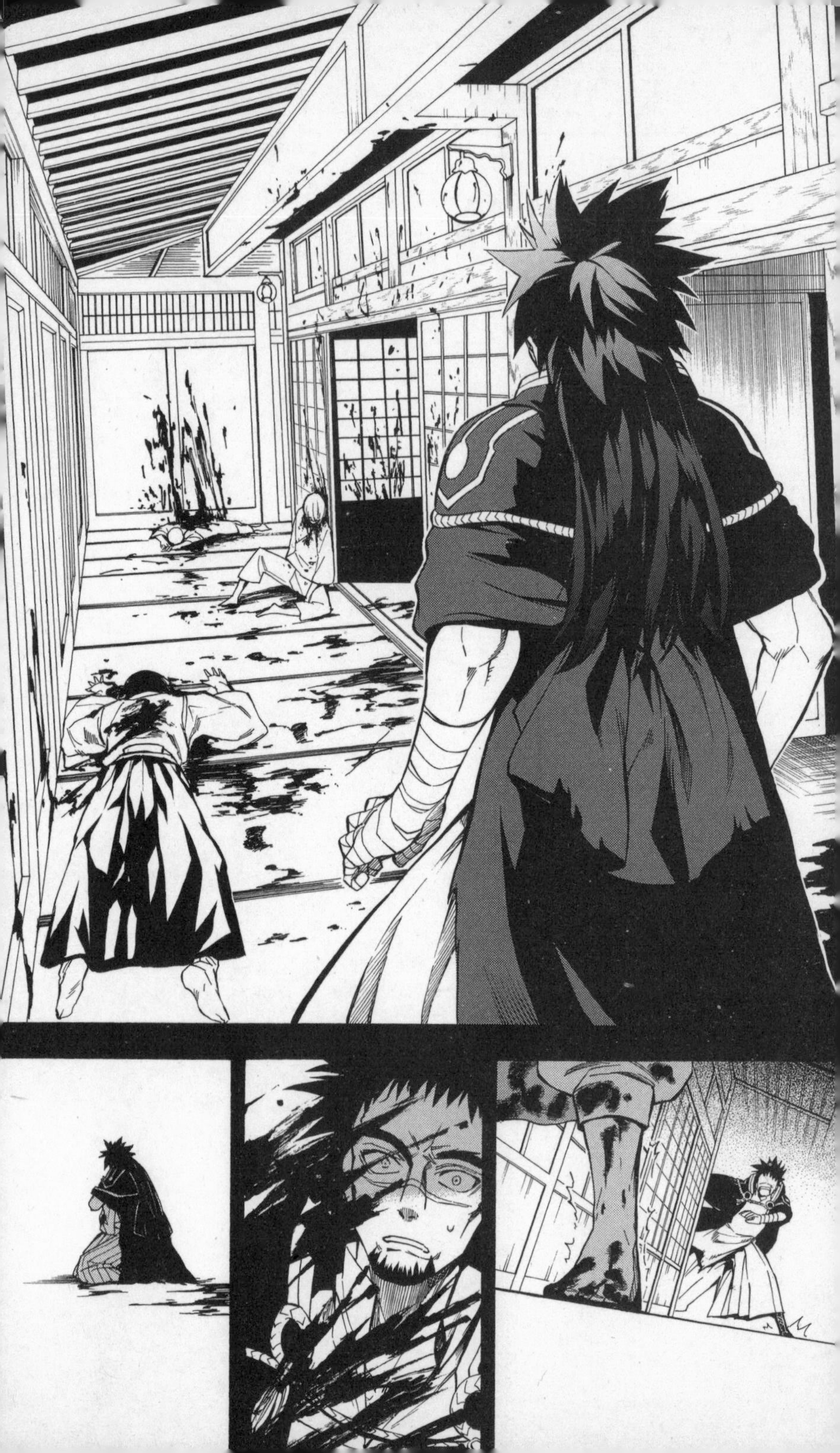

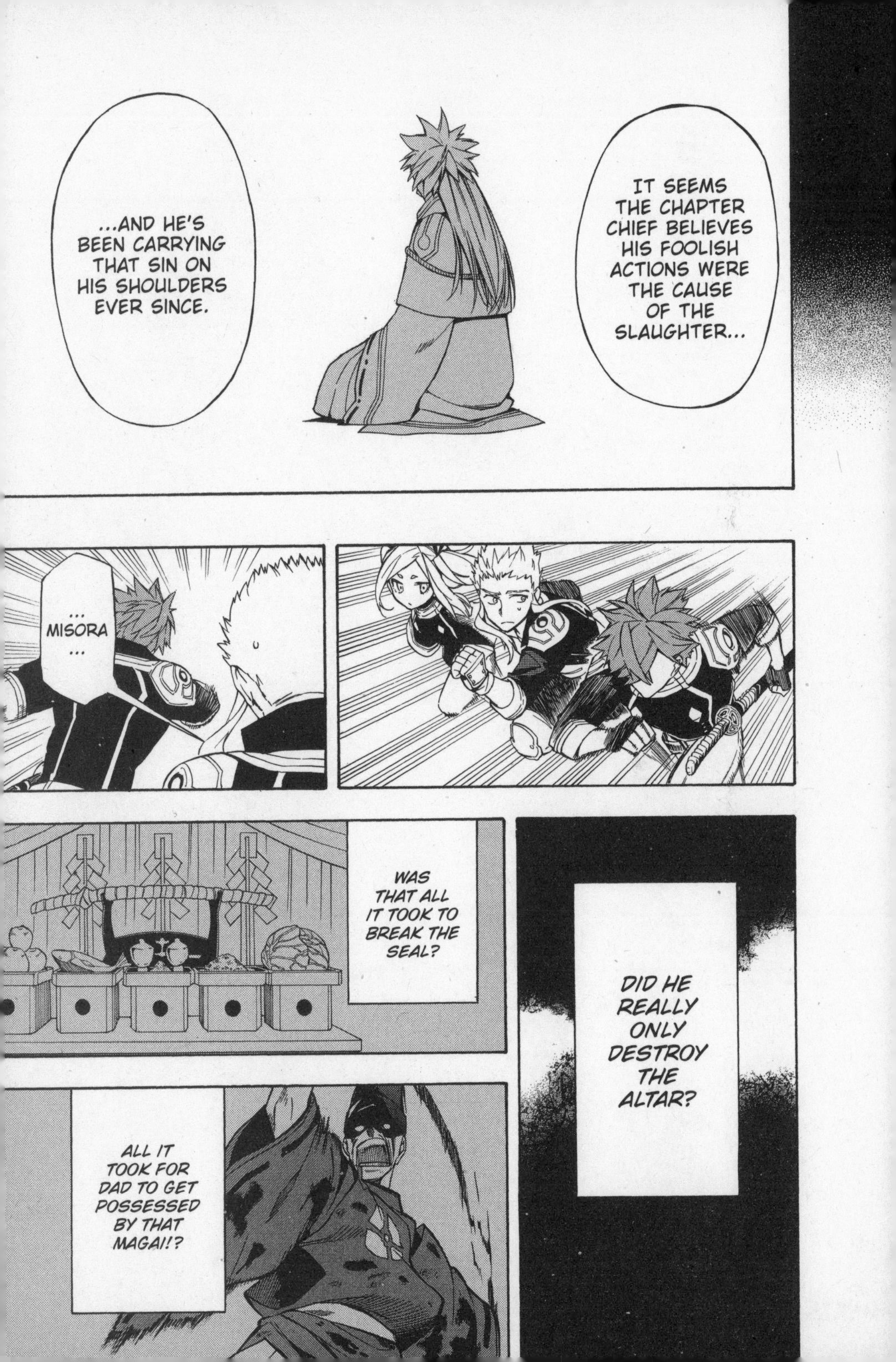
IT SEEMS THE CHAPTER CHIEF BELIEVES HIS FOOLISH ACTIONS WERE THE CAUSE OF THE SLAUGHTER...
...AND HE'S BEEN CARRYING THAT SIN ON HIS SHOULDERS EVER SINCE.
... MISORA ...
DID HE REALLY ONLY DESTROY THE ALTAR?
WAS THAT ALL IT TOOK TO BREAK THE SEAL?
ALL IT TOOK FOR DAD TO GET POSSESSED BY THAT MAGAI!?

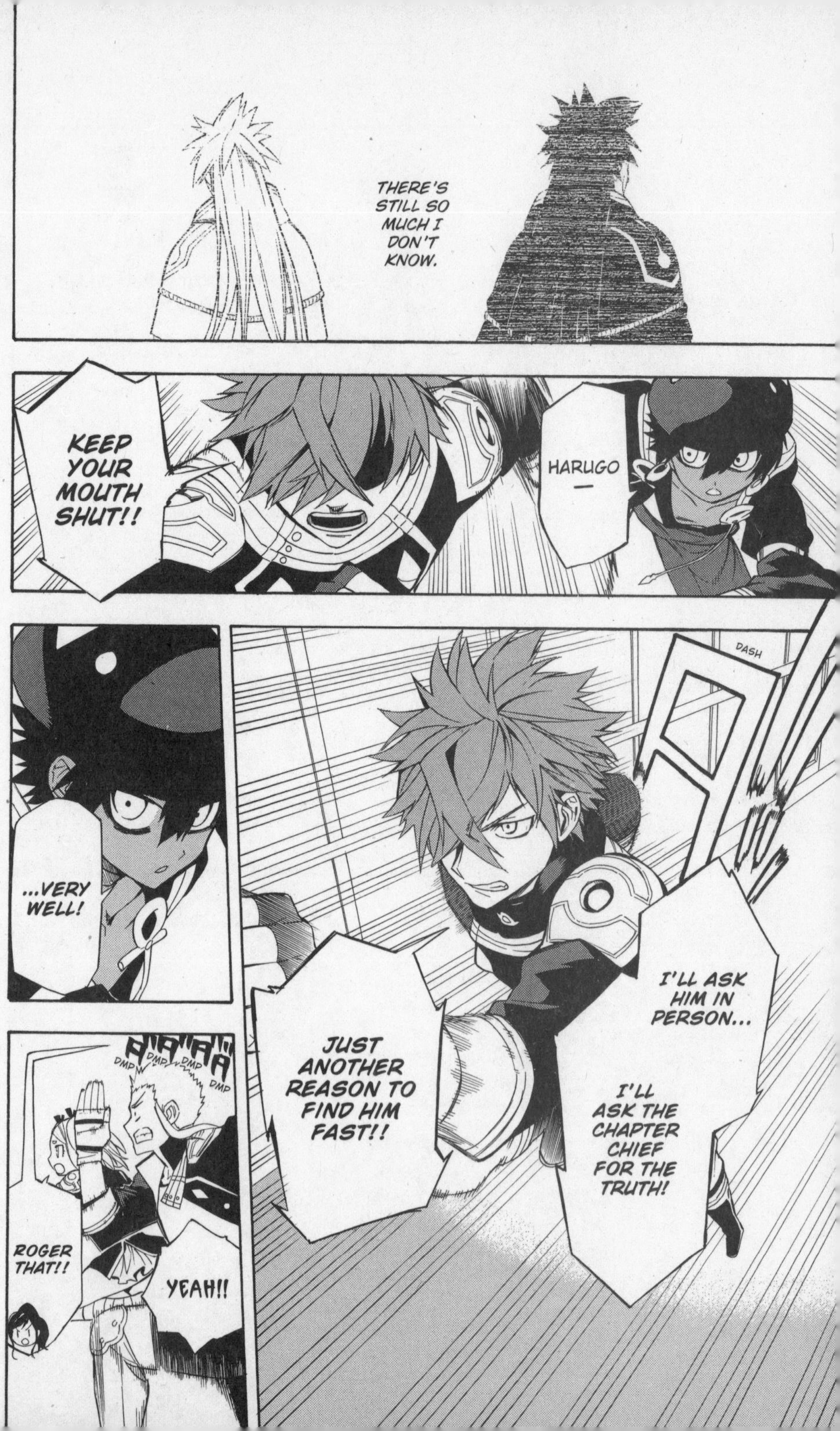
THERE'S STILL SO MUCH I DON'T KNOW.
HARUGO —
KEEP YOUR MOUTH SHUT!!
DASH
I'LL ASK HIM IN PERSON...
I'LL ASK THE CHAPTER CHIEF FOR THE TRUTH!
JUST ANOTHER REASON TO FIND HIM FAST!!
...VERY WELL!
DMP DMP DMP DMP
ROGER THAT!!
YEAH!!

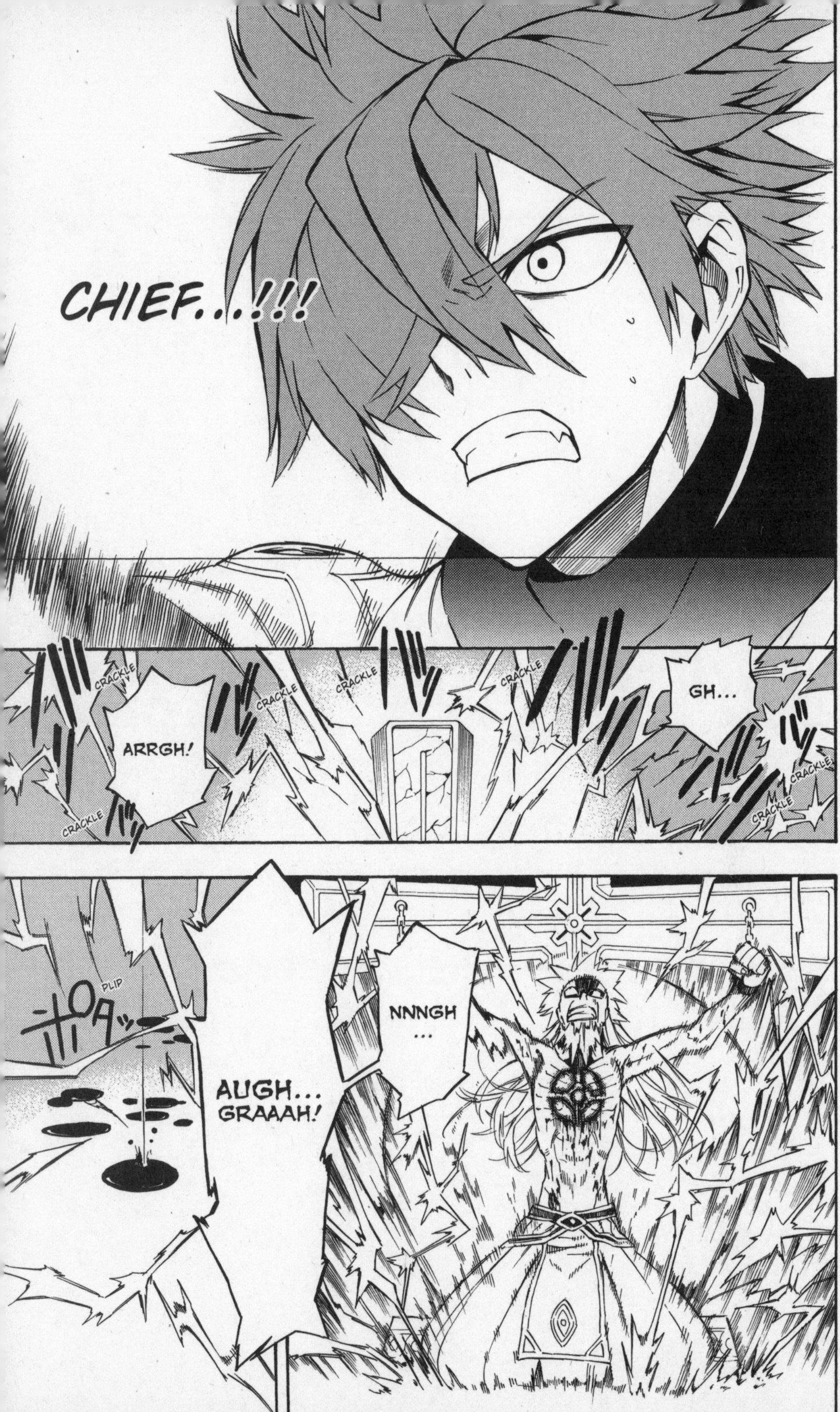
CHIEF...!!!
GH...
CRACKLE
CRACKLE
CRACKLE
CRACKLE
CRACKLE
CRACKLE
ARRGH!
CRACKLE
NNNGH
...
AUGH...
GRAAAH!
PLIP

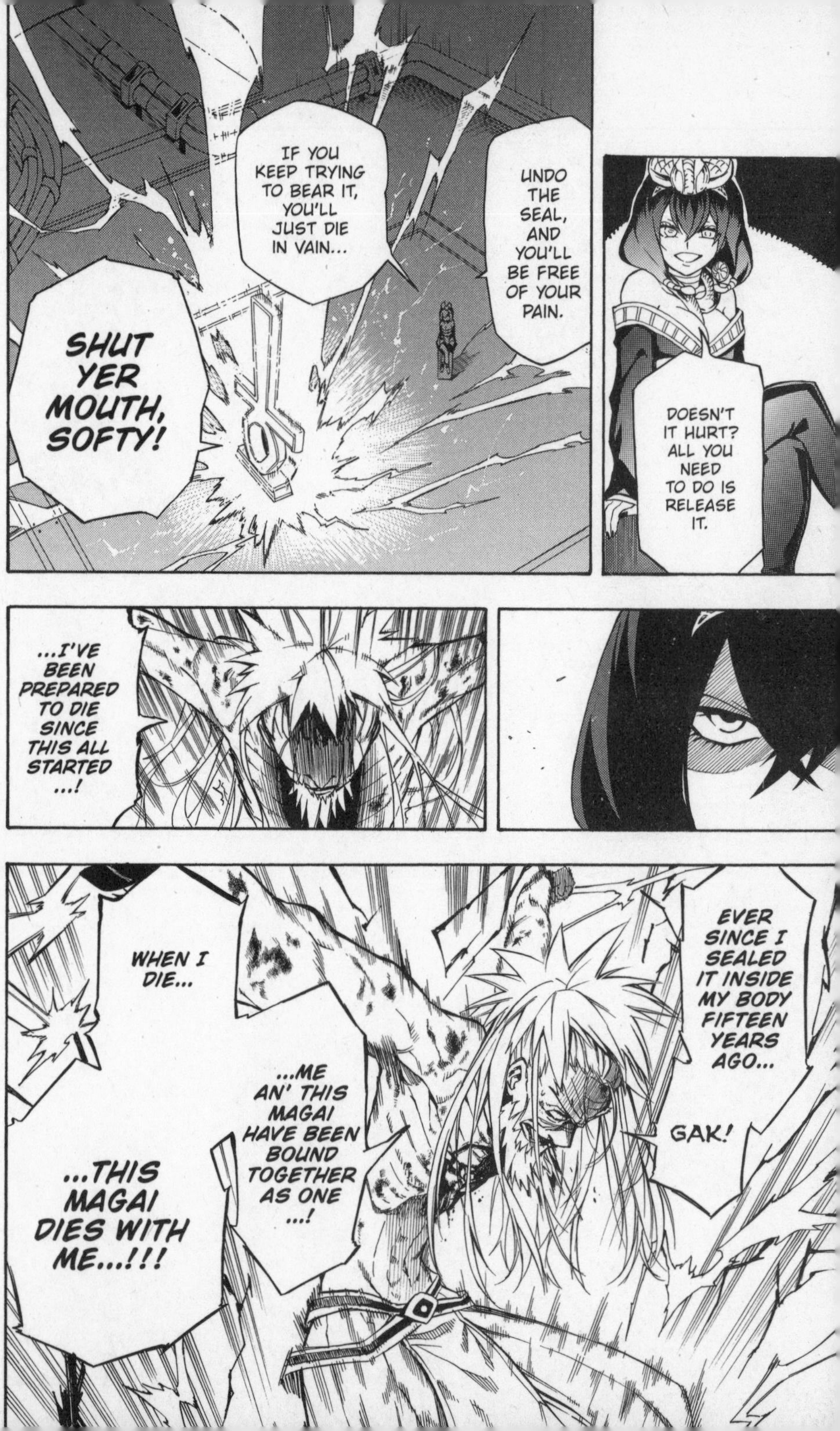
DOESN'T IT HURT? ALL YOU NEED TO DO IS RELEASE IT.
UNDO THE SEAL, AND YOU'LL BE FREE OF YOUR PAIN.
IF YOU KEEP TRYING TO BEAR IT, YOU'LL JUST DIE IN VAIN...
SHUT YER MOUTH, SOFTY!
...I'VE BEEN PREPARED TO DIE SINCE THIS ALL STARTED ...!
EVER SINCE I SEALED IT INSIDE MY BODY FIFTEEN YEARS AGO...
GAK!
...ME AN' THIS MAGAI HAVE BEEN BOUND TOGETHER AS ONE ...!
WHEN I DIE...
...THIS MAGAI DIES WITH ME...!!!

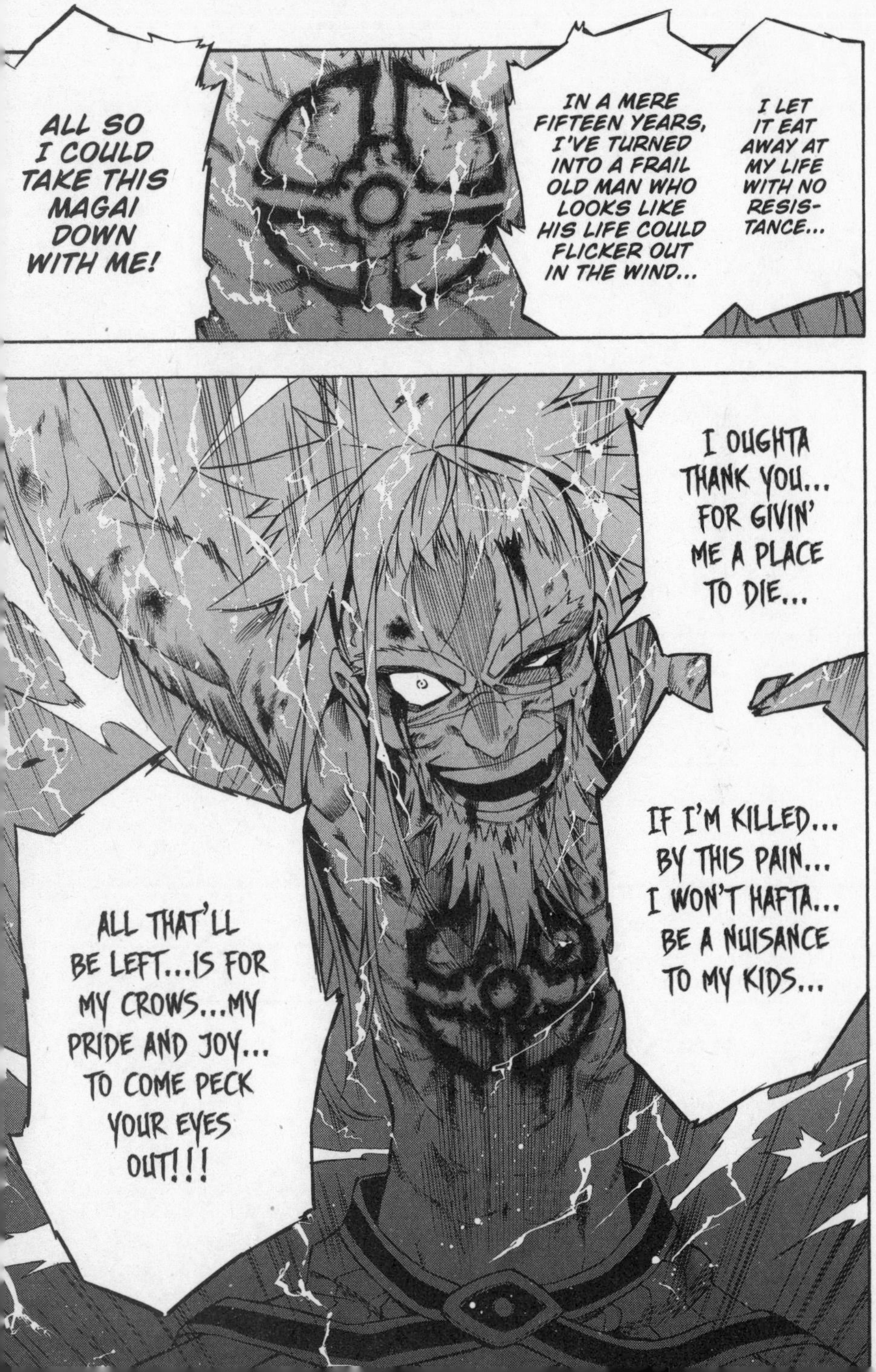
I LET IT EAT AWAY AT MY LIFE WITH NO RESIS-TANCE...
IN A MERE FIFTEEN YEARS, I'VE TURNED INTO A FRAIL OLD MAN WHO LOOKS LIKE HIS LIFE COULD FLICKER OUT IN THE WIND...
ALL SO I COULD TAKE THIS MAGAI DOWN WITH ME!
I OUGHTA THANK YOU... FOR GIVIN' ME A PLACE TO DIE...
IF I'M KILLED... BY THIS PAIN... I WON'T HAFTA... BE A NUISANCE TO MY KIDS...
ALL THAT'LL BE LEFT...IS FOR MY CROWS...MY PRIDE AND JOY... TO COME PECK YOUR EYES OUT!!!

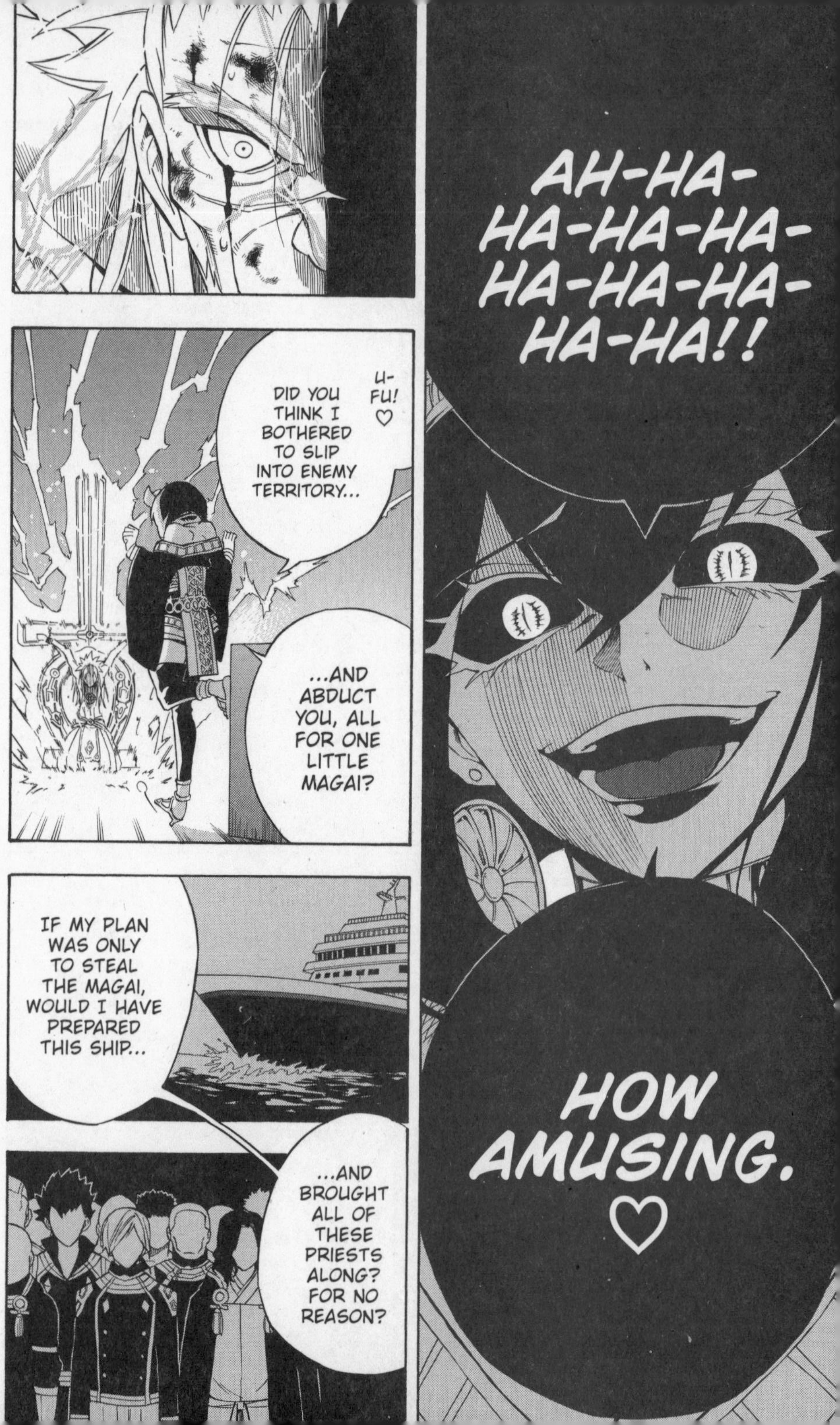
AH-HA-HA-HA-HA-HA-HA-HA-HA-HA!!
HOW AMUSING. ♡
U-FU! ♡
DID YOU THINK I BOTHERED TO SLIP INTO ENEMY TERRITORY...
...AND ABDUCT YOU, ALL FOR ONE LITTLE MAGAI?
IF MY PLAN WAS ONLY TO STEAL THE MAGAI, WOULD I HAVE PREPARED THIS SHIP...
...AND BROUGHT ALL OF THESE PRIESTS ALONG? FOR NO REASON?

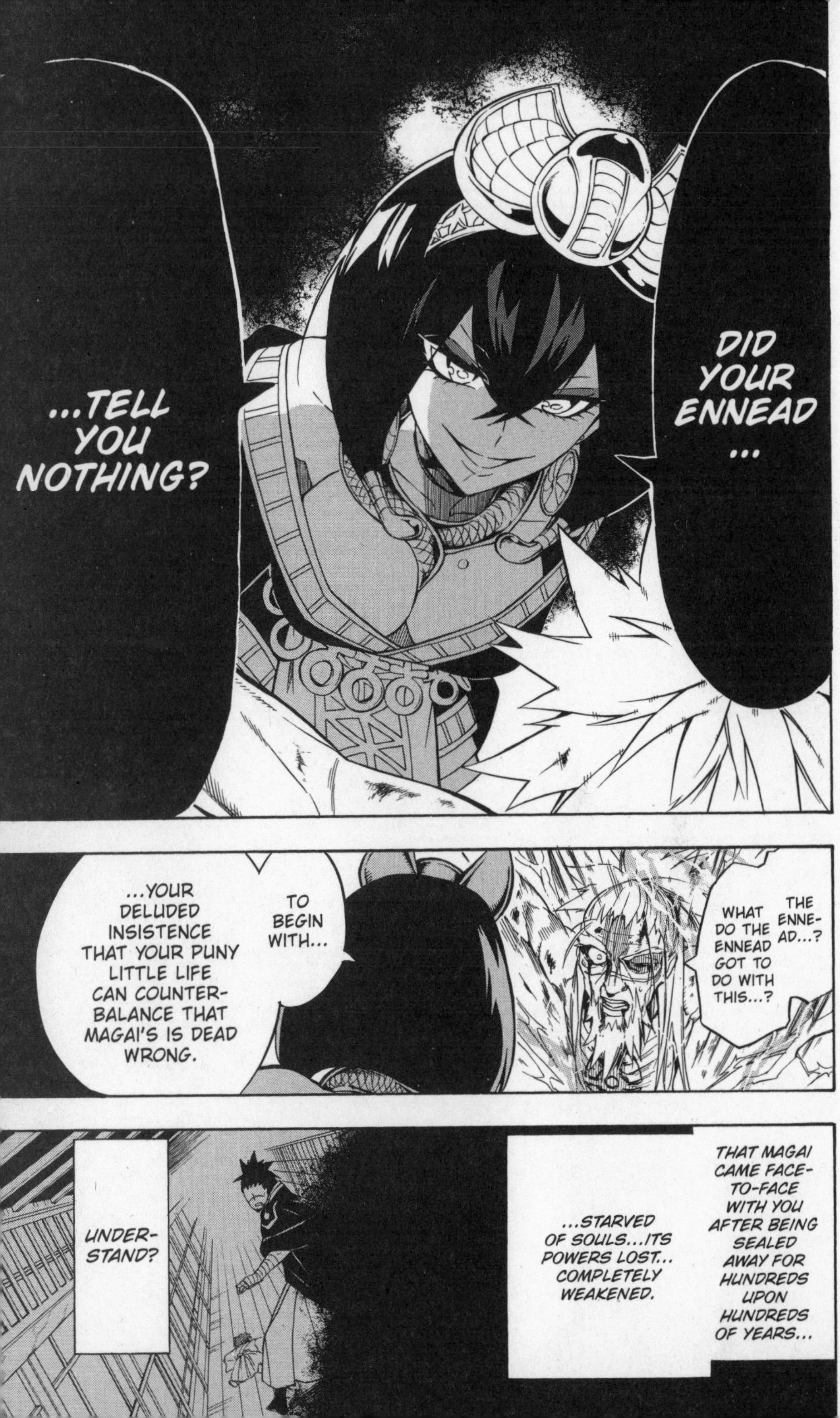
DID YOUR ENNEAD ...
...TELL YOU NOTHING?
THE ENNE-AD...?
WHAT DO THE ENNEAD GOT TO DO WITH THIS...?
TO BEGIN WITH...
...YOUR DELUDED INSISTENCE THAT YOUR PUNY LITTLE LIFE CAN COUNTER-BALANCE THAT MAGAI'S IS DEAD WRONG.
THAT MAGAI CAME FACE-TO-FACE WITH YOU AFTER BEING SEALED AWAY FOR HUNDREDS UPON HUNDREDS OF YEARS...
...STARVED OF SOULS...ITS POWERS LOST... COMPLETELY WEAKENED.
UNDER-STAND?

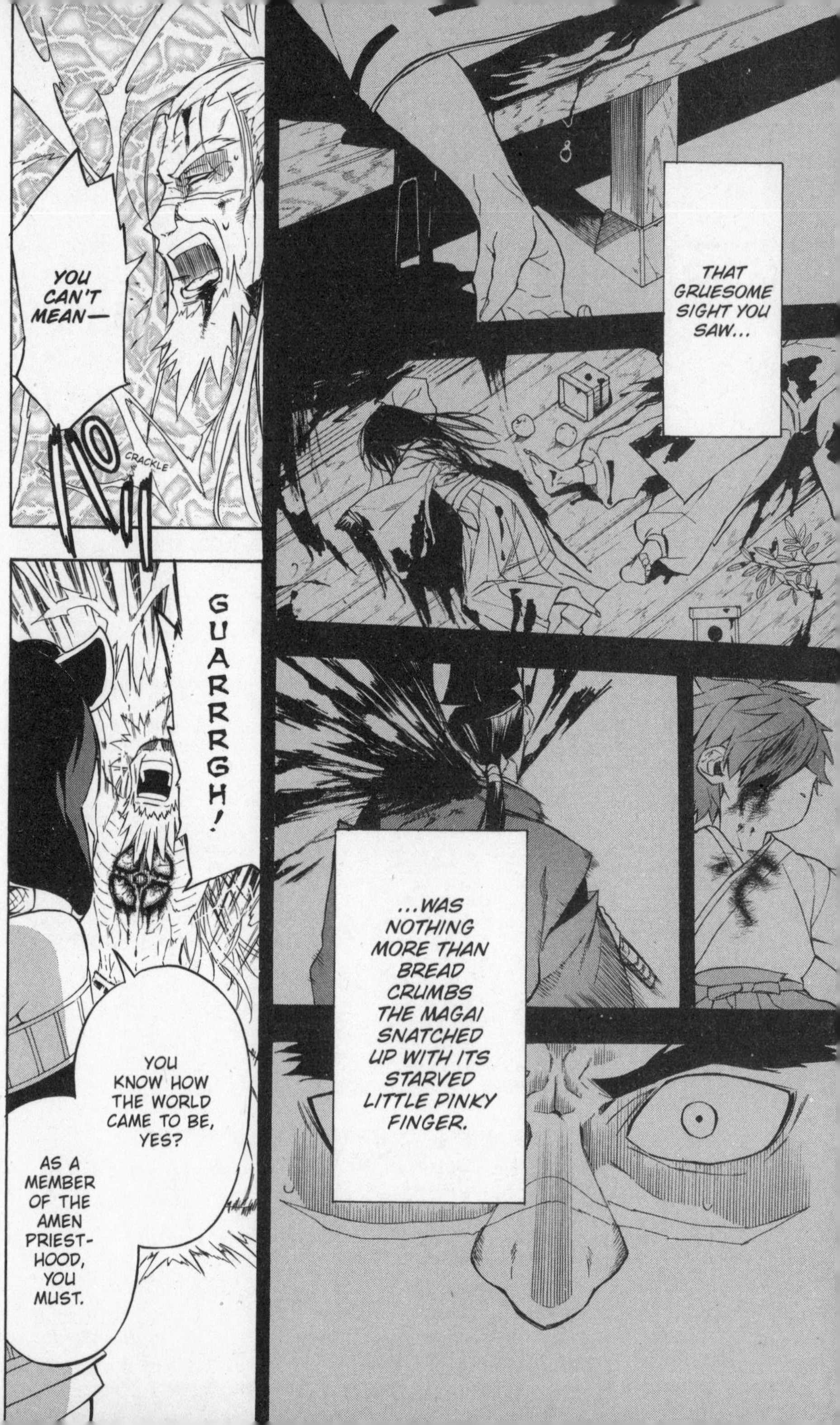
THAT GRUESOME SIGHT YOU SAW...
...WAS NOTHING MORE THAN BREAD CRUMBS THE MAGAI SNATCHED UP WITH ITS STARVED LITTLE PINKY FINGER.
YOU CAN'T MEAN—
CRACKLE
GUARRRGH!
YOU KNOW HOW THE WORLD CAME TO BE, YES?
AS A MEMBER OF THE AMEN PRIEST-HOOD, YOU MUST.

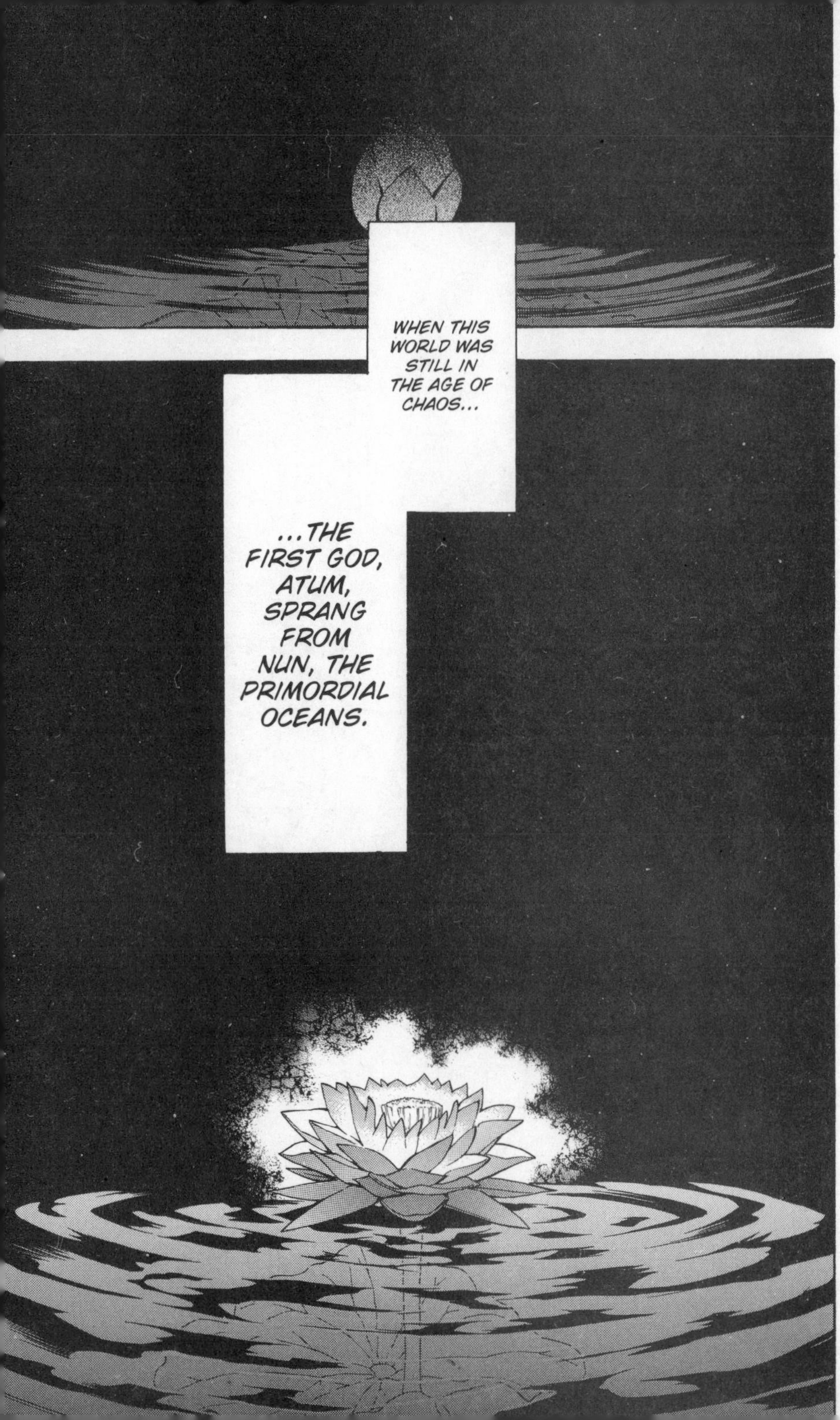
WHEN THIS WORLD WAS STILL IN THE AGE OF CHAOS...
...THE FIRST GOD, ATUM, SPRANG FROM NUN, THE PRIMORDIAL OCEANS.

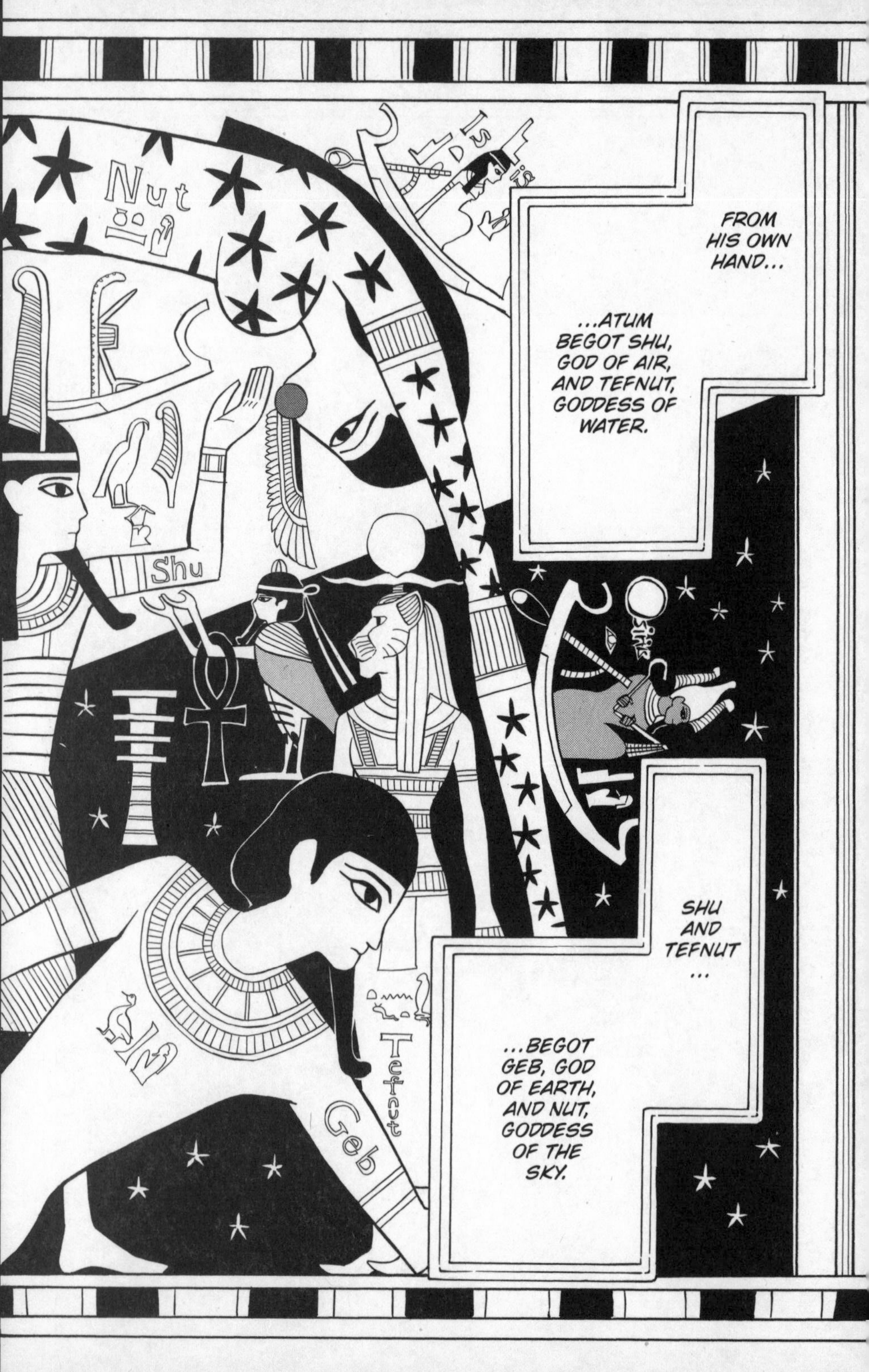
FROM HIS OWN HAND...
...ATUM BEGOT SHU, GOD OF AIR, AND TEFNUT, GODDESS OF WATER.
Nut
Shu
SHU AND TEFNUT ...
...BEGOT GEB, GOD OF EARTH, AND NUT, GODDESS OF THE SKY.
Tefnut
Geb

THEN, FROM THE UNION OF THE WEDDED GODS GEB AND NUT...

...CAME FOUR MORE GODS.

OSIRIS...

...ISIS...

...SETH...

...AND NEPHTHYS.

THESE NINE GODS ARE THE ORIGINAL GODS WHO WOULD LATER CREATE THE WORLD OF LIGHT IN WHICH WE LIVE—

THE ENNEAD.

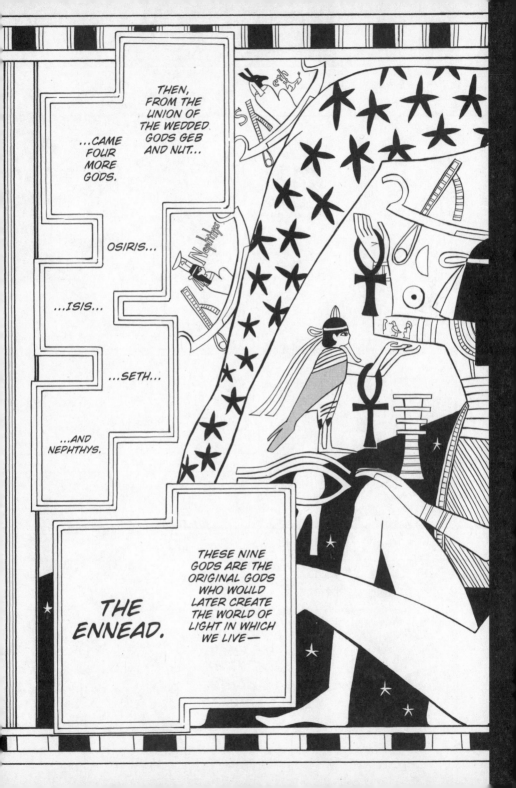

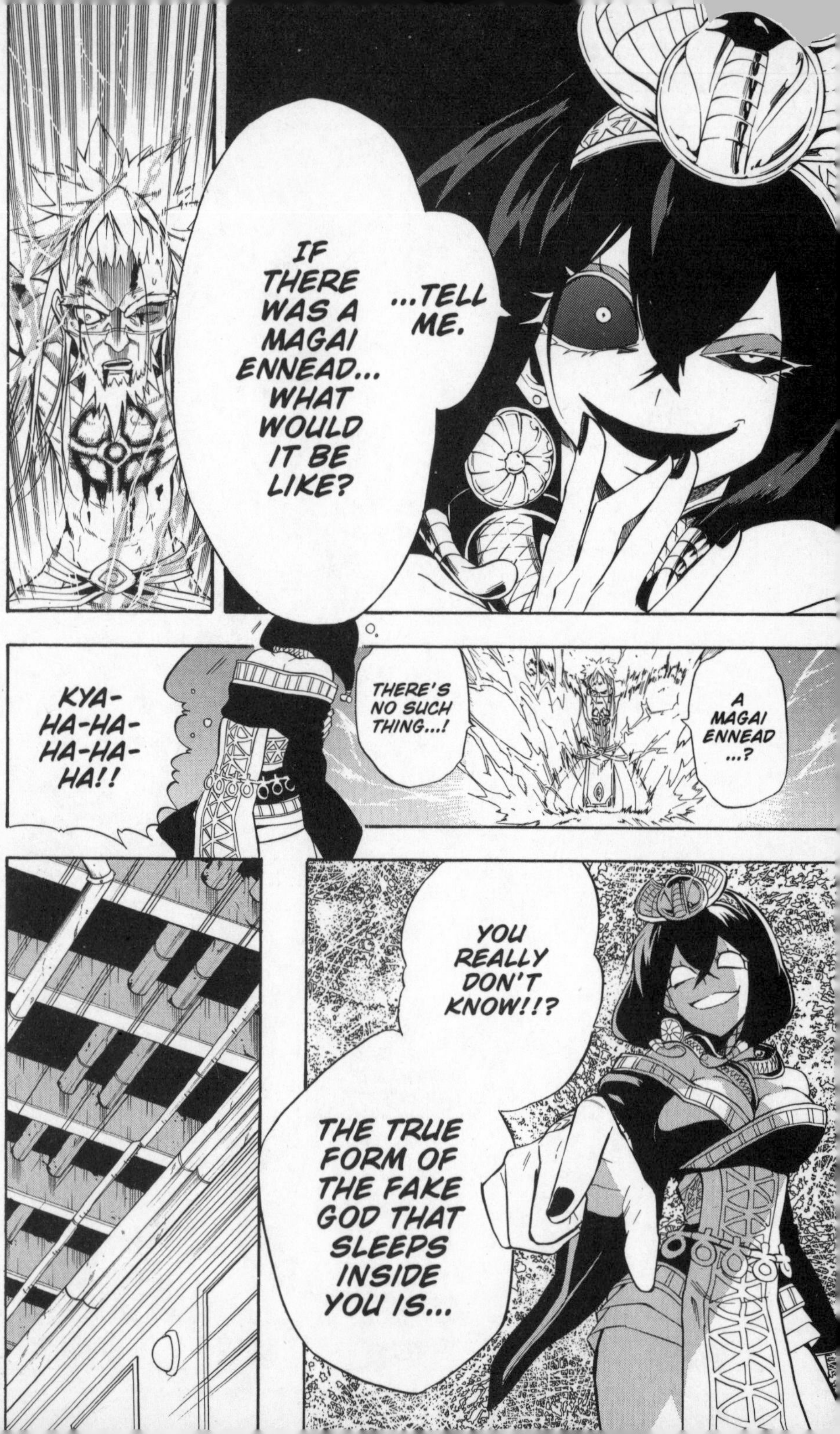
...TELL ME.
IF THERE WAS A MAGAI ENNEAD... WHAT WOULD IT BE LIKE?
A MAGAI ENNEAD ...?
THERE'S NO SUCH THING...!
KYA-HA-HA-HA-HA-HA!!
YOU REALLY DON'T KNOW!!?
THE TRUE FORM OF THE FAKE GOD THAT SLEEPS INSIDE YOU IS...

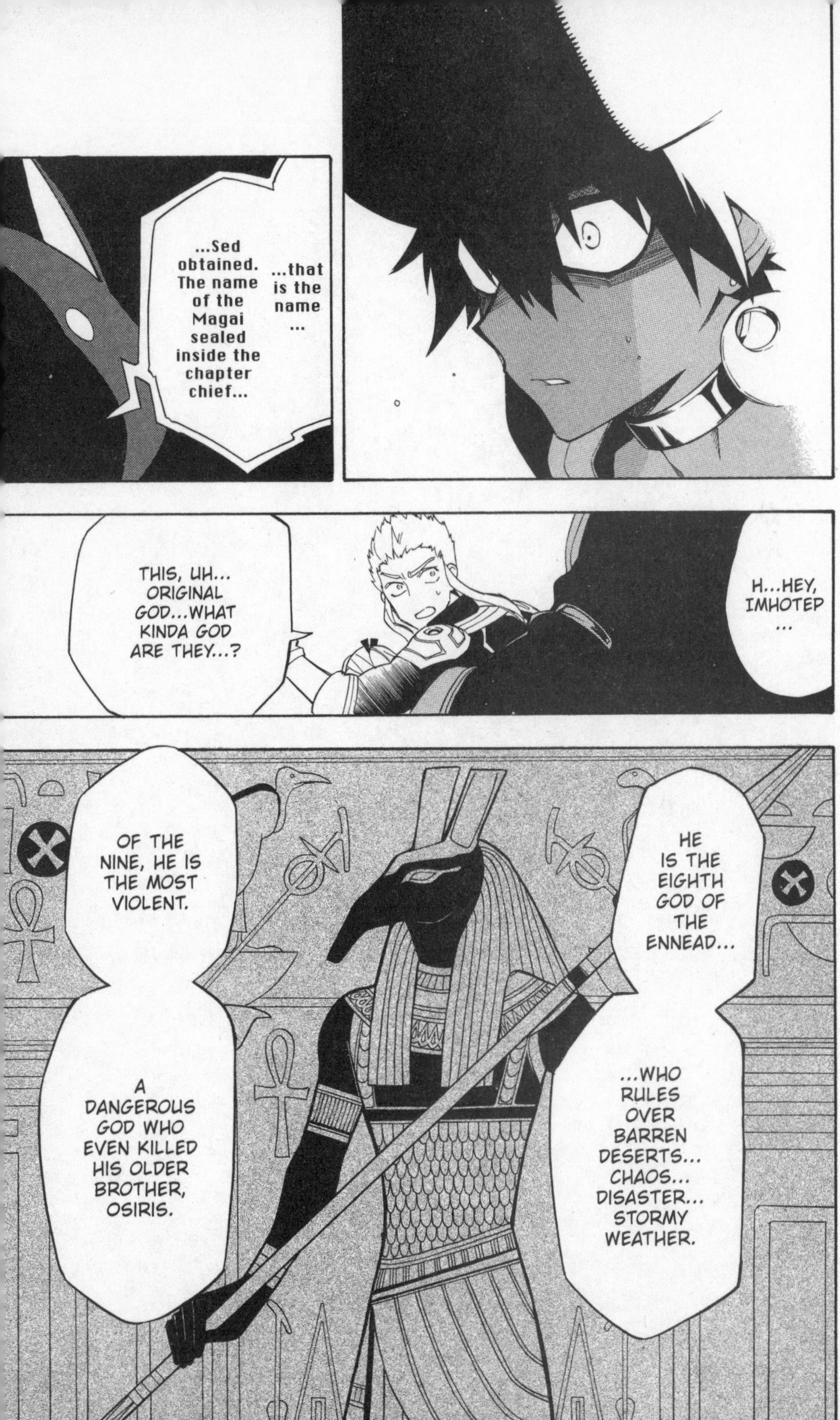
...that is the name ...
...Sed obtained. The name of the Magai sealed inside the chapter chief...
H...HEY, IMHOTEP ...
THIS, UH... ORIGINAL GOD...WHAT KINDA GOD ARE THEY...?
HE IS THE EIGHTH GOD OF THE ENNEAD...
...WHO RULES OVER BARREN DESERTS... CHAOS... DISASTER... STORMY WEATHER.
OF THE NINE, HE IS THE MOST VIOLENT.
A DANGEROUS GOD WHO EVEN KILLED HIS OLDER BROTHER, OSIRIS.

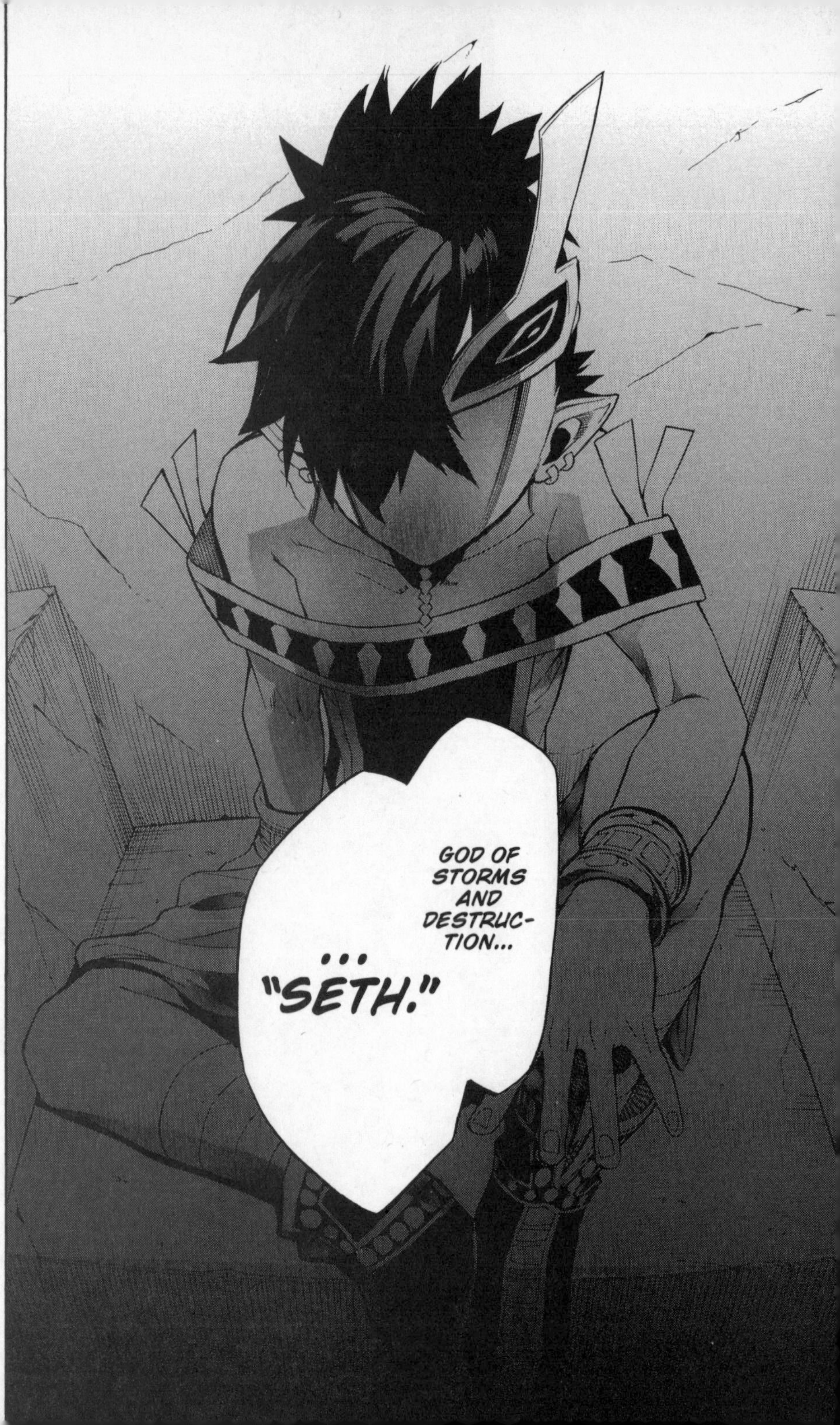
GOD OF STORMS AND DESTRUCTION...
... "SETH."

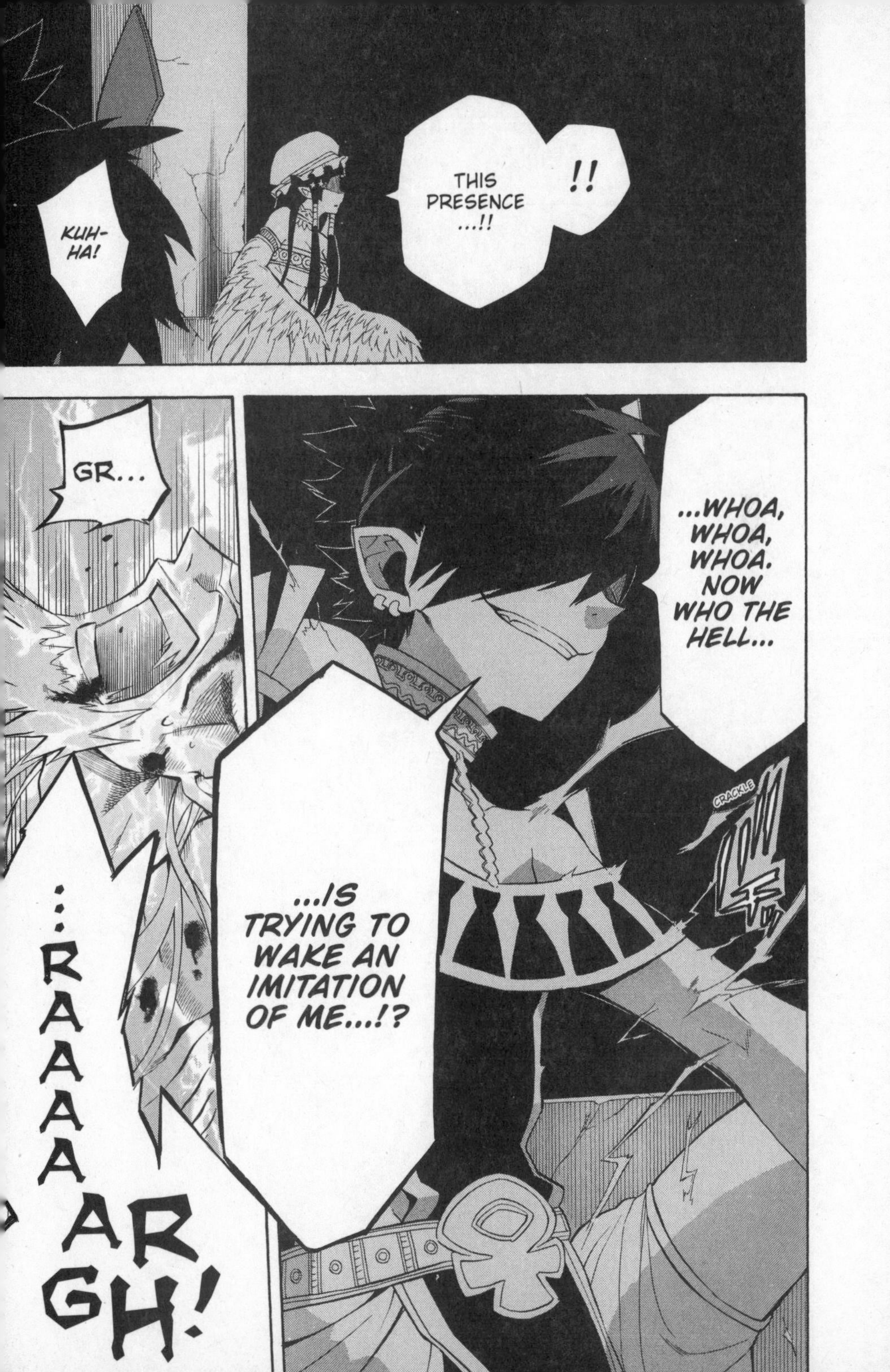
!!
THIS PRESENCE ...!!
KUH-HA!
...WHOA, WHOA, WHOA. NOW WHO THE HELL...
CRACKLE
...IS TRYING TO WAKE AN IMITATION OF ME...!?
GR...
...RAAAAARGH!

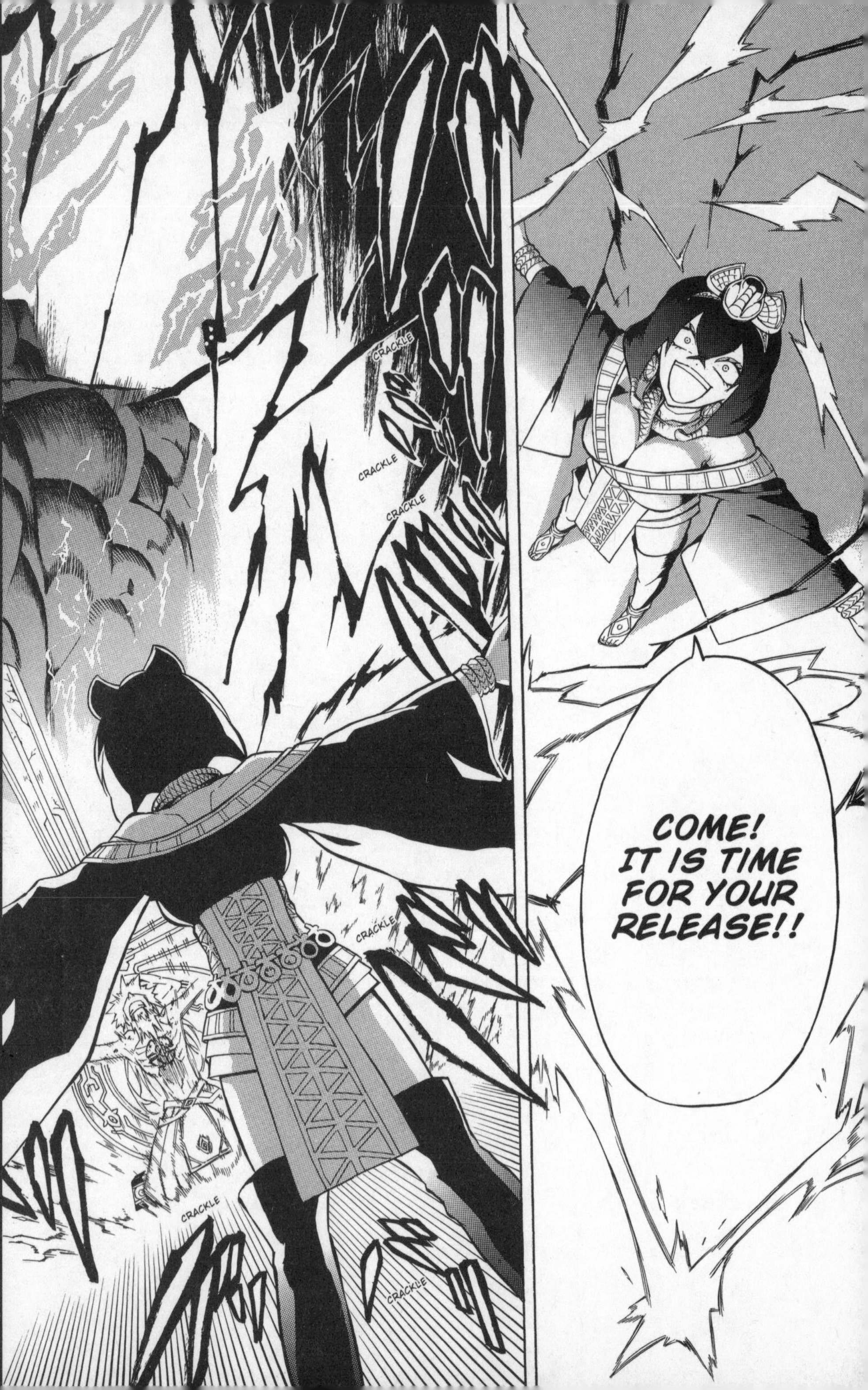
COME! IT IS TIME FOR YOUR RELEASE!!
CRACKLE
CRACKLE
CRACKLE
CRACKLE
CRACKLE
CRACKLE

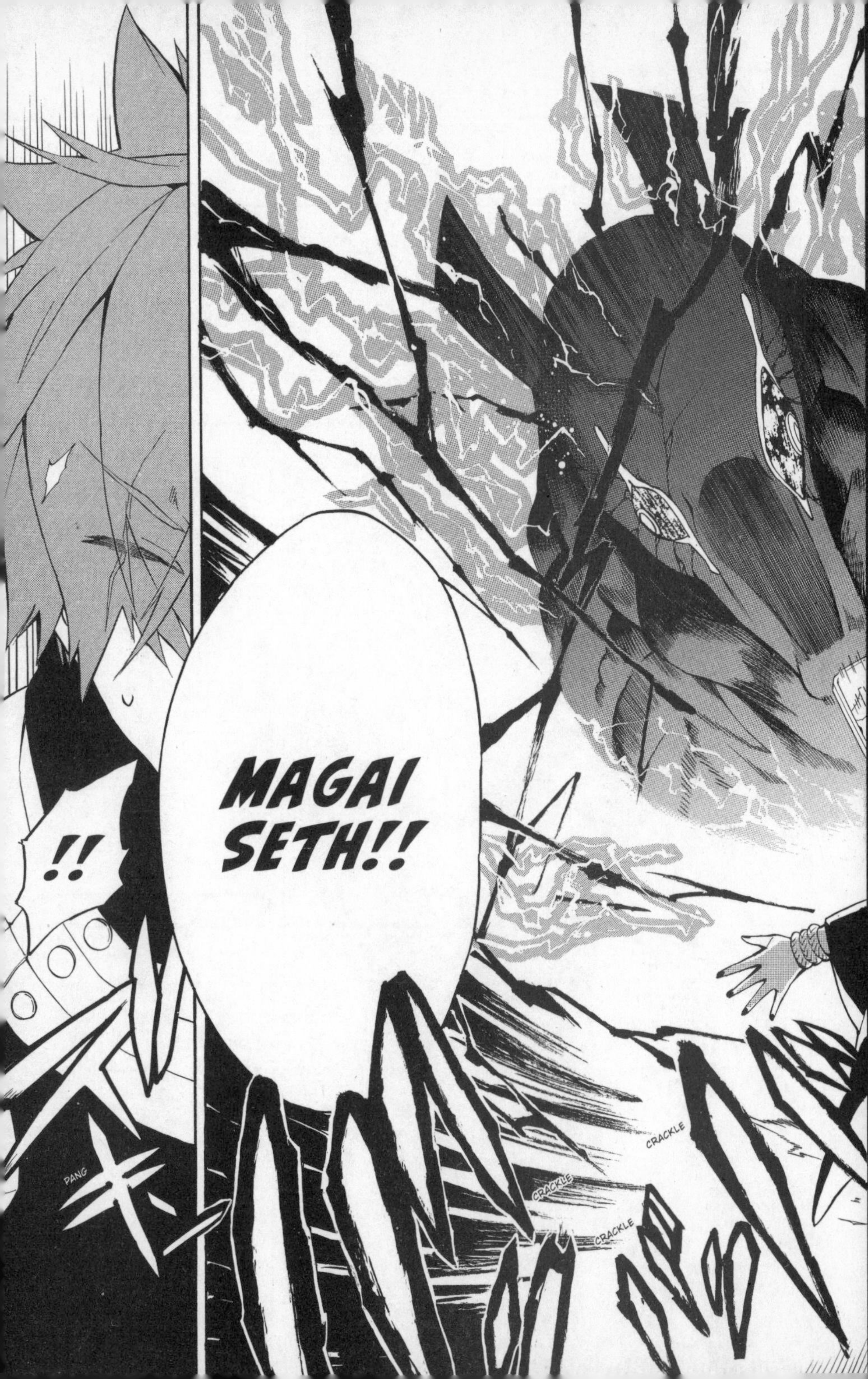
MAGAI SETH!!
CRACKLE
CRACKLE
CRACKLE
!!
PANG

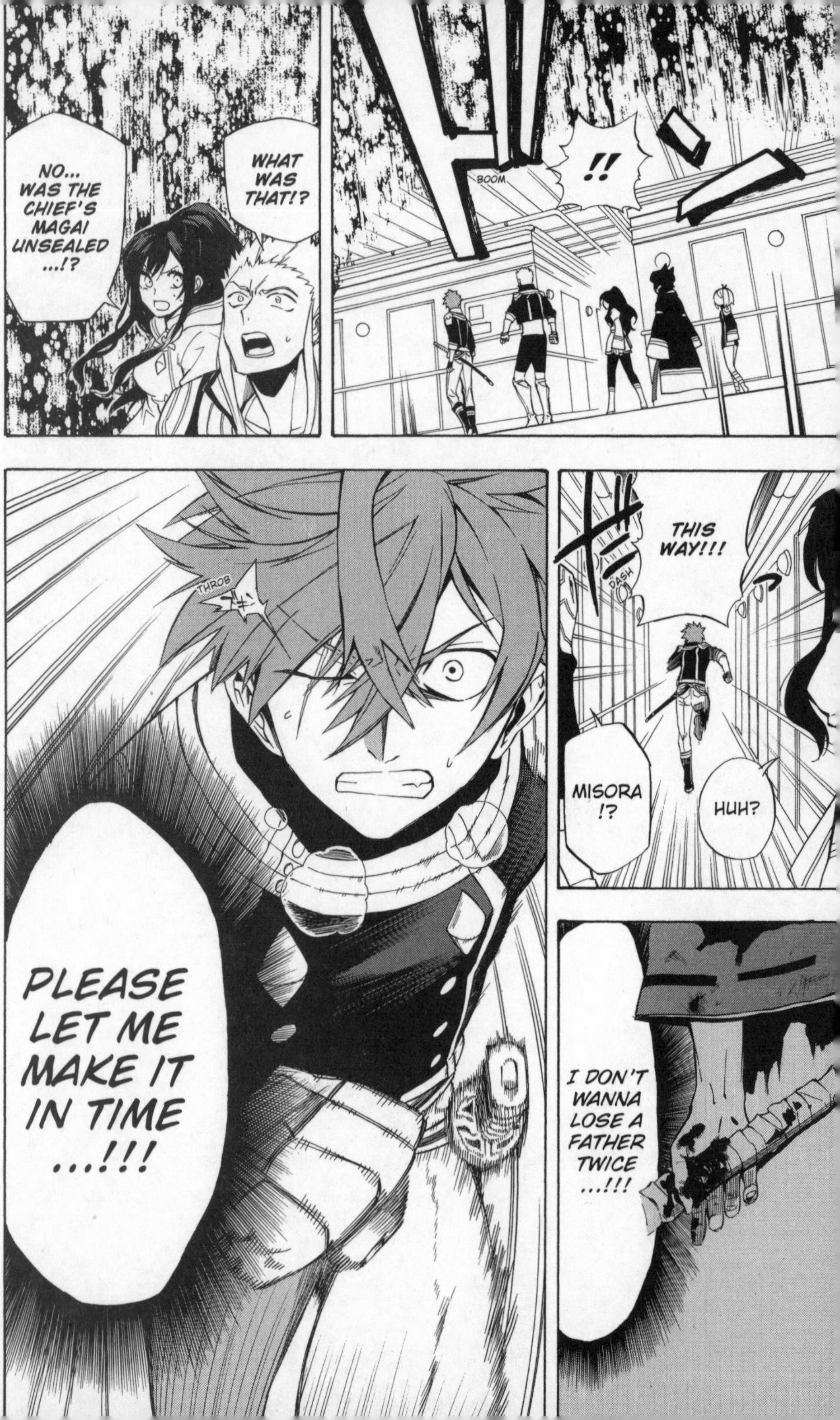
!!
BOOM
WHAT WAS THAT!?
NO... WAS THE CHIEF'S MAGAI UNSEALED ...!?
THIS WAY!!!
DASH
HUH?
MISORA !?
I DON'T WANNA LOSE A FATHER TWICE ...!!!
THROB
PLEASE LET ME MAKE IT IN TIME ...!!!

Great Priest Imhotep

Great Priest Imhotep

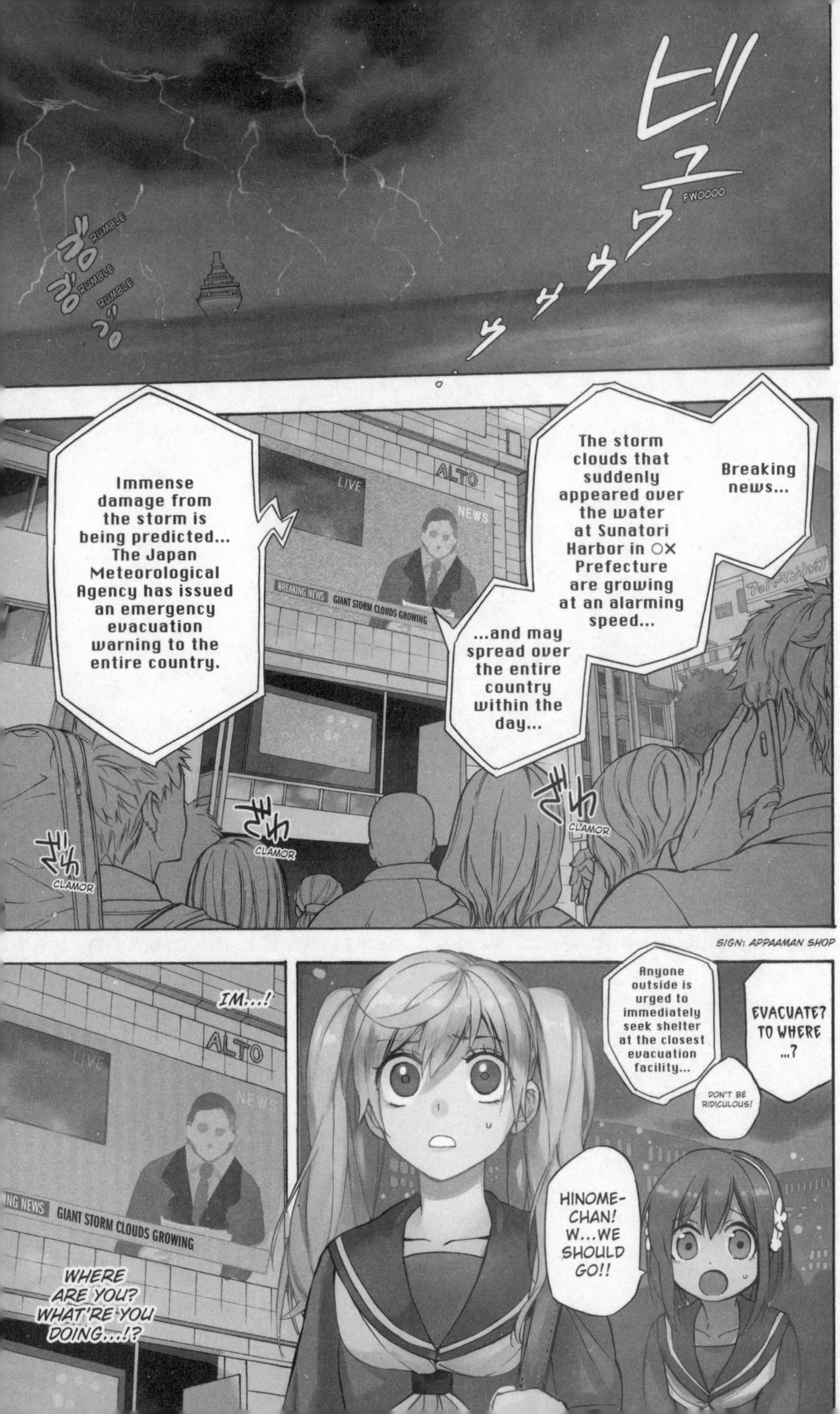
FWOOOO
RUMBLE
RUMBLE
RUMBLE
Breaking news...
The storm clouds that suddenly appeared over the water at Sunatori Harbor in ○✕ Prefecture are growing at an alarming speed...
...and may spread over the entire country within the day...
Immense damage from the storm is being predicted... The Japan Meteorological Agency has issued an emergency evacuation warning to the entire country.
ALTO
LIVE
NEWS
BREAKING NEWS
GIANT STORM CLOUDS GROWING
CLAMOR
CLAMOR
CLAMOR
SIGN: APPAAMAN SHOP
EVACUATE? TO WHERE ...?
Anyone outside is urged to immediately seek shelter at the closest evacuation facility...
DON'T BE RIDICULOUS!
HINOME-CHAN! W...WE SHOULD GO!!
IM...!
ALTO
LIVE
NEWS
GIANT STORM CLOUDS GROWING
WHERE ARE YOU? WHAT'RE YOU DOING...!?

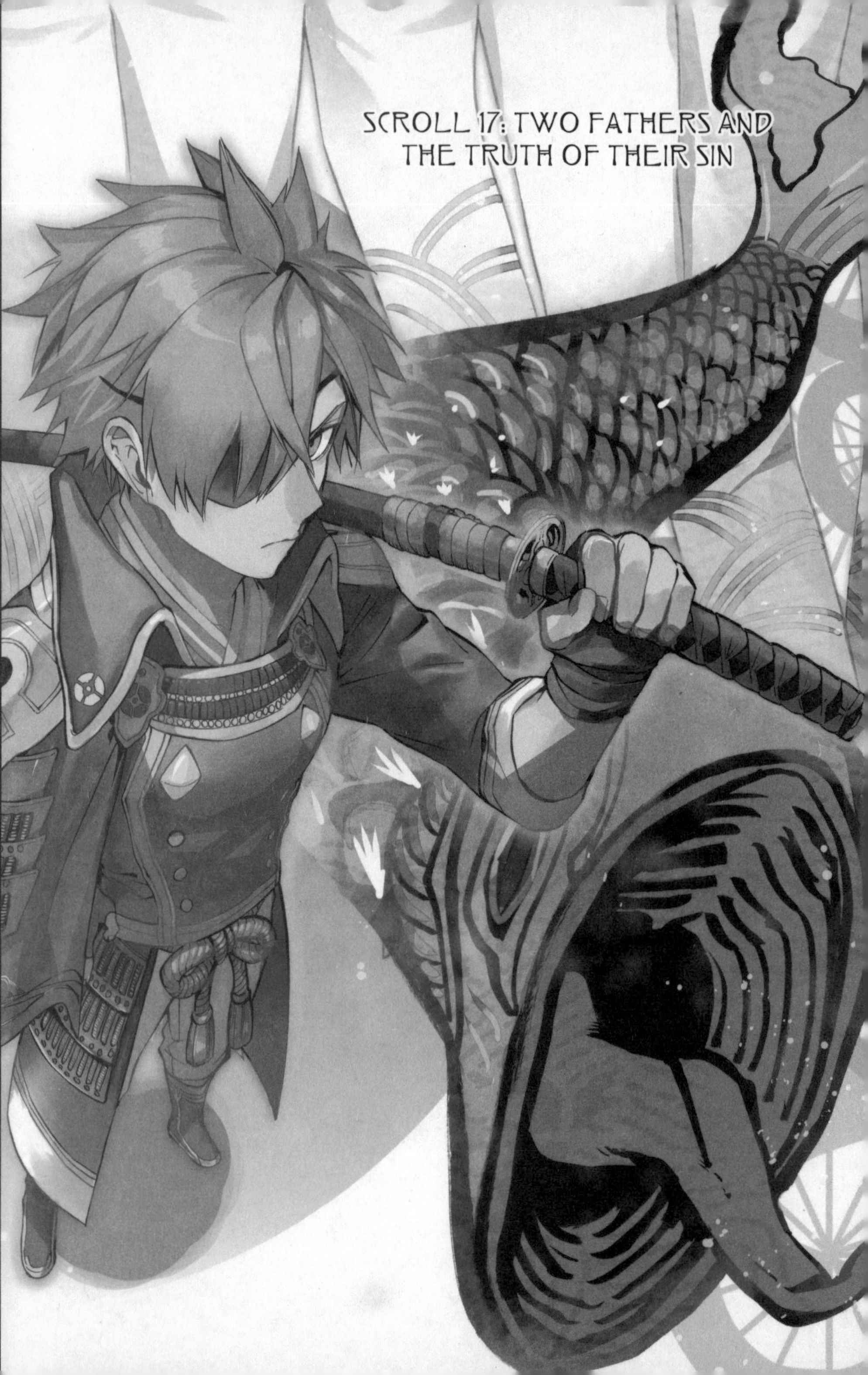
SCROLL 17: TWO FATHERS AND THE TRUTH OF THEIR SIN

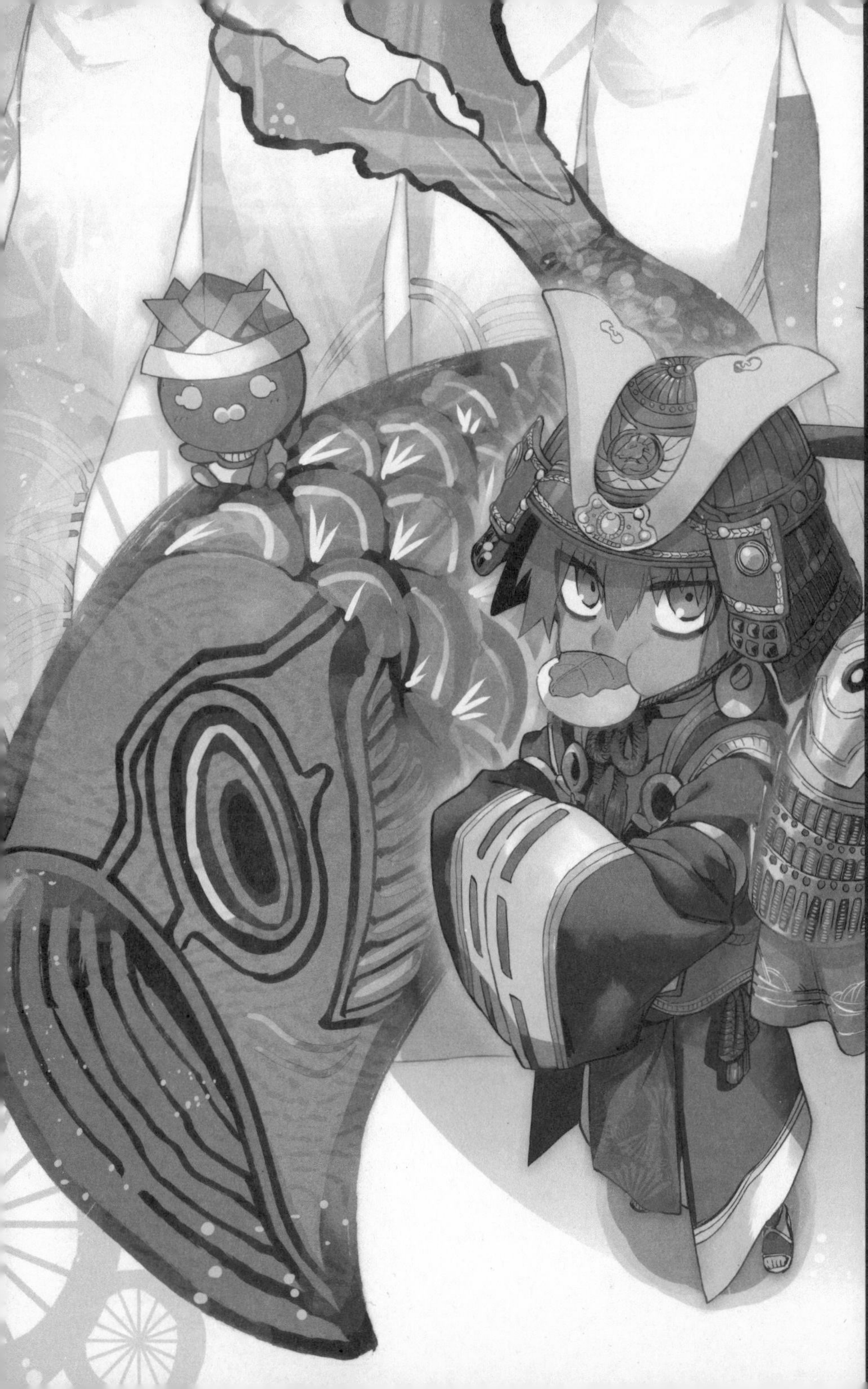

Great Priest Imhotep

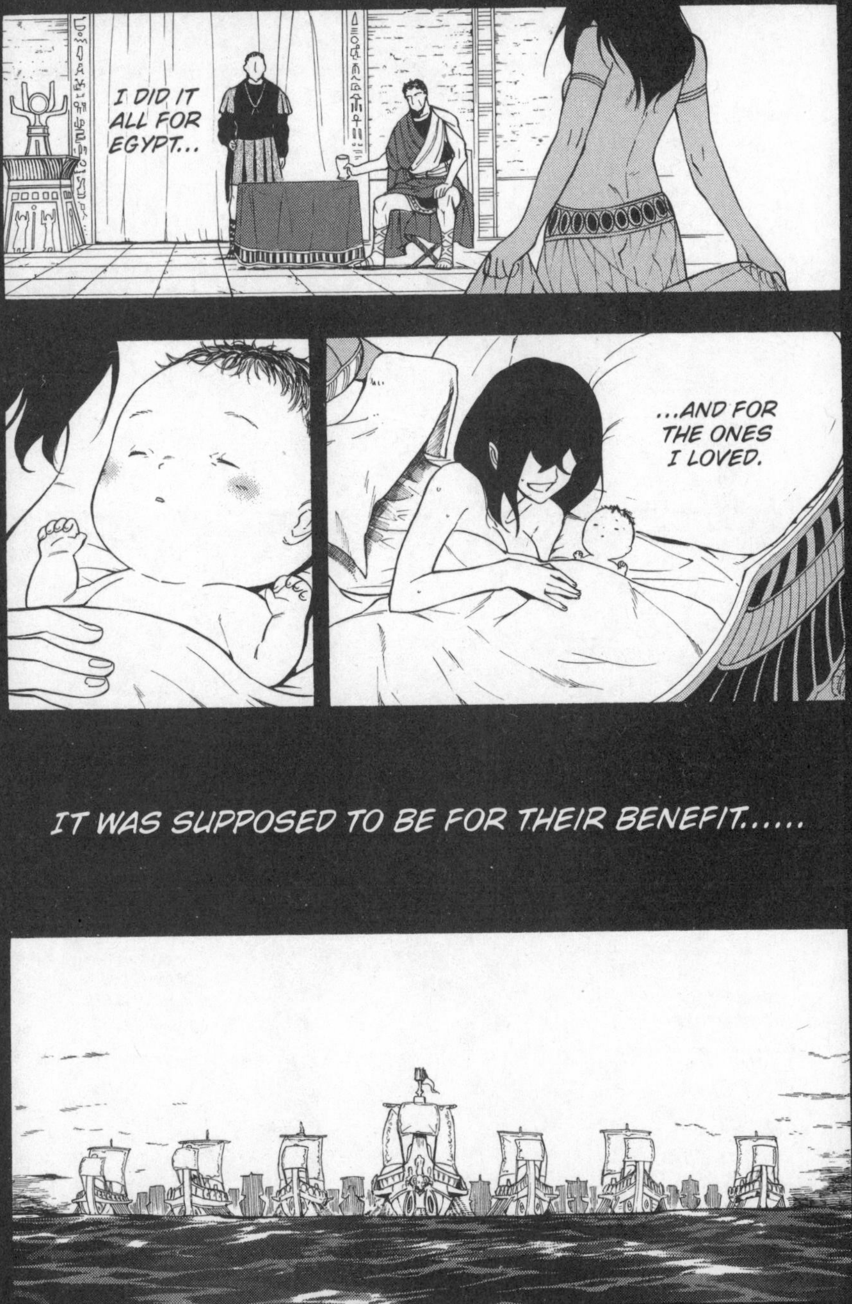
I DID IT ALL FOR EGYPT...
...AND FOR THE ONES I LOVED.
IT WAS SUPPOSED TO BE FOR THEIR BENEFIT......

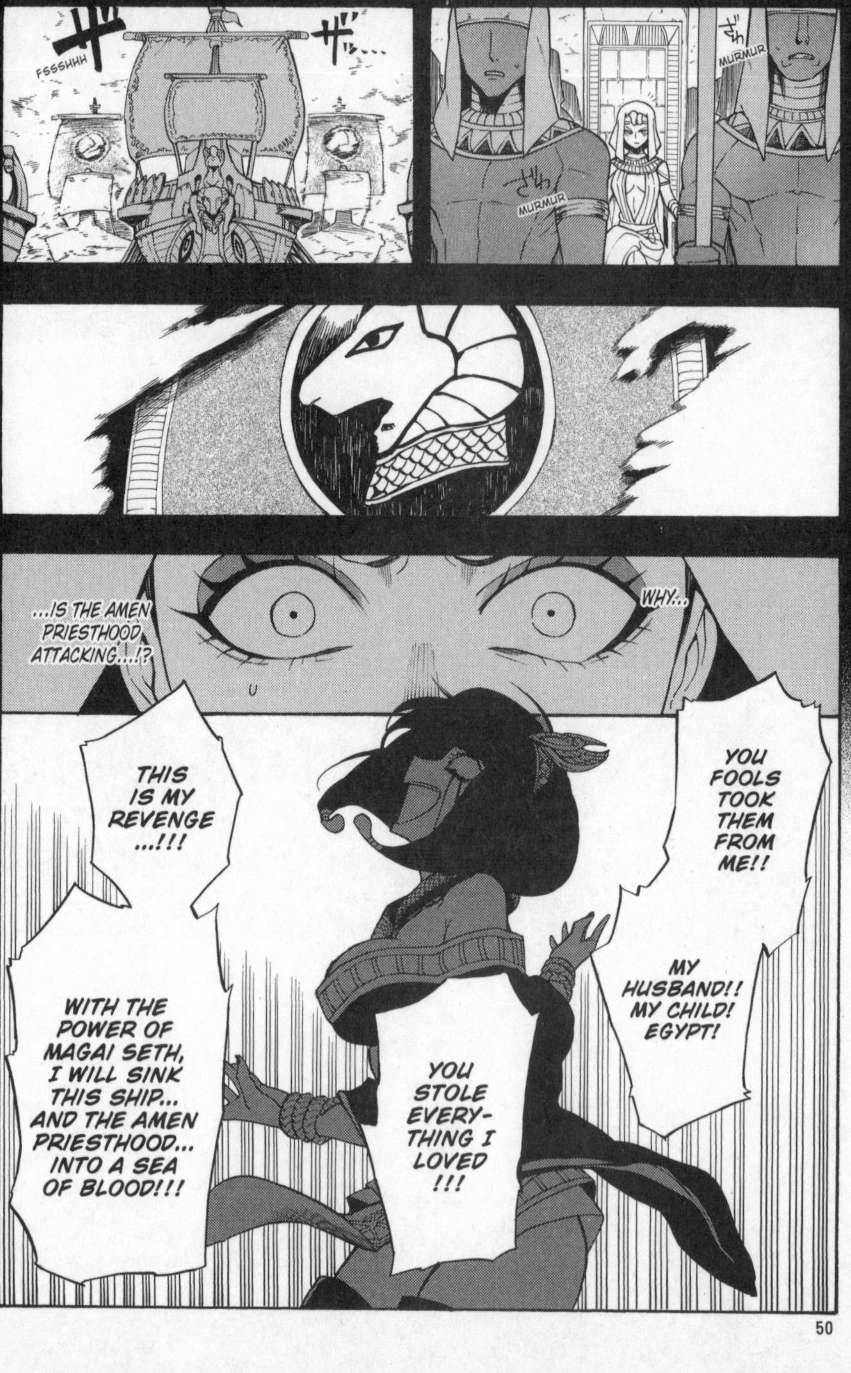
MURMUR
MURMUR
FSSSHHH
WHY...
...IS THE AMEN PRIESTHOOD ATTACKING...!?
YOU FOOLS TOOK THEM FROM ME!!
MY HUSBAND!! MY CHILD! EGYPT!
THIS IS MY REVENGE ...!!!
YOU STOLE EVERYTHING I LOVED !!!
WITH THE POWER OF MAGAI SETH, I WILL SINK THIS SHIP... AND THE AMEN PRIESTHOOD... INTO A SEA OF BLOOD!!!

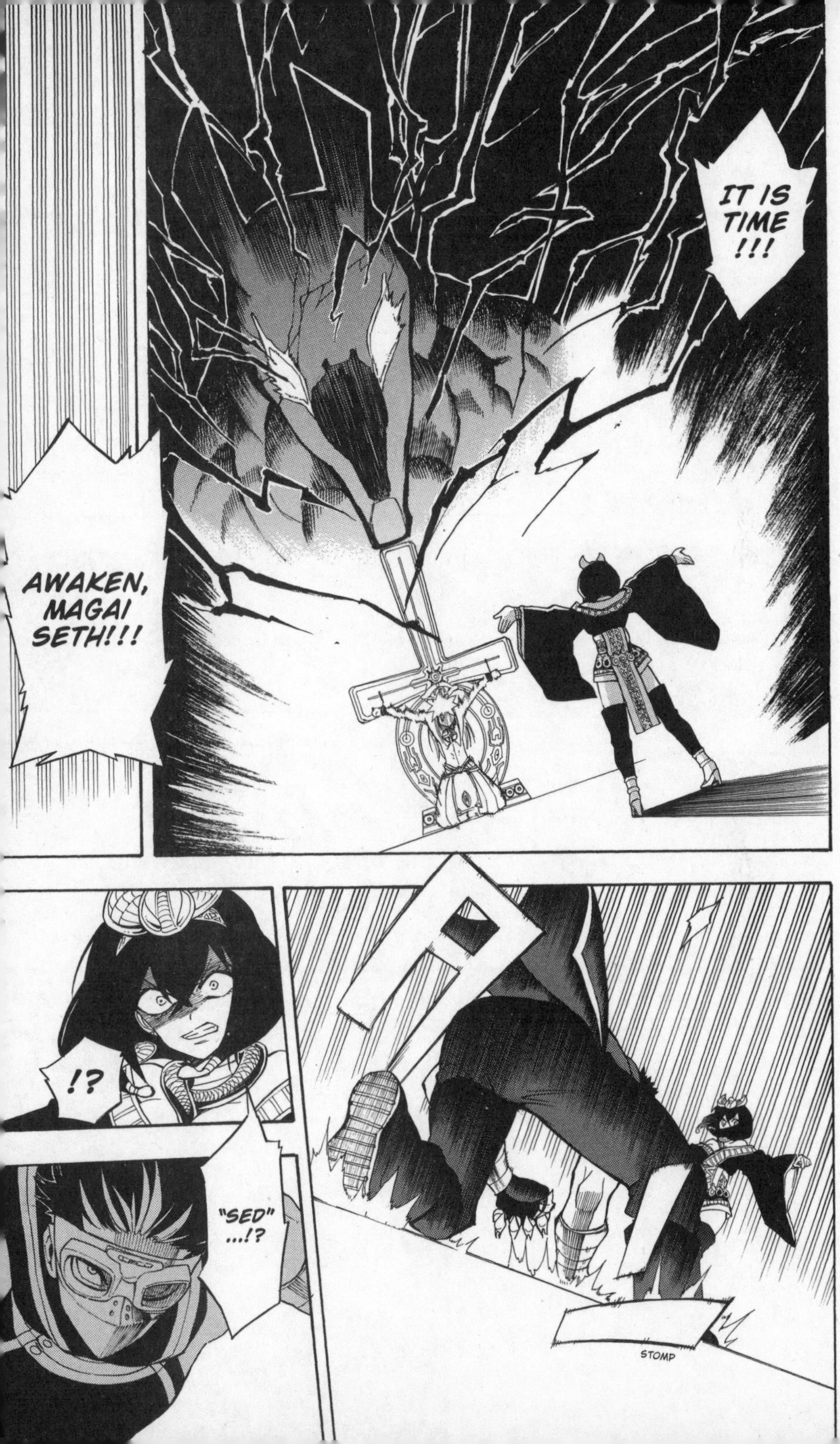
IT IS TIME!!!
AWAKEN, MAGAI SETH!!!
STOMP
!?
"SED" ...!?

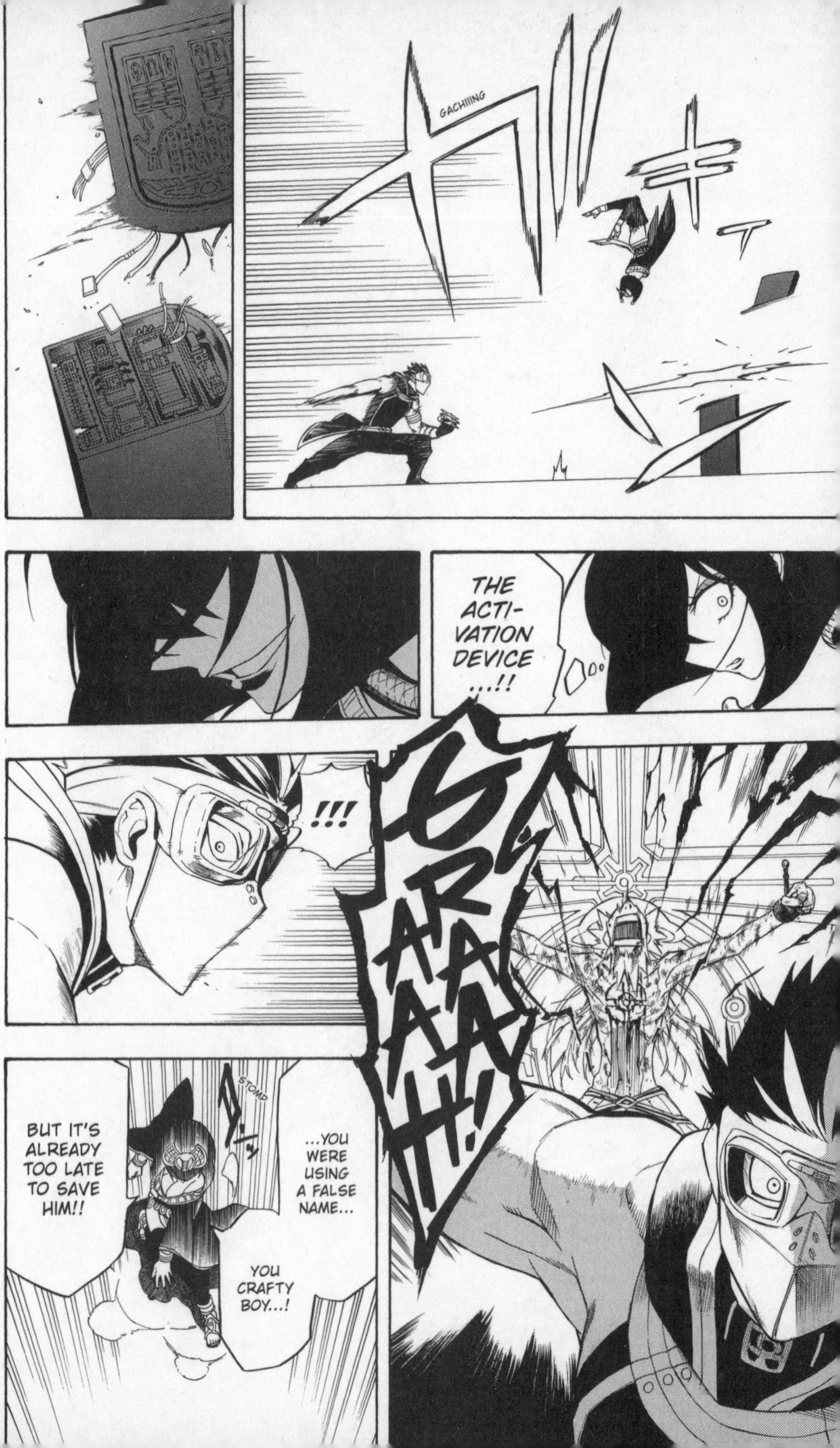
GACHIIING
THE ACTIVATION DEVICE ...!!
SARAAAH!!
!!!
STOMP
...YOU WERE USING A FALSE NAME...
YOU CRAFTY BOY...!
BUT IT'S ALREADY TOO LATE TO SAVE HIM!!

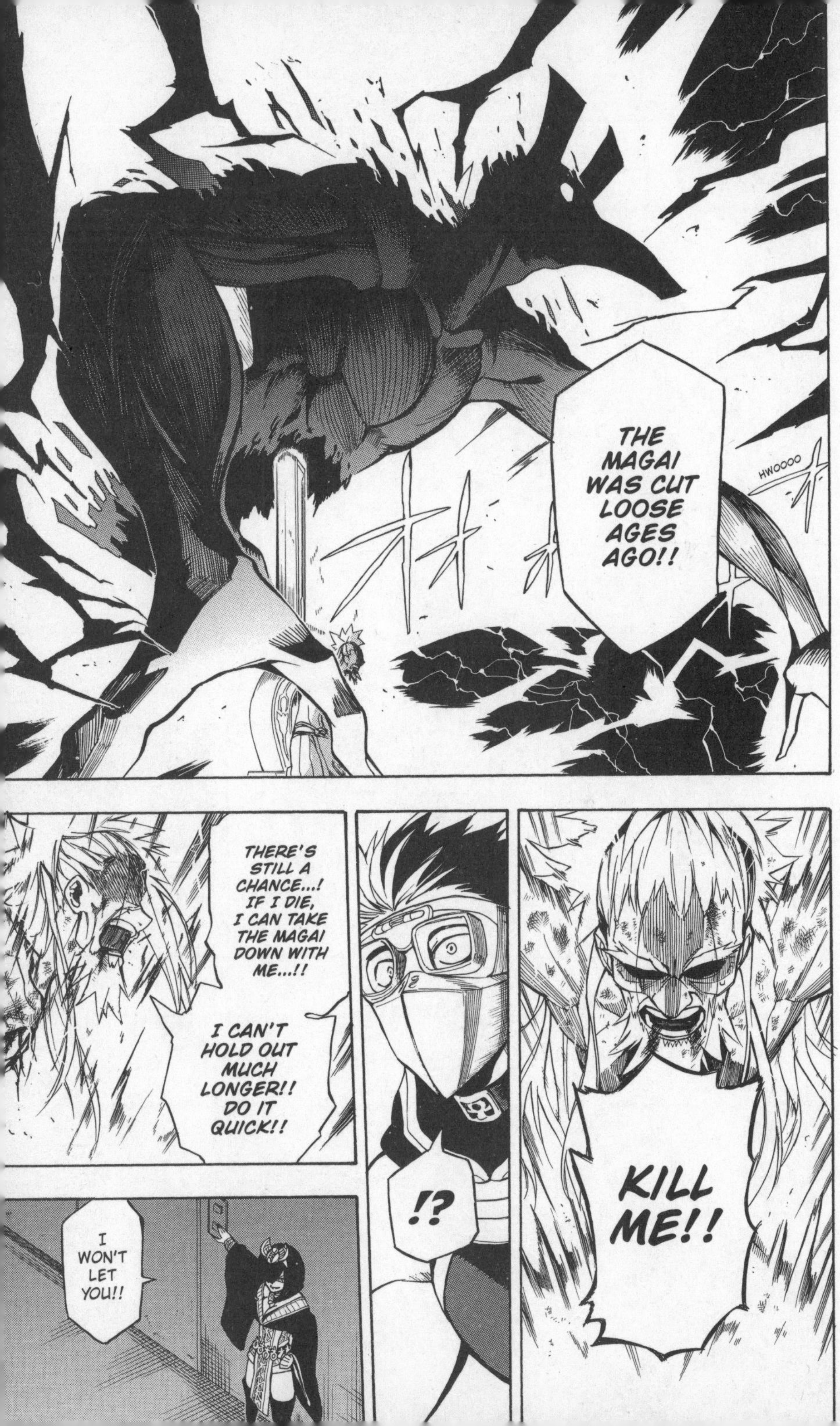
THE MAGAI WAS CUT LOOSE AGES AGO!!
HWOOOO
KILL ME!!
!?
THERE'S STILL A CHANCE...! IF I DIE, I CAN TAKE THE MAGAI DOWN WITH ME...!!
I CAN'T HOLD OUT MUCH LONGER!! DO IT QUICK!!
I WON'T LET YOU!!

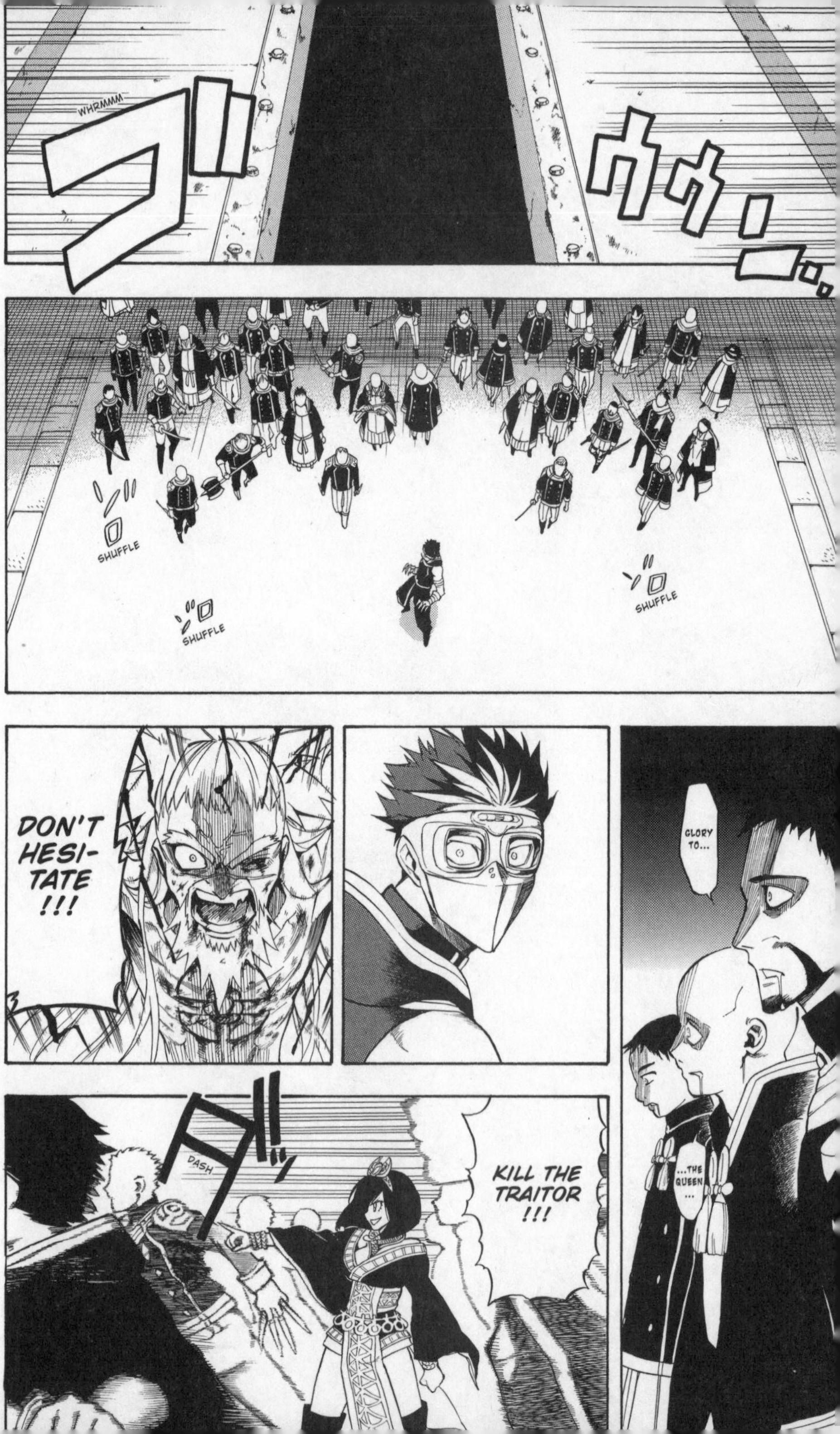
WHRMMM
SHUFFLE
SHUFFLE
SHUFFLE
GLORY TO...
...THE QUEEN...
DON'T HESI-TATE!!!
KILL THE TRAITOR!!!
DASH

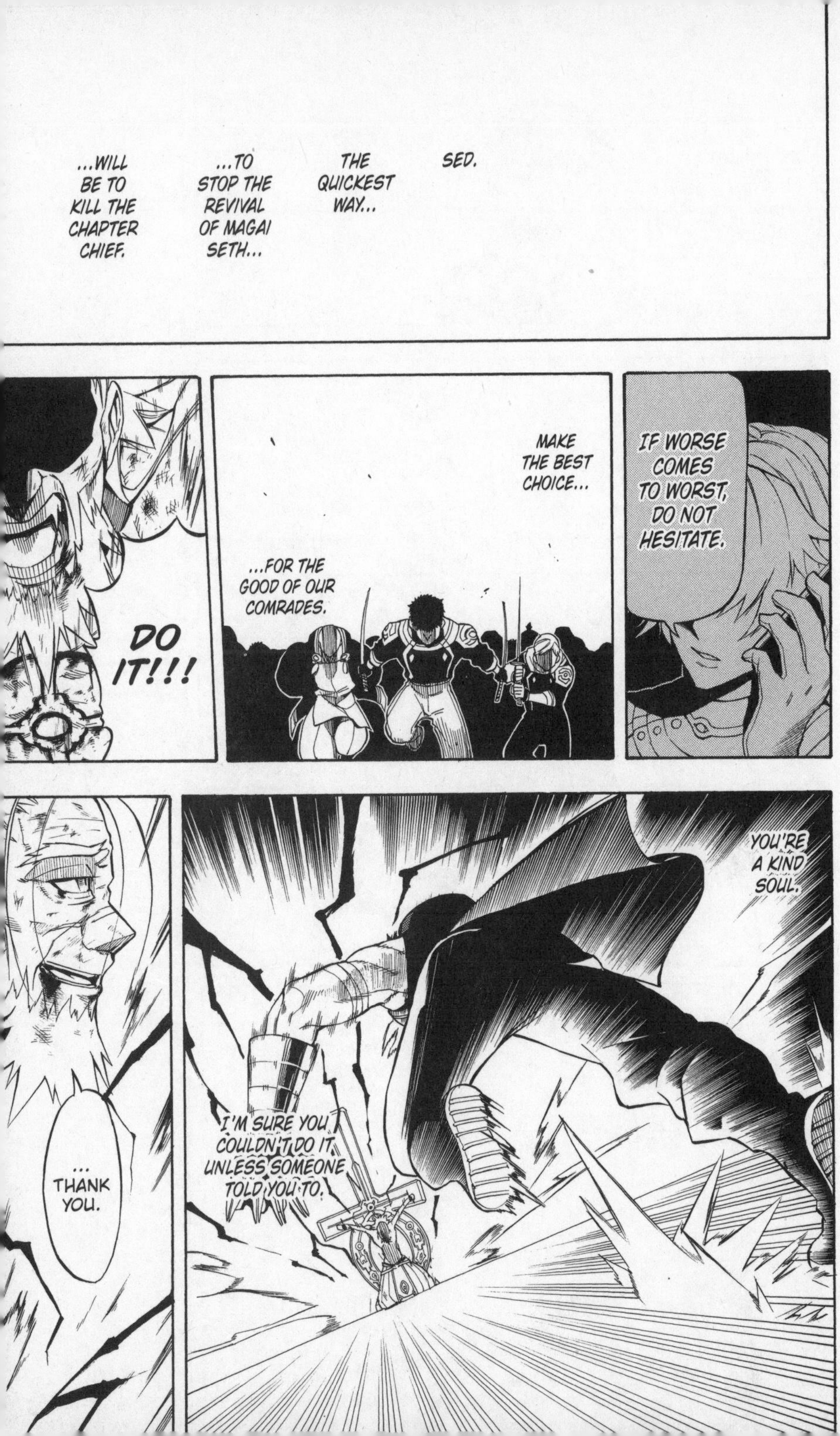
SED.
THE QUICKEST WAY...
...TO STOP THE REVIVAL OF MAGAI SETH...
...WILL BE TO KILL THE CHAPTER CHIEF.
IF WORSE COMES TO WORST, DO NOT HESITATE.
MAKE THE BEST CHOICE...
...FOR THE GOOD OF OUR COMRADES.
DO IT!!!
YOU'RE A KIND SOUL.
I'M SURE YOU COULDN'T DO IT UNLESS SOMEONE TOLD YOU TO.
... THANK YOU.

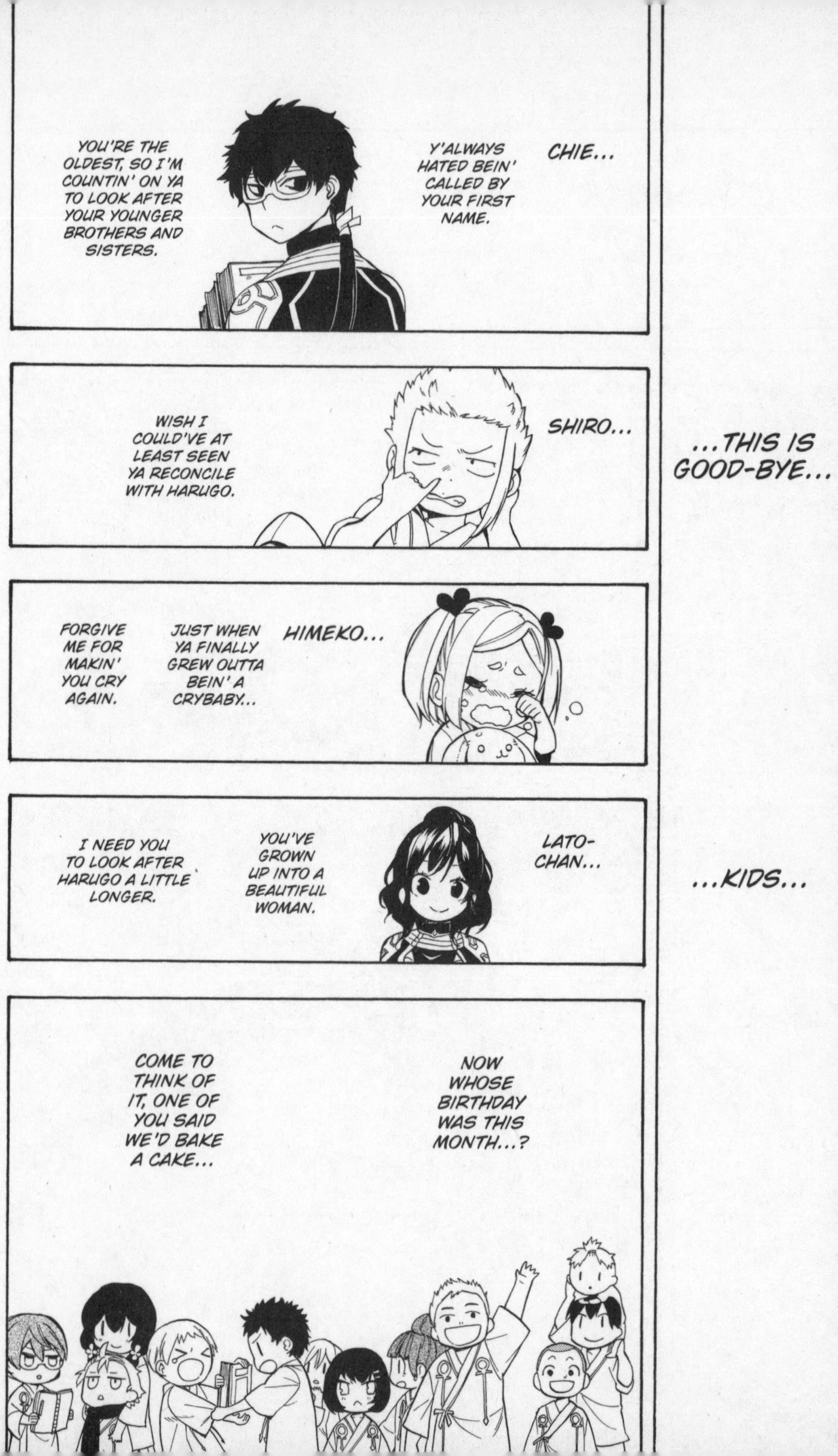
...THIS IS GOOD-BYE...
...KIDS...
CHIE...
Y'ALWAYS HATED BEIN' CALLED BY YOUR FIRST NAME.
YOU'RE THE OLDEST, SO I'M COUNTIN' ON YA TO LOOK AFTER YOUR YOUNGER BROTHERS AND SISTERS.
SHIRO...
WISH I COULD'VE AT LEAST SEEN YA RECONCILE WITH HARUGO.
HIMEKO...
JUST WHEN YA FINALLY GREW OUTTA BEIN' A CRYBABY...
FORGIVE ME FOR MAKIN' YOU CRY AGAIN.
LATO-CHAN...
YOU'VE GROWN UP INTO A BEAUTIFUL WOMAN.
I NEED YOU TO LOOK AFTER HARUGO A LITTLE LONGER.
NOW WHOSE BIRTHDAY WAS THIS MONTH...?
COME TO THINK OF IT, ONE OF YOU SAID WE'D BAKE A CAKE...

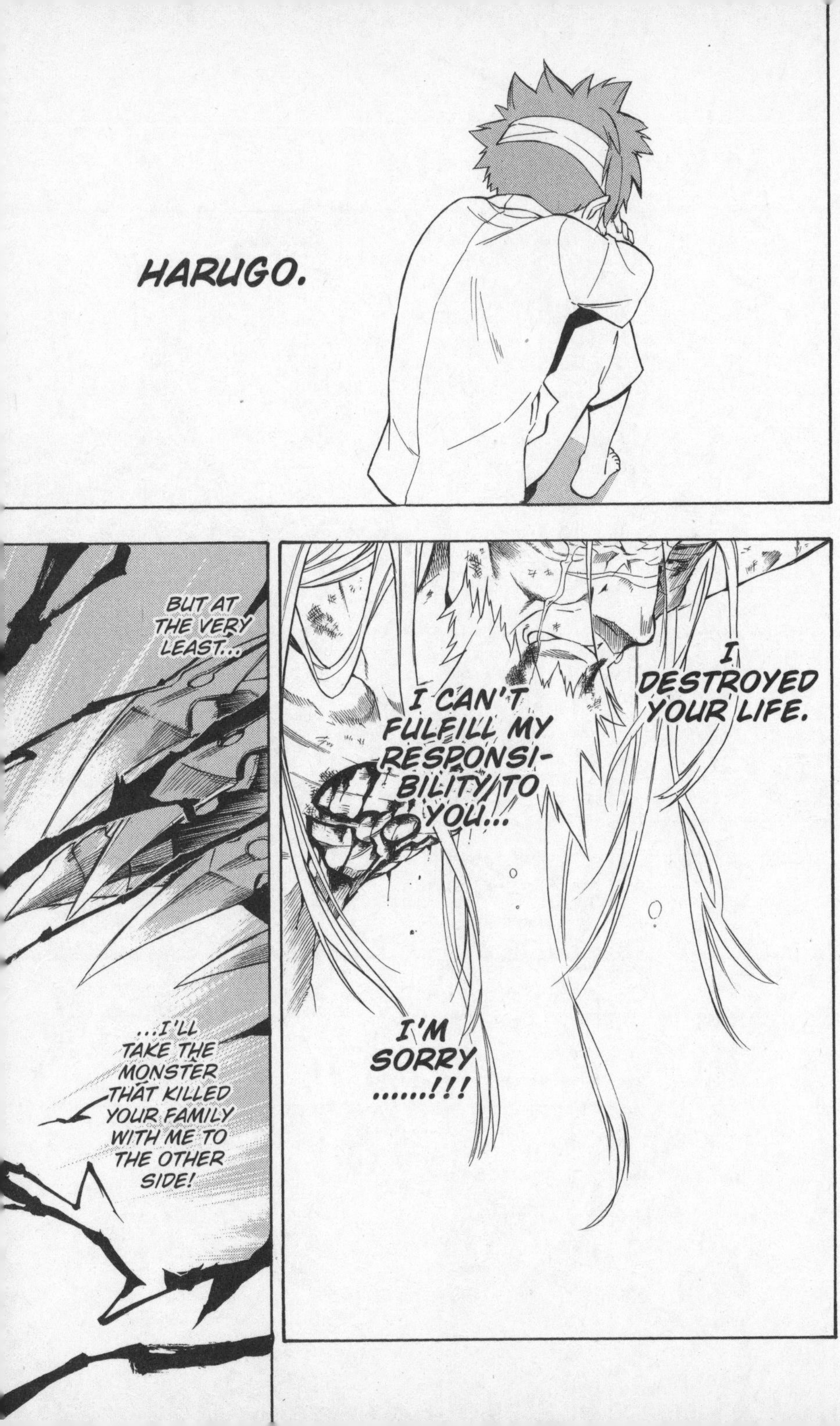
HARUGO.
I DESTROYED YOUR LIFE.
I CAN'T FULFILL MY RESPONSIBILITY TO YOU...
I'M SORRY ......!!!
BUT AT THE VERY LEAST...
...I'LL TAKE THE MONSTER THAT KILLED YOUR FAMILY WITH ME TO THE OTHER SIDE!

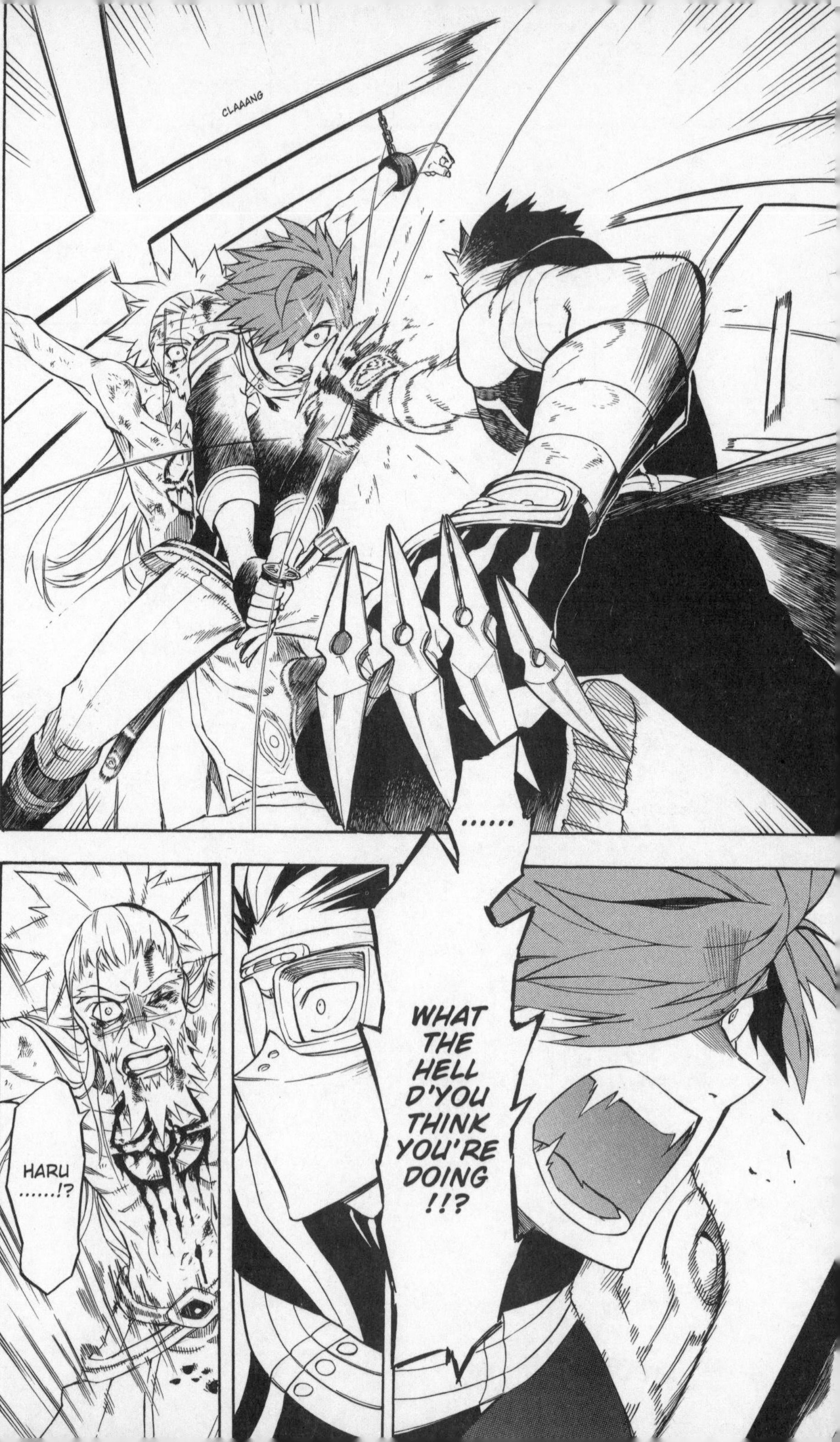
CLAAANG
......
WHAT THE HELL D'YOU THINK YOU'RE DOING !!?
HARU ......!?

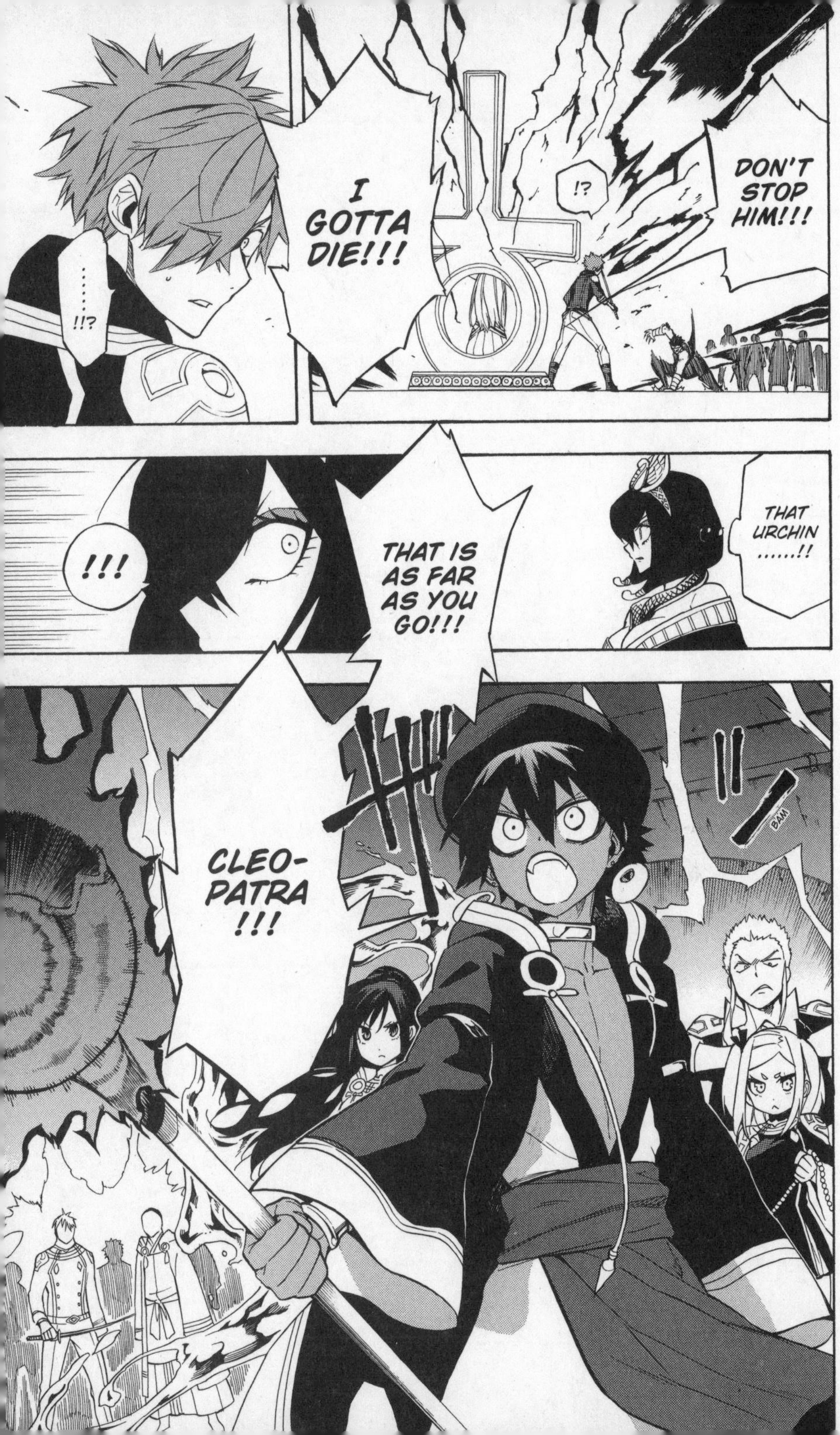

DON'T STOP HIM!!!
!?
I GOTTA DIE!!!
......!!?
THAT URCHIN ......!!
THAT IS AS FAR AS YOU GO!!!
!!!
BAM
CLEO-PATRA!!!

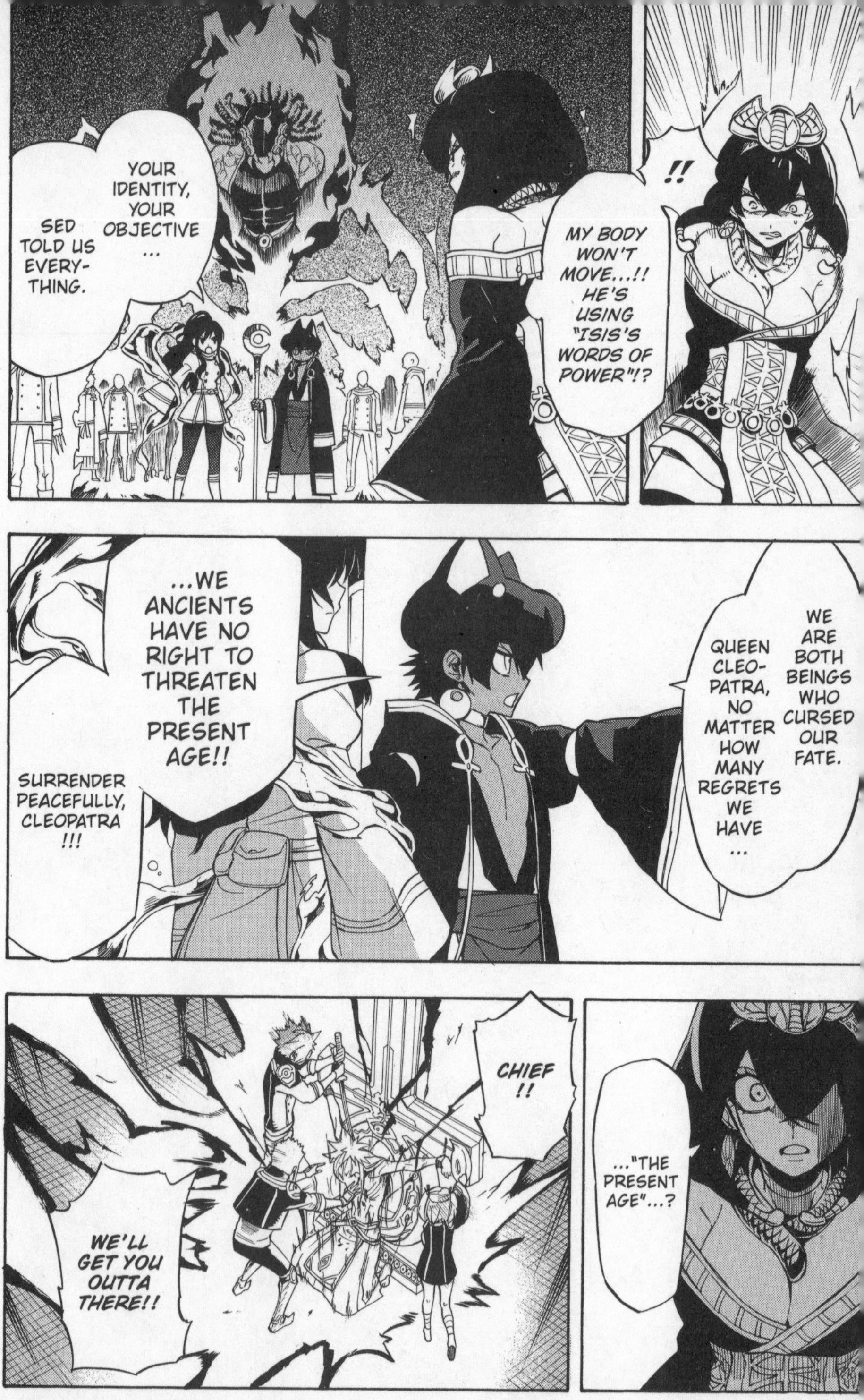
!!
MY BODY WON'T MOVE...!! HE'S USING "ISIS'S WORDS OF POWER"!?
YOUR IDENTITY, YOUR OBJECTIVE ...
SED TOLD US EVERY-THING.
WE ARE BOTH BEINGS WHO CURSED OUR FATE.
QUEEN CLEO-PATRA, NO MATTER HOW MANY REGRETS WE HAVE ...
...WE ANCIENTS HAVE NO RIGHT TO THREATEN THE PRESENT AGE!!
SURRENDER PEACEFULLY, CLEOPATRA !!!
..."THE PRESENT AGE"...?
CHIEF !!
WE'LL GET YOU OUTTA THERE!!

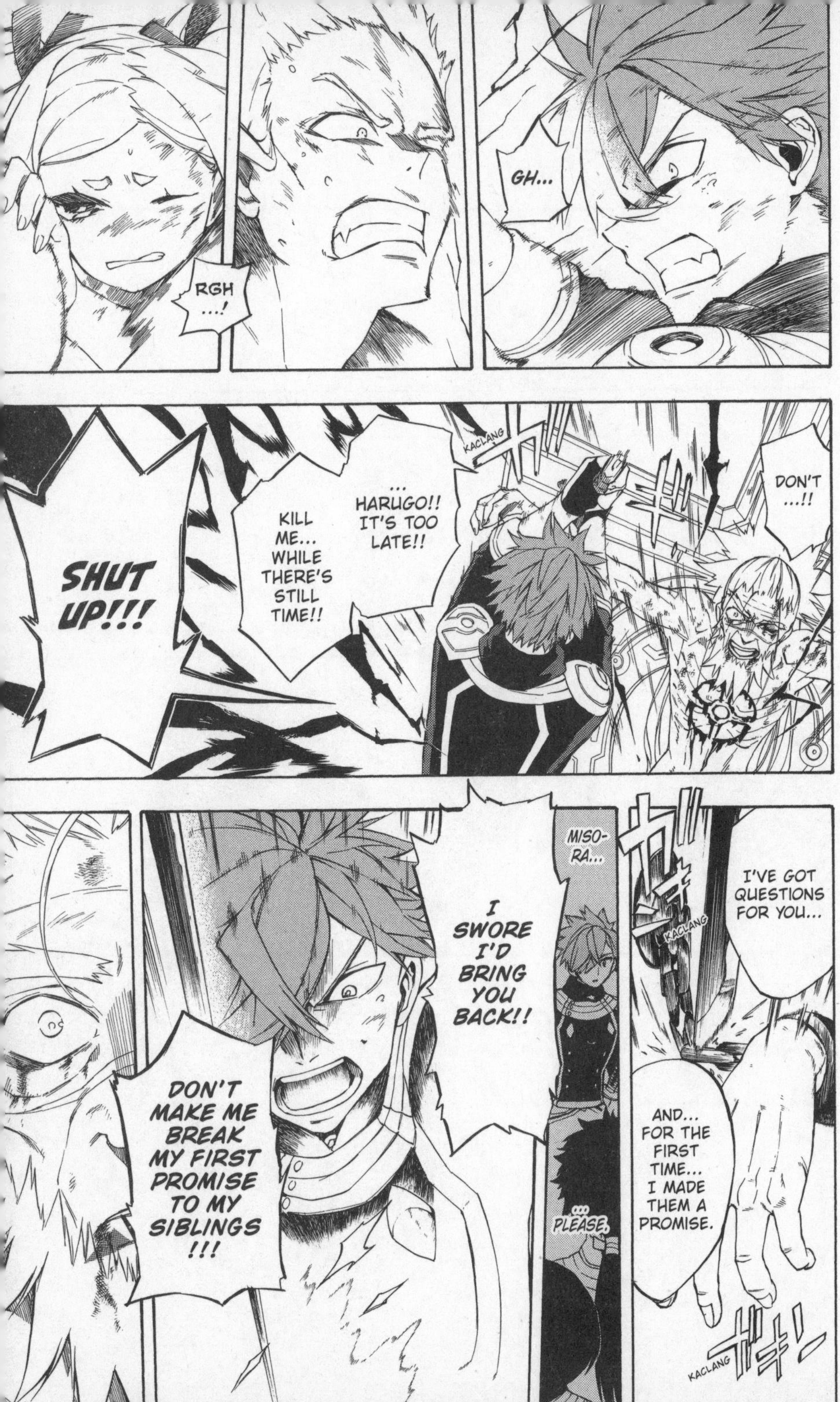
GH...
RGH ....!
DON'T ...!!
KACLANG
... HARUGO!! IT'S TOO LATE!!
KILL ME... WHILE THERE'S STILL TIME!!
SHUT UP!!!
I'VE GOT QUESTIONS FOR YOU...
KACLANG
AND... FOR THE FIRST TIME... I MADE THEM A PROMISE.
KACLANG
MISO-RA...
...PLEASE.
I SWORE I'D BRING YOU BACK!!
DON'T MAKE ME BREAK MY FIRST PROMISE TO MY SIBLINGS!!!

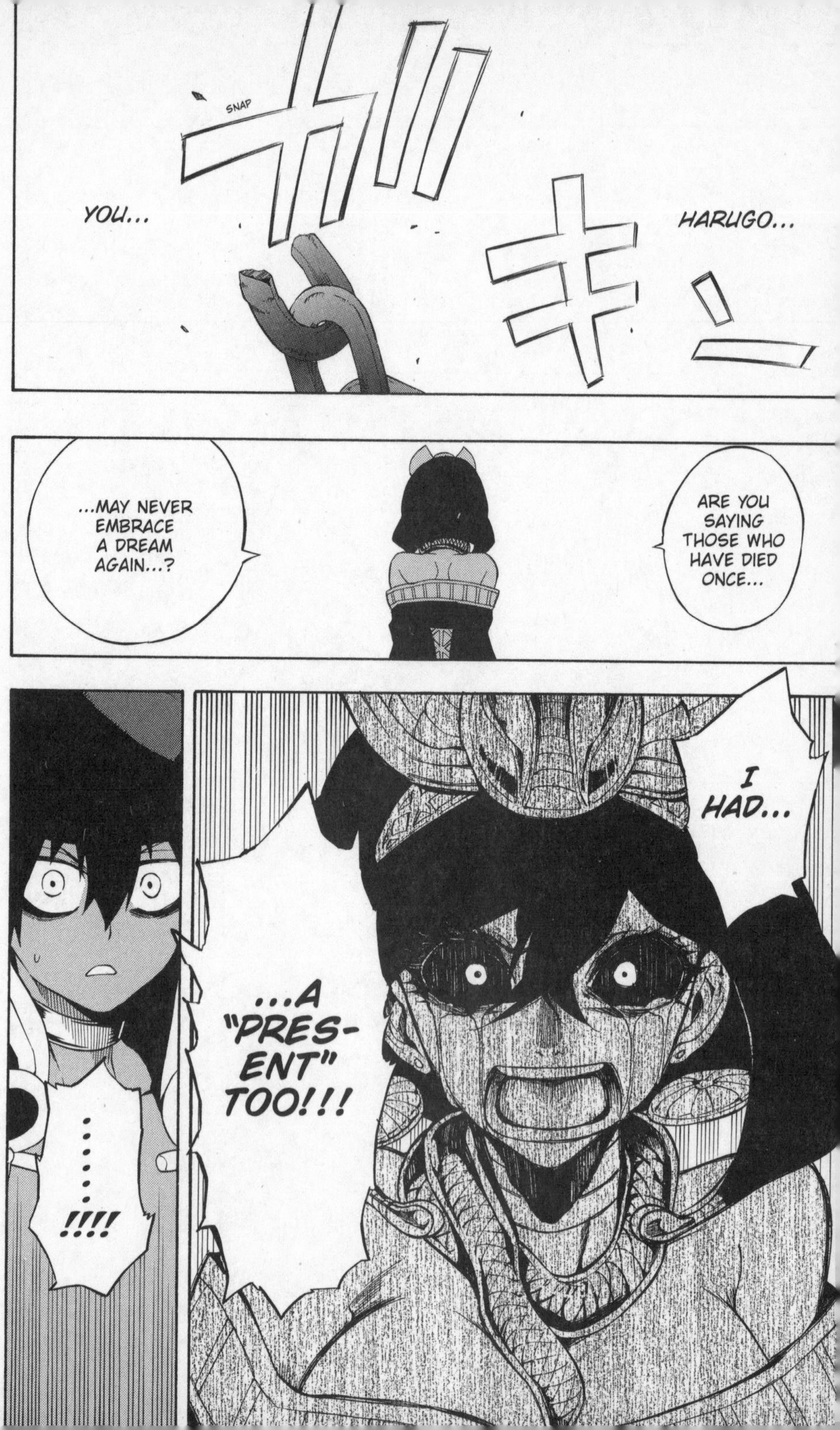
HARUGO...
SNAP
YOU...
ARE YOU SAYING THOSE WHO HAVE DIED ONCE...
...MAY NEVER EMBRACE A DREAM AGAIN...?
I HAD...
...A "PRES-ENT" TOO!!!
......
!!!!

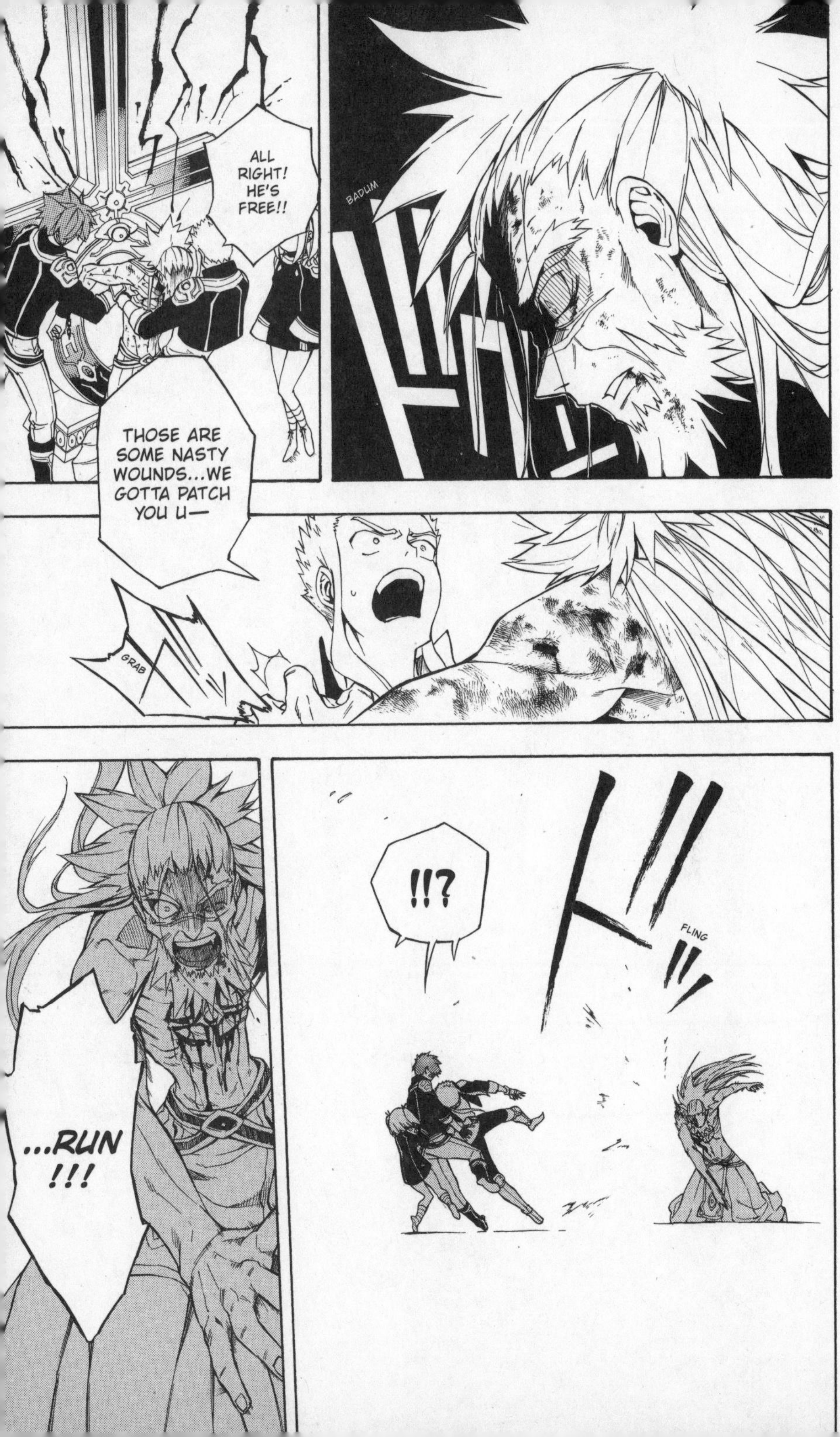
BADUM
ALL RIGHT! HE'S FREE!!
THOSE ARE SOME NASTY WOUNDS...WE GOTTA PATCH YOU U—
GRAB
!!?
FLING
...RUN !!!

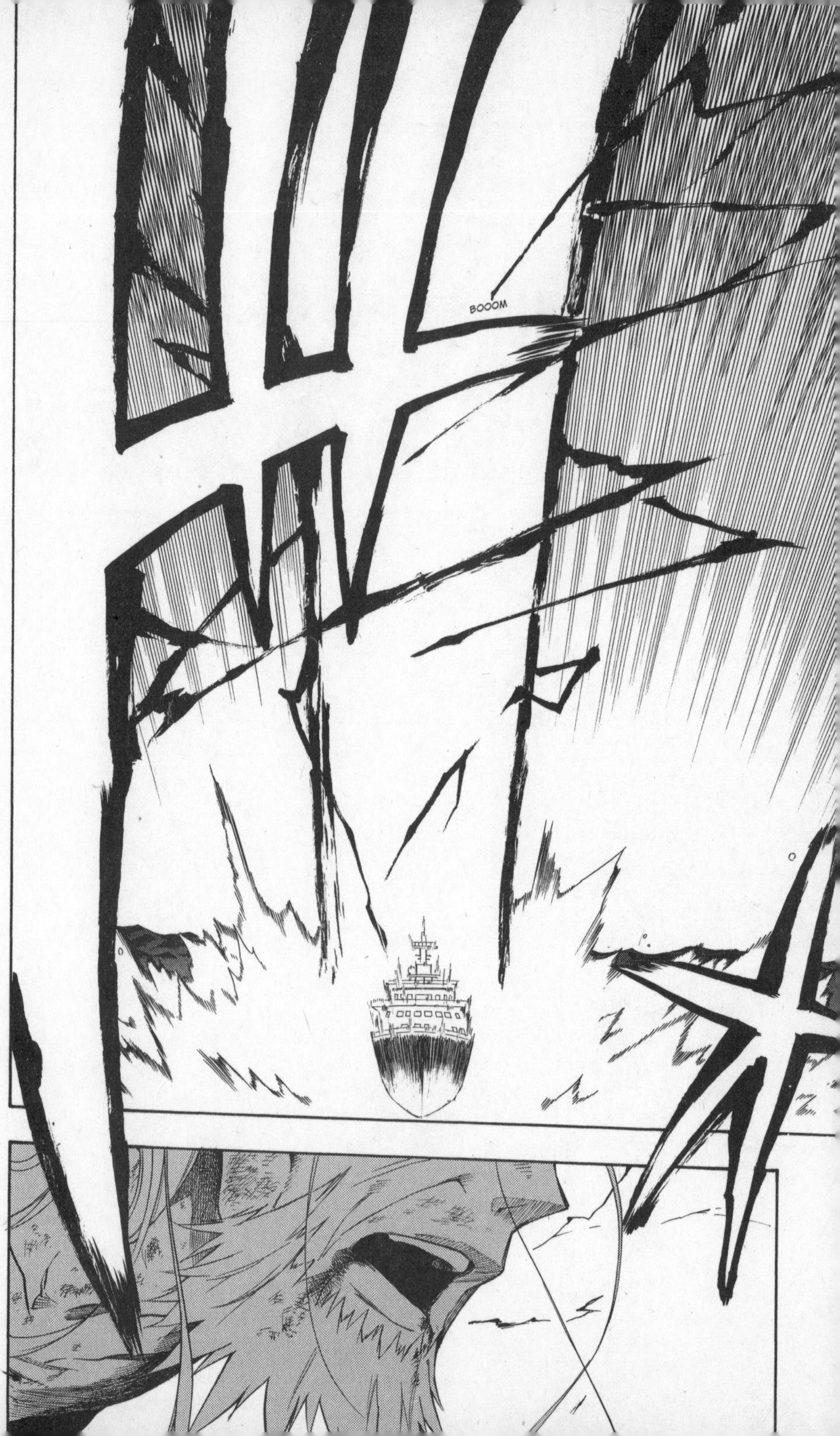
BOOOM

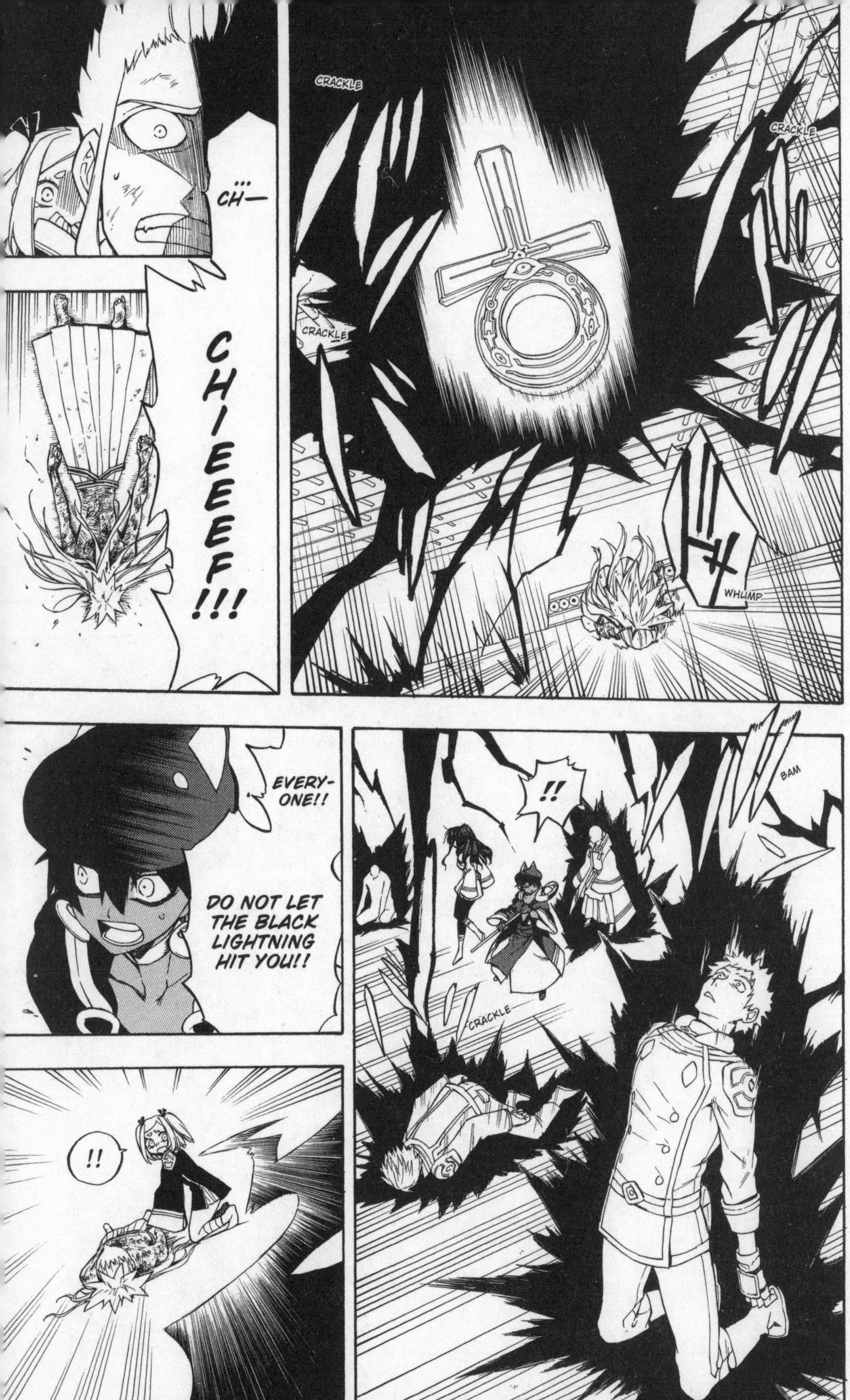
CRACKLE
CRACKLE
CRACKLE
WHLUMP
...CH—
CHIEEEEF!!!
!!
BAM
CRACKLE
EVERY-ONE!!
DO NOT LET THE BLACK LIGHTNING HIT YOU!!
!!

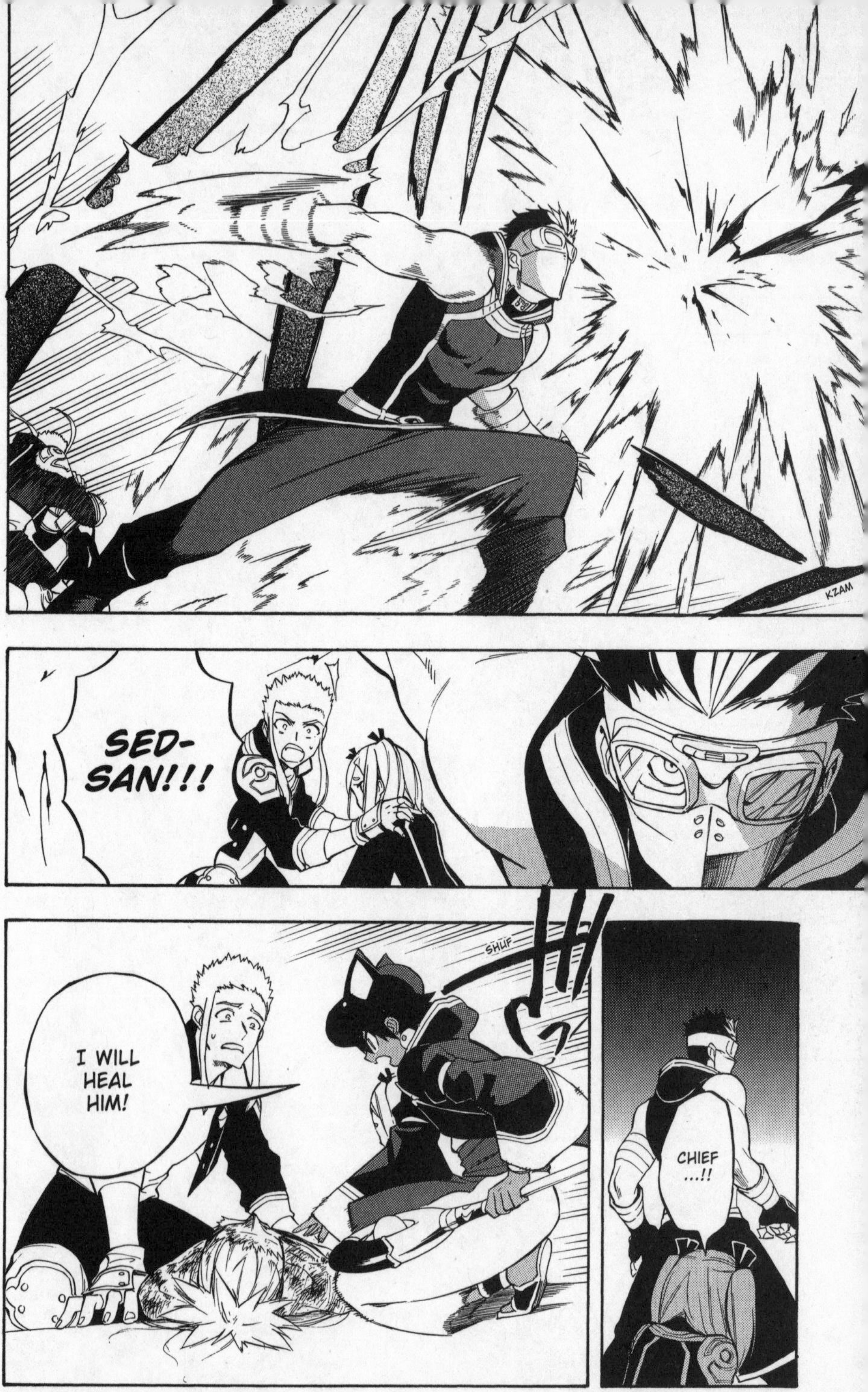
KZAM
SED-SAN!!!
SHUF
CHIEF ...!!
I WILL HEAL HIM!

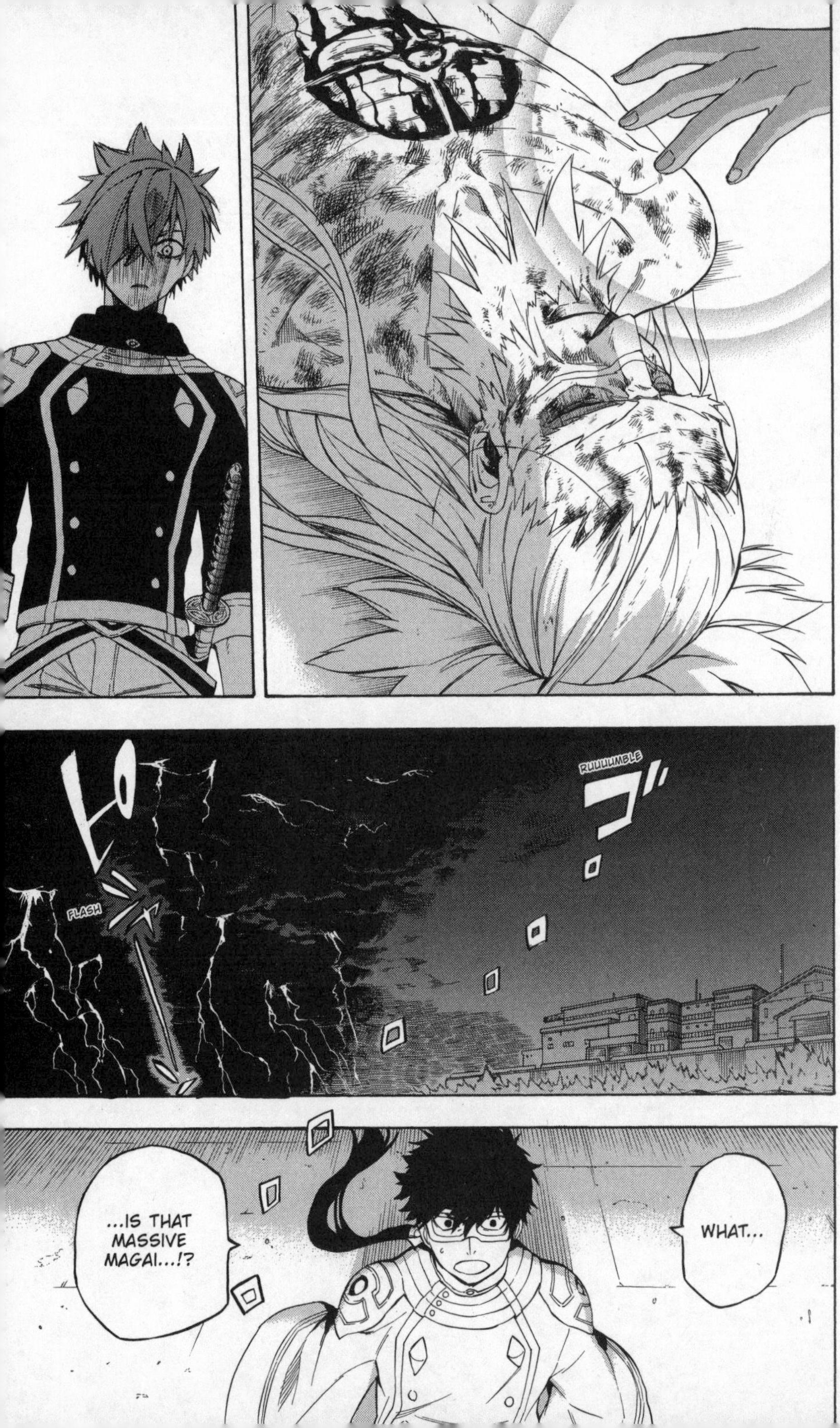
RUUUUMBLE
FLASH
WHAT...
...IS THAT MASSIVE MAGAI...!?

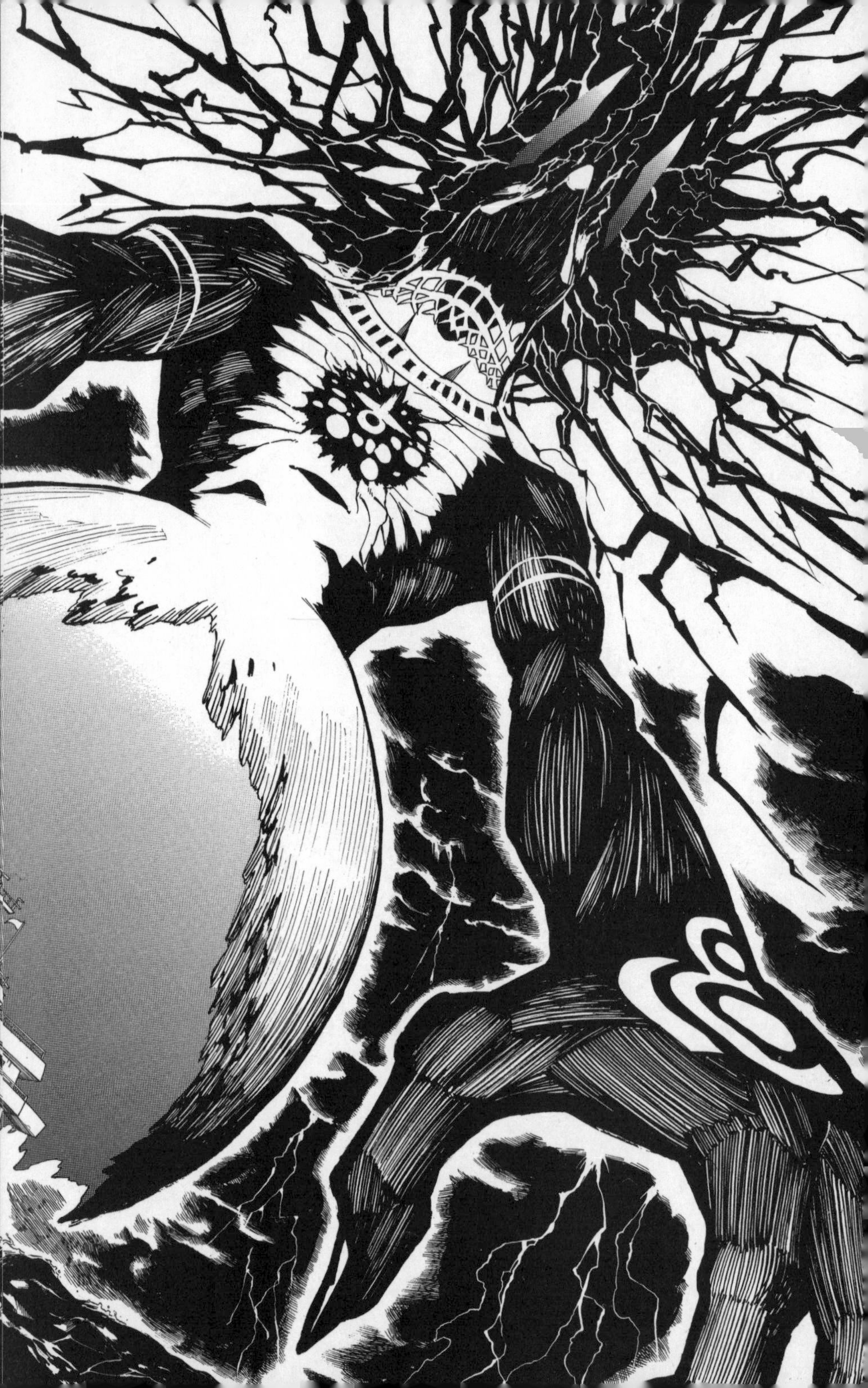

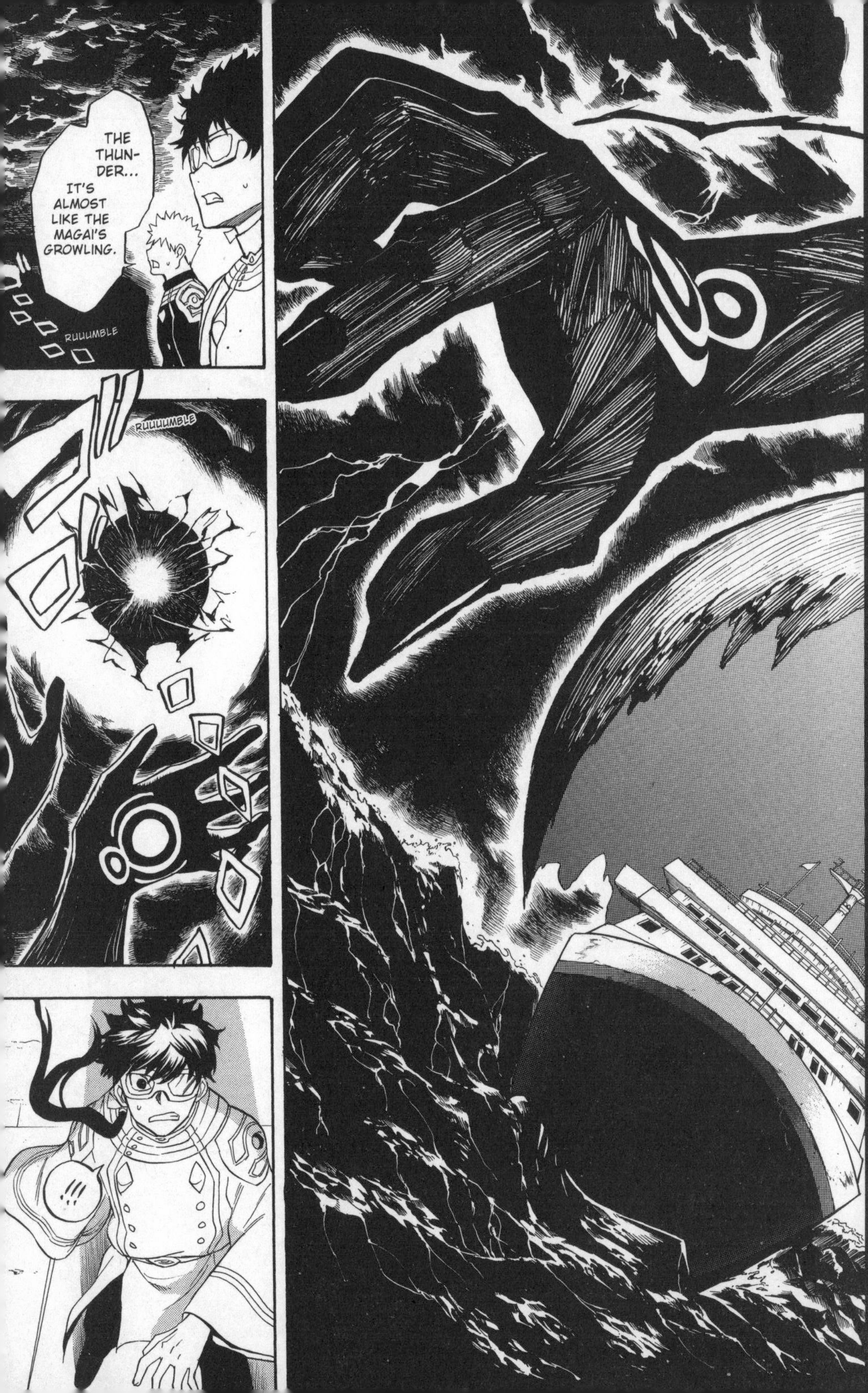
THE THUNDER... IT'S ALMOST LIKE THE MAGAI'S GROWLING.
RUUUMBLE
RUUUUMBLE
!!!

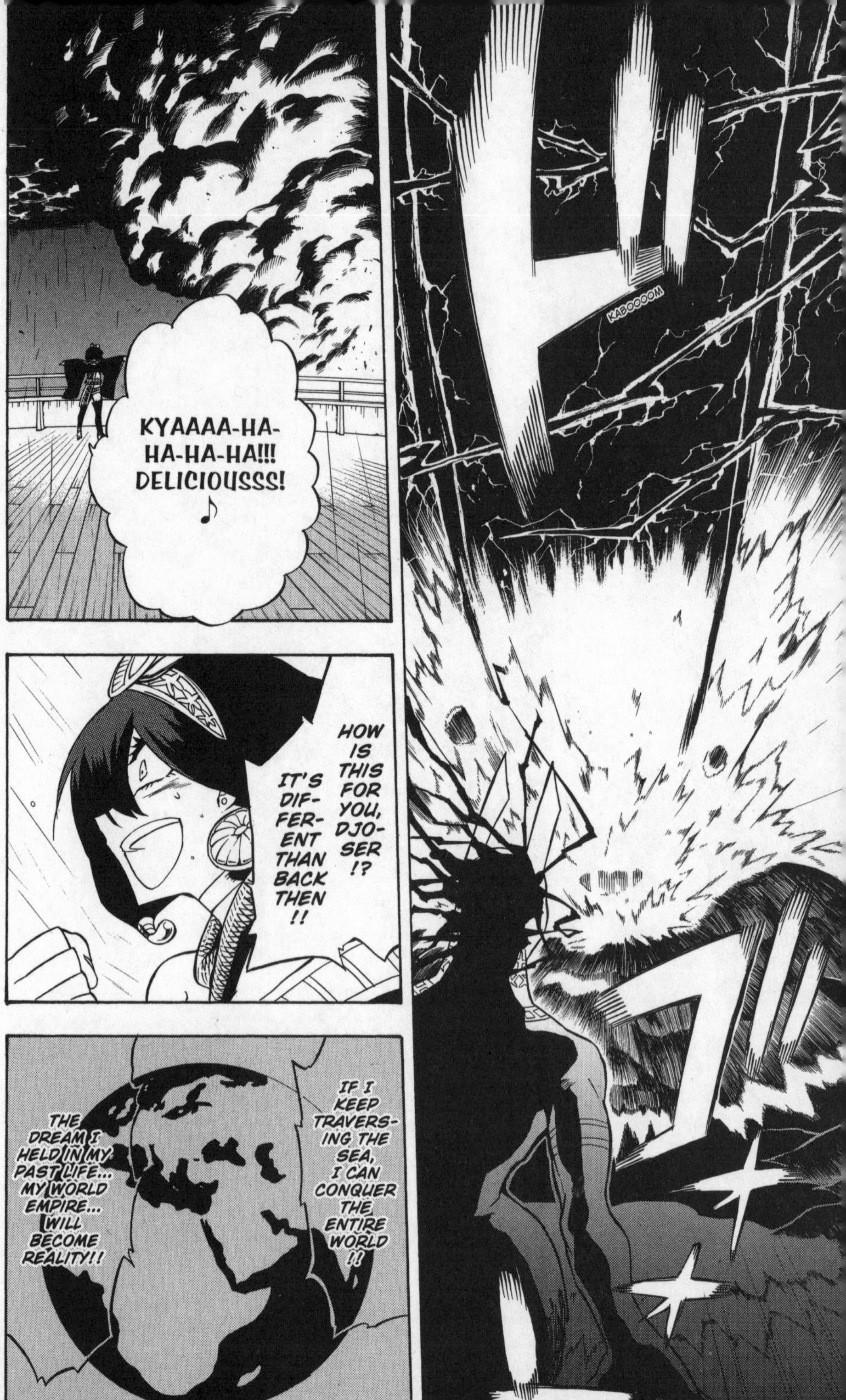
KABOOOOM
KYAAAA-HA-HA-HA-HA!!! DELICIOUSSS! ♪
HOW IS THIS FOR YOU, DJOSER!?
IT'S DIFFERENT THAN BACK THEN!!
IF I KEEP TRAVERSING THE SEA, I CAN CONQUER THE ENTIRE WORLD!!
THE DREAM I HELD IN MY PAST LIFE... MY WORLD EMPIRE... WILL BECOME REALITY!!

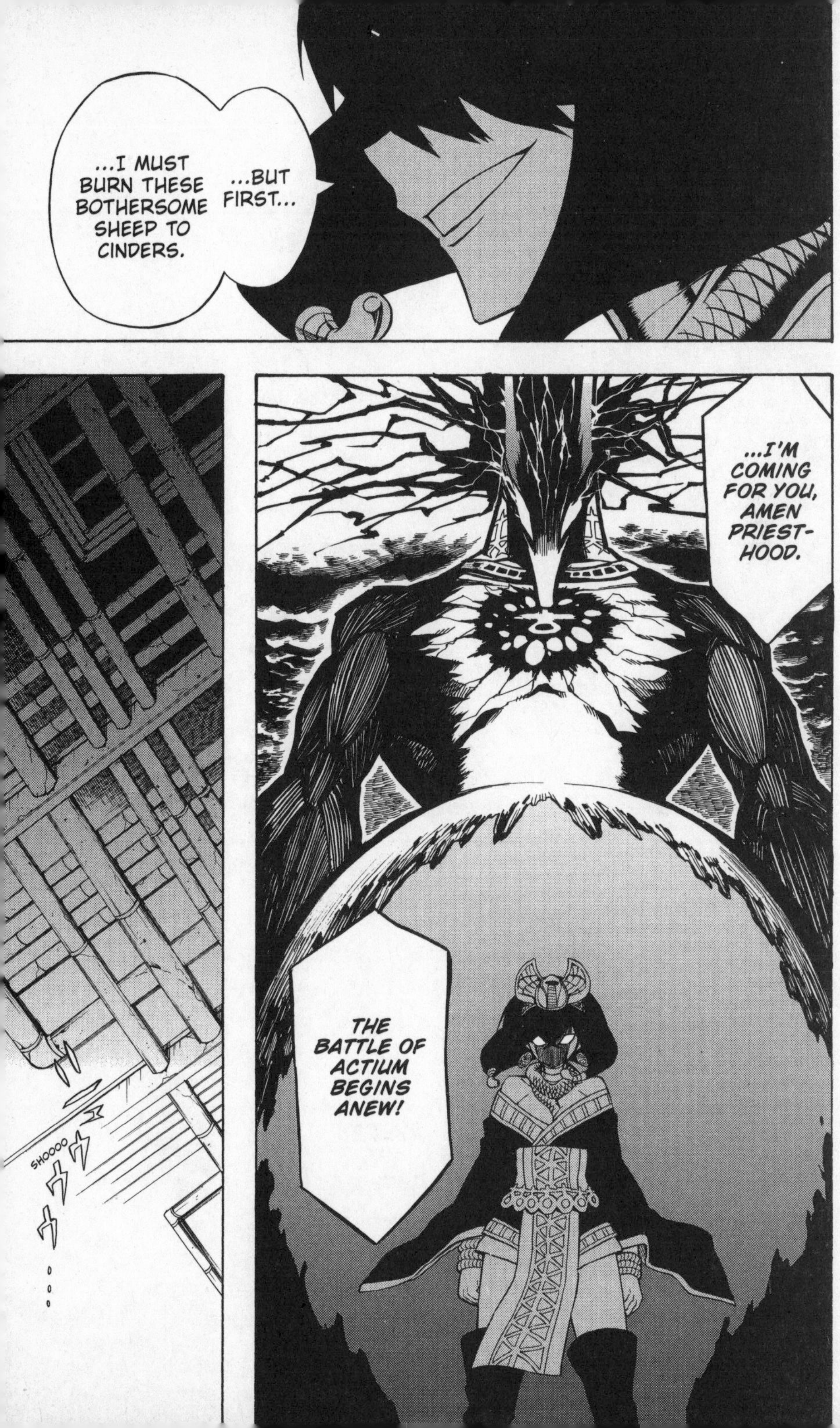
...BUT FIRST...
...I MUST BURN THESE BOTHERSOME SHEEP TO CINDERS.
...I'M COMING FOR YOU, AMEN PRIEST-HOOD.
THE BATTLE OF ACTIUM BEGINS ANEW!
SHOOOO

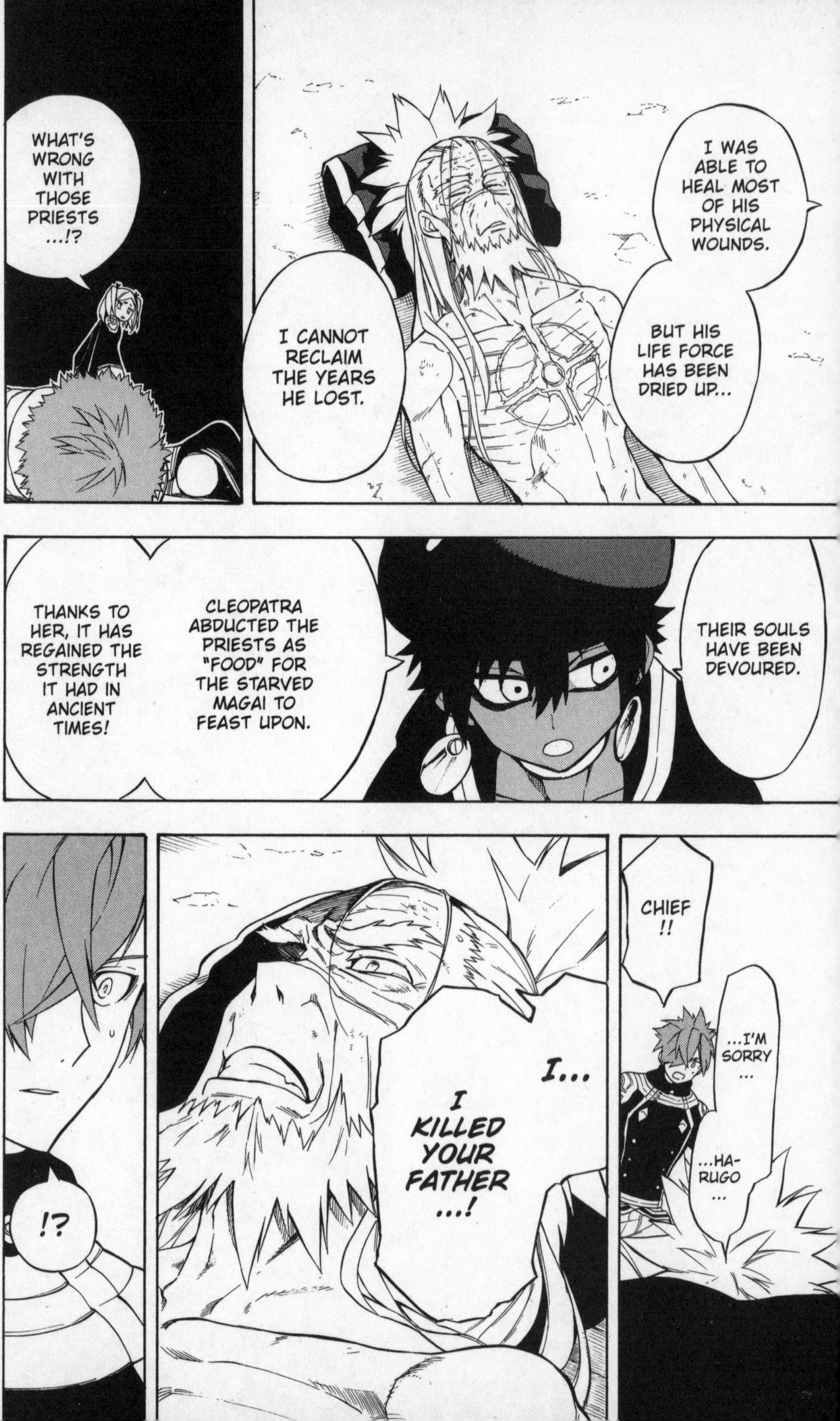
I WAS ABLE TO HEAL MOST OF HIS PHYSICAL WOUNDS.
BUT HIS LIFE FORCE HAS BEEN DRIED UP...
I CANNOT RECLAIM THE YEARS HE LOST.
WHAT'S WRONG WITH THOSE PRIESTS ...!?
THEIR SOULS HAVE BEEN DEVOURED.
CLEOPATRA ABDUCTED THE PRIESTS AS "FOOD" FOR THE STARVED MAGAI TO FEAST UPON.
THANKS TO HER, IT HAS REGAINED THE STRENGTH IT HAD IN ANCIENT TIMES!
CHIEF !!
...I'M SORRY ...
...HA-RUGO ...
I... I KILLED YOUR FATHER ...!
!?

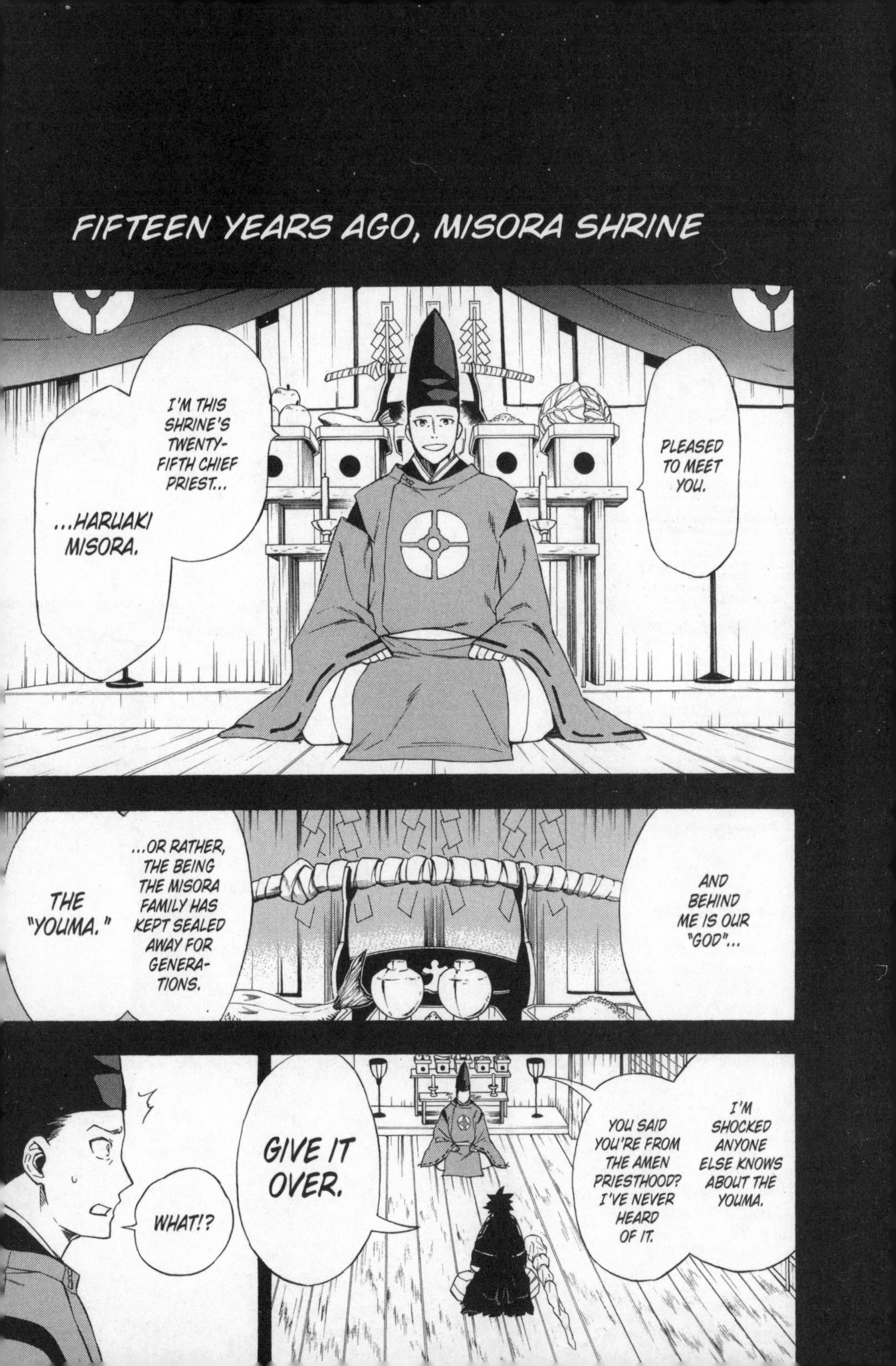
FIFTEEN YEARS AGO, MISORA SHRINE
PLEASED TO MEET YOU.
I'M THIS SHRINE'S TWENTY-FIFTH CHIEF PRIEST...
...HARUAKI MISORA.
AND BEHIND ME IS OUR "GOD"...
...OR RATHER, THE BEING THE MISORA FAMILY HAS KEPT SEALED AWAY FOR GENERA-TIONS.
THE "YOUMA."
I'M SHOCKED ANYONE ELSE KNOWS ABOUT THE YOUMA.
YOU SAID YOU'RE FROM THE AMEN PRIESTHOOD? I'VE NEVER HEARD OF IT.
GIVE IT OVER.
WHAT!?

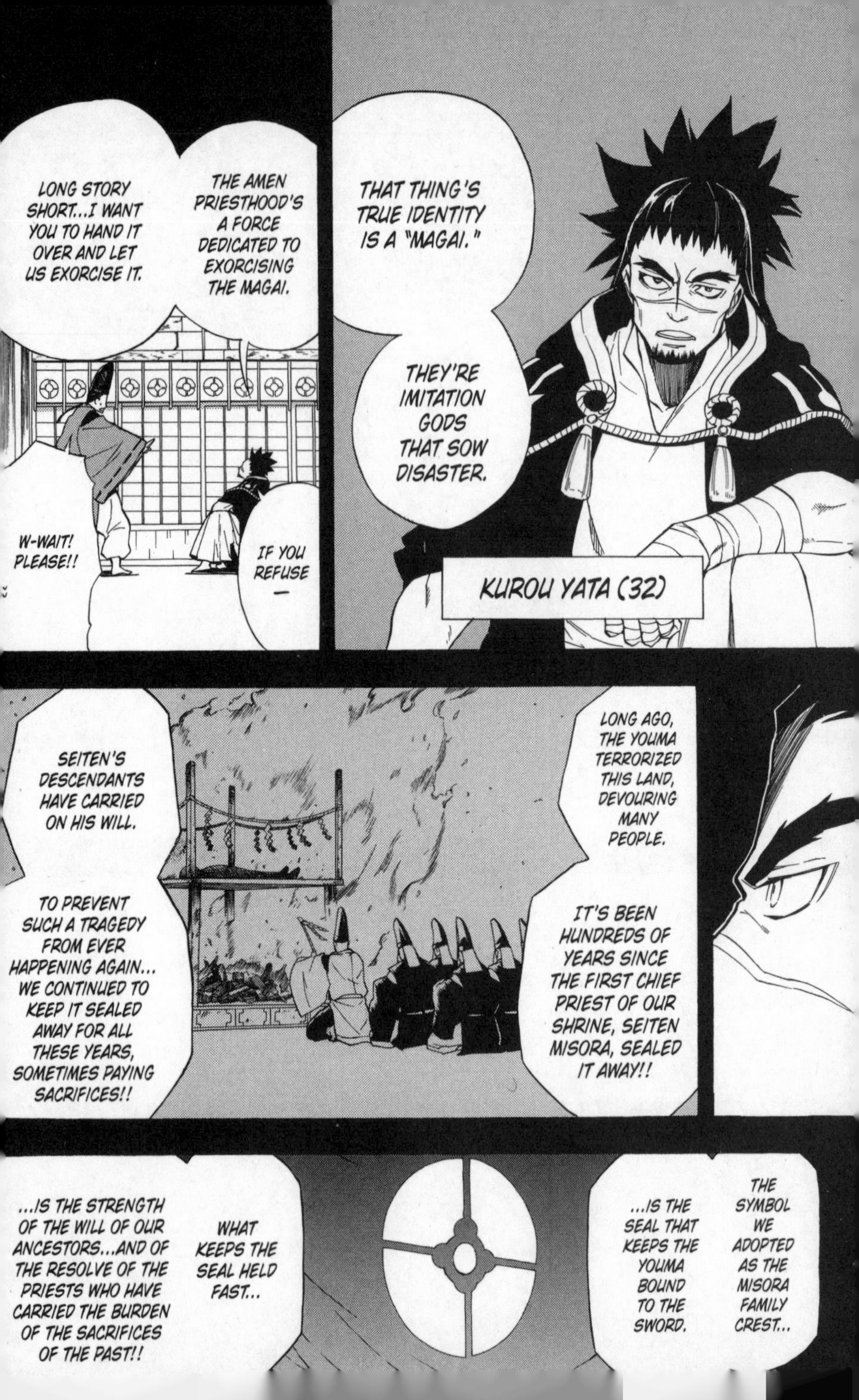
THAT THING'S TRUE IDENTITY IS A "MAGAI."
THEY'RE IMITATION GODS THAT SOW DISASTER.
KUROU YATA (32)
THE AMEN PRIESTHOOD'S A FORCE DEDICATED TO EXORCISING THE MAGAI.
LONG STORY SHORT...I WANT YOU TO HAND IT OVER AND LET US EXORCISE IT.
IF YOU REFUSE—
W-WAIT! PLEASE!!
LONG AGO, THE YOUMA TERRORIZED THIS LAND, DEVOURING MANY PEOPLE.
IT'S BEEN HUNDREDS OF YEARS SINCE THE FIRST CHIEF PRIEST OF OUR SHRINE, SEITEN MISORA, SEALED IT AWAY!!
SEITEN'S DESCENDANTS HAVE CARRIED ON HIS WILL.
TO PREVENT SUCH A TRAGEDY FROM EVER HAPPENING AGAIN... WE CONTINUED TO KEEP IT SEALED AWAY FOR ALL THESE YEARS, SOMETIMES PAYING SACRIFICES!!
THE SYMBOL WE ADOPTED AS THE MISORA FAMILY CREST...
...IS THE SEAL THAT KEEPS THE YOUMA BOUND TO THE SWORD.
WHAT KEEPS THE SEAL HELD FAST...
...IS THE STRENGTH OF THE WILL OF OUR ANCESTORS...AND OF THE RESOLVE OF THE PRIESTS WHO HAVE CARRIED THE BURDEN OF THE SACRIFICES OF THE PAST!!

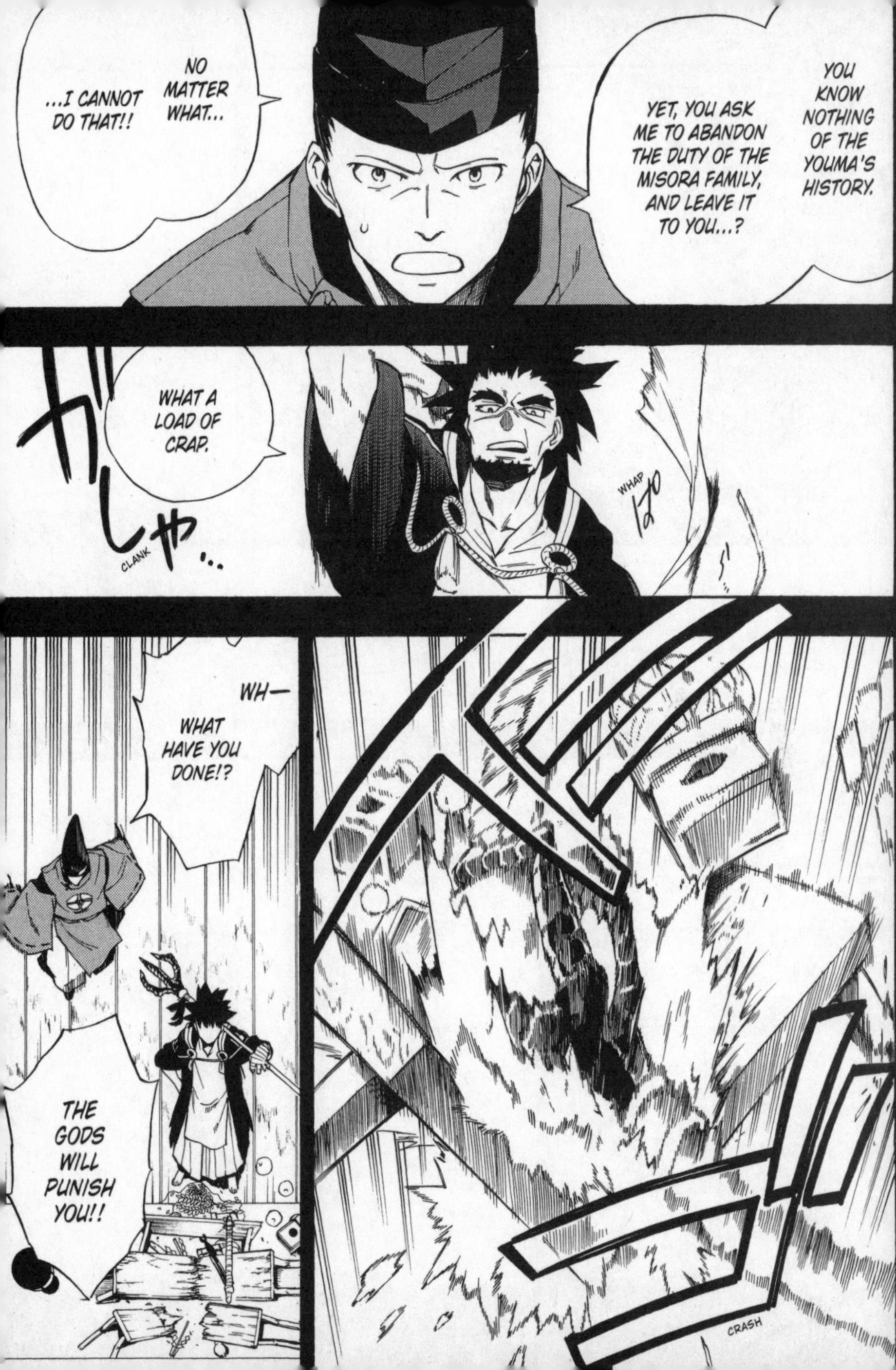
YOU KNOW NOTHING OF THE YOUMA'S HISTORY.
YET, YOU ASK ME TO ABANDON THE DUTY OF THE MISORA FAMILY, AND LEAVE IT TO YOU...?
NO MATTER WHAT...
...I CANNOT DO THAT!!
WHAP ぱ
WHAT A LOAD OF CRAP.
がしゃ... CLANK
CRASH
WH—
WHAT HAVE YOU DONE!?
THE GODS WILL PUNISH YOU!!

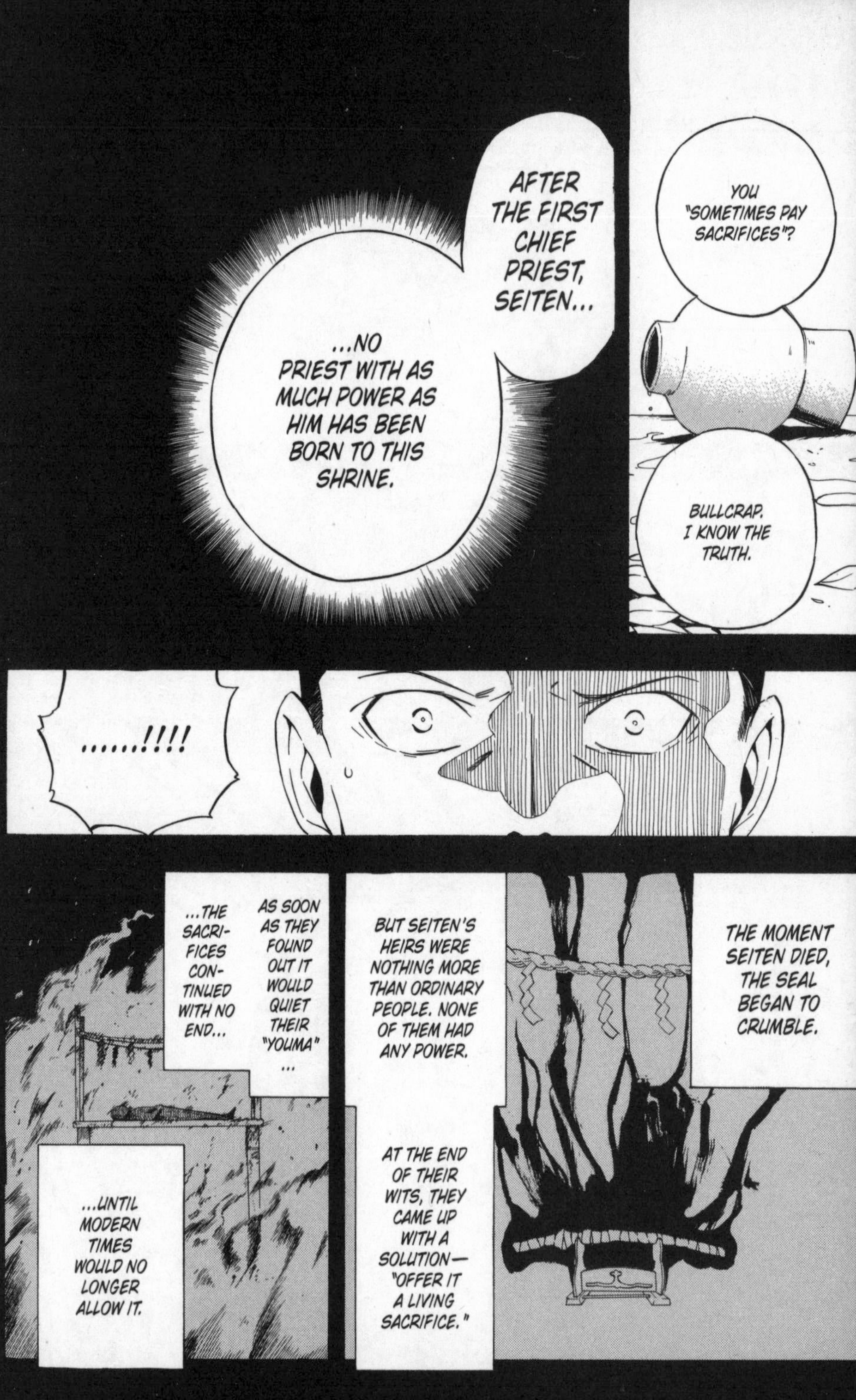
YOU "SOMETIMES PAY SACRIFICES"?
BULLCRAP. I KNOW THE TRUTH.
AFTER THE FIRST CHIEF PRIEST, SEITEN...
...NO PRIEST WITH AS MUCH POWER AS HIM HAS BEEN BORN TO THIS SHRINE.
......!!!!
THE MOMENT SEITEN DIED, THE SEAL BEGAN TO CRUMBLE.
BUT SEITEN'S HEIRS WERE NOTHING MORE THAN ORDINARY PEOPLE. NONE OF THEM HAD ANY POWER.
AT THE END OF THEIR WITS, THEY CAME UP WITH A SOLUTION—"OFFER IT A LIVING SACRIFICE."
AS SOON AS THEY FOUND OUT IT WOULD QUIET THEIR "YOUMA"...
...THE SACRI-FICES CON-TINUED WITH NO END...
...UNTIL MODERN TIMES WOULD NO LONGER ALLOW IT.

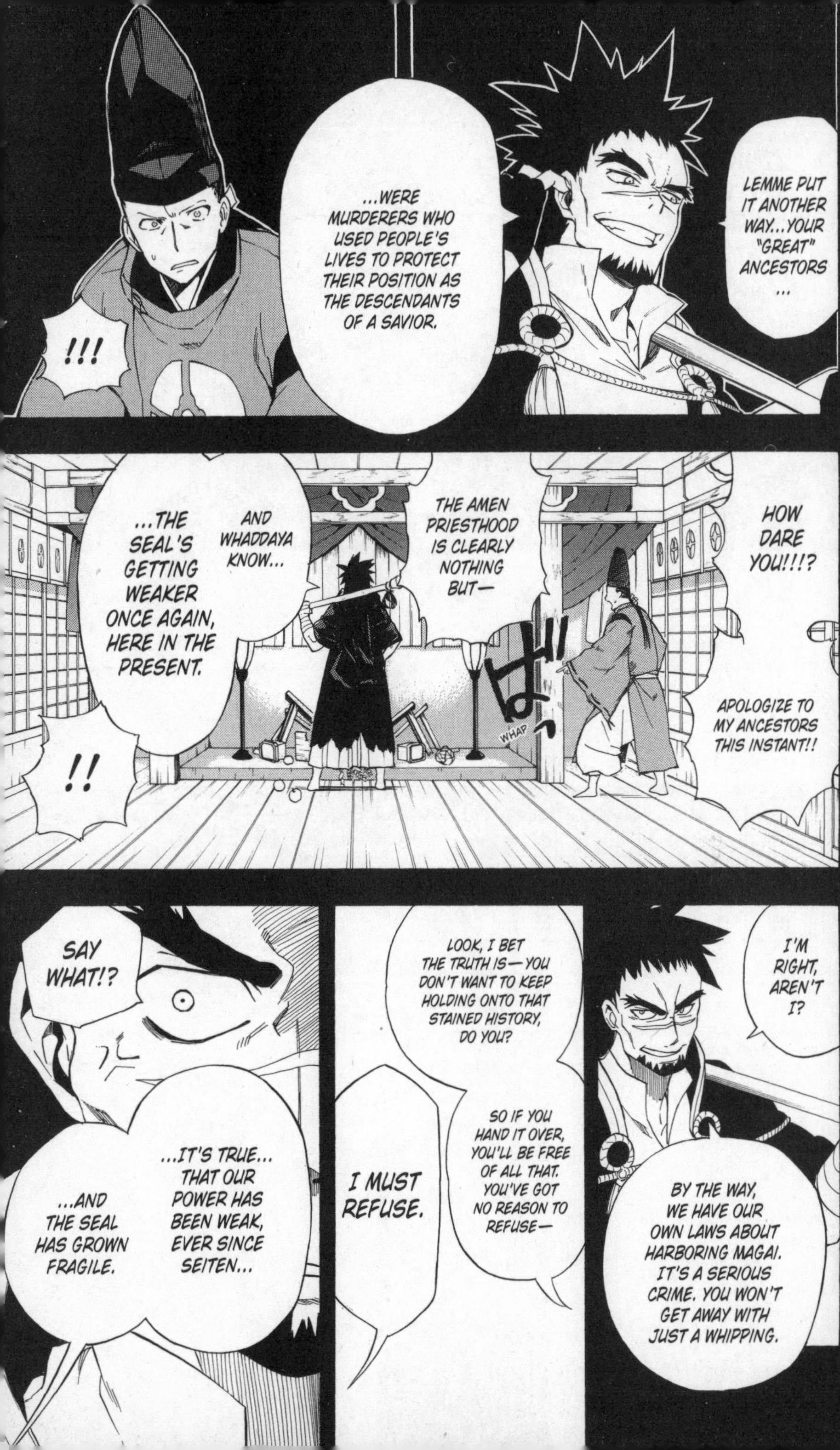
LEMME PUT IT ANOTHER WAY...YOUR "GREAT" ANCESTORS ...
...WERE MURDERERS WHO USED PEOPLE'S LIVES TO PROTECT THEIR POSITION AS THE DESCENDANTS OF A SAVIOR.
!!!
HOW DARE YOU!!!?
APOLOGIZE TO MY ANCESTORS THIS INSTANT!!
THE AMEN PRIESTHOOD IS CLEARLY NOTHING BUT—
AND WHADDAYA KNOW...
...THE SEAL'S GETTING WEAKER ONCE AGAIN, HERE IN THE PRESENT.
WHAP
!!
I'M RIGHT, AREN'T I?
LOOK, I BET THE TRUTH IS—YOU DON'T WANT TO KEEP HOLDING ONTO THAT STAINED HISTORY, DO YOU?
SO IF YOU HAND IT OVER, YOU'LL BE FREE OF ALL THAT. YOU'VE GOT NO REASON TO REFUSE—
BY THE WAY, WE HAVE OUR OWN LAWS ABOUT HARBORING MAGAI. IT'S A SERIOUS CRIME. YOU WON'T GET AWAY WITH JUST A WHIPPING.
I MUST REFUSE.
SAY WHAT!?
...IT'S TRUE... THAT OUR POWER HAS BEEN WEAK, EVER SINCE SEITEN...
...AND THE SEAL HAS GROWN FRAGILE.

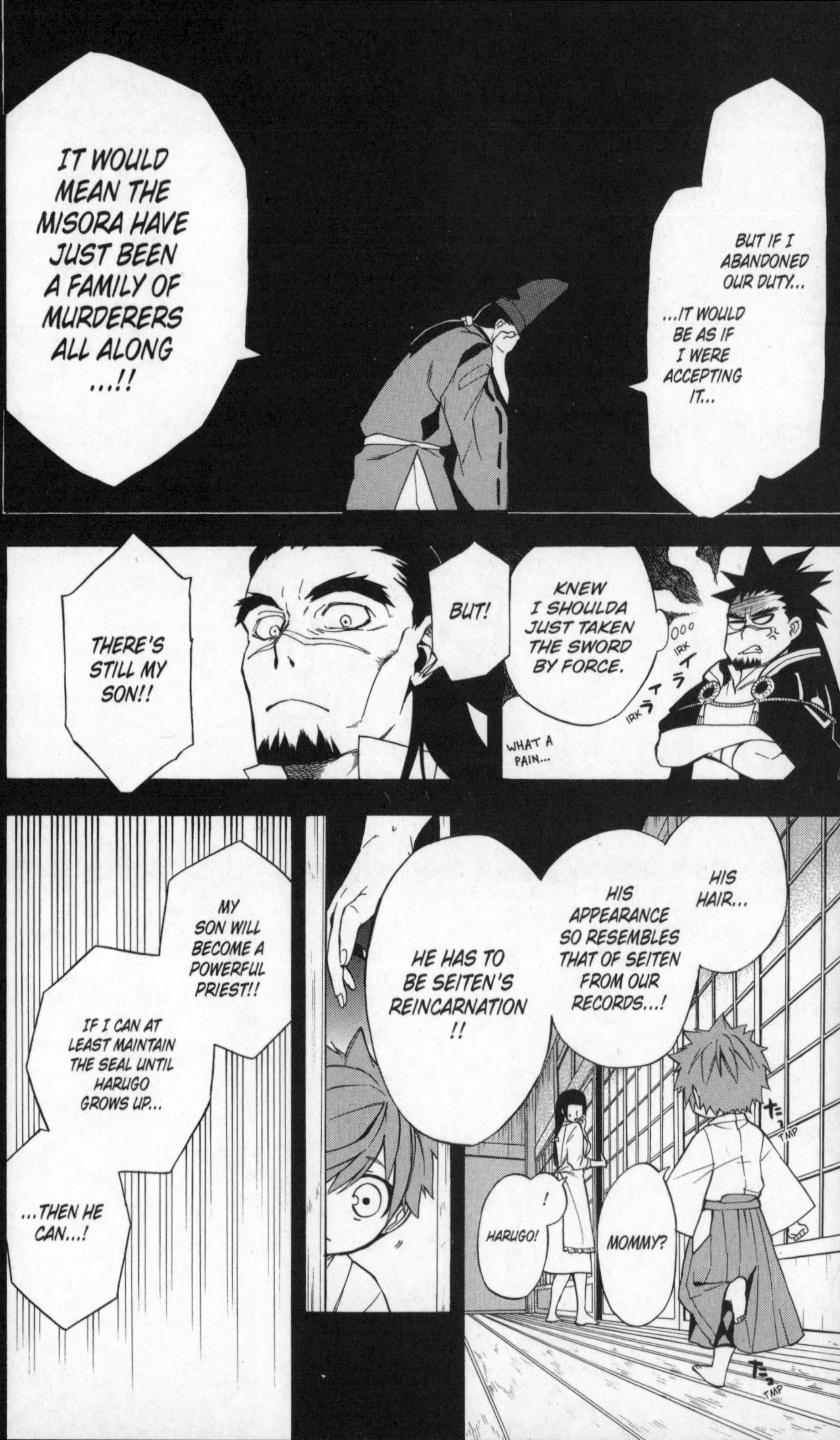
BUT IF I ABANDONED OUR DUTY...
...IT WOULD BE AS IF I WERE ACCEPTING IT...
IT WOULD MEAN THE MISORA HAVE JUST BEEN A FAMILY OF MURDERERS ALL ALONG ...!!
KNEW I SHOULDA JUST TAKEN THE SWORD BY FORCE.
IRK
IRK
WHAT A PAIN...
BUT!
THERE'S STILL MY SON!!
HIS HAIR...
HIS APPEARANCE SO RESEMBLES THAT OF SEITEN FROM OUR RECORDS...!
HE HAS TO BE SEITEN'S REINCARNATION!!
TMP
MOMMY?
!
HARUGO!
TMP
MY SON WILL BECOME A POWERFUL PRIEST!!
IF I CAN AT LEAST MAINTAIN THE SEAL UNTIL HARUGO GROWS UP...
...THEN HE CAN...!

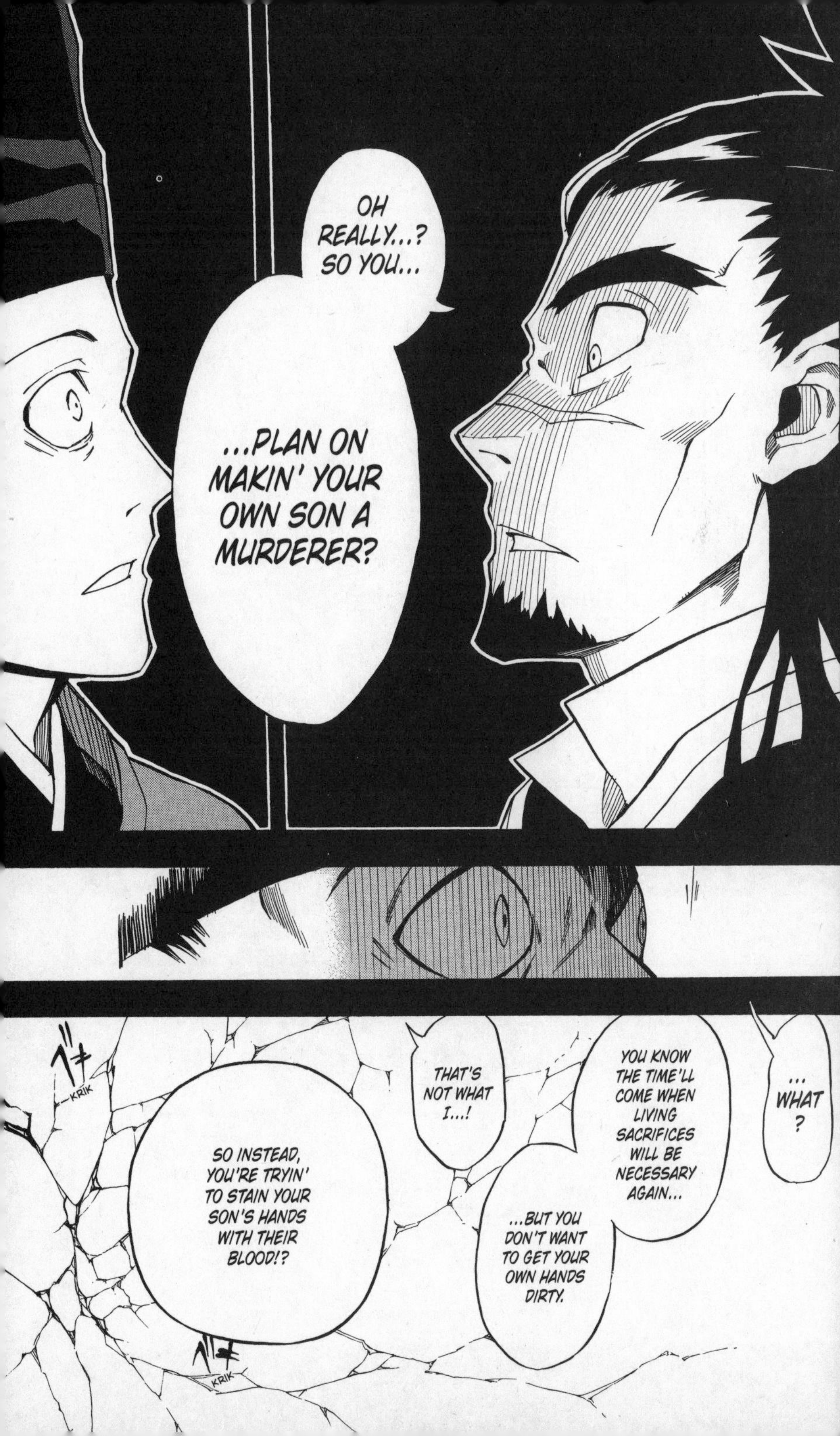
OH REALLY...? SO YOU...
...PLAN ON MAKIN' YOUR OWN SON A MURDERER?
...WHAT?
YOU KNOW THE TIME'LL COME WHEN LIVING SACRIFICES WILL BE NECESSARY AGAIN...
...BUT YOU DON'T WANT TO GET YOUR OWN HANDS DIRTY.
THAT'S NOT WHAT I...!
SO INSTEAD, YOU'RE TRYIN' TO STAIN YOUR SON'S HANDS WITH THEIR BLOOD!?
KRIK
KRIK

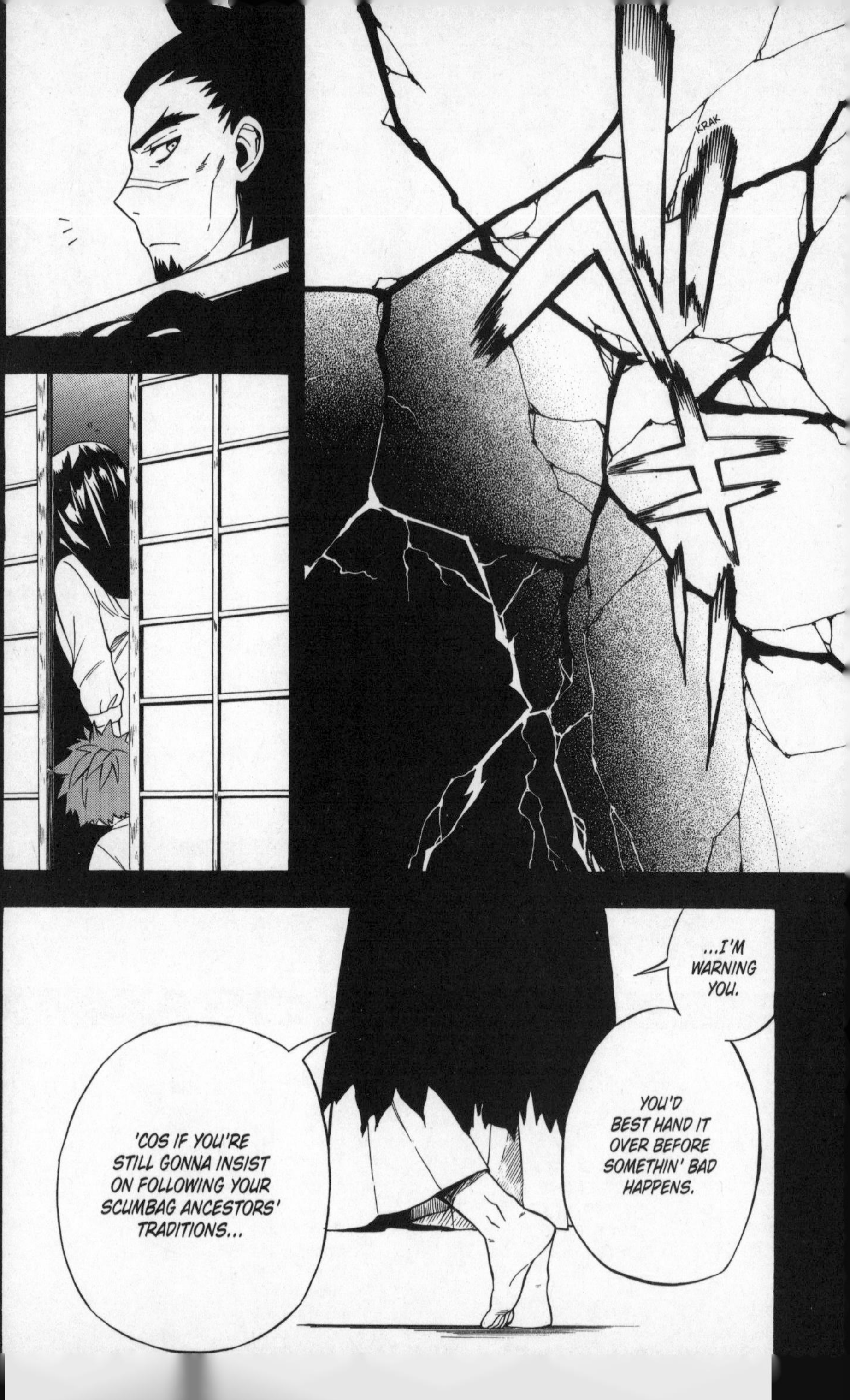
KRAK
...I'M WARNING YOU.
YOU'D BEST HAND IT OVER BEFORE SOMETHIN' BAD HAPPENS.
'COS IF YOU'RE STILL GONNA INSIST ON FOLLOWING YOUR SCUMBAG ANCESTORS' TRADITIONS...

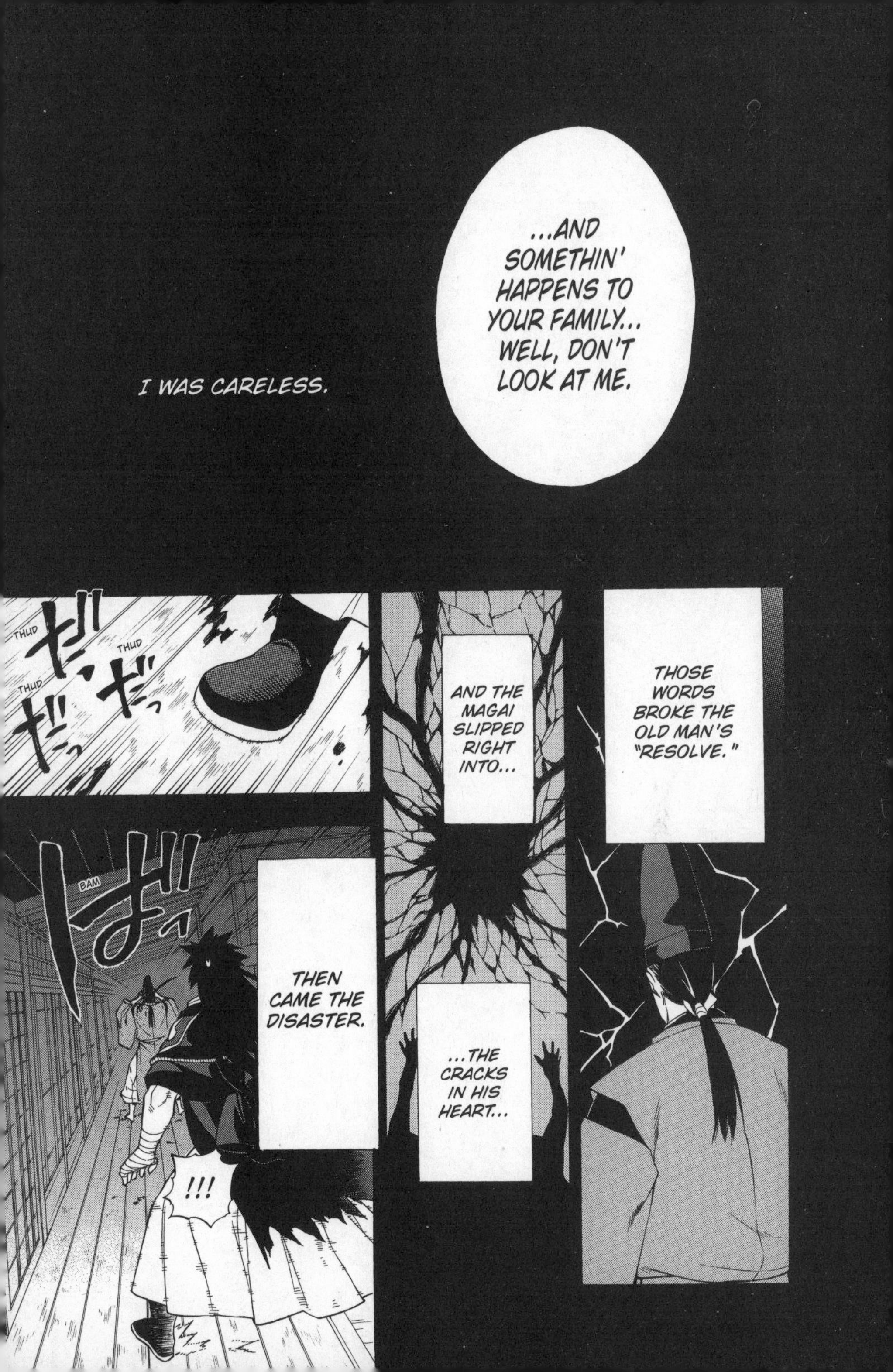

...AND SOMETHIN' HAPPENS TO YOUR FAMILY... WELL, DON'T LOOK AT ME.
I WAS CARELESS.
THOSE WORDS BROKE THE OLD MAN'S "RESOLVE."
AND THE MAGAI SLIPPED RIGHT INTO...
...THE CRACKS IN HIS HEART...
THUD
THUD
THUD
BAM
THEN CAME THE DISASTER.
!!!

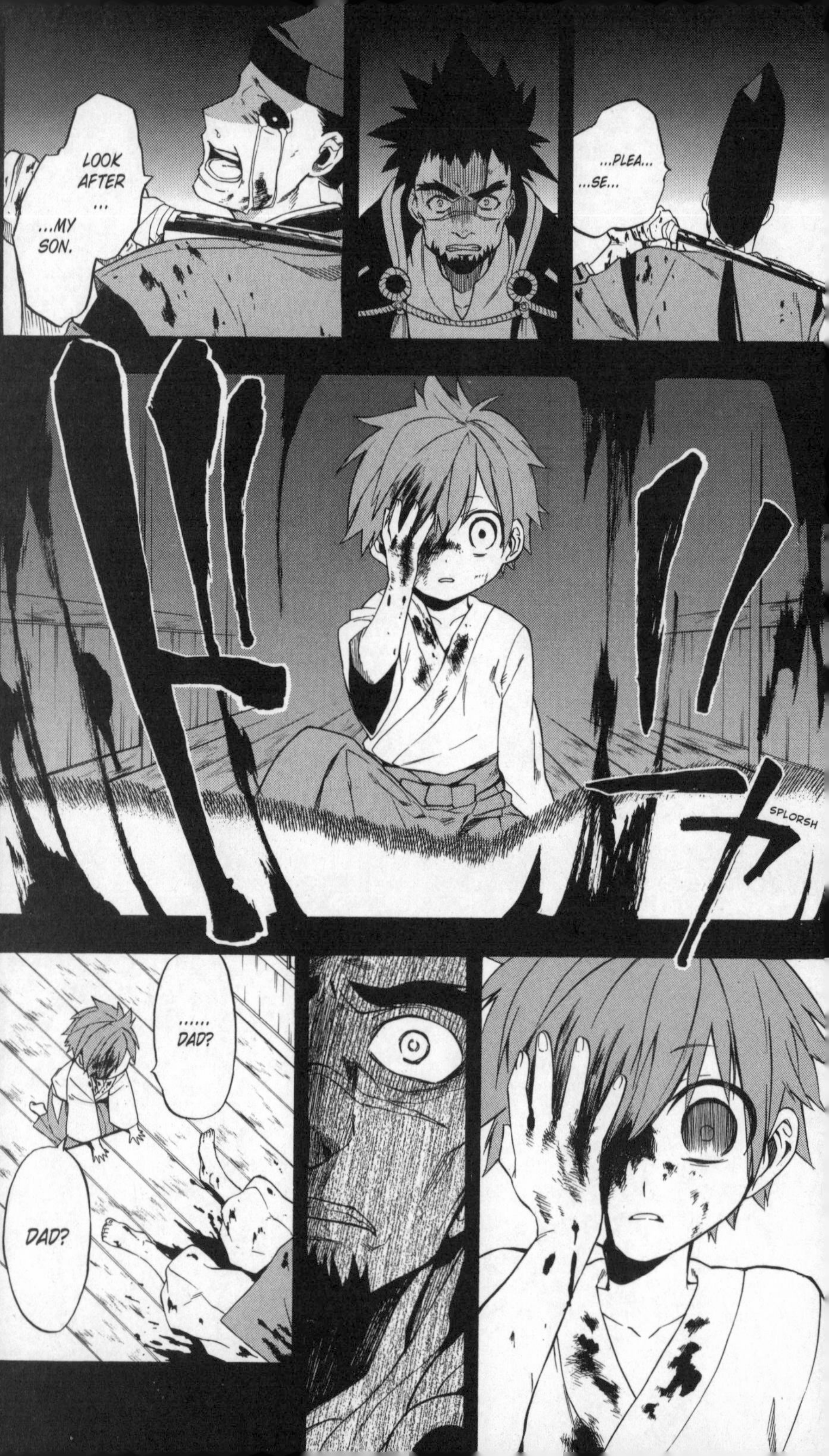
...PLEA... ...SE...
LOOK AFTER ... ...MY SON.
SPLORSH
...... DAD?
DAD?

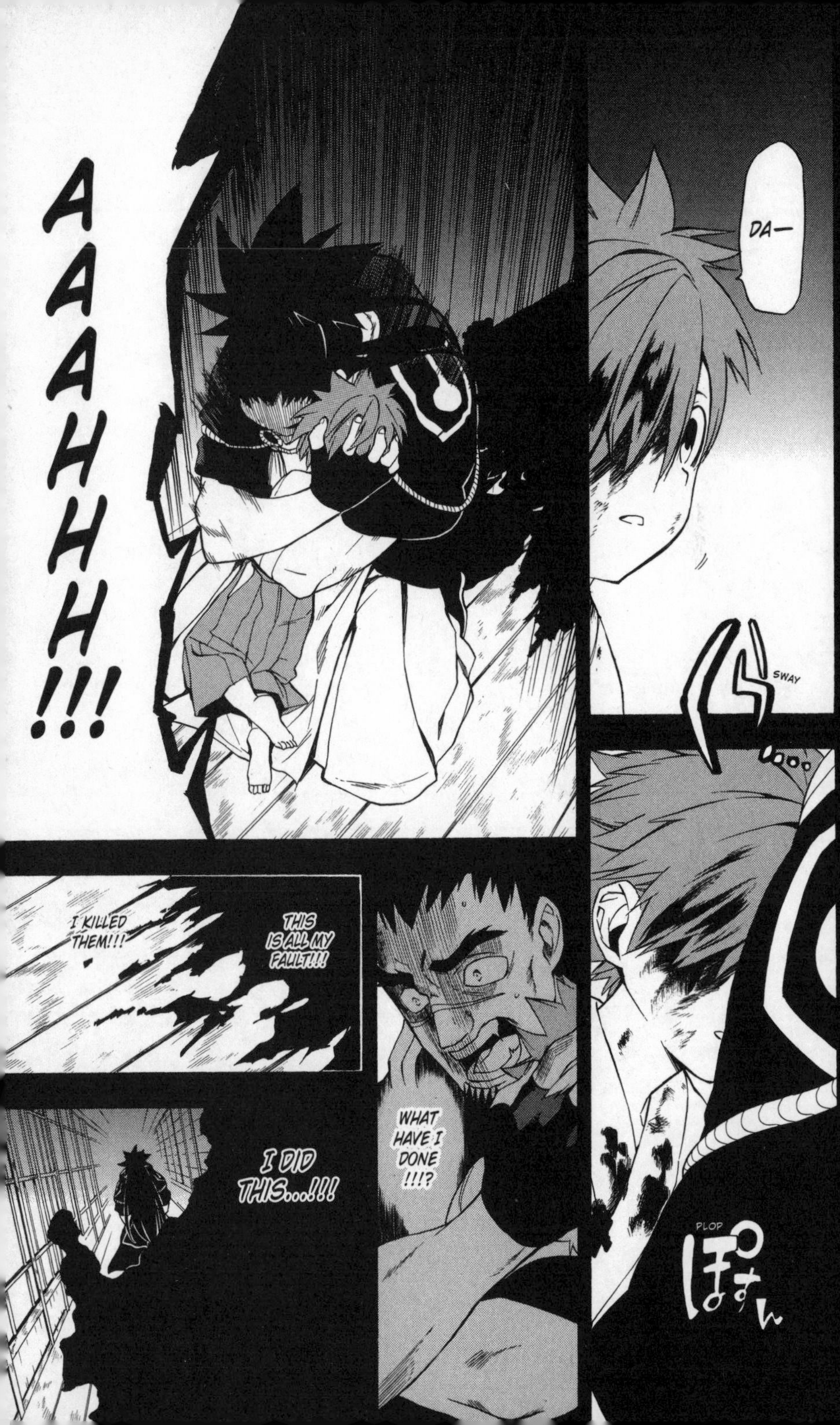
DA—
SWAY
AAAAHHHH!!!
...
PLOP
ぽすん
WHAT HAVE I DONE!!!?
THIS IS ALL MY FAULT!!!
I KILLED THEM!!!
I DID THIS...!!!

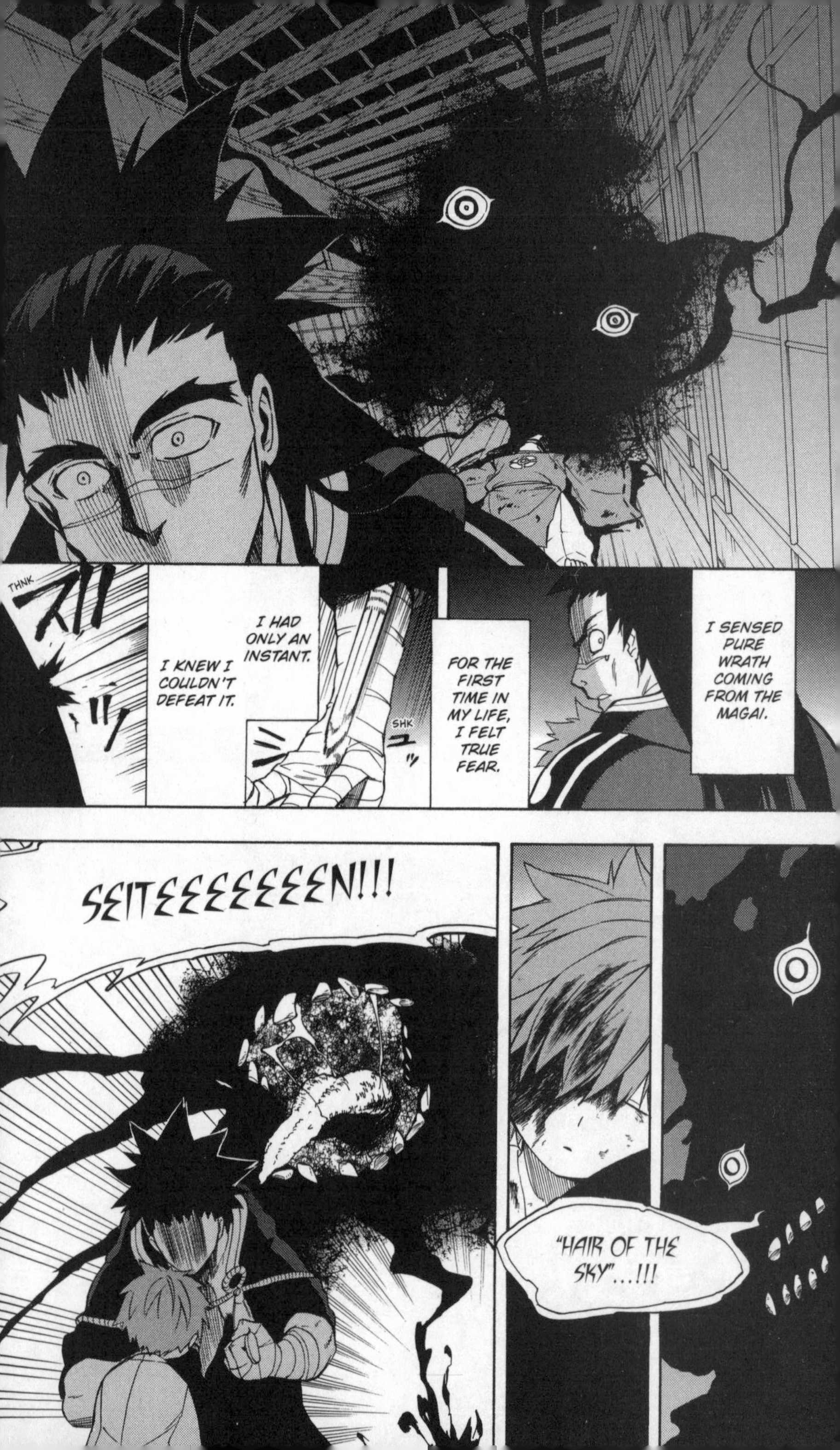
I SENSED PURE WRATH COMING FROM THE MAGAI.
FOR THE FIRST TIME IN MY LIFE, I FELT TRUE FEAR.
SHK
I HAD ONLY AN INSTANT.
I KNEW I COULDN'T DEFEAT IT.
THNK
"HAIR OF THE SKY"...!!!
SEITEEEEEEEN!!!

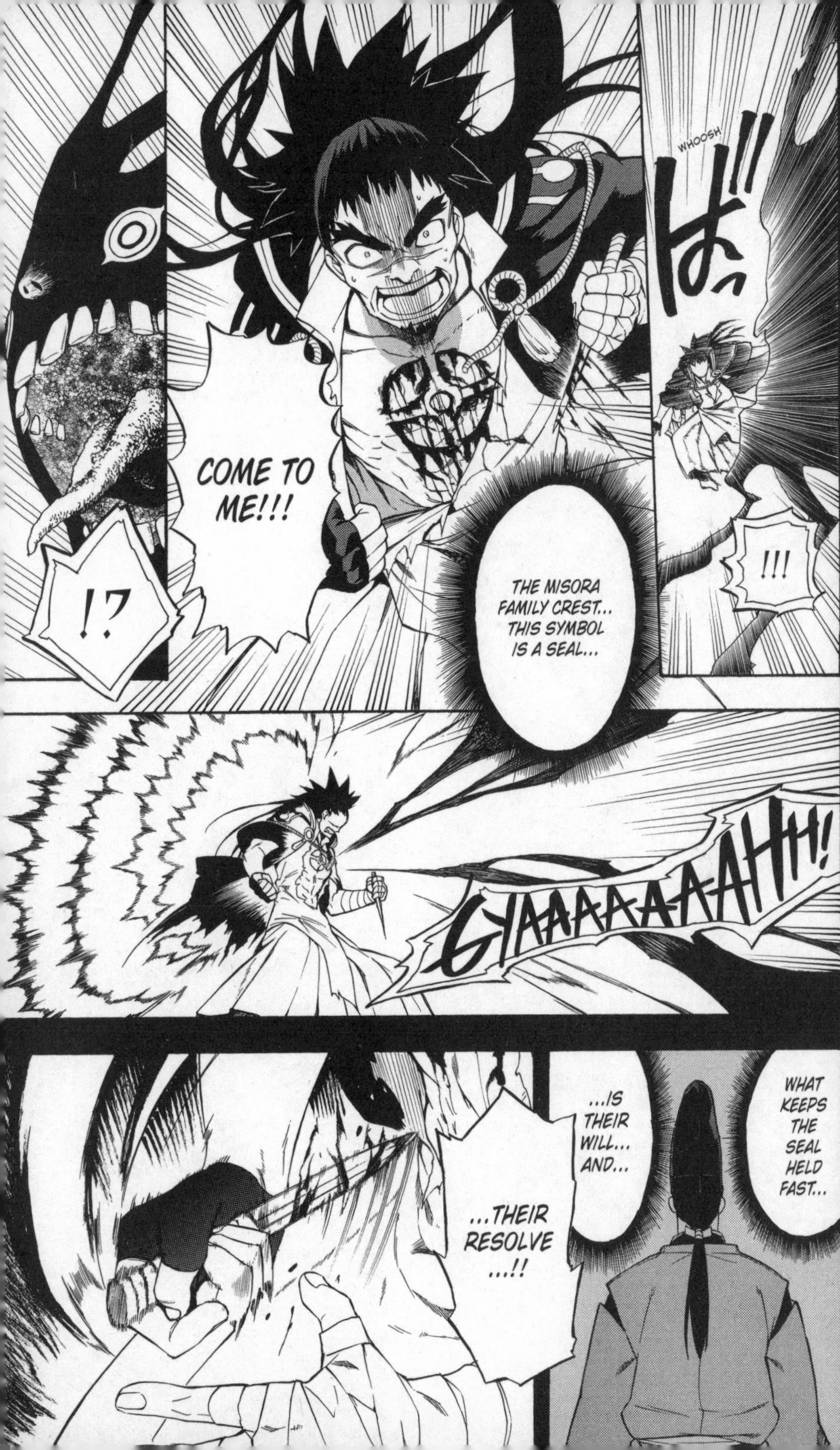
WHOOSH
ぱっ!!
!!!
THE MISORA FAMILY CREST... THIS SYMBOL IS A SEAL...
COME TO ME!!!
!?
GYAAAAAAAAHH!
WHAT KEEPS THE SEAL HELD FAST...
...IS THEIR WILL... AND...
...THEIR RESOLVE ...!!

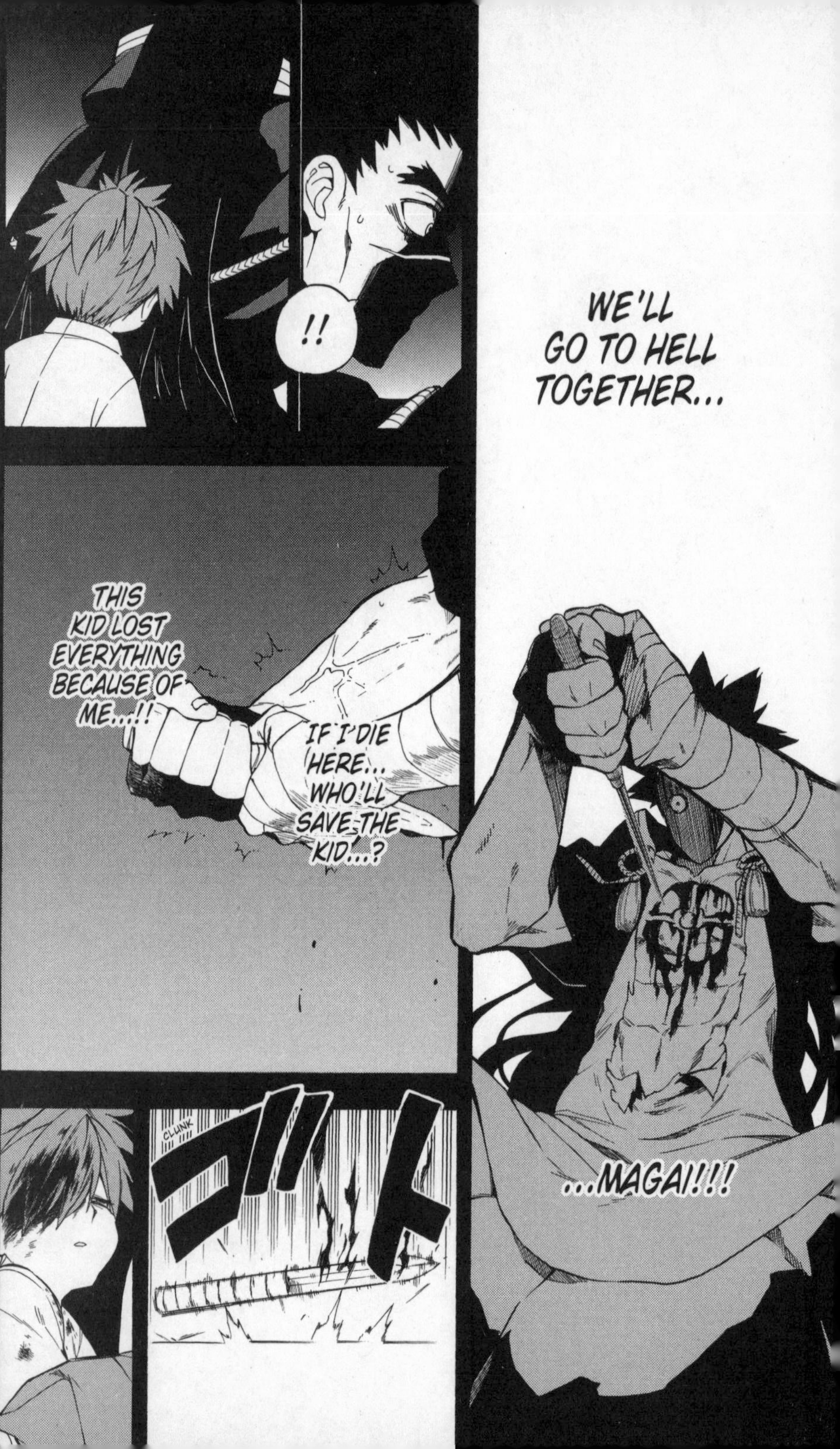

WE'LL GO TO HELL TOGETHER...
...MAGAI!!!
!!
THIS KID LOST EVERYTHING BECAUSE OF ME...!!
IF I DIE HERE... WHO'LL SAVE THE KID...?
CLUNK

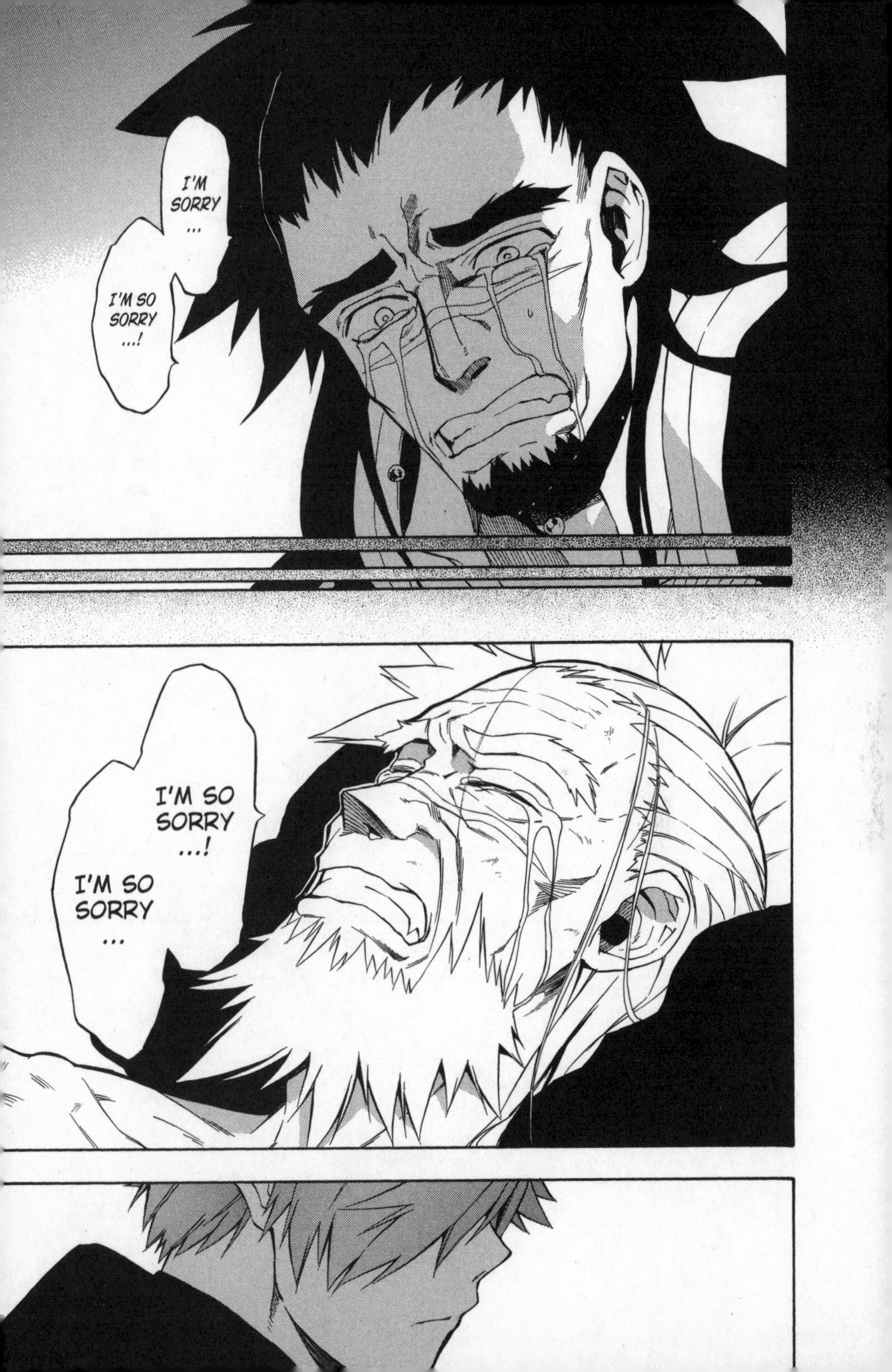
I'M SORRY ...
I'M SO SORRY ...!
I'M SO SORRY ...!
I'M SO SORRY ...

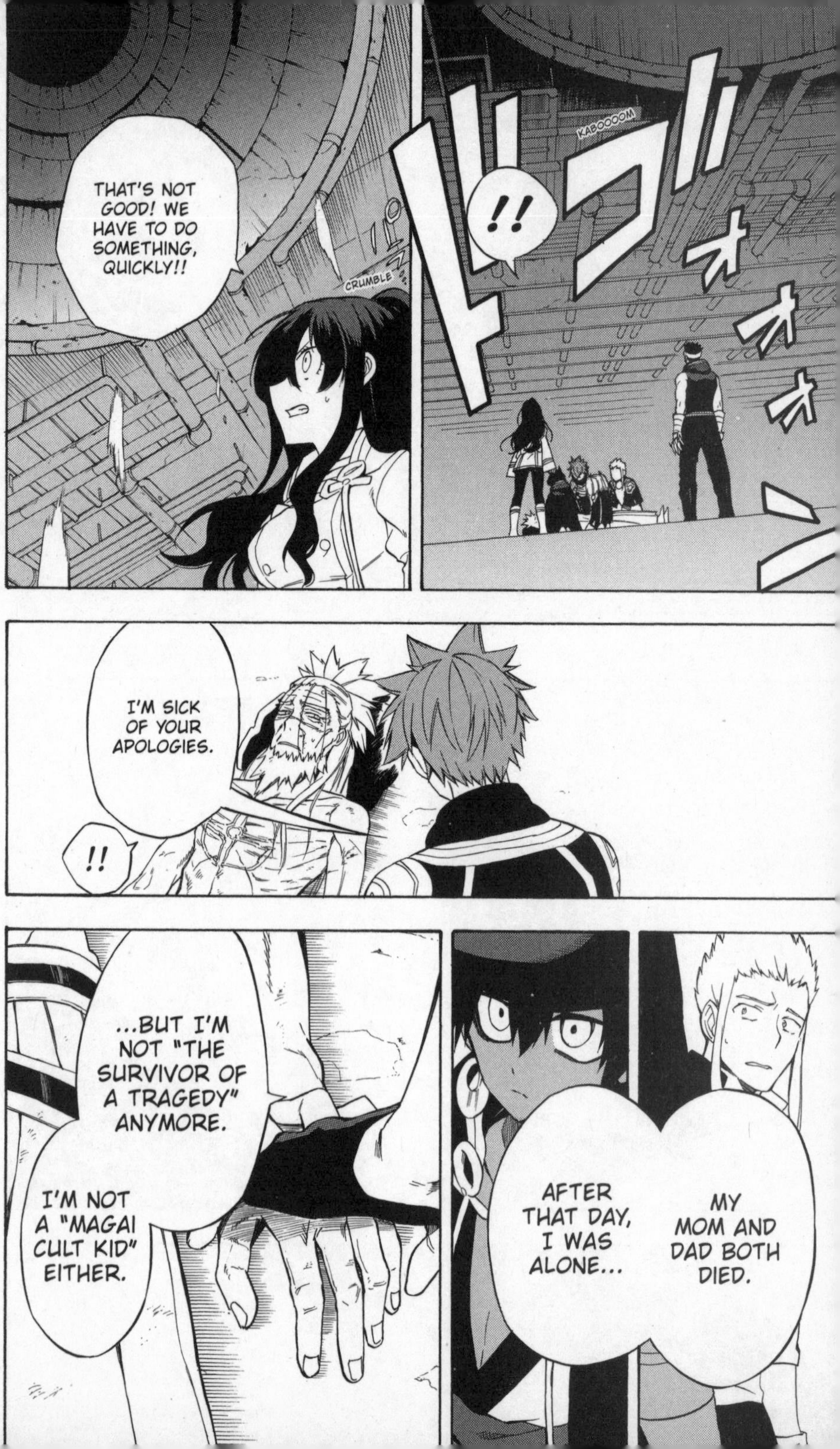
KABOOOOM
!!
THAT'S NOT GOOD! WE HAVE TO DO SOMETHING, QUICKLY!!
CRUMBLE
I'M SICK OF YOUR APOLOGIES.
!!
MY MOM AND DAD BOTH DIED.
AFTER THAT DAY, I WAS ALONE...
...BUT I'M NOT "THE SURVIVOR OF A TRAGEDY" ANYMORE.
I'M NOT A "MAGAI CULT KID" EITHER.

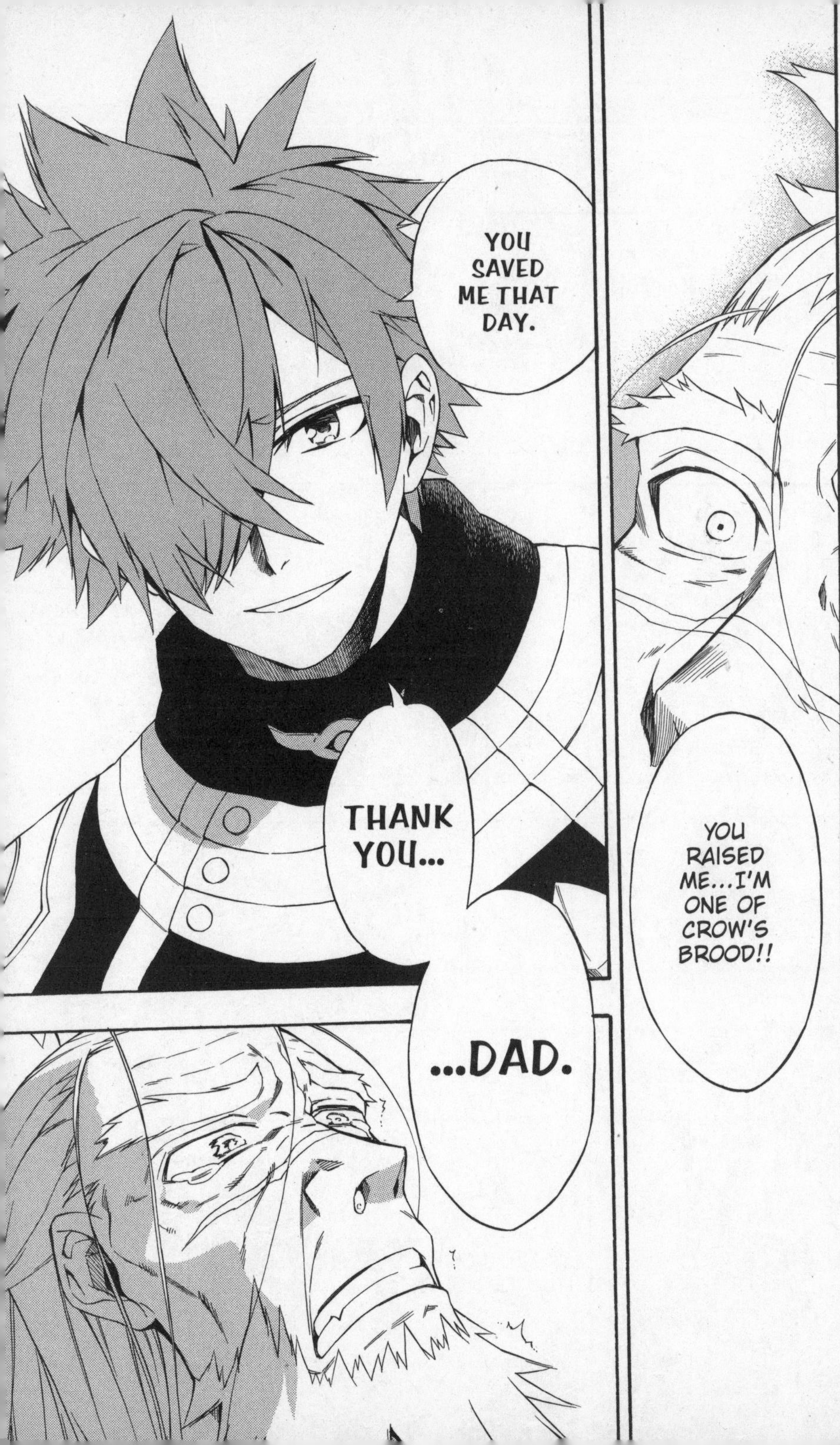
YOU SAVED ME THAT DAY.
YOU RAISED ME...I'M ONE OF CROW'S BROOD!!
THANK YOU...
...DAD.

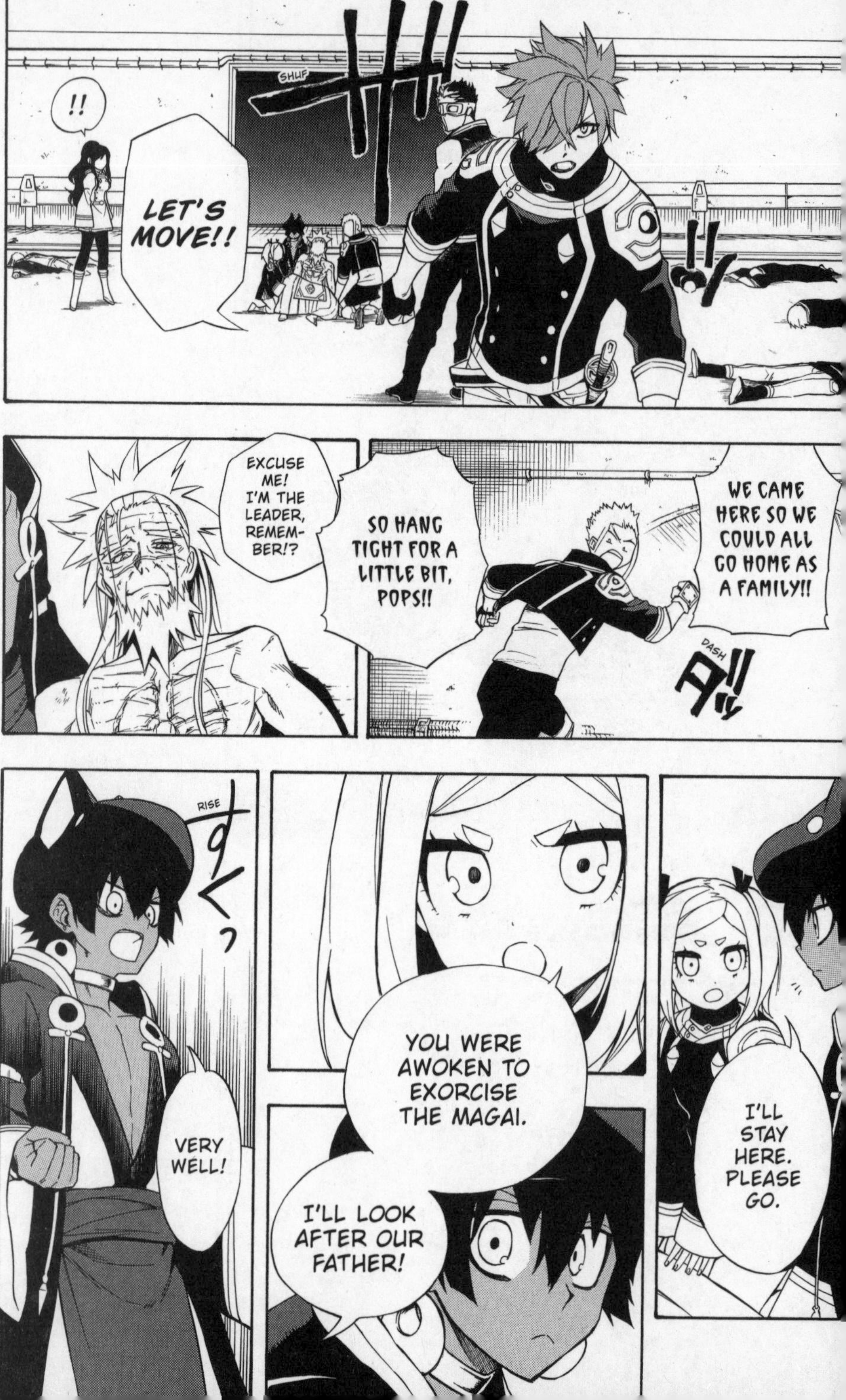
SHUF
!!
LET'S MOVE!!
WE CAME HERE SO WE COULD ALL GO HOME AS A FAMILY!!
SO HANG TIGHT FOR A LITTLE BIT, POPS!!
DASH
EXCUSE ME! I'M THE LEADER, REMEMBER!?
I'LL STAY HERE. PLEASE GO.
YOU WERE AWOKEN TO EXORCISE THE MAGAI.
I'LL LOOK AFTER OUR FATHER!
RISE
VERY WELL!

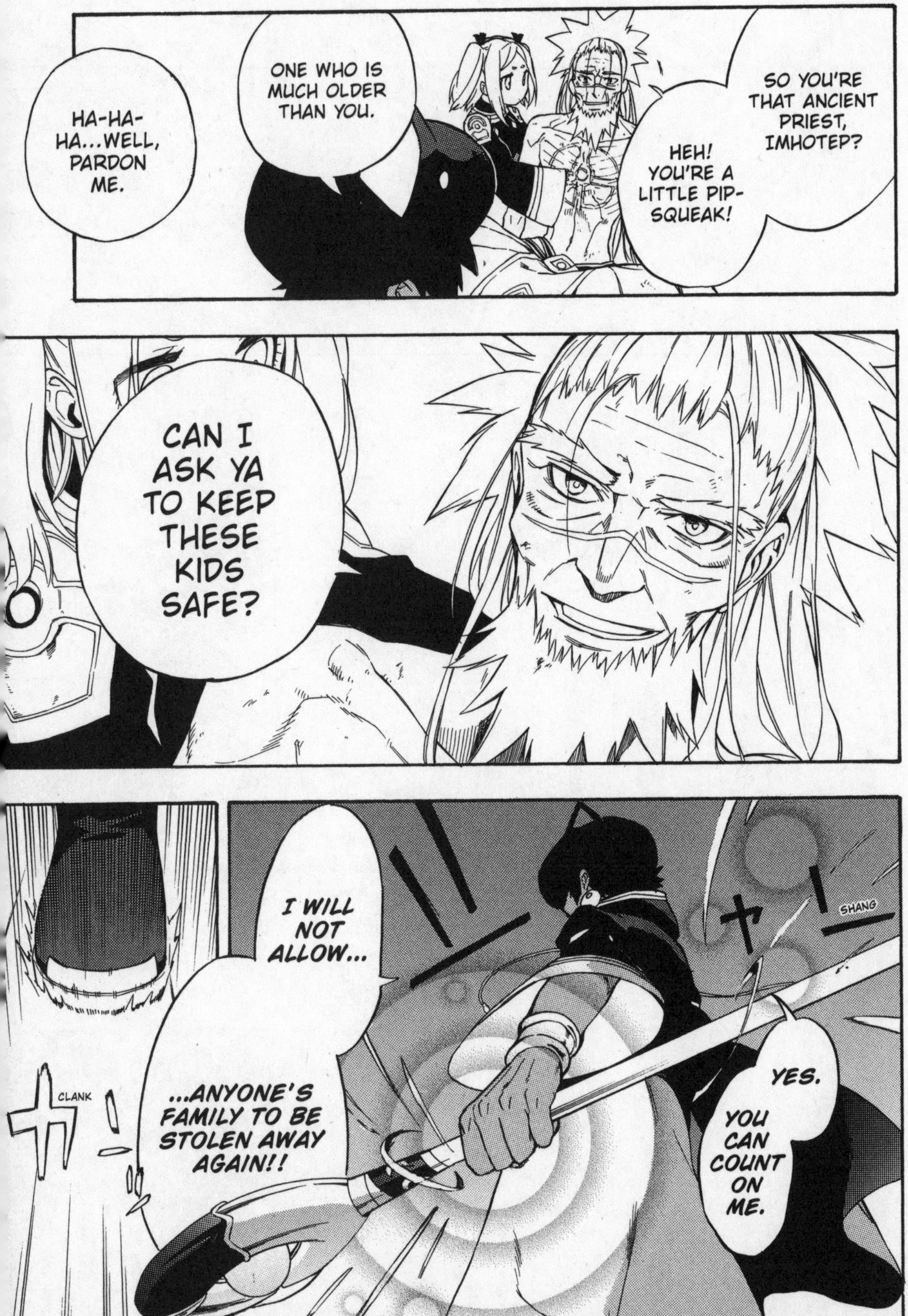
SO YOU'RE THAT ANCIENT PRIEST, IMHOTEP?
HEH! YOU'RE A LITTLE PIP-SQUEAK!
ONE WHO IS MUCH OLDER THAN YOU.
HA-HA-HA...WELL, PARDON ME.
CAN I ASK YA TO KEEP THESE KIDS SAFE?
SHANG
YES.
YOU CAN COUNT ON ME.
I WILL NOT ALLOW...
...ANYONE'S FAMILY TO BE STOLEN AWAY AGAIN!!
CLANK

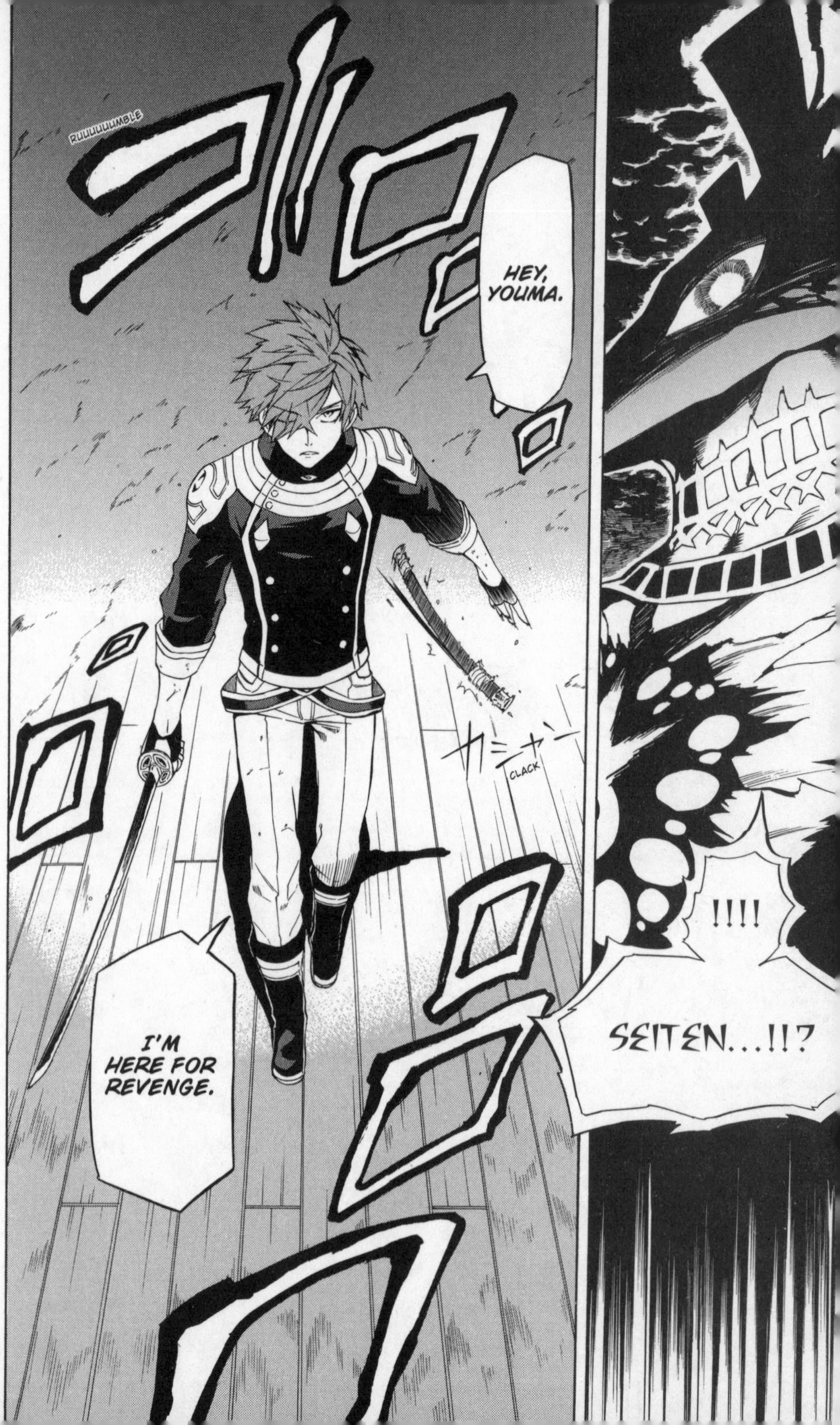
!!!!
SEITEN...!!?
RUUUUUUUMBLE
HEY, YOUMA.
CLACK
I'M HERE FOR REVENGE.

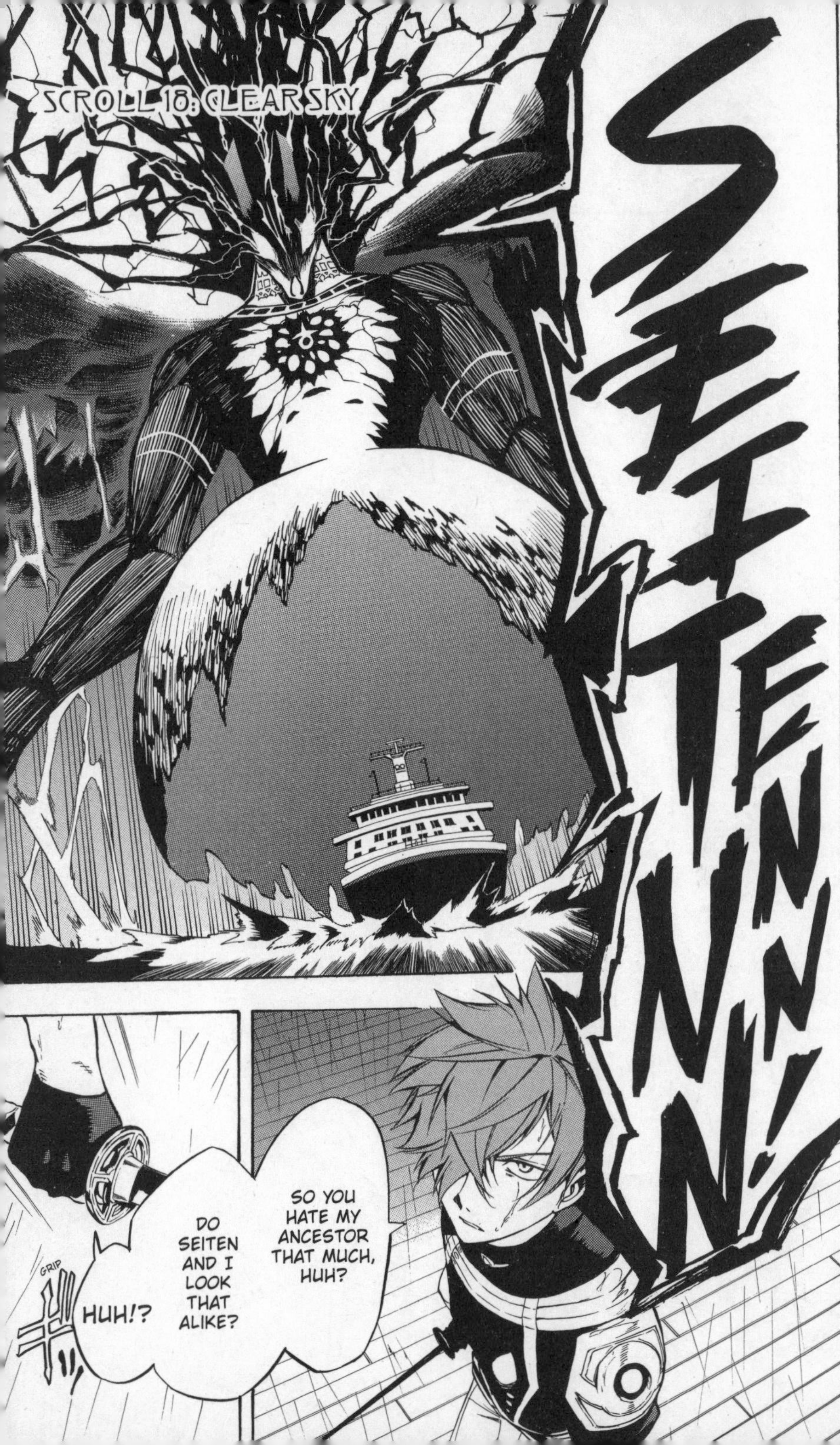
SCROLL 18: CLEAR SKY
SEITENNNN!
SO YOU HATE MY ANCESTOR THAT MUCH, HUH?
DO SEITEN AND I LOOK THAT ALIKE?
HUH!?
GRIP

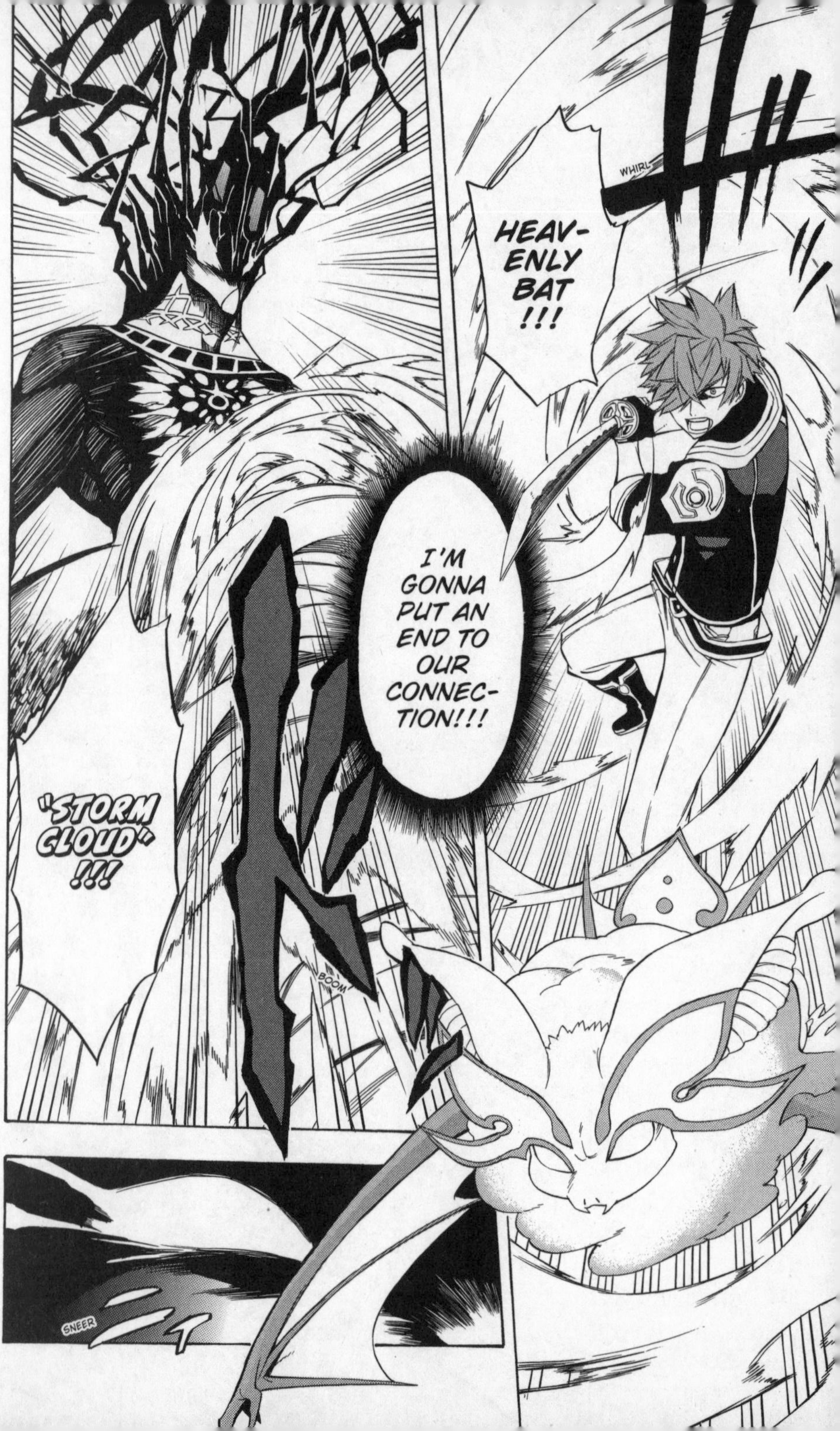
WHIRL
HEAV-ENLY BAT!!!
I'M GONNA PUT AN END TO OUR CONNECTION!!!
"STORM CLOUD"!!!
BOOM
SNEER

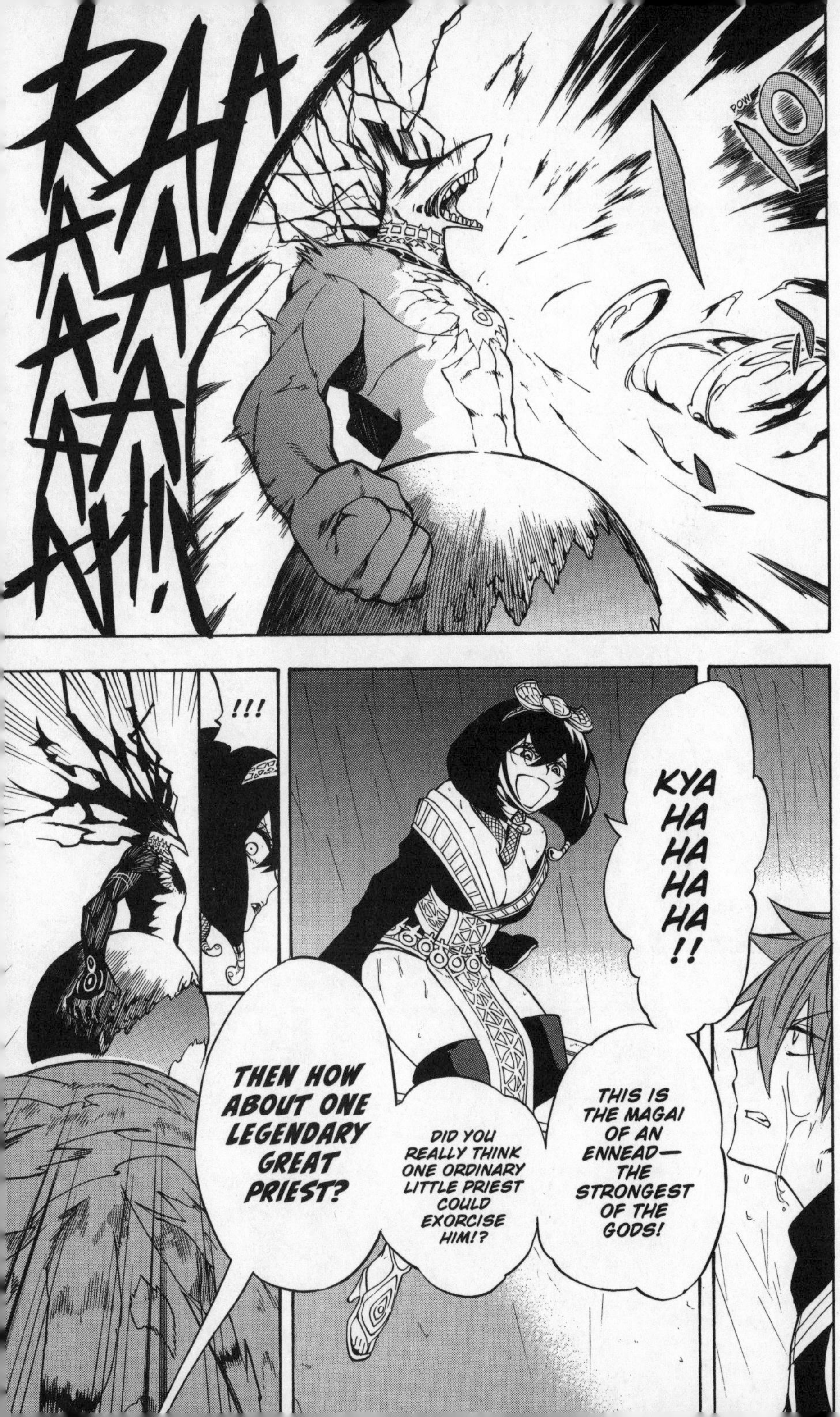
POW
RAAAAAAAAH!!
KYA HA HA HA HA!!
THIS IS THE MAGAI OF AN ENNEAD—THE STRONGEST OF THE GODS!
DID YOU REALLY THINK ONE ORDINARY LITTLE PRIEST COULD EXORCISE HIM!?
THEN HOW ABOUT ONE LEGENDARY GREAT PRIEST?
!!!

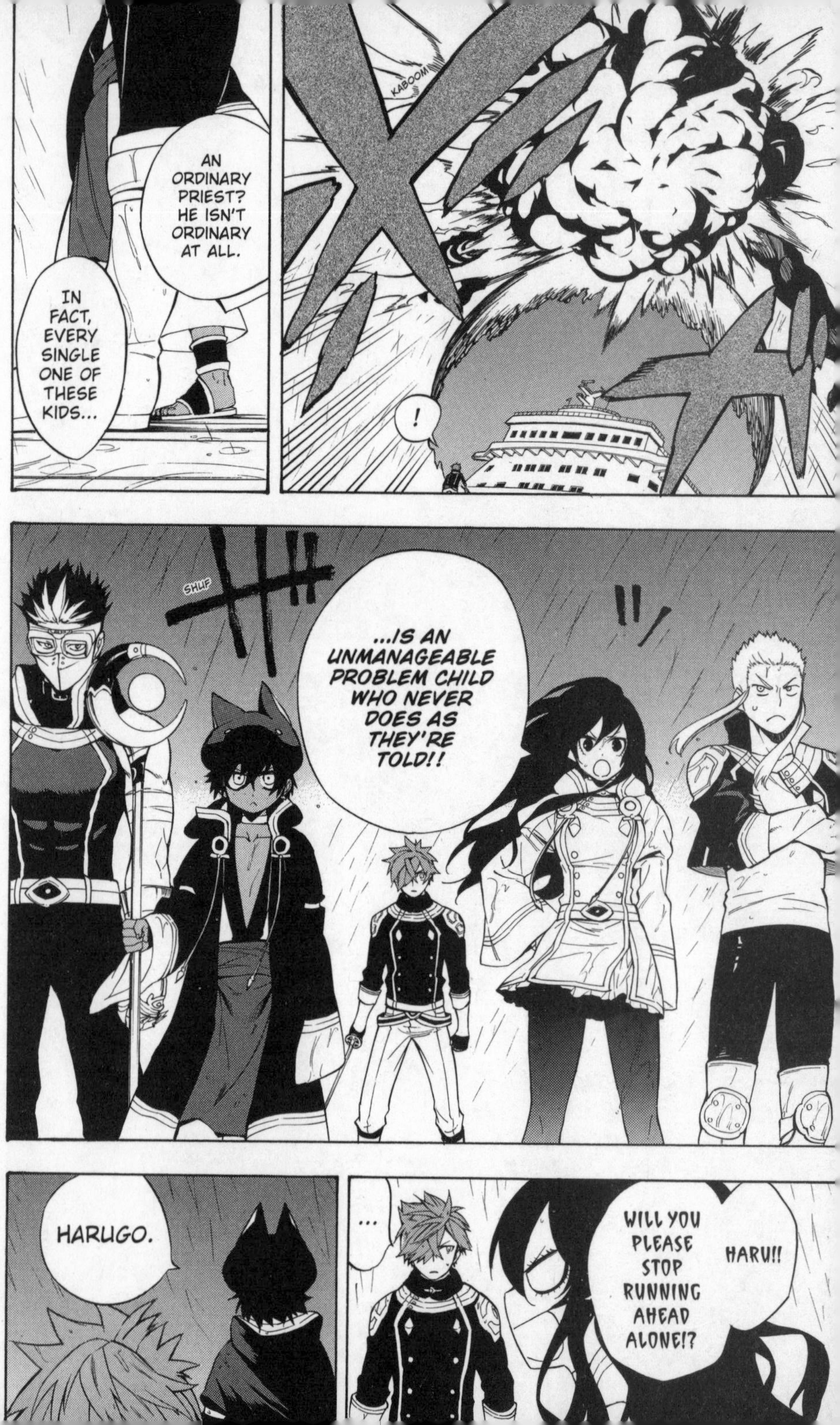
KABOOM
!
AN ORDINARY PRIEST? HE ISN'T ORDINARY AT ALL.
IN FACT, EVERY SINGLE ONE OF THESE KIDS...
SHUF
...IS AN UNMANAGEABLE PROBLEM CHILD WHO NEVER DOES AS THEY'RE TOLD!!
HARU!!
WILL YOU PLEASE STOP RUNNING AHEAD ALONE!?
...
HARUGO.

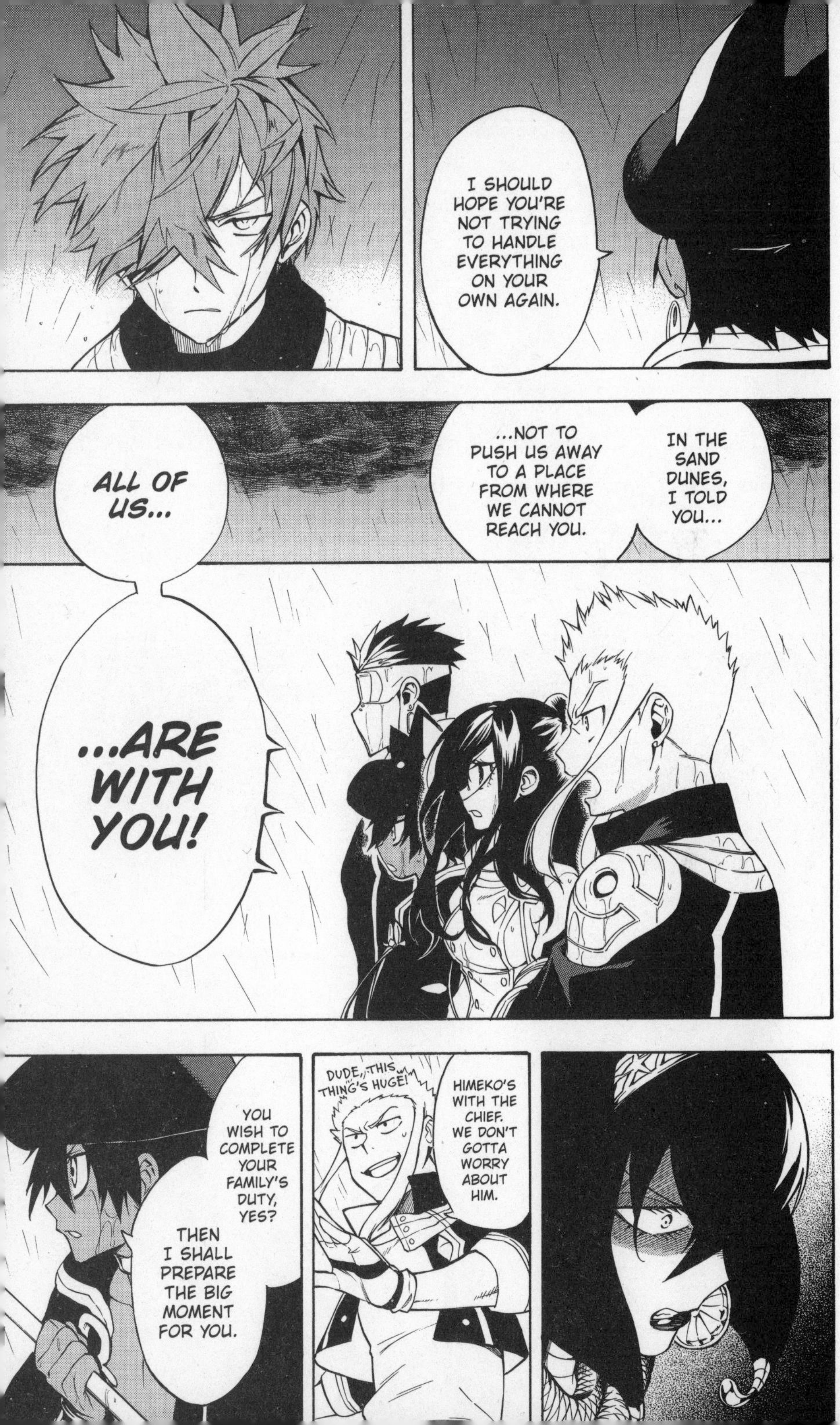
I SHOULD HOPE YOU'RE NOT TRYING TO HANDLE EVERYTHING ON YOUR OWN AGAIN.
IN THE SAND DUNES, I TOLD YOU...
...NOT TO PUSH US AWAY TO A PLACE FROM WHERE WE CANNOT REACH YOU.
ALL OF US...
...ARE WITH YOU!
HIMEKO'S WITH THE CHIEF. WE DON'T GOTTA WORRY ABOUT HIM.
DUDE, THIS THING'S HUGE!
YOU WISH TO COMPLETE YOUR FAMILY'S DUTY, YES?
THEN I SHALL PREPARE THE BIG MOMENT FOR YOU.

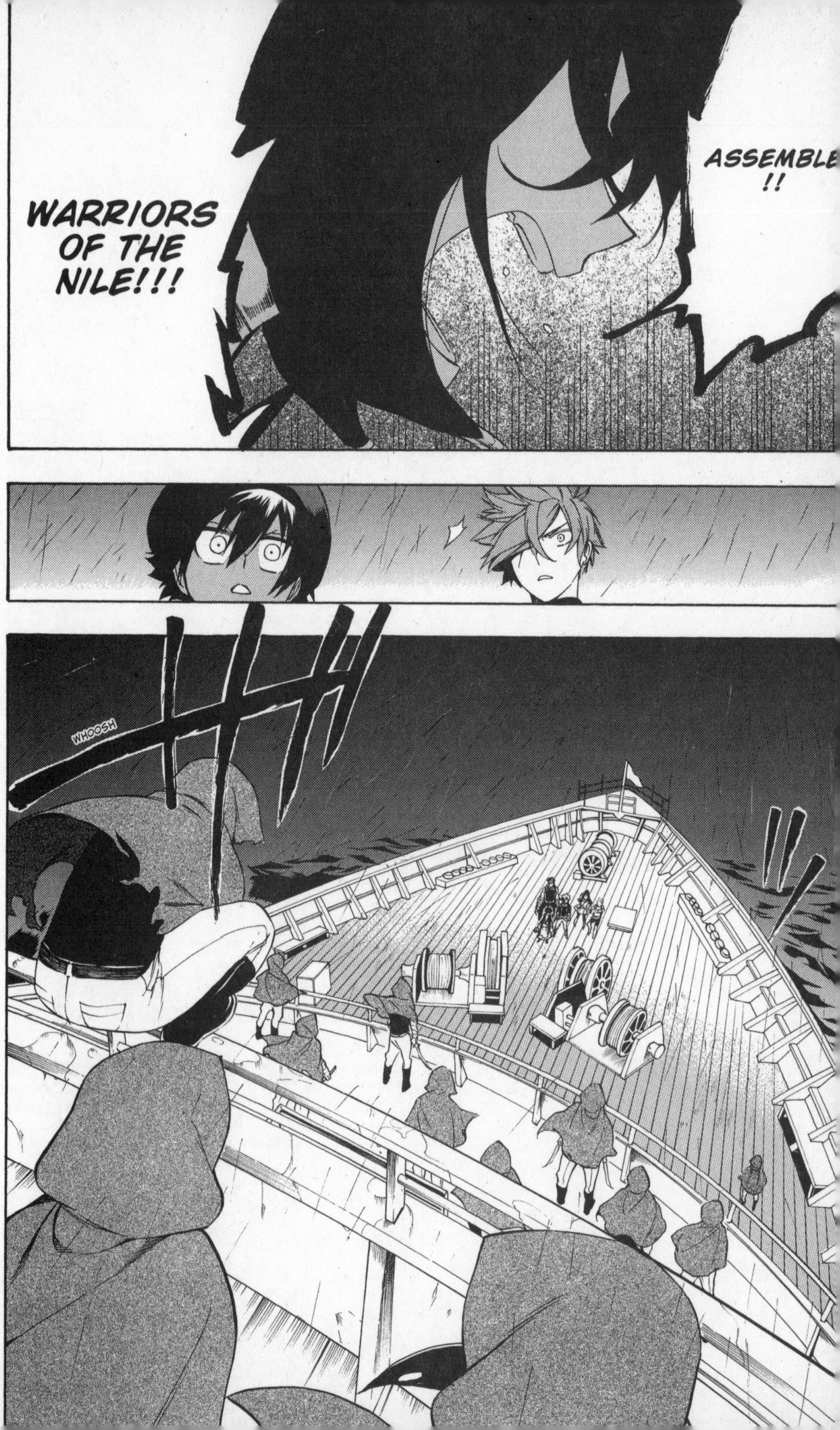
ASSEMBLE !!
WARRIORS OF THE NILE!!!
WHOOSH

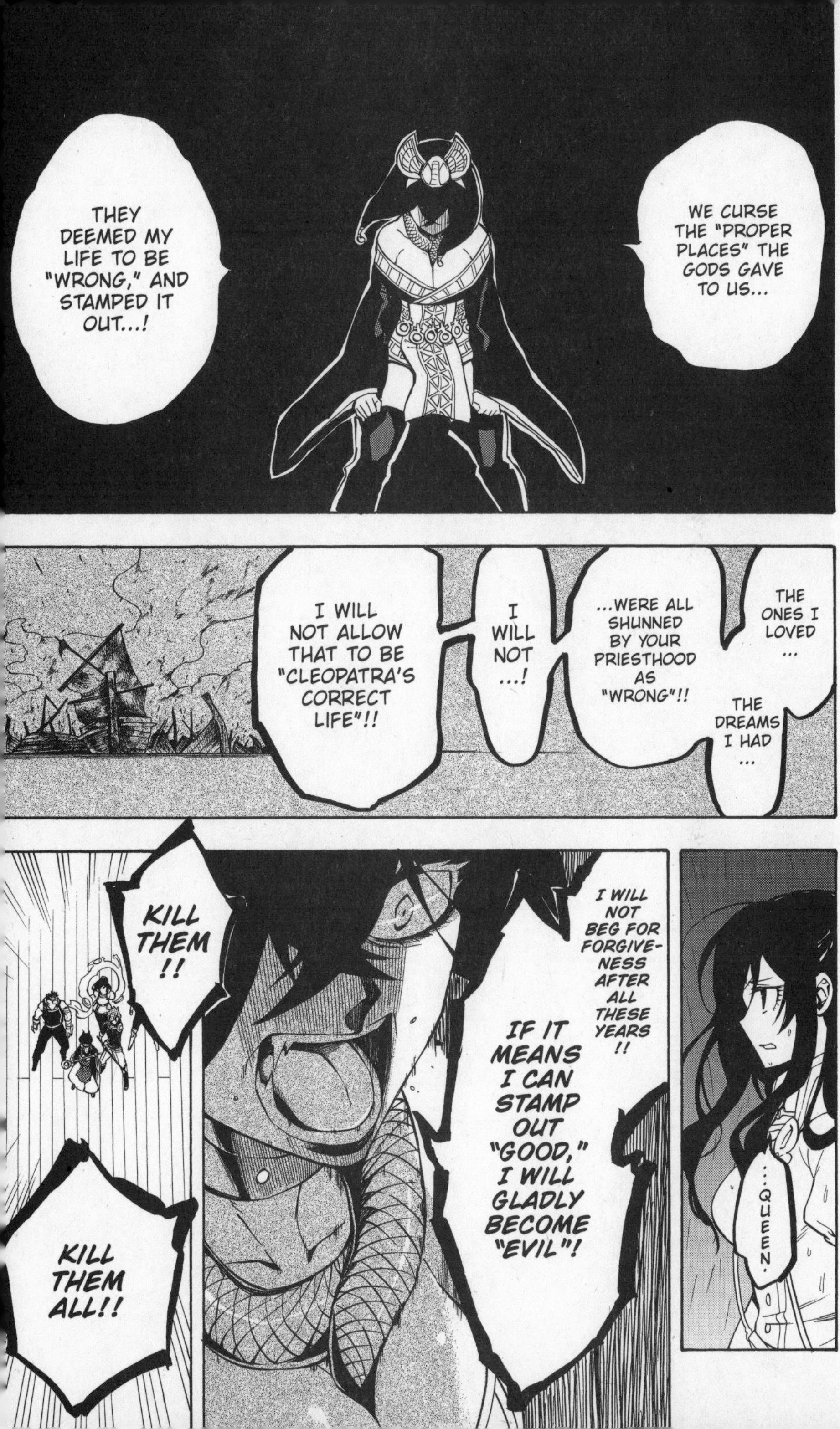
WE CURSE THE "PROPER PLACES" THE GODS GAVE TO US...
THEY DEEMED MY LIFE TO BE "WRONG," AND STAMPED IT OUT...!
THE ONES I LOVED ...
THE DREAMS I HAD ...
...WERE ALL SHUNNED BY YOUR PRIESTHOOD AS "WRONG"!!
I WILL NOT ...!
I WILL NOT ALLOW THAT TO BE "CLEOPATRA'S CORRECT LIFE"!!
...QUEEN.
I WILL NOT BEG FOR FORGIVE-NESS AFTER ALL THESE YEARS!!
IF IT MEANS I CAN STAMP OUT "GOOD," I WILL GLADLY BECOME "EVIL"!
KILL THEM!!
KILL THEM ALL!!

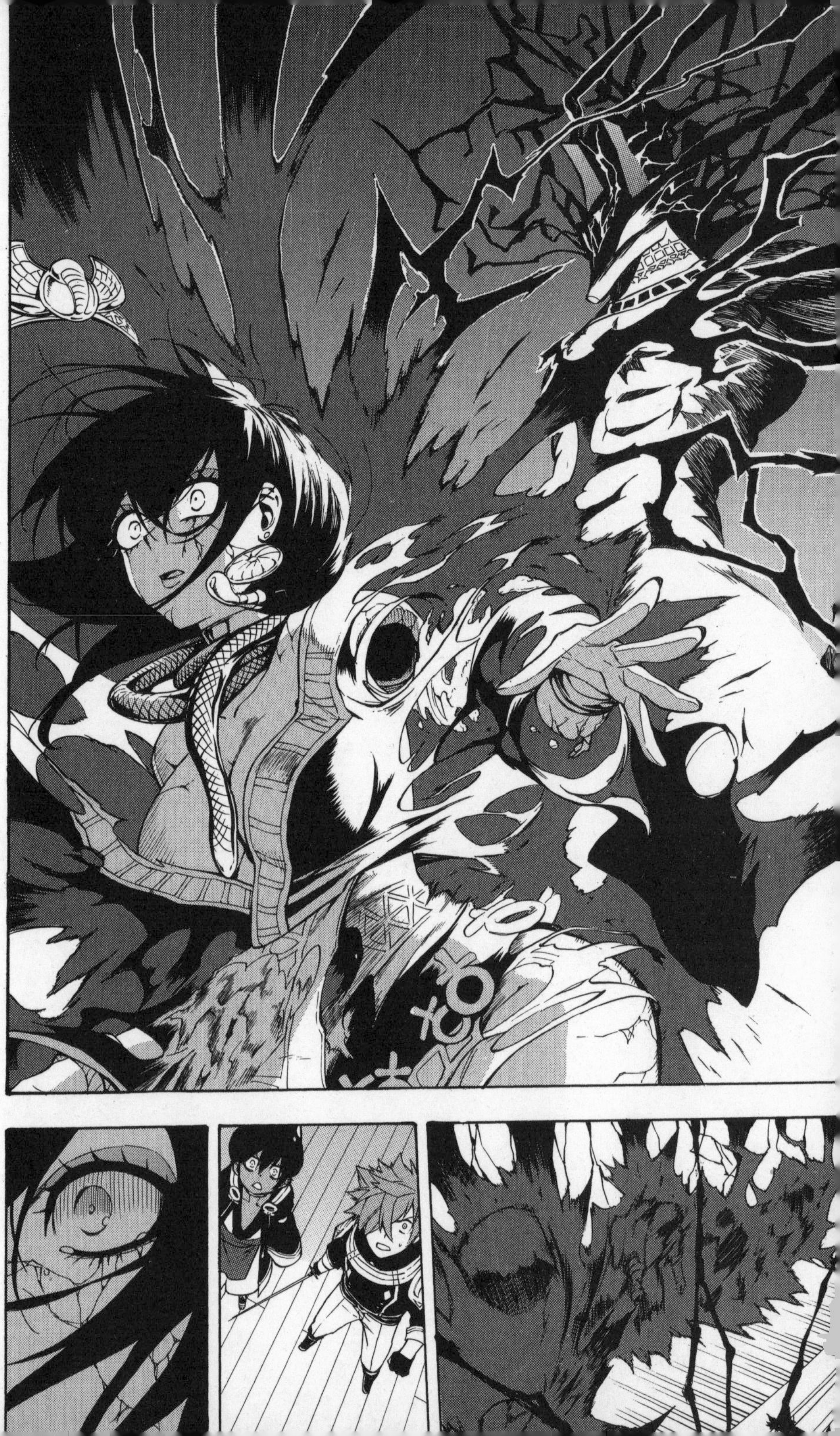

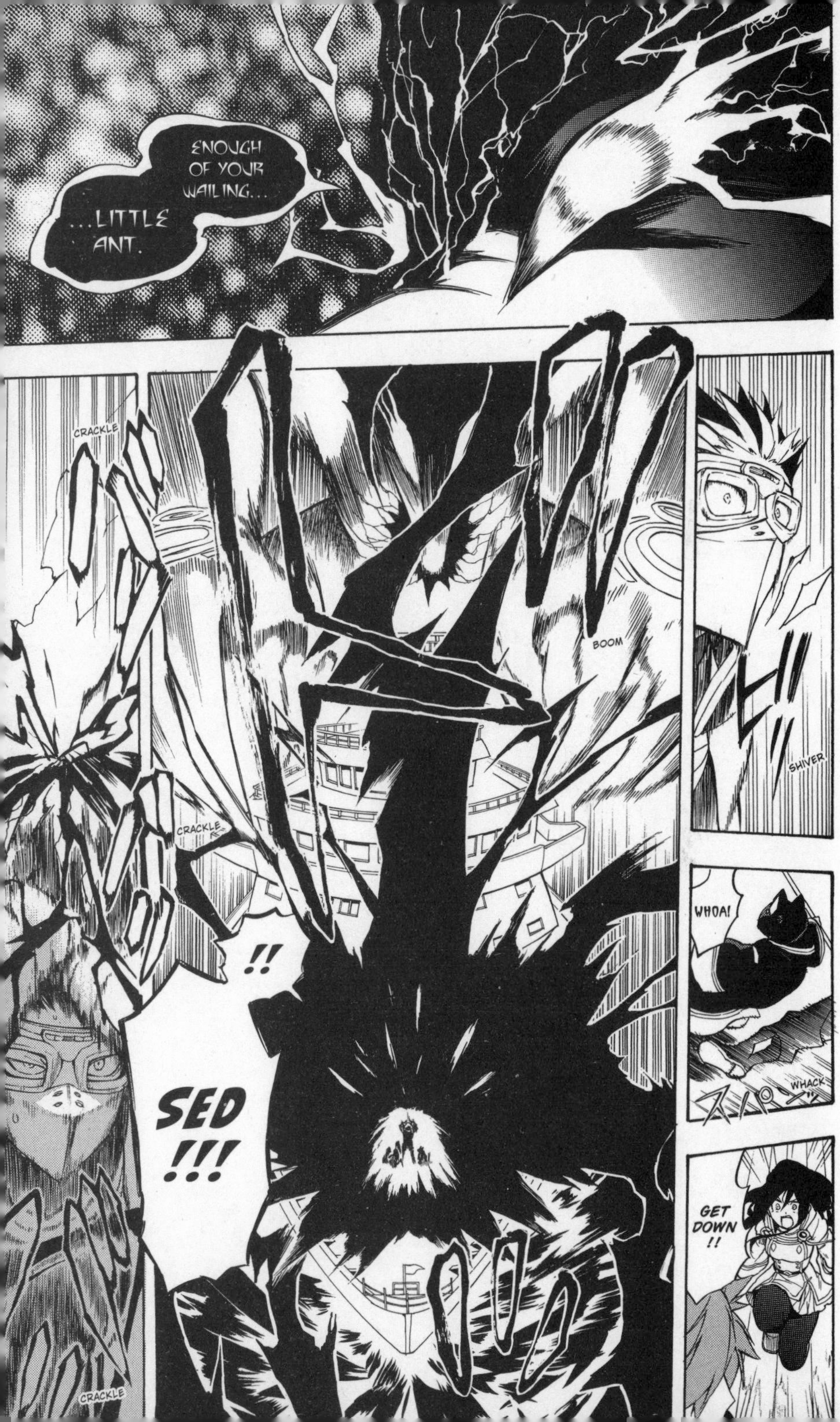
ENOUGH OF YOUR WAILING...
...LITTLE ANT.
SHIVER
WHOA!
WHACK
GET DOWN!!
BOOM
CRACKLE
CRACKLE
!!
SED!!!
CRACKLE

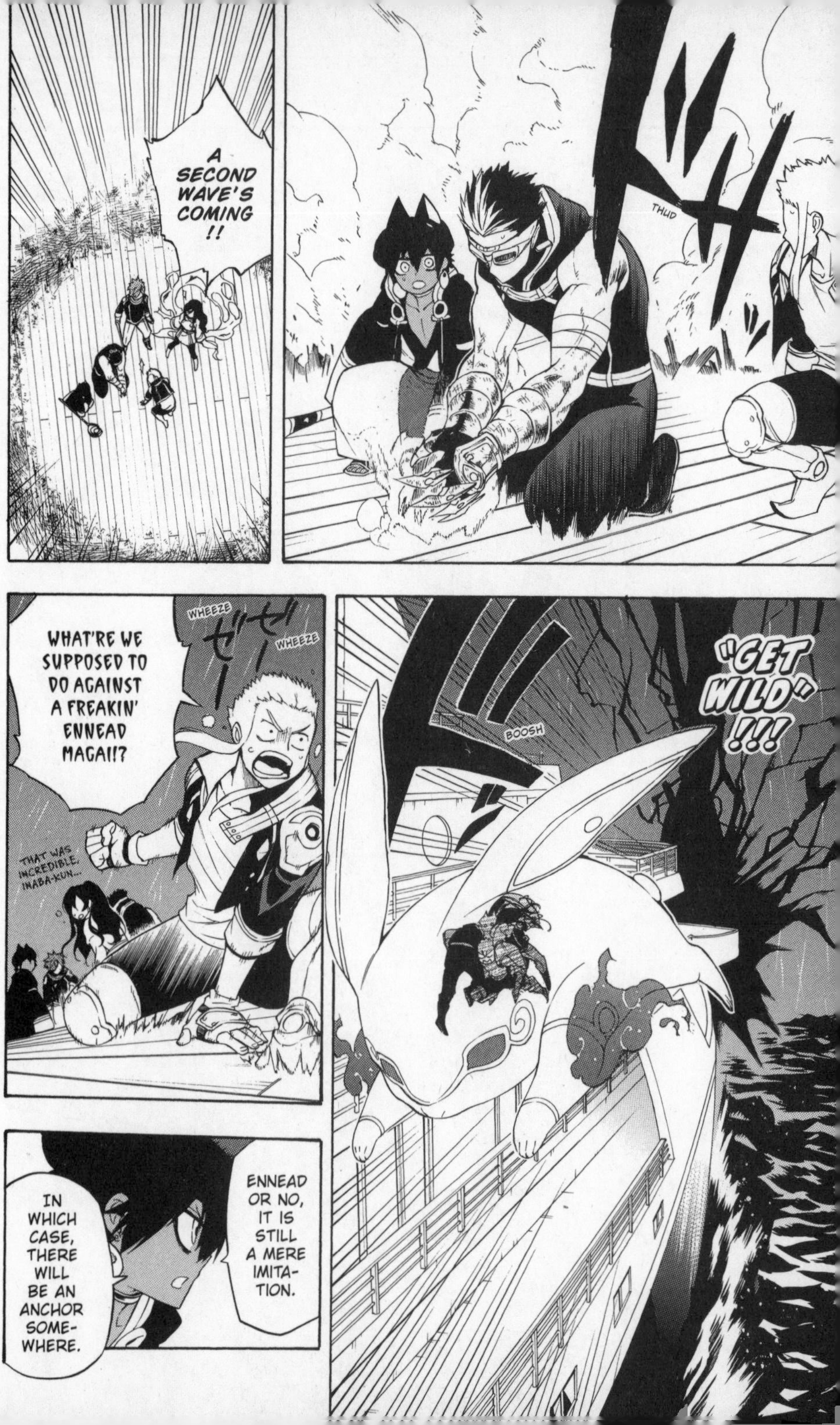
THUD
A SECOND WAVE'S COMING!!
"GET WILD"!!!
BOOSH
WHEEZE
WHEEZE
WHAT'RE WE SUPPOSED TO DO AGAINST A FREAKIN' ENNEAD MAGAI!?
THAT WAS INCREDIBLE, INABA-KUN...
ENNEAD OR NO, IT IS STILL A MERE IMITATION.
IN WHICH CASE, THERE WILL BE AN ANCHOR SOMEWHERE.

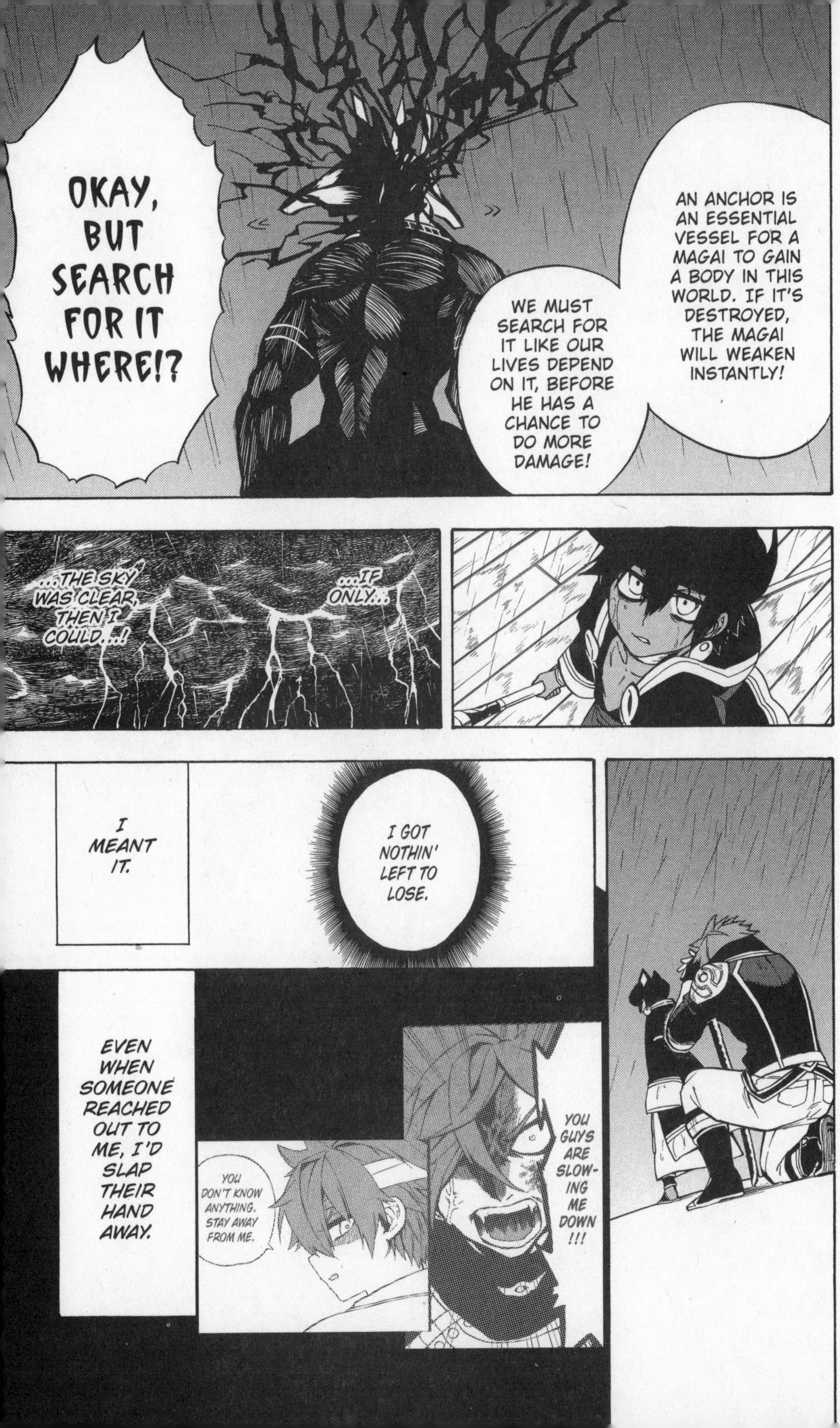

AN ANCHOR IS AN ESSENTIAL VESSEL FOR A MAGAI TO GAIN A BODY IN THIS WORLD. IF IT'S DESTROYED, THE MAGAI WILL WEAKEN INSTANTLY!
WE MUST SEARCH FOR IT LIKE OUR LIVES DEPEND ON IT, BEFORE HE HAS A CHANCE TO DO MORE DAMAGE!
OKAY, BUT SEARCH FOR IT WHERE!?
...IF ONLY...
...THE SKY WAS CLEAR, THEN I COULD...!
I GOT NOTHIN' LEFT TO LOSE.
I MEANT IT.
YOU GUYS ARE SLOWING ME DOWN!!!
YOU DON'T KNOW ANYTHING. STAY AWAY FROM ME.
EVEN WHEN SOMEONE REACHED OUT TO ME, I'D SLAP THEIR HAND AWAY.

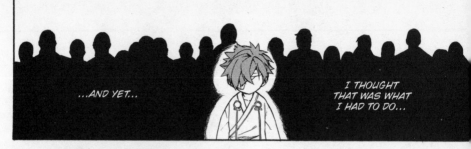

I THOUGHT THAT WAS WHAT I HAD TO DO...
...AND YET...
IF YOU WANTED ME TO KNOW, THEN TELL IT ALL TO ME NOW!!!!
I WILL DRAG YOU OUT INTO THE SUNLIGHT, EVEN IF I MUST USE FORCE TO DO SO!
I WILL TAKE OFF YOUR TOUGH-GUY MASK!!
EVEN THOUGH I'D IGNORED HIM...
EVEN THOUGH I'D HATED HIM...

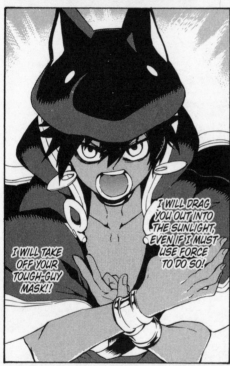

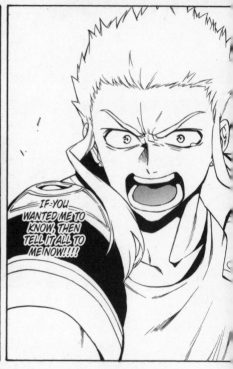

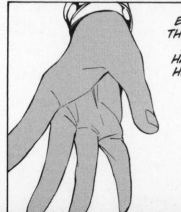

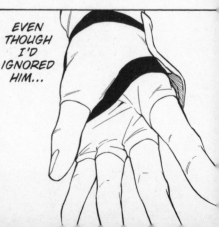

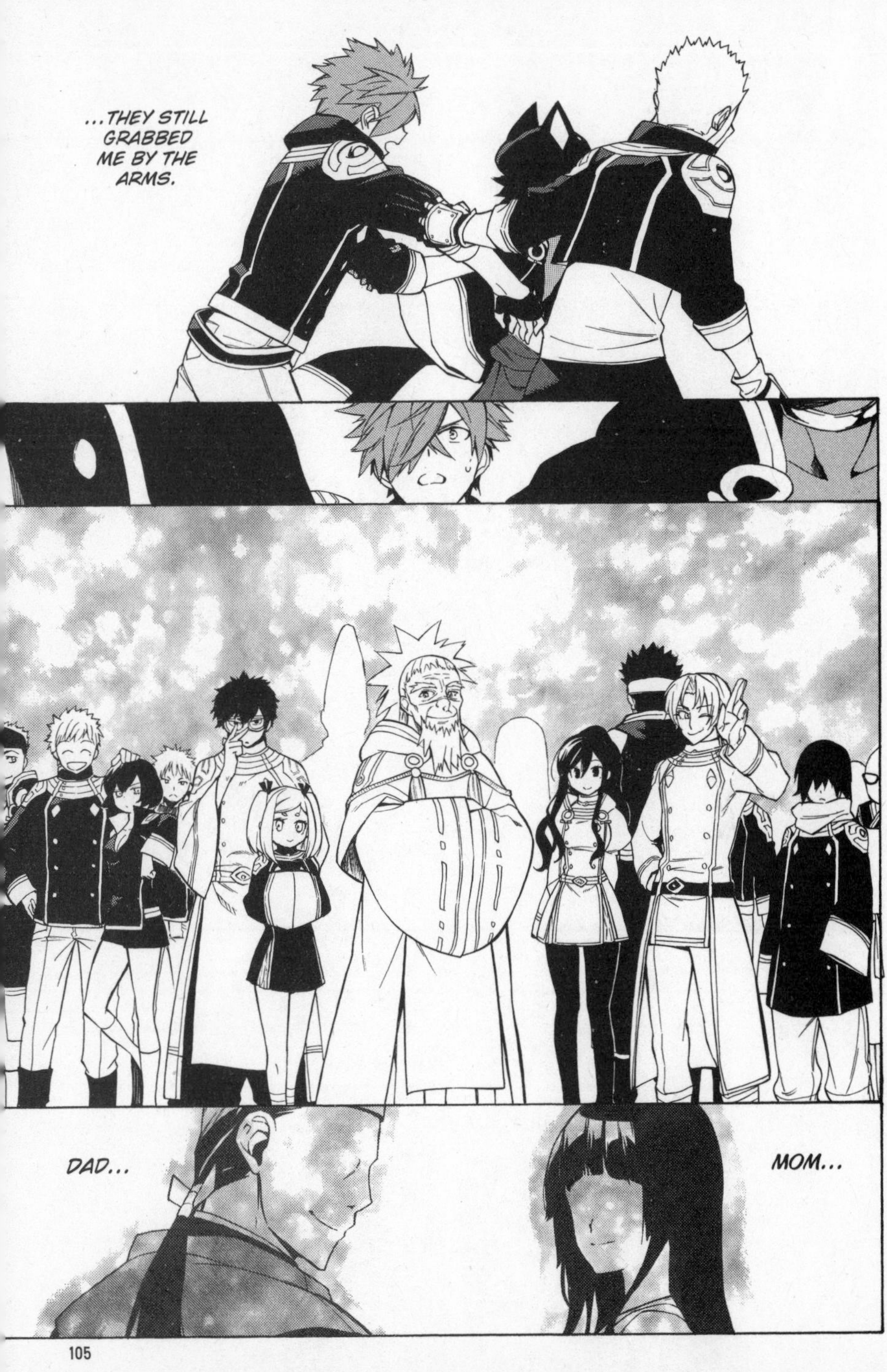
...THEY STILL GRABBED ME BY THE ARMS.
MOM...
DAD...

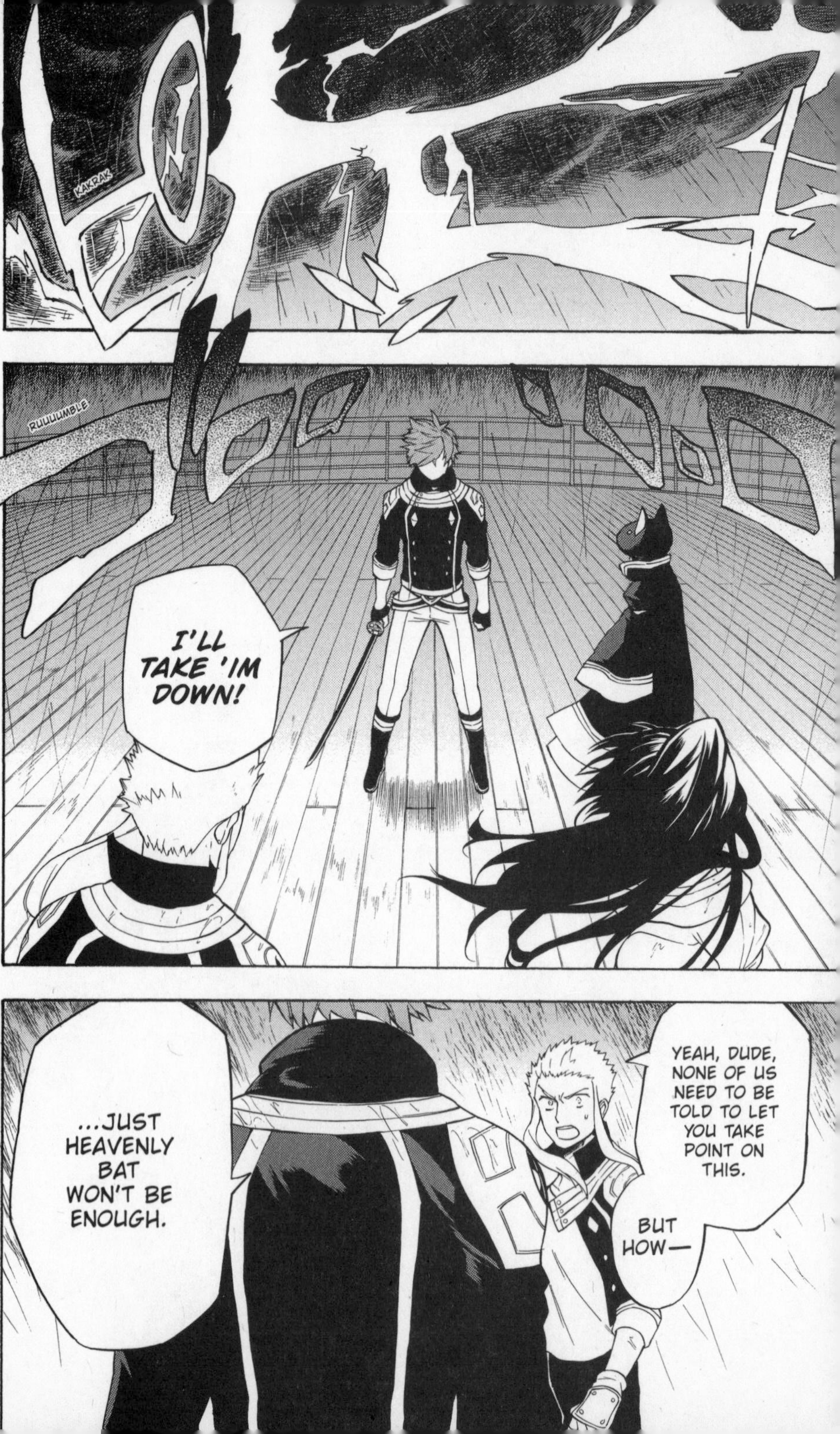
KAKRAK
RUUUUMBLE
I'LL TAKE 'IM DOWN!
YEAH, DUDE, NONE OF US NEED TO BE TOLD TO LET YOU TAKE POINT ON THIS.
BUT HOW—
...JUST HEAVENLY BAT WON'T BE ENOUGH.

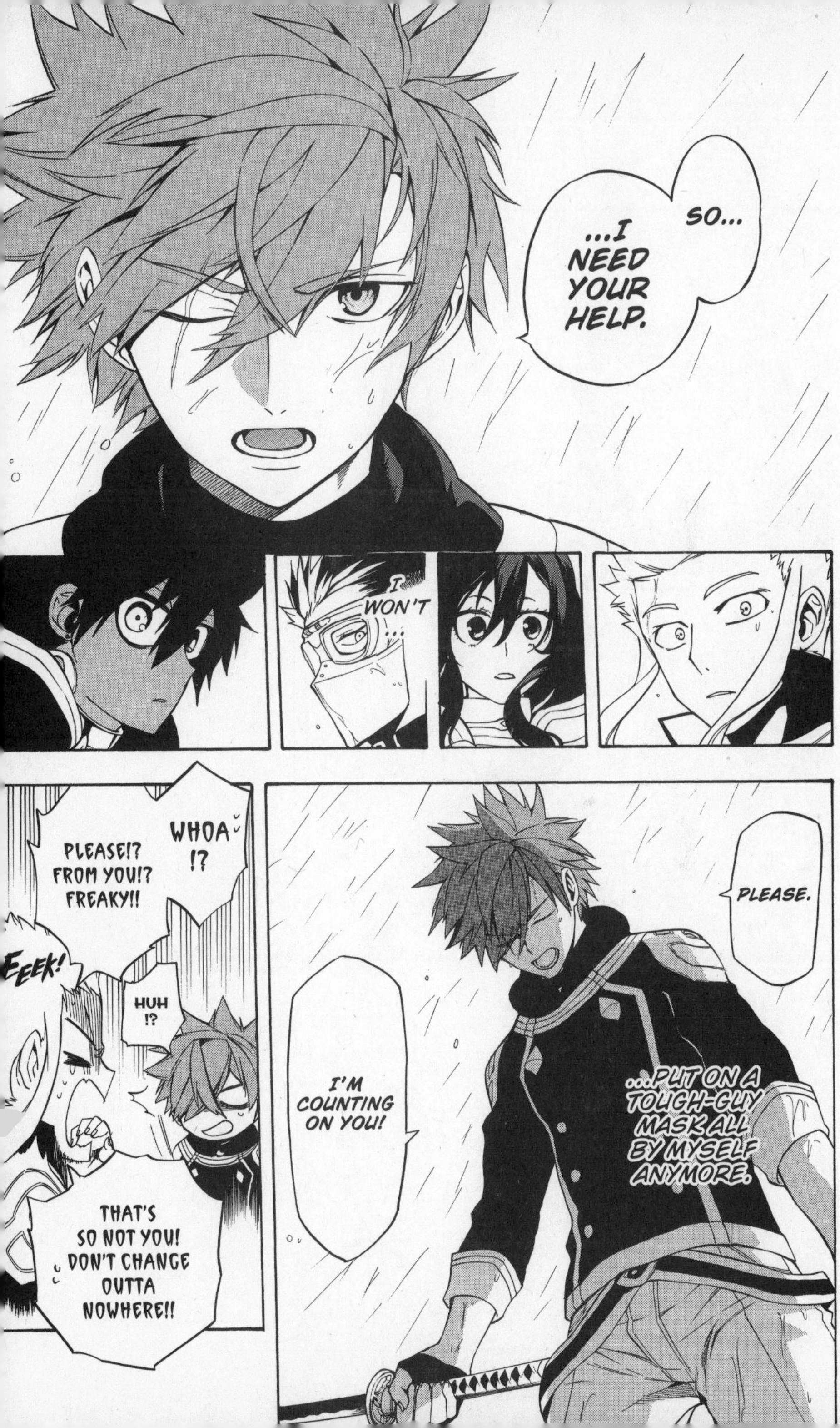
SO...
...I NEED YOUR HELP.
I WON'T ...
PLEASE.
...PUT ON A TOUGH-GUY MASK ALL BY MYSELF ANYMORE.
I'M COUNTING ON YOU!
WHOA !?
PLEASE!? FROM YOU!? FREAKY!!
EEEK!
HUH !?
THAT'S SO NOT YOU! DON'T CHANGE OUTTA NOWHERE!!

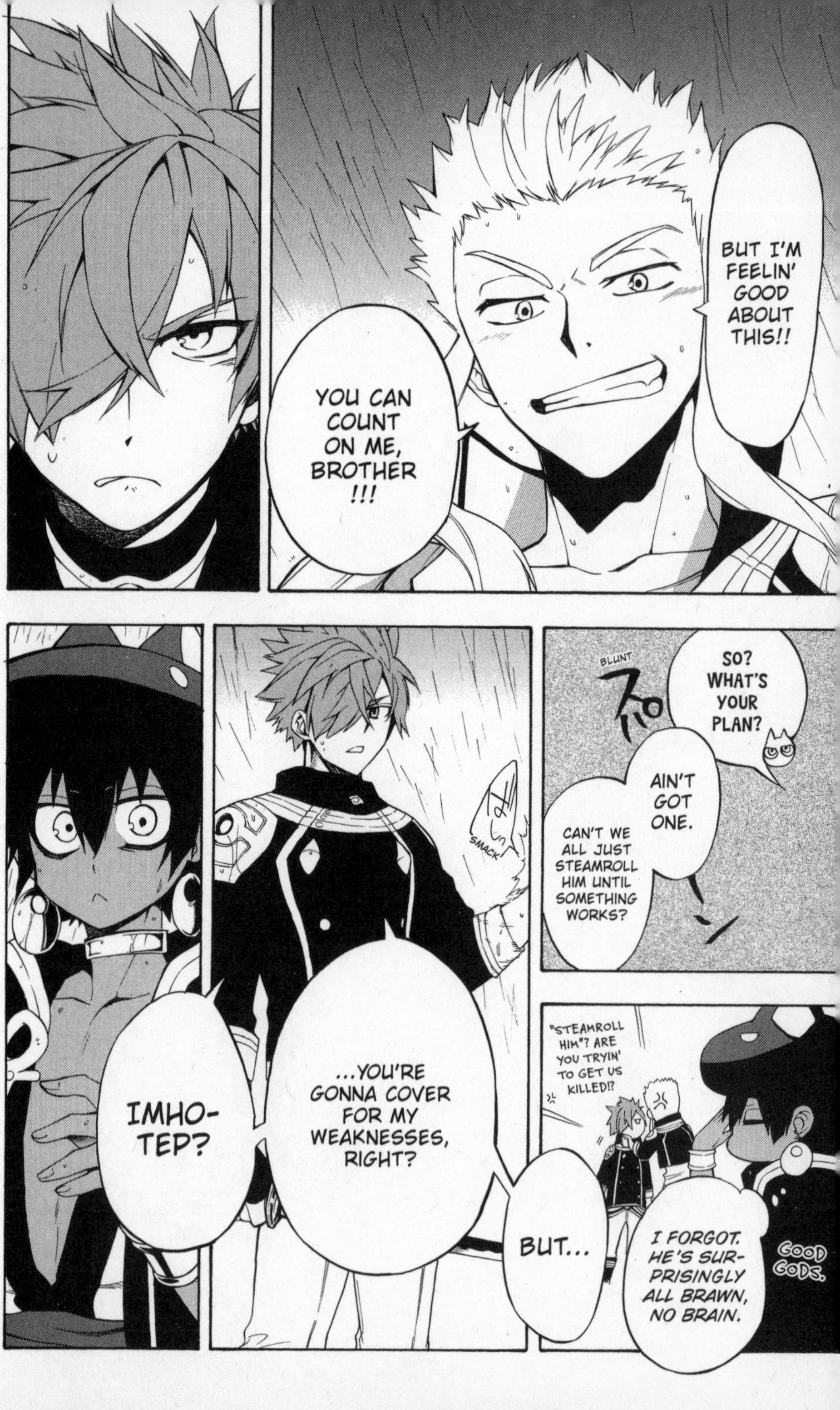
BUT I'M FEELIN' GOOD ABOUT THIS!!
YOU CAN COUNT ON ME, BROTHER!!!
BLUNT
SO? WHAT'S YOUR PLAN?
AIN'T GOT ONE.
CAN'T WE ALL JUST STEAMROLL HIM UNTIL SOMETHING WORKS?
"STEAMROLL HIM"? ARE YOU TRYIN' TO GET US KILLED!?
GOOD GODS.
I FORGOT. HE'S SURPRISINGLY ALL BRAWN, NO BRAIN.
BUT...
SMACK
...YOU'RE GONNA COVER FOR MY WEAKNESSES, RIGHT?
IMHOTEP?

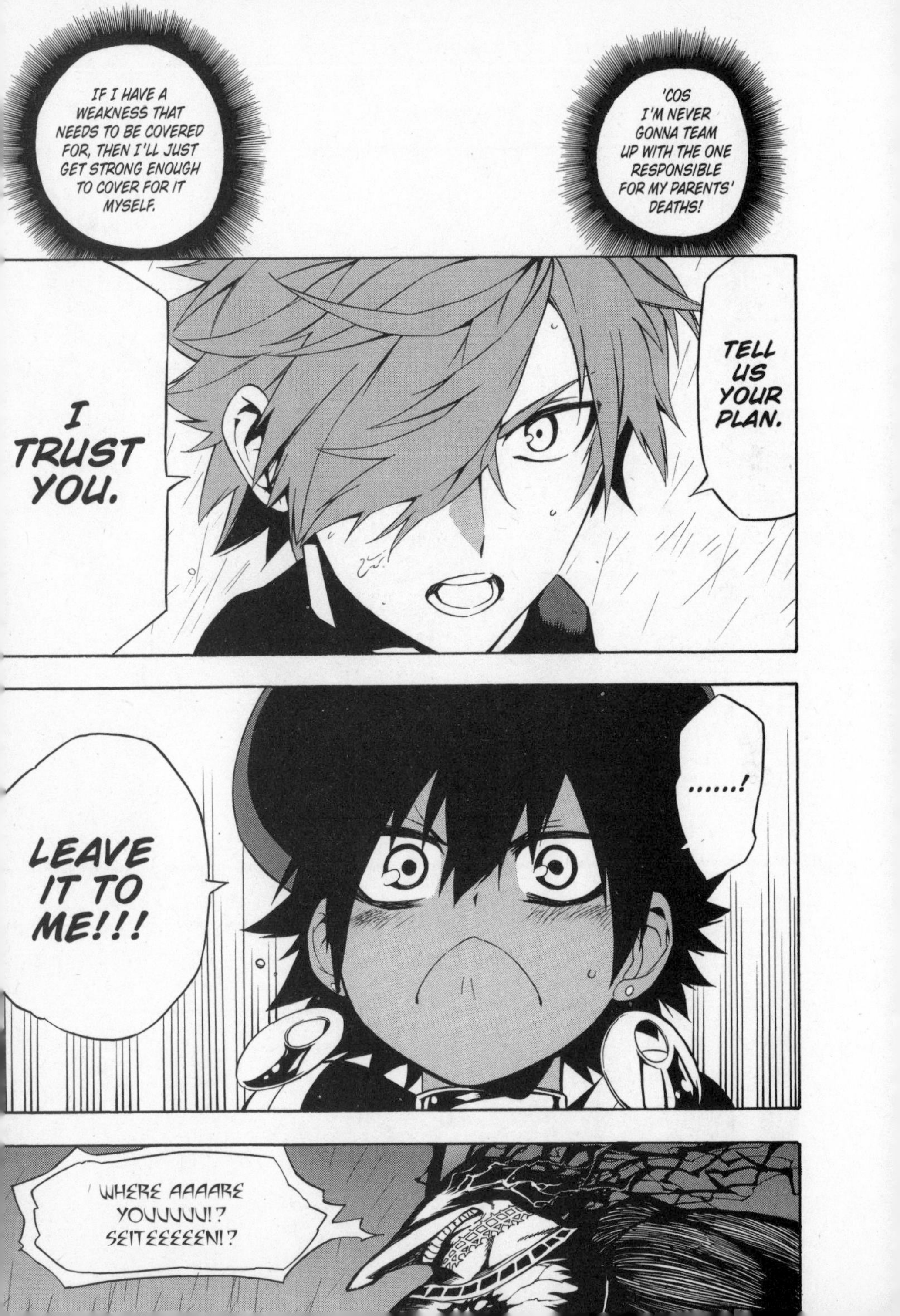
'COS I'M NEVER GONNA TEAM UP WITH THE ONE RESPONSIBLE FOR MY PARENTS' DEATHS!
IF I HAVE A WEAKNESS THAT NEEDS TO BE COVERED FOR, THEN I'LL JUST GET STRONG ENOUGH TO COVER FOR IT MYSELF.
TELL US YOUR PLAN.
I TRUST YOU.
......!
LEAVE IT TO ME!!!
WHERE AAAARE YOUUUUU!? SEITEEEEEN!?

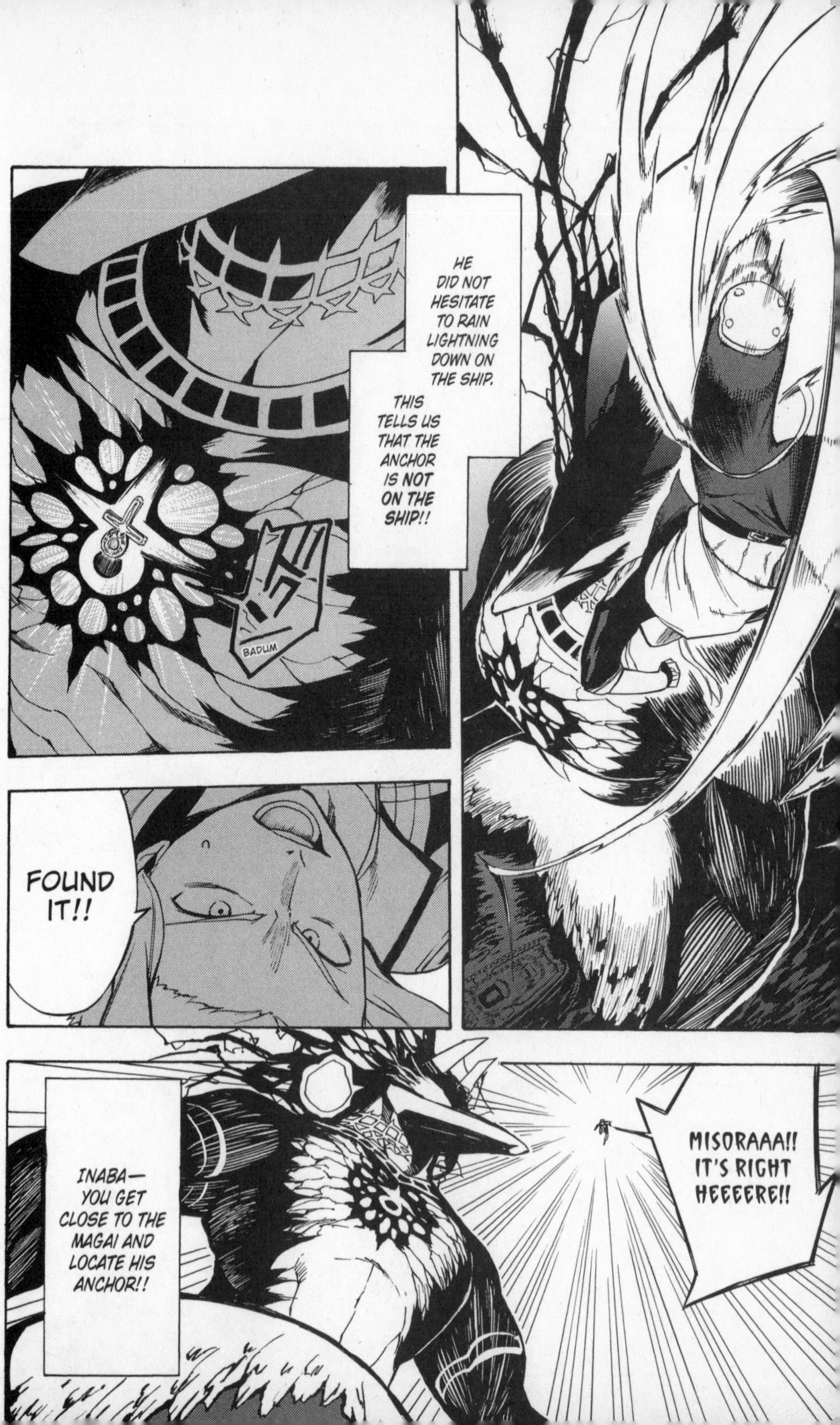
HE DID NOT HESITATE TO RAIN LIGHTNING DOWN ON THE SHIP.
THIS TELLS US THAT THE ANCHOR IS NOT ON THE SHIP!!
BADUM
FOUND IT!!
MISORAAA!! IT'S RIGHT HEEEERE!!
INABA— YOU GET CLOSE TO THE MAGAI AND LOCATE HIS ANCHOR!!

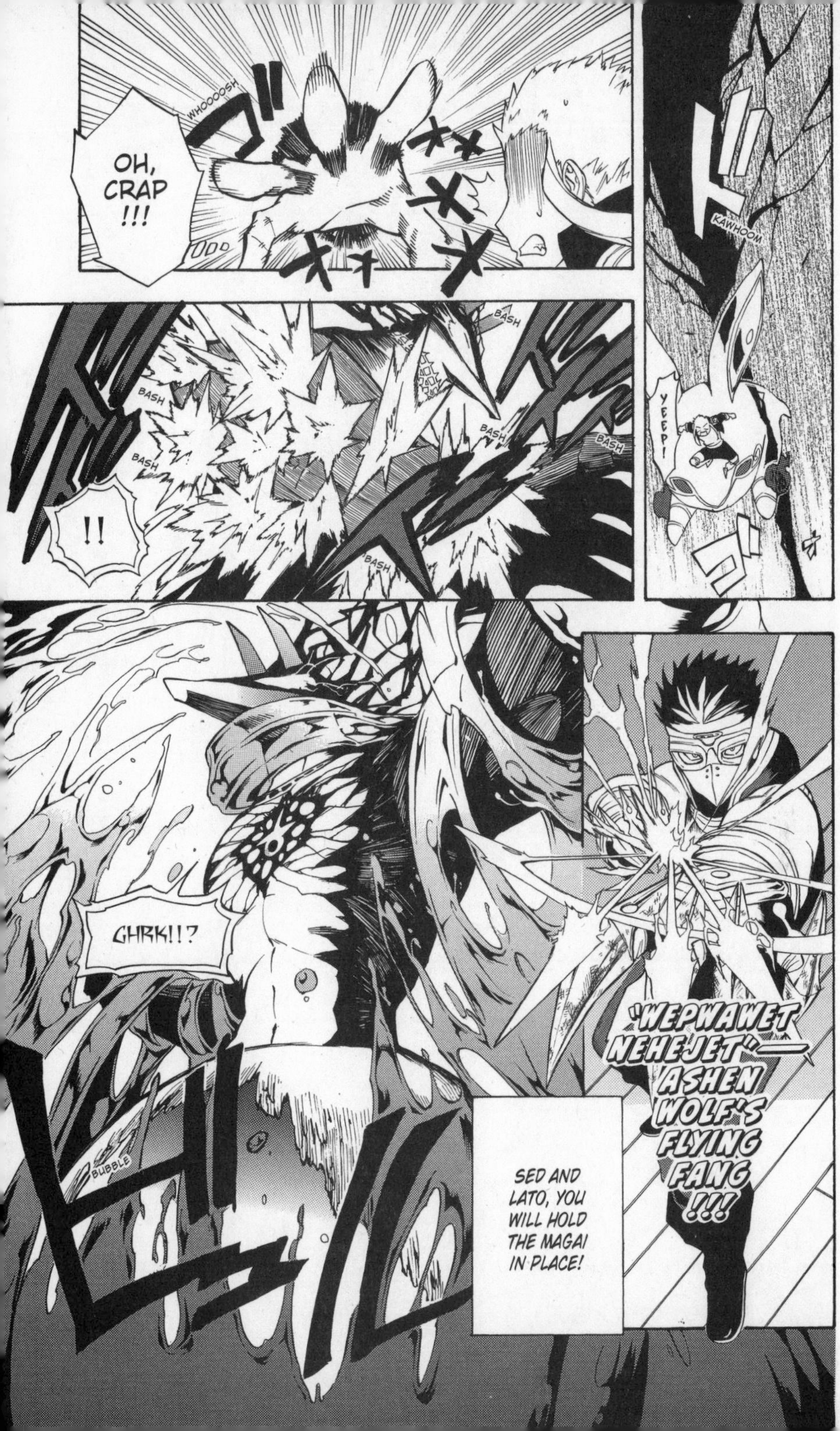
KAWHOOM
YEEP!
WHOOOOSH
OH, CRAP!!!
BASH
BASH
BASH
BASH
BASH
BASH
!!
"WEPWAWET NEHEJET"— ASHEN WOLF'S FLYING FANG!!!
SED AND LATO, YOU WILL HOLD THE MAGAI IN PLACE!
GHRK!!?
BUBBLE

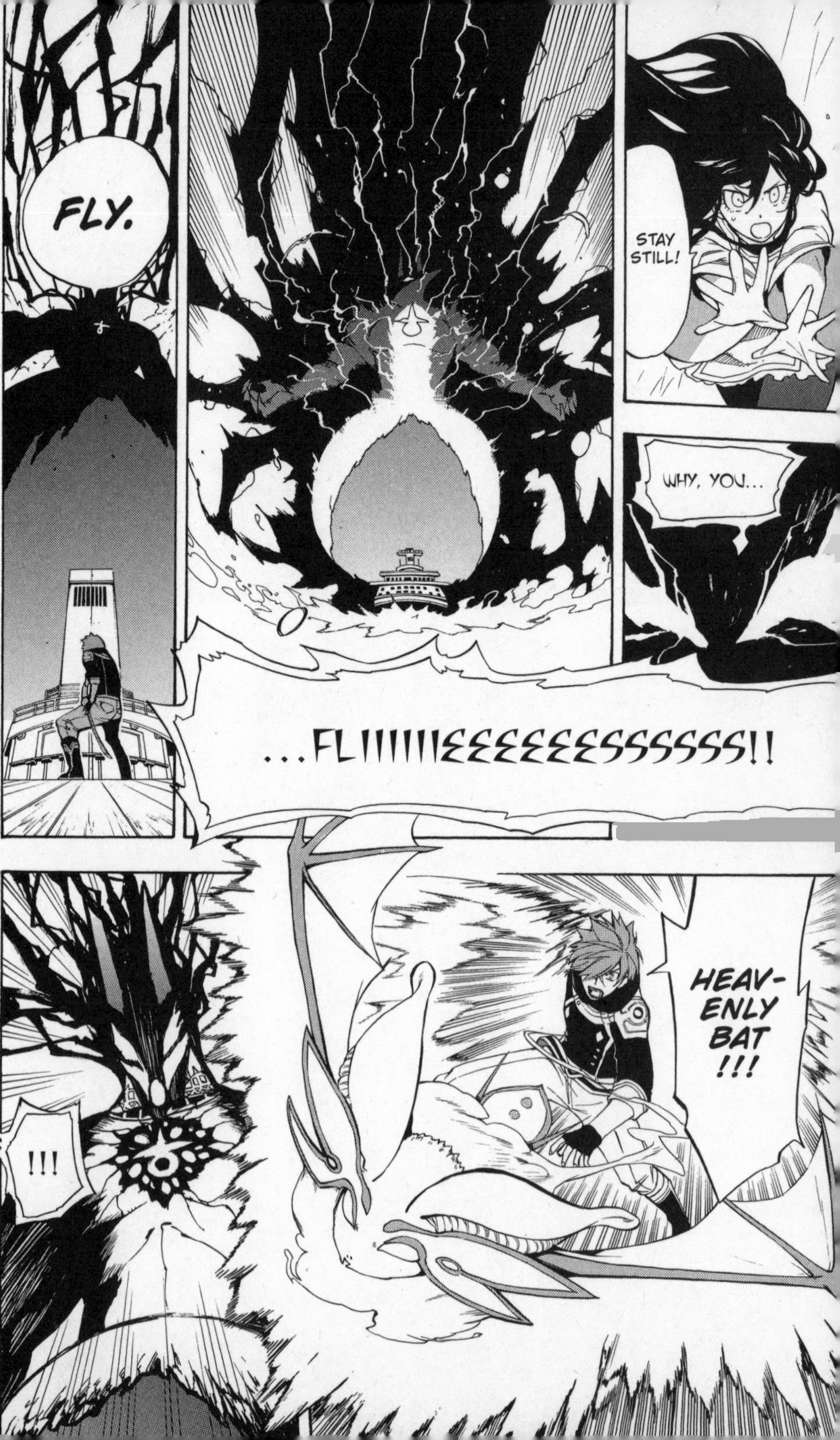
STAY STILL!
WHY, YOU...
FLY.
...FLIIIIIIEEEEEEESSSSSS!!
HEAV-ENLY BAT!!!
!!!

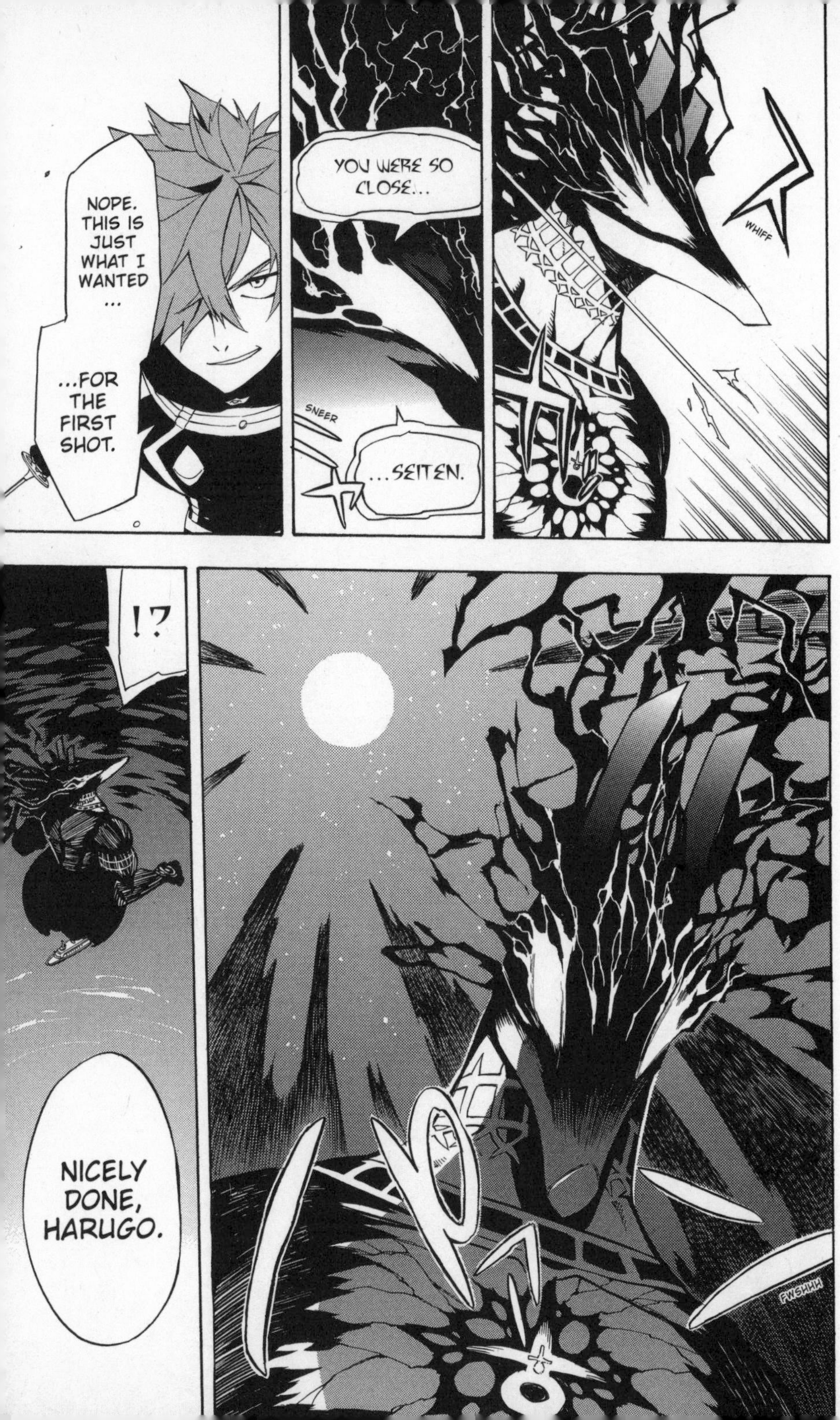
WHIFF
YOU WERE SO CLOSE...
SNEER
...SEITEN.
NOPE. THIS IS JUST WHAT I WANTED ...
...FOR THE FIRST SHOT.
FWSHHH
!?
NICELY DONE, HARUGO.

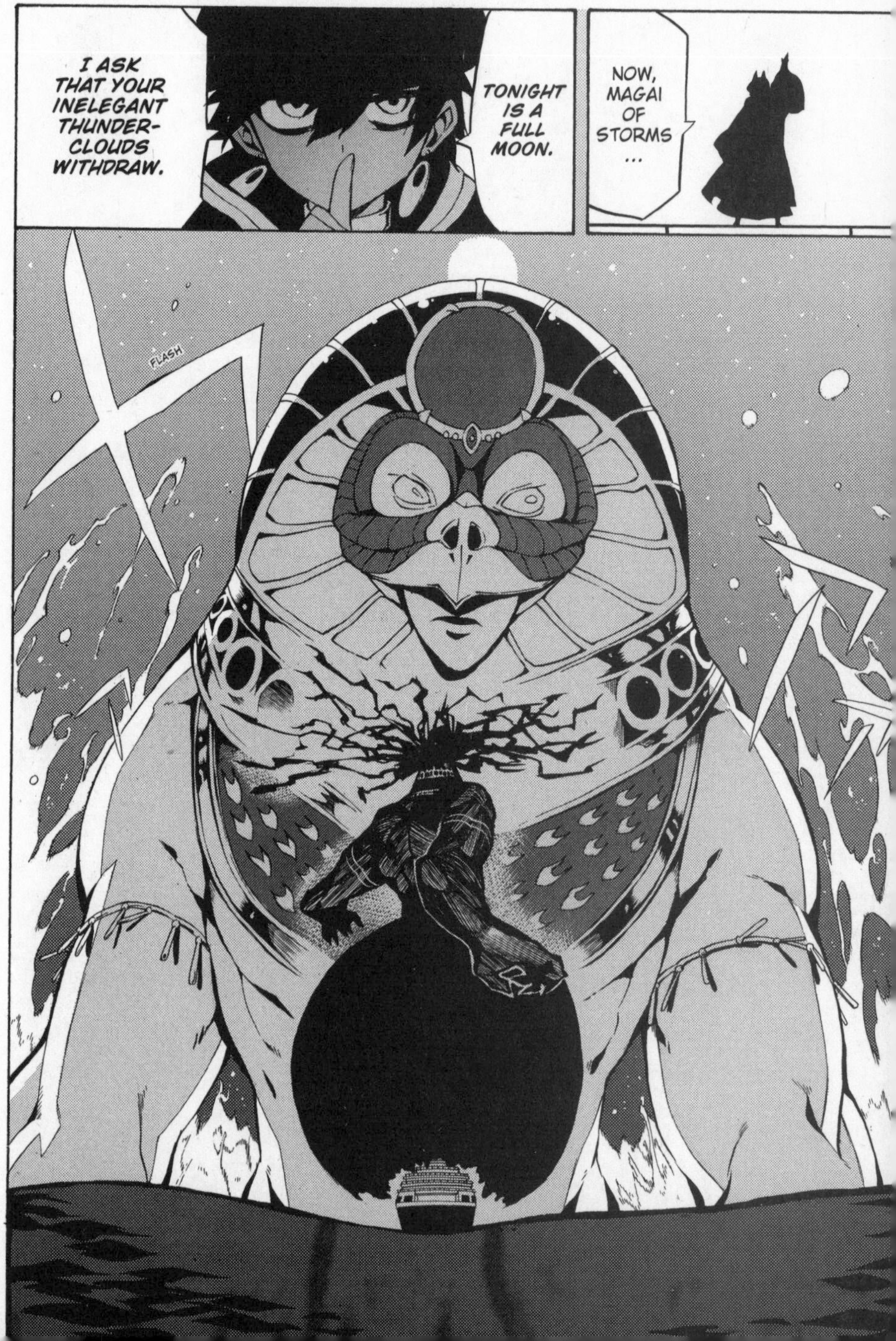
NOW, MAGAI OF STORMS ...
TONIGHT IS A FULL MOON.
I ASK THAT YOUR INELEGANT THUNDER-CLOUDS WITHDRAW.
FLASH

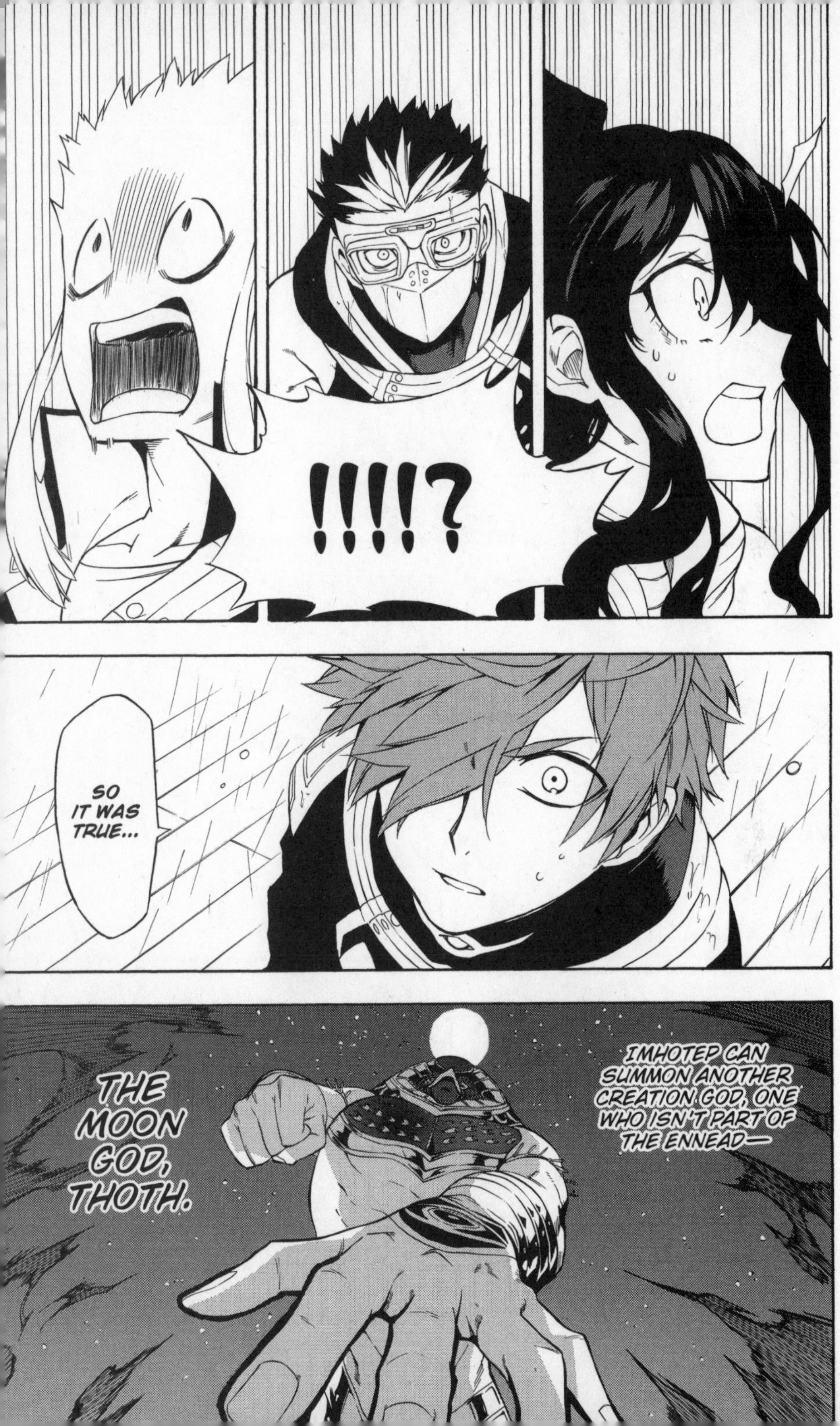
!!!!?
SO IT WAS TRUE...
IMHOTEP CAN SUMMON ANOTHER CREATION GOD, ONE WHO ISN'T PART OF THE ENNEAD—
THE MOON GOD, THOTH.

WHAT...!!?

WHY ARE YOU— !!?

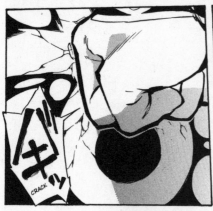

CRACK

SHOOM

I HAVE FINISHED MY PART.

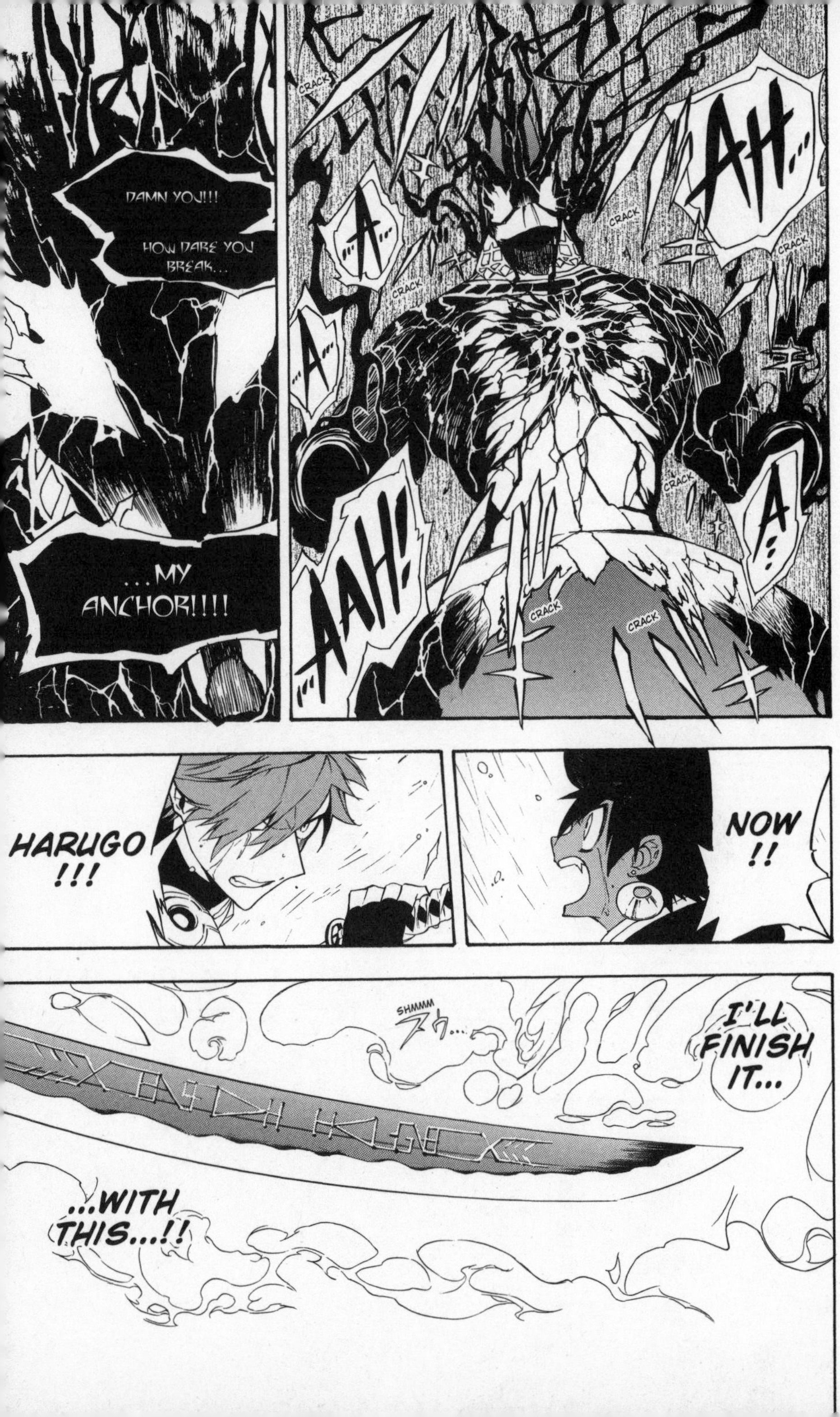
CRACK
AH...
CRACK
CRACK
A...
CRACK
A...
CRACK
A...
CRACK
CRACK
AAH!!
DAMN YOU!!!
HOW DARE YOU BREAK...
...MY ANCHOR!!!!
NOW !!
HARUGO !!!
I'LL FINISH IT...
SHMMM
...WITH THIS...!!

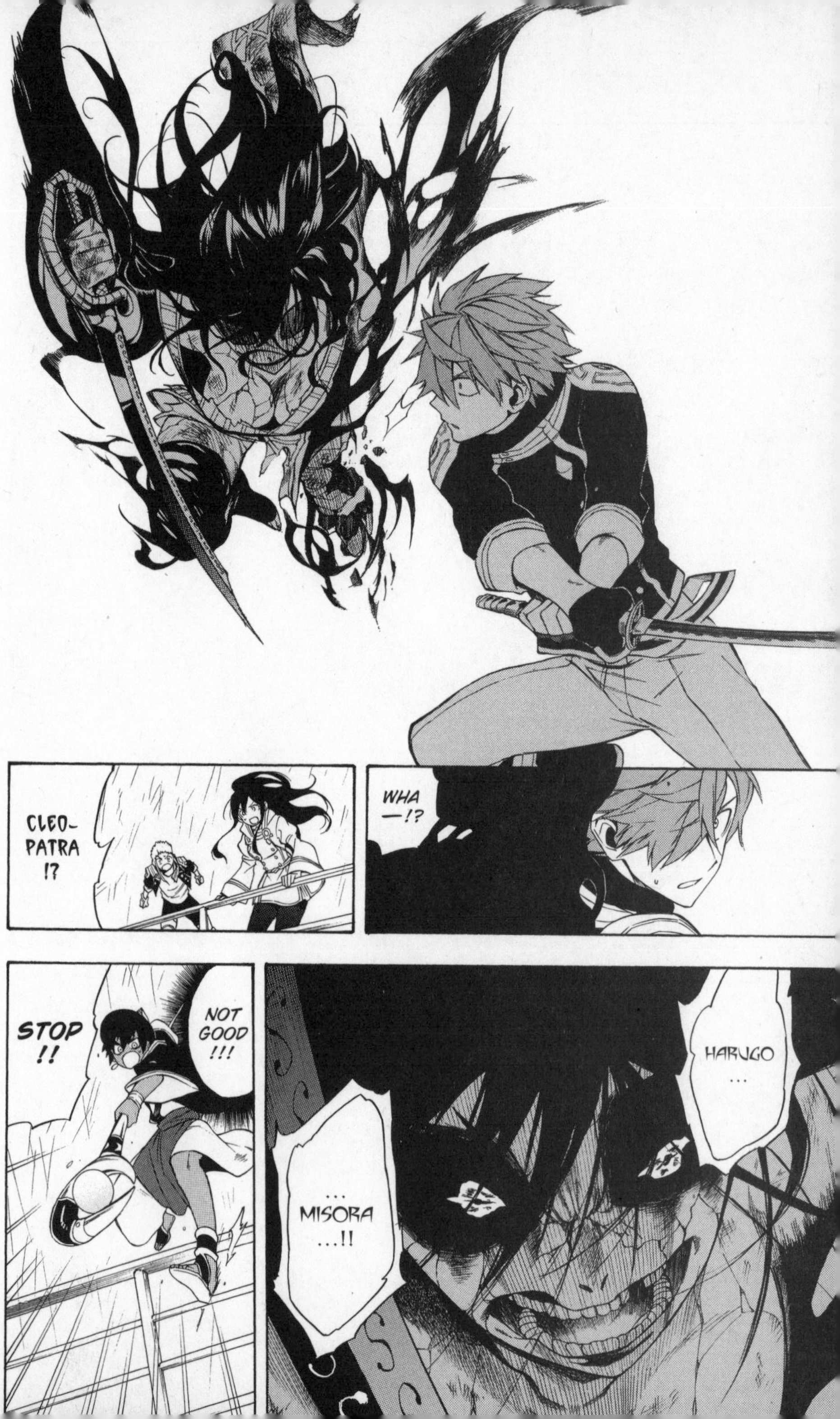
WHA—!?
CLEO-PATRA!?
HARUGO...
...MISORA...!!
NOT GOOD!!!
STOP!!

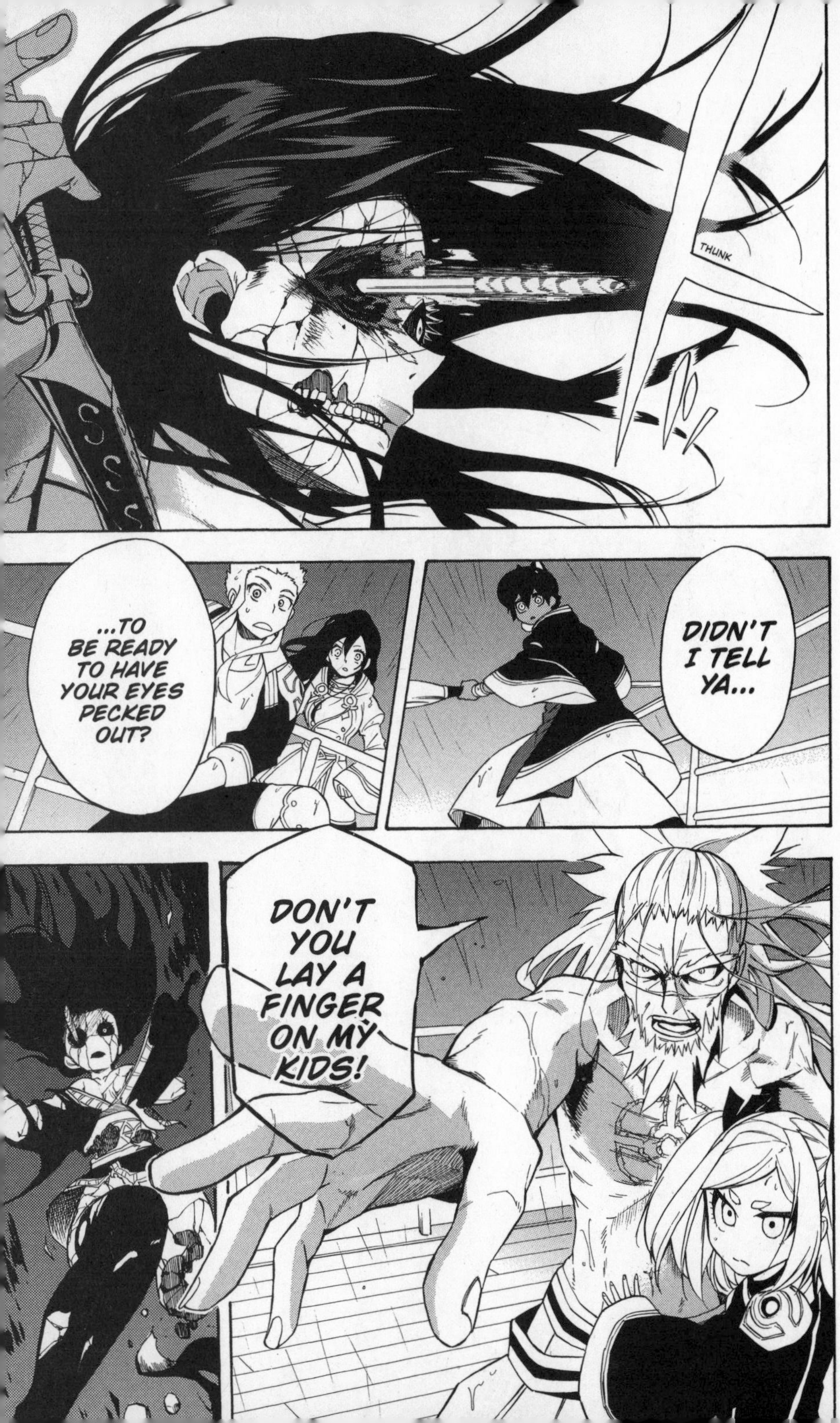
THUNK
DIDN'T I TELL YA...
...TO BE READY TO HAVE YOUR EYES PECKED OUT?
DON'T YOU LAY A FINGER ON MY KIDS!

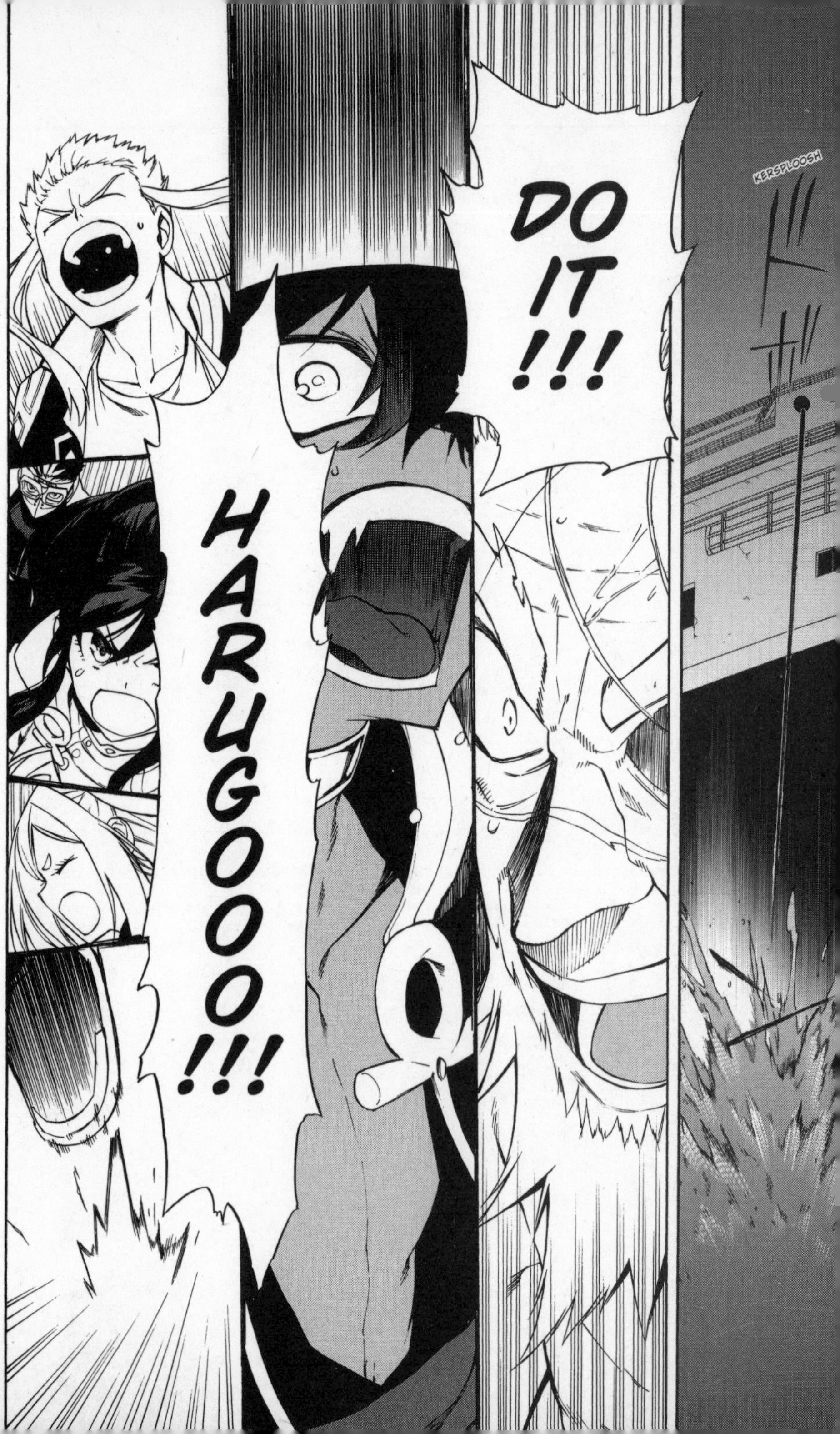
KERSPLOOSH
DO IT!!!
HARUGOOOO!!!

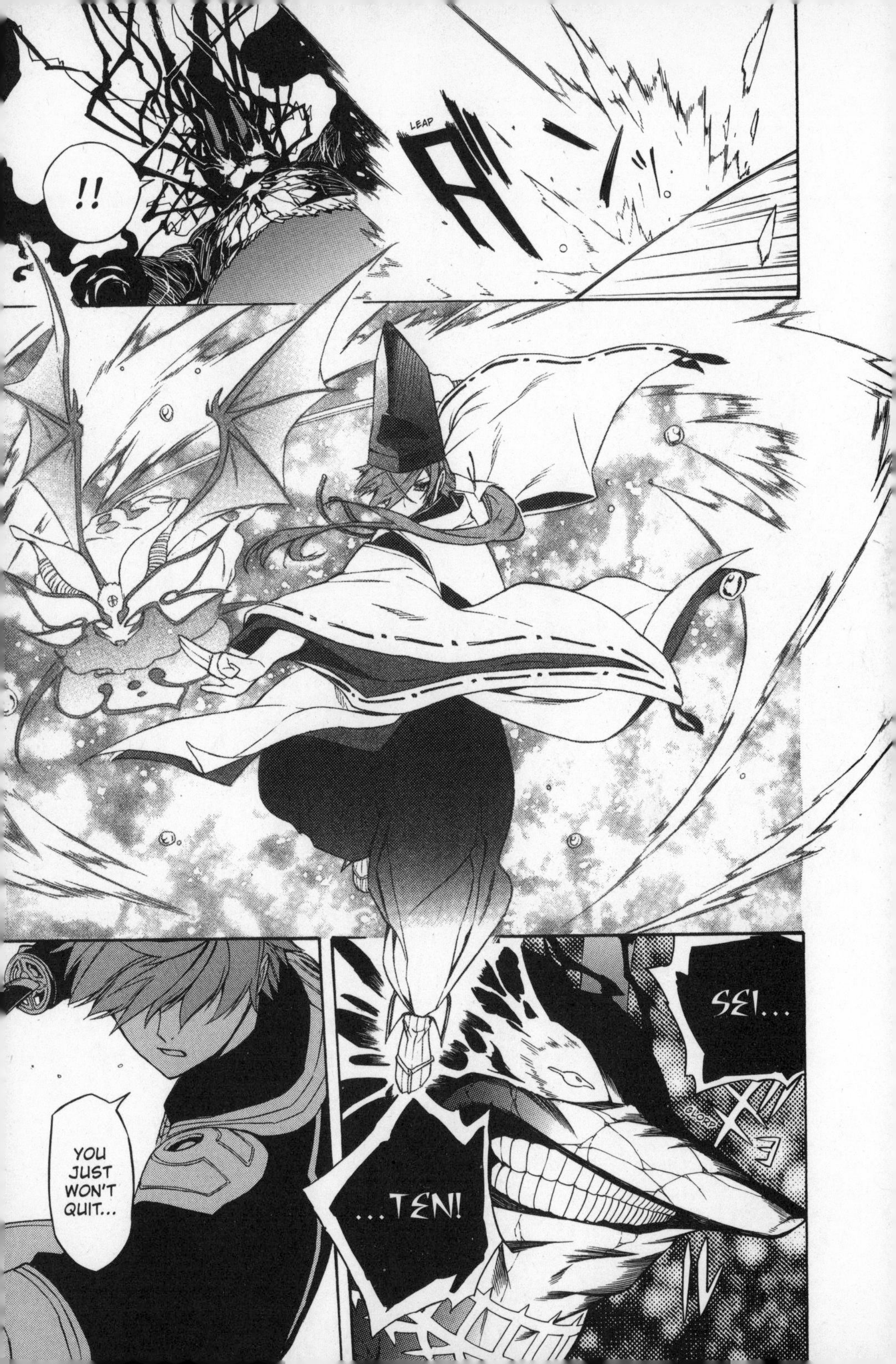
LEAP
!!
SEI...
GLORP
...TEN!
YOU JUST WON'T QUIT...

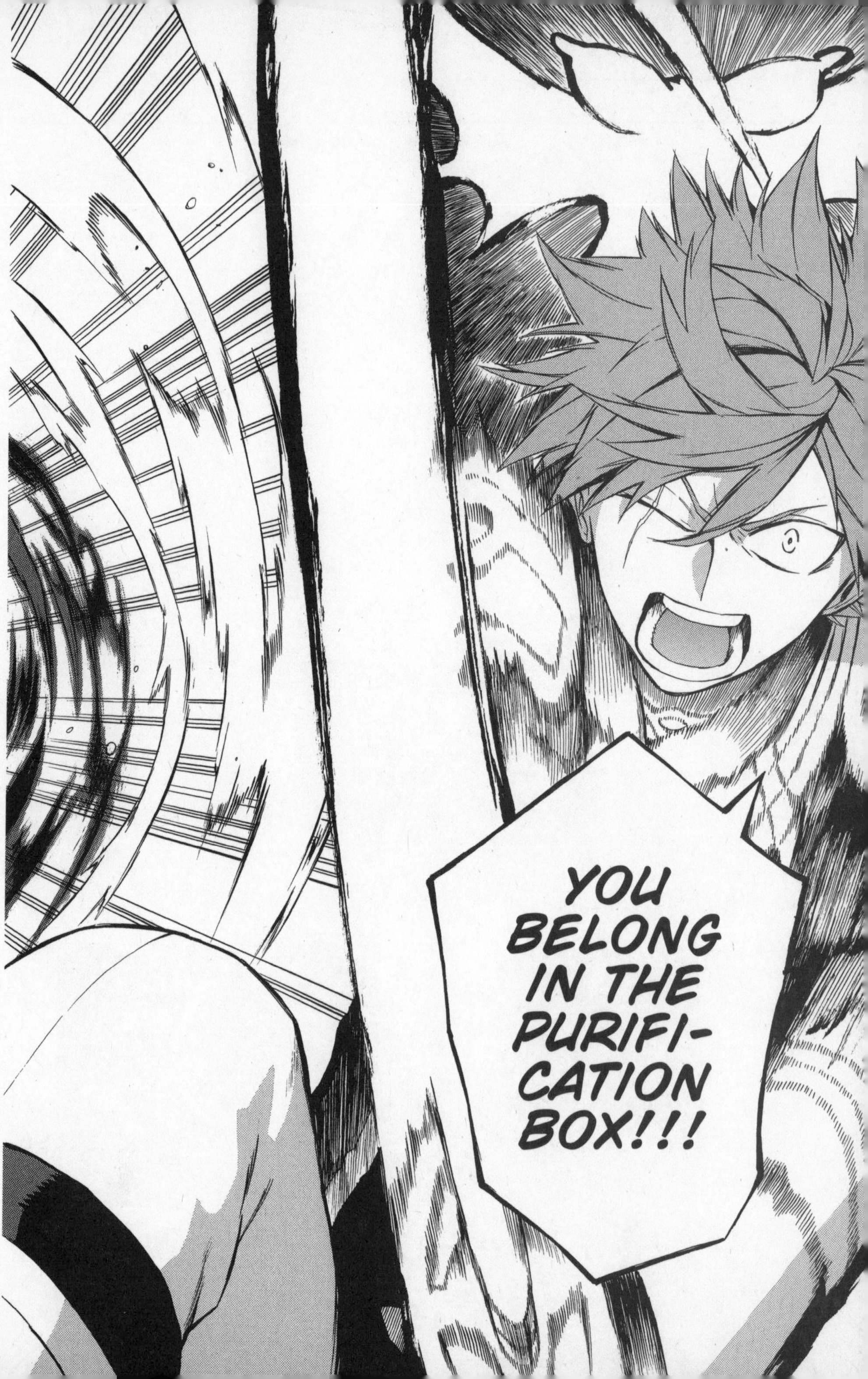
YOU BELONG IN THE PURIFI-CATION BOX!!!

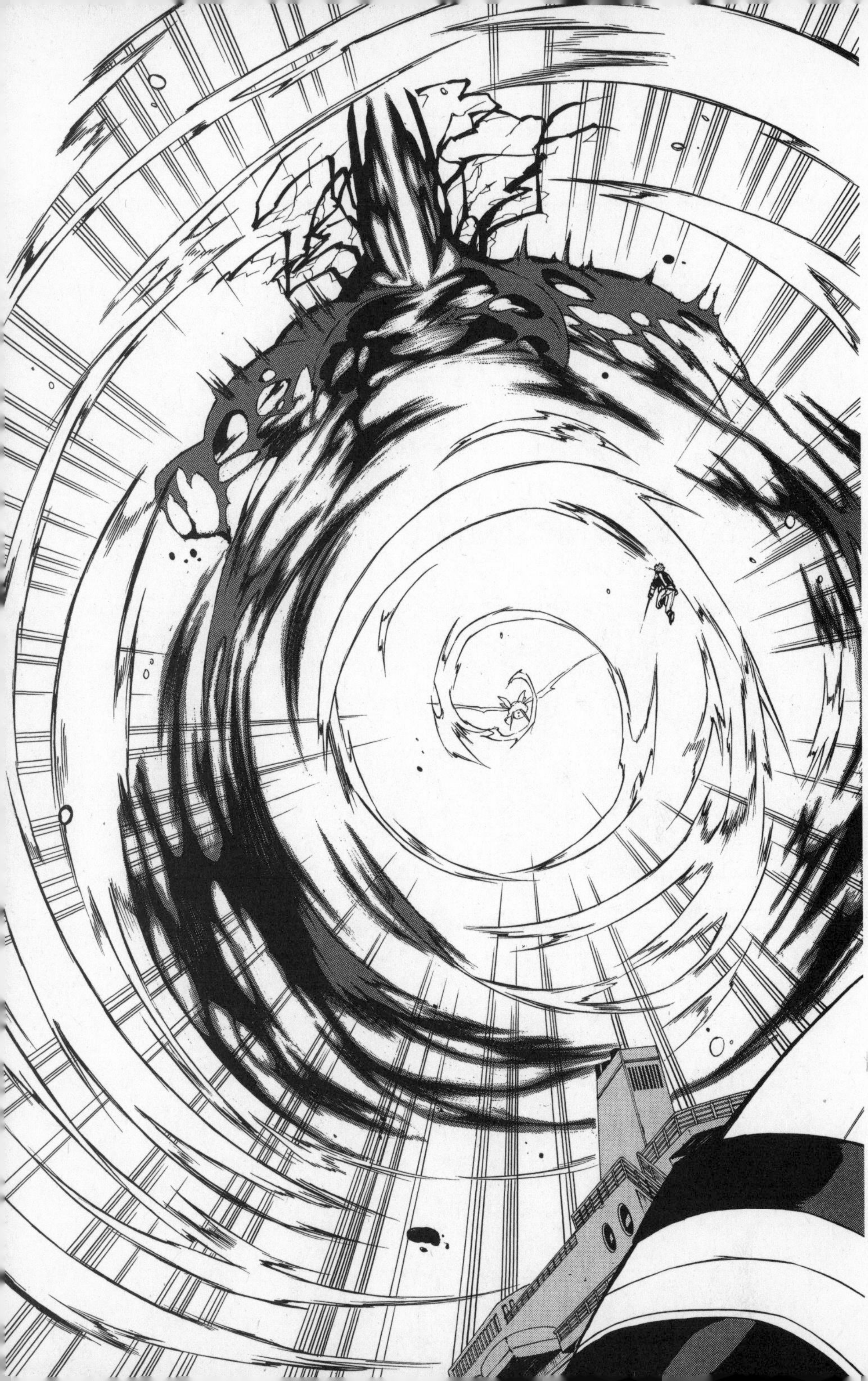

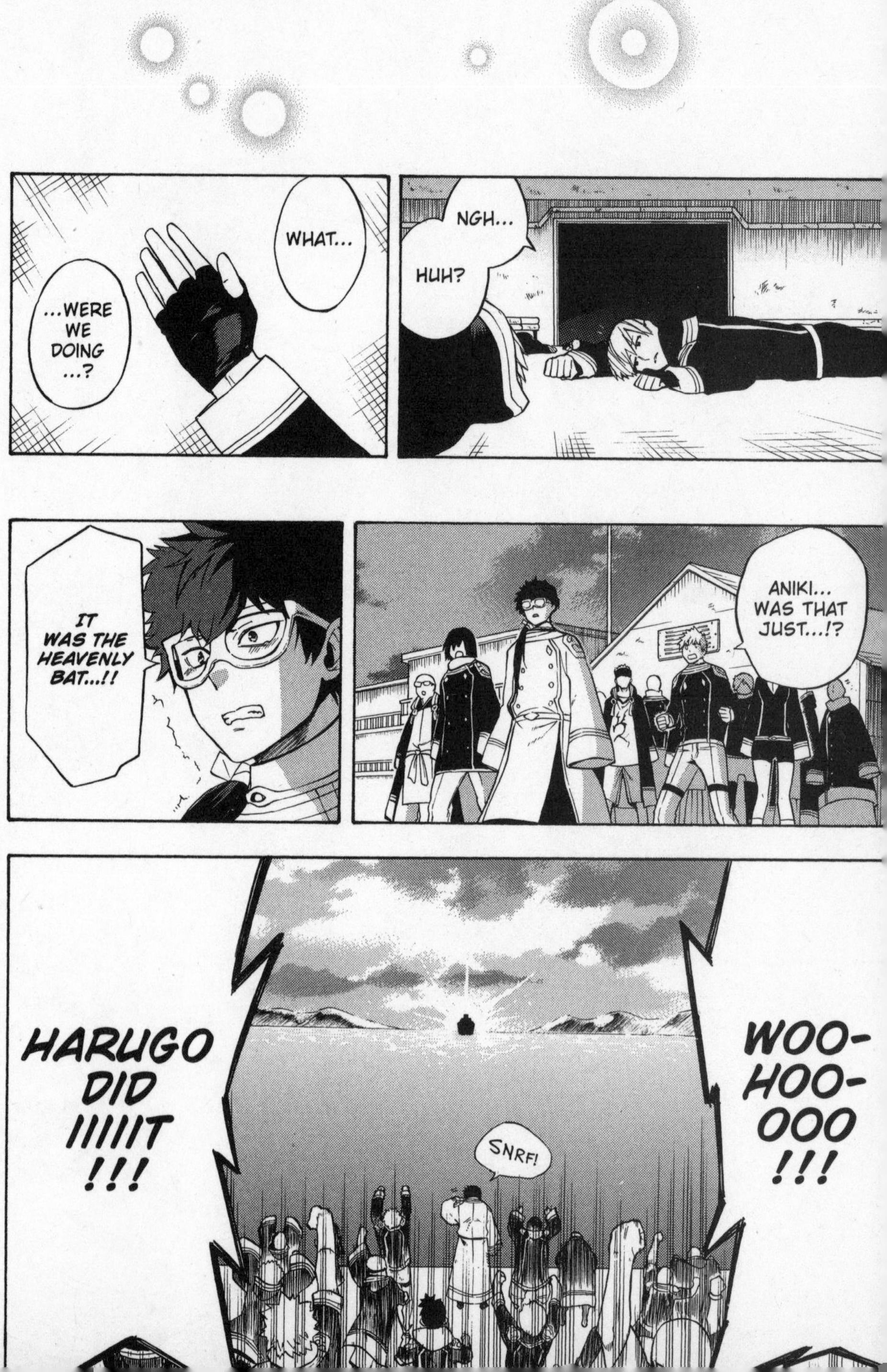
NGH...
HUH?
WHAT...
...WERE WE DOING ...?
ANIKI... WAS THAT JUST...!?
IT WAS THE HEAVENLY BAT...!!
WOO-HOO-OOO !!!
SNRF!
HARUGO DID IIIIIT !!!

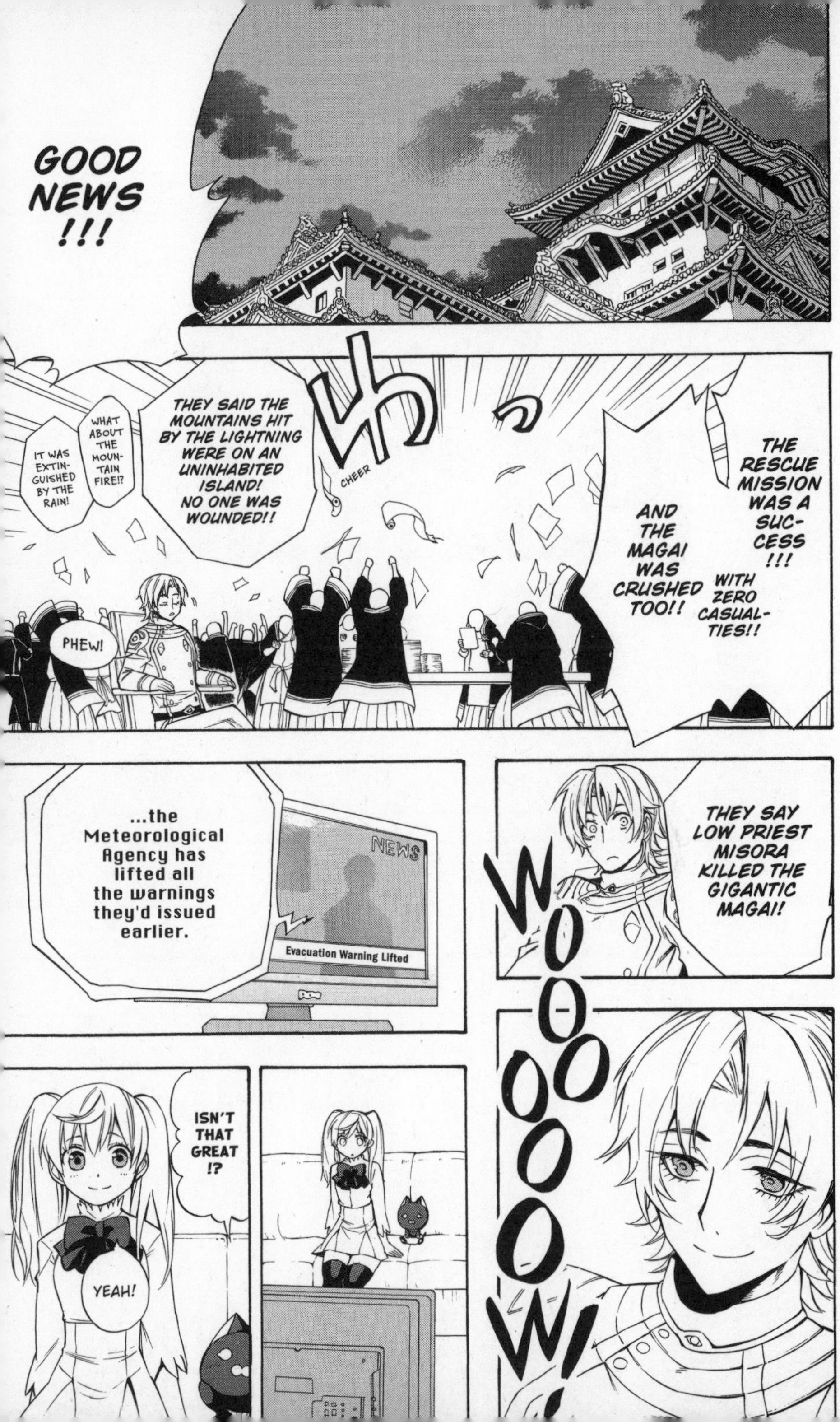
GOOD NEWS!!!
THE RESCUE MISSION WAS A SUCCESS!!!
WITH ZERO CASUALTIES!!
AND THE MAGAI WAS CRUSHED TOO!!
わっ
CHEER
THEY SAID THE MOUNTAINS HIT BY THE LIGHTNING WERE ON AN UNINHABITED ISLAND! NO ONE WAS WOUNDED!!
WHAT ABOUT THE MOUNTAIN FIRE!?
IT WAS EXTINGUISHED BY THE RAIN!
PHEW!
THEY SAY LOW PRIEST MISORA KILLED THE GIGANTIC MAGAI!
...the Meteorological Agency has lifted all the warnings they'd issued earlier.
NEWS
Evacuation Warning Lifted
WOOOOOW!
ISN'T THAT GREAT!?
YEAH!

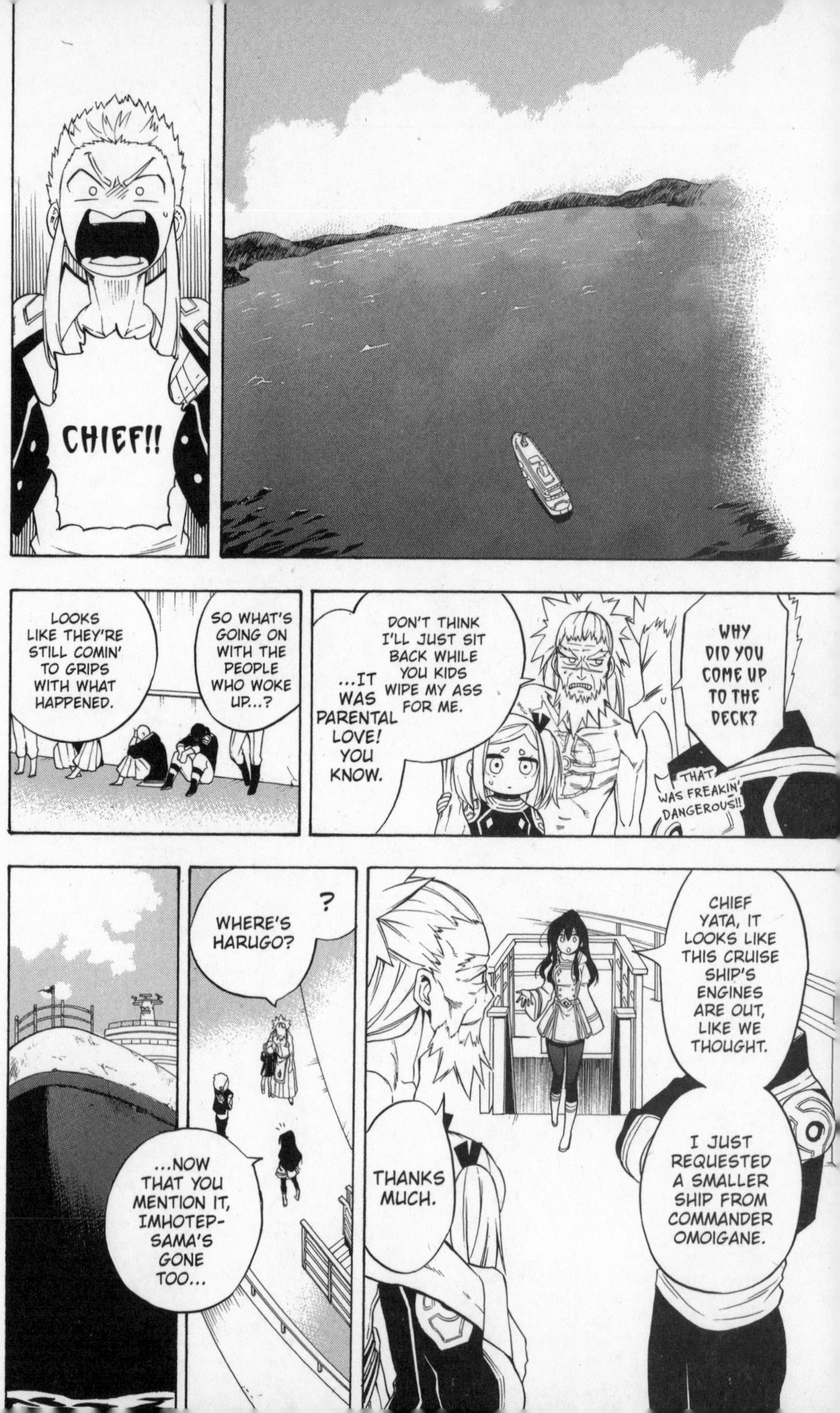
CHIEF!!
WHY DID YOU COME UP TO THE DECK?
THAT WAS FREAKIN' DANGEROUS!!
DON'T THINK I'LL JUST SIT BACK WHILE YOU KIDS WIPE MY ASS FOR ME.
...IT WAS PARENTAL LOVE! YOU KNOW.
SO WHAT'S GOING ON WITH THE PEOPLE WHO WOKE UP...?
LOOKS LIKE THEY'RE STILL COMIN' TO GRIPS WITH WHAT HAPPENED.
CHIEF YATA, IT LOOKS LIKE THIS CRUISE SHIP'S ENGINES ARE OUT, LIKE WE THOUGHT.
I JUST REQUESTED A SMALLER SHIP FROM COMMANDER OMOIGANE.
THANKS MUCH.
?
WHERE'S HARUGO?
...NOW THAT YOU MENTION IT, IMHOTEP-SAMA'S GONE TOO...

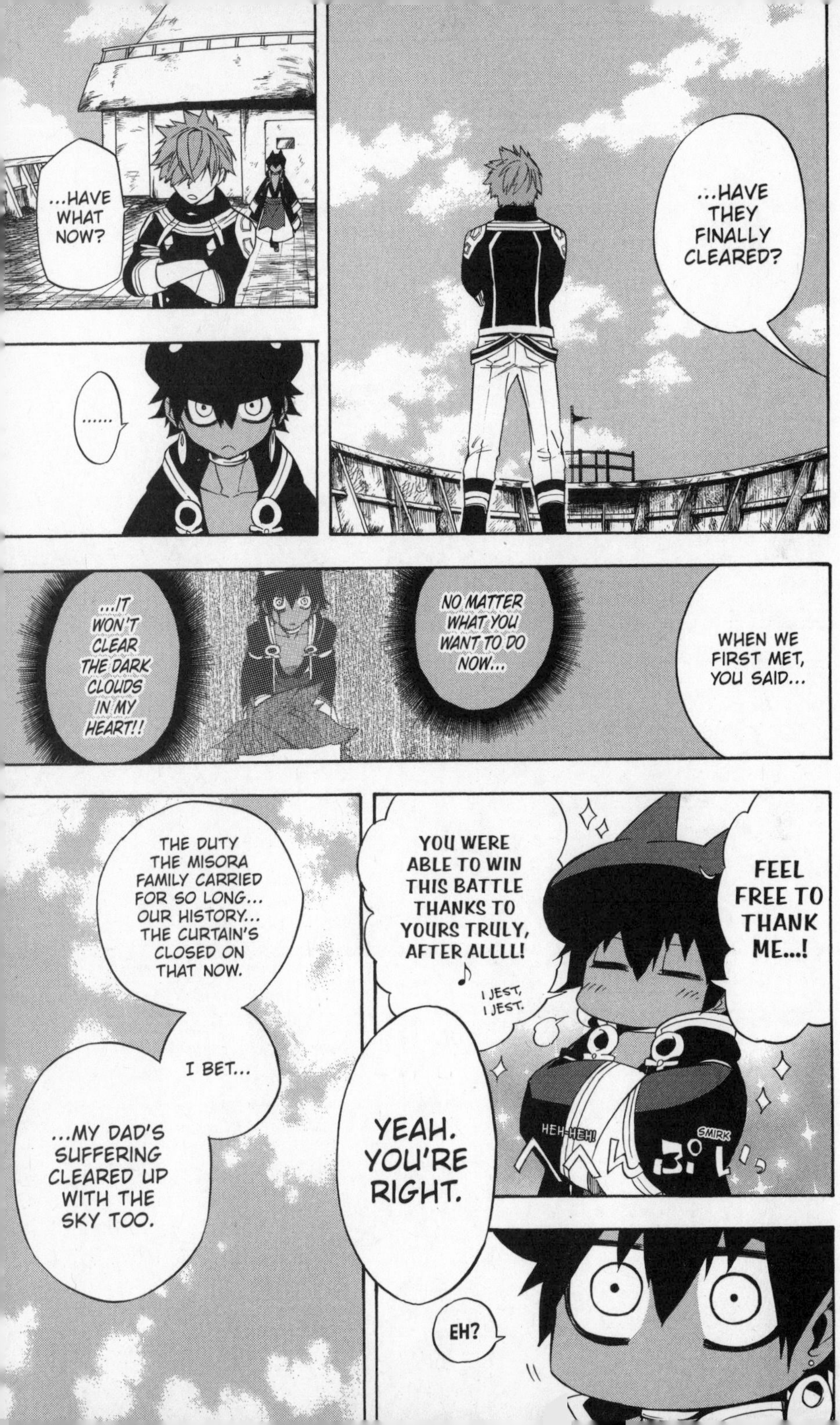
...HAVE THEY FINALLY CLEARED?
...HAVE WHAT NOW?
......
WHEN WE FIRST MET, YOU SAID...
NO MATTER WHAT YOU WANT TO DO NOW...
...IT WON'T CLEAR THE DARK CLOUDS IN MY HEART!!
FEEL FREE TO THANK ME...!
YOU WERE ABLE TO WIN THIS BATTLE THANKS TO YOURS TRULY, AFTER ALLLL! ♪
I JEST, I JEST.
HEH-HEH!
SMIRK
EH?
THE DUTY THE MISORA FAMILY CARRIED FOR SO LONG... OUR HISTORY... THE CURTAIN'S CLOSED ON THAT NOW.
I BET...
...MY DAD'S SUFFERING CLEARED UP WITH THE SKY TOO.
YEAH. YOU'RE RIGHT.

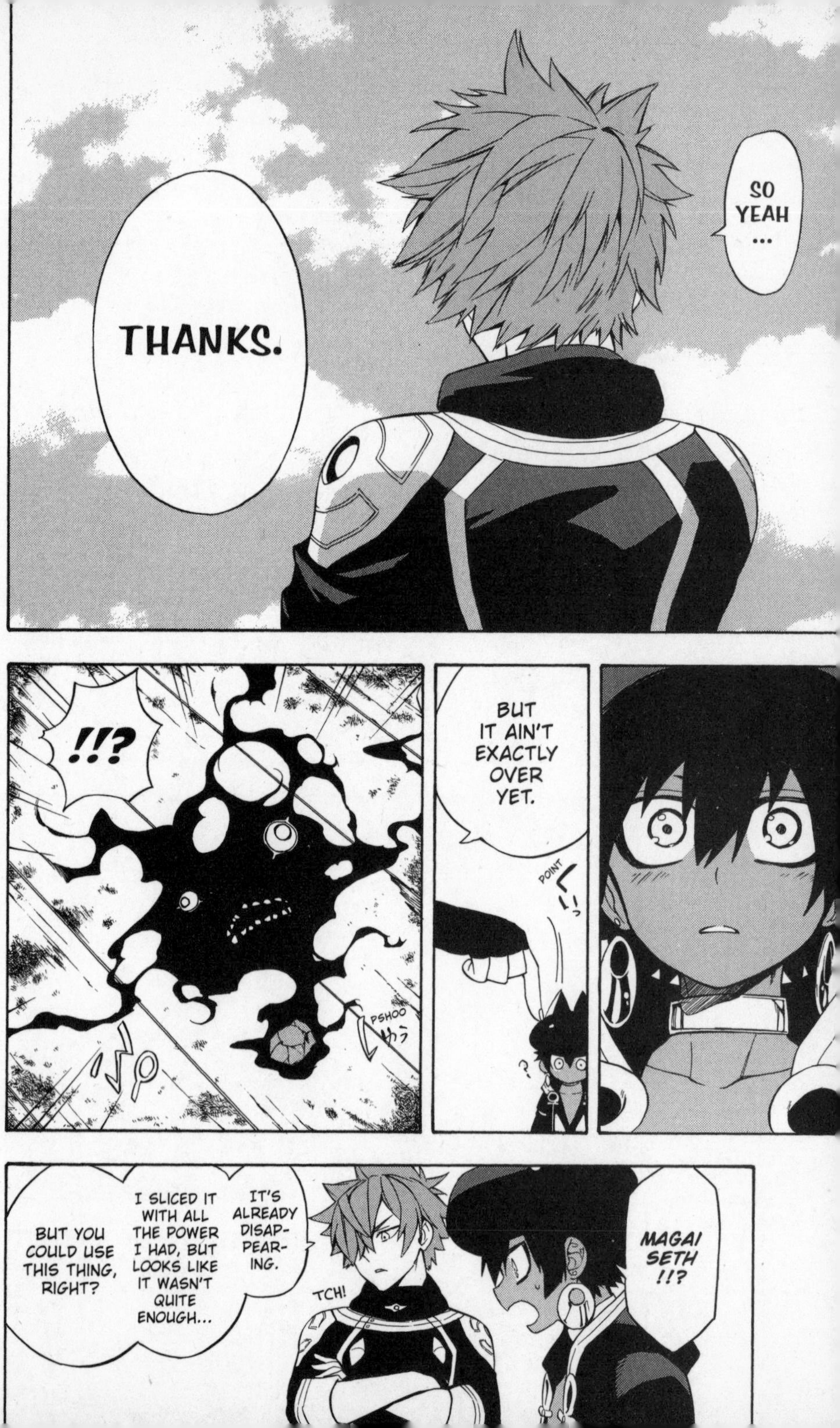
SO YEAH ...
THANKS.
BUT IT AIN'T EXACTLY OVER YET.
POINT
!!?
PSHOO
MAGAI SETH !!?
IT'S ALREADY DISAP-PEAR-ING.
TCH!
I SLICED IT WITH ALL THE POWER I HAD, BUT LOOKS LIKE IT WASN'T QUITE ENOUGH...
BUT YOU COULD USE THIS THING, RIGHT?

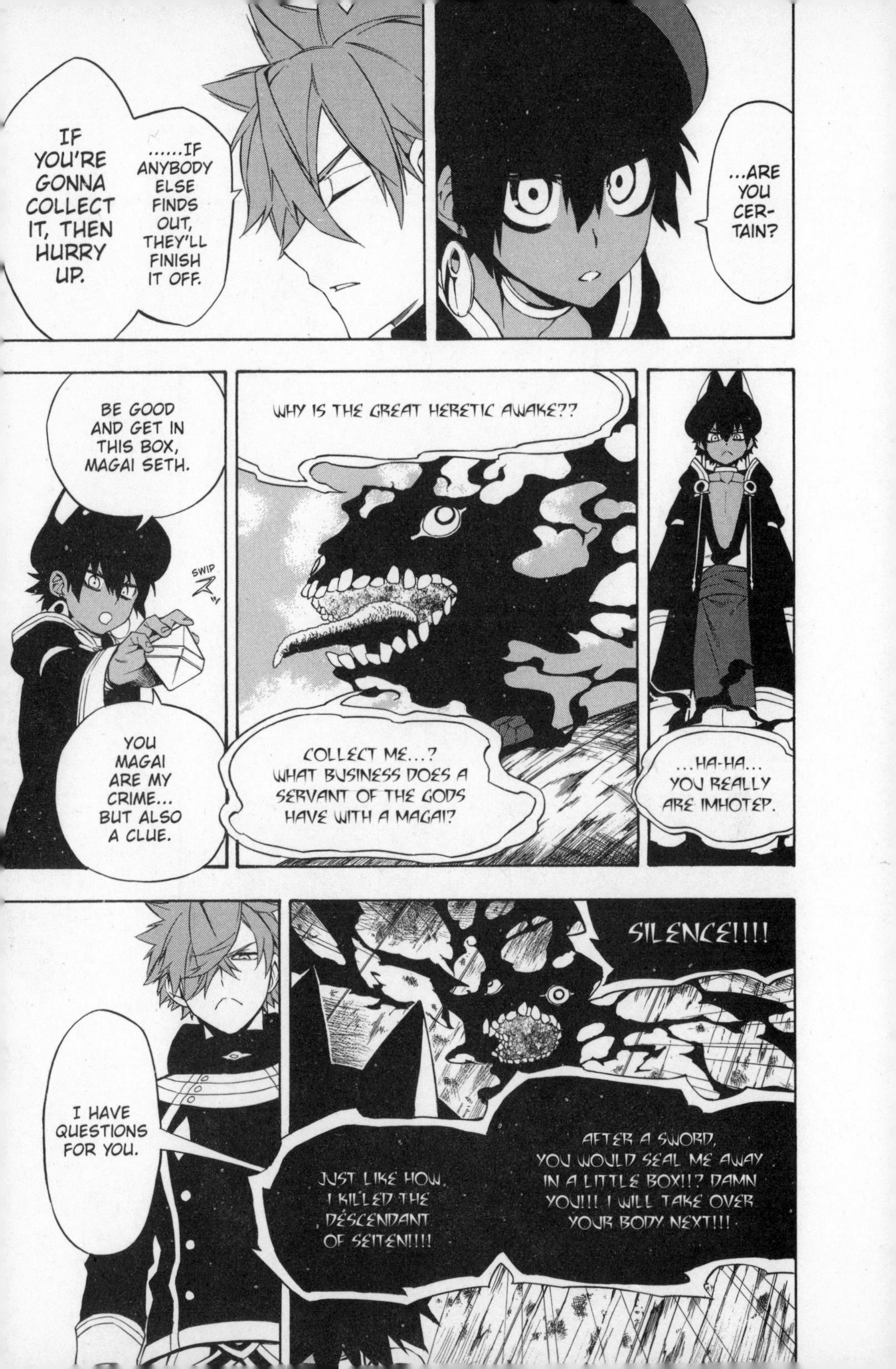
...ARE YOU CER-TAIN?
......IF ANYBODY ELSE FINDS OUT, THEY'LL FINISH IT OFF.
IF YOU'RE GONNA COLLECT IT, THEN HURRY UP.
...HA-HA... YOU REALLY ARE IMHOTEP.
WHY IS THE GREAT HERETIC AWAKE??
COLLECT ME...? WHAT BUSINESS DOES A SERVANT OF THE GODS HAVE WITH A MAGAI?
BE GOOD AND GET IN THIS BOX, MAGAI SETH.
SWIP
YOU MAGAI ARE MY CRIME... BUT ALSO A CLUE.
SILENCE!!!!
AFTER A SWORD, YOU WOULD SEAL ME AWAY IN A LITTLE BOX!!? DAMN YOU!!! I WILL TAKE OVER YOUR BODY NEXT!!!
JUST LIKE HOW I KILLED THE DESCENDANT OF SEITEN!!!!
I HAVE QUESTIONS FOR YOU.

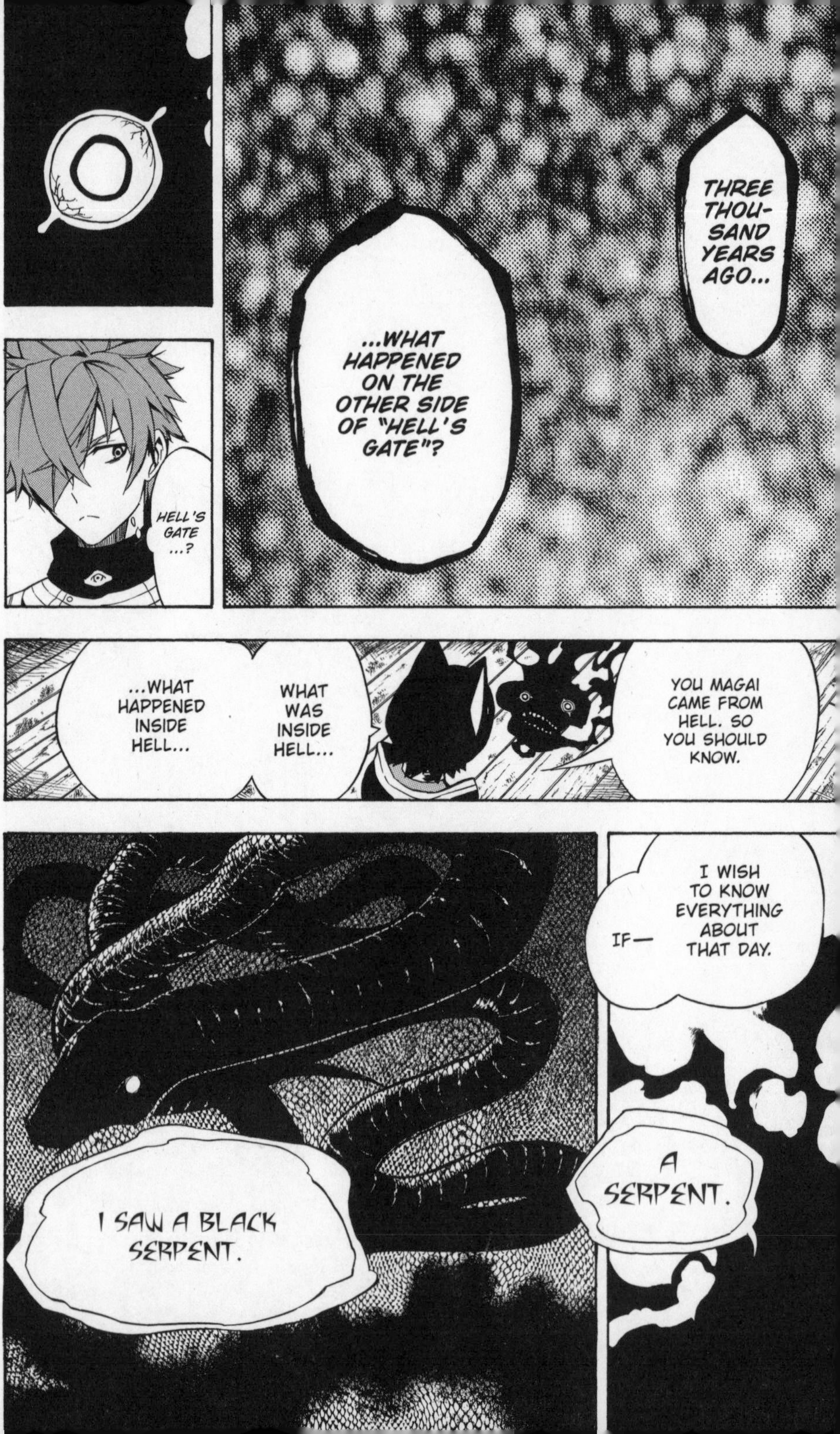
THREE THOU-SAND YEARS AGO...
...WHAT HAPPENED ON THE OTHER SIDE OF "HELL'S GATE"?
HELL'S GATE ...?
YOU MAGAI CAME FROM HELL. SO YOU SHOULD KNOW.
WHAT WAS INSIDE HELL...
...WHAT HAPPENED INSIDE HELL...
I WISH TO KNOW EVERYTHING ABOUT THAT DAY.
IF—
A SERPENT.
I SAW A BLACK SERPENT.

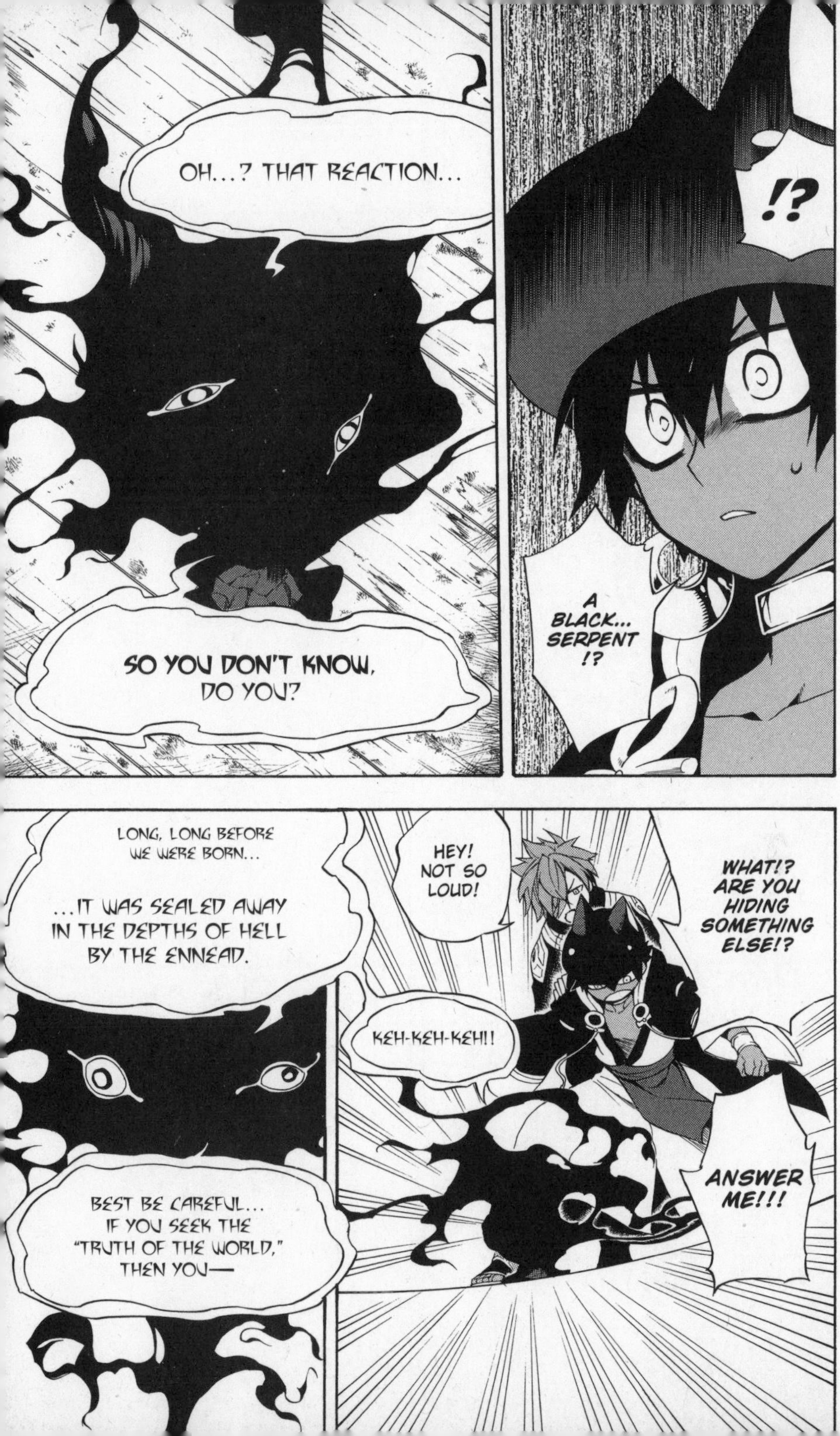
!?
A BLACK... SERPENT !?
OH...? THAT REACTION...
SO YOU DON'T KNOW, DO YOU?
WHAT!? ARE YOU HIDING SOMETHING ELSE!?
HEY! NOT SO LOUD!
KEH-KEH-KEH!!
ANSWER ME!!!
LONG, LONG BEFORE WE WERE BORN...
...IT WAS SEALED AWAY IN THE DEPTHS OF HELL BY THE ENNEAD.
BEST BE CAREFUL... IF YOU SEEK THE "TRUTH OF THE WORLD," THEN YOU—

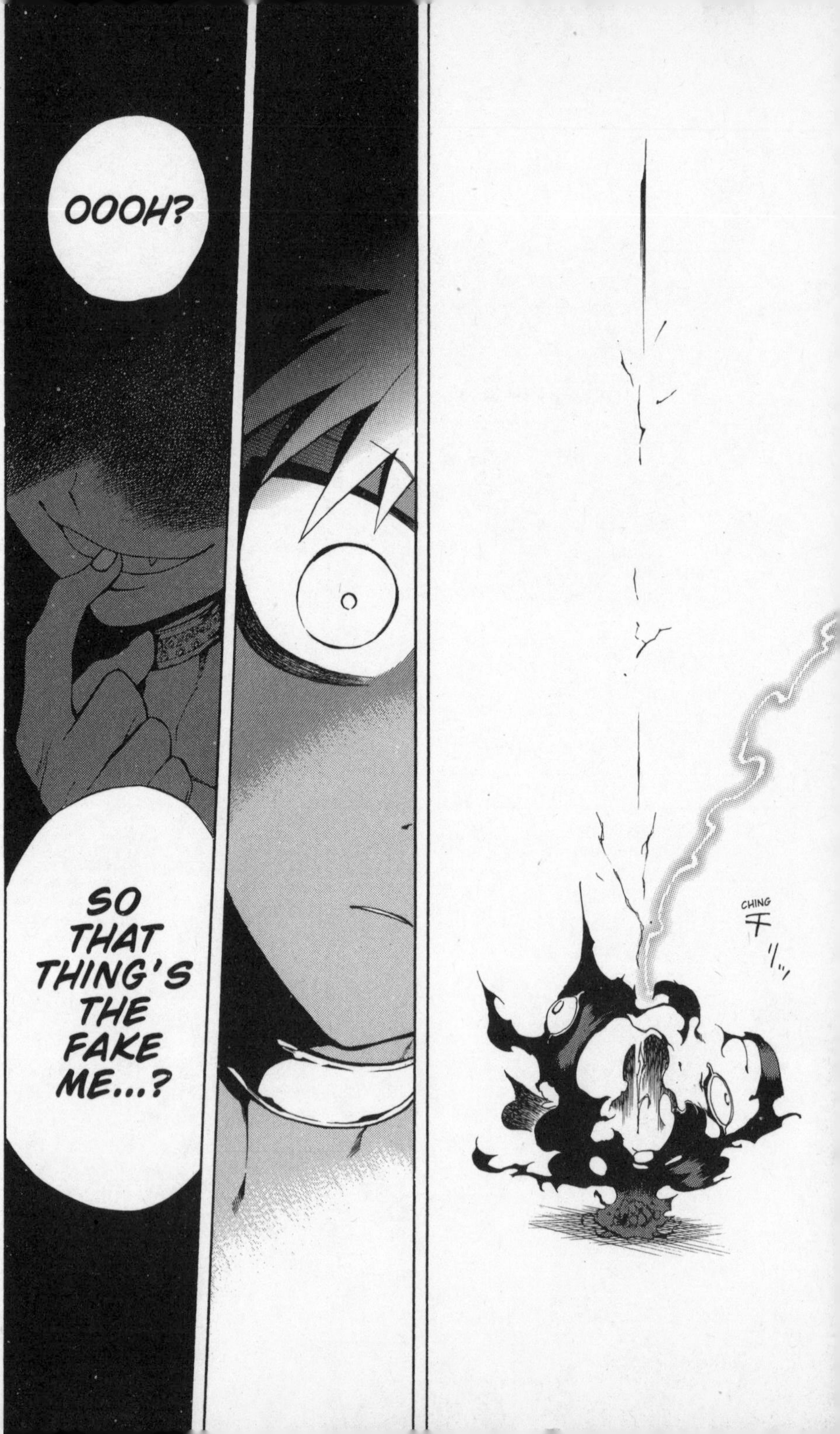

CHING
OOOH?
SO THAT THING'S THE FAKE ME...?

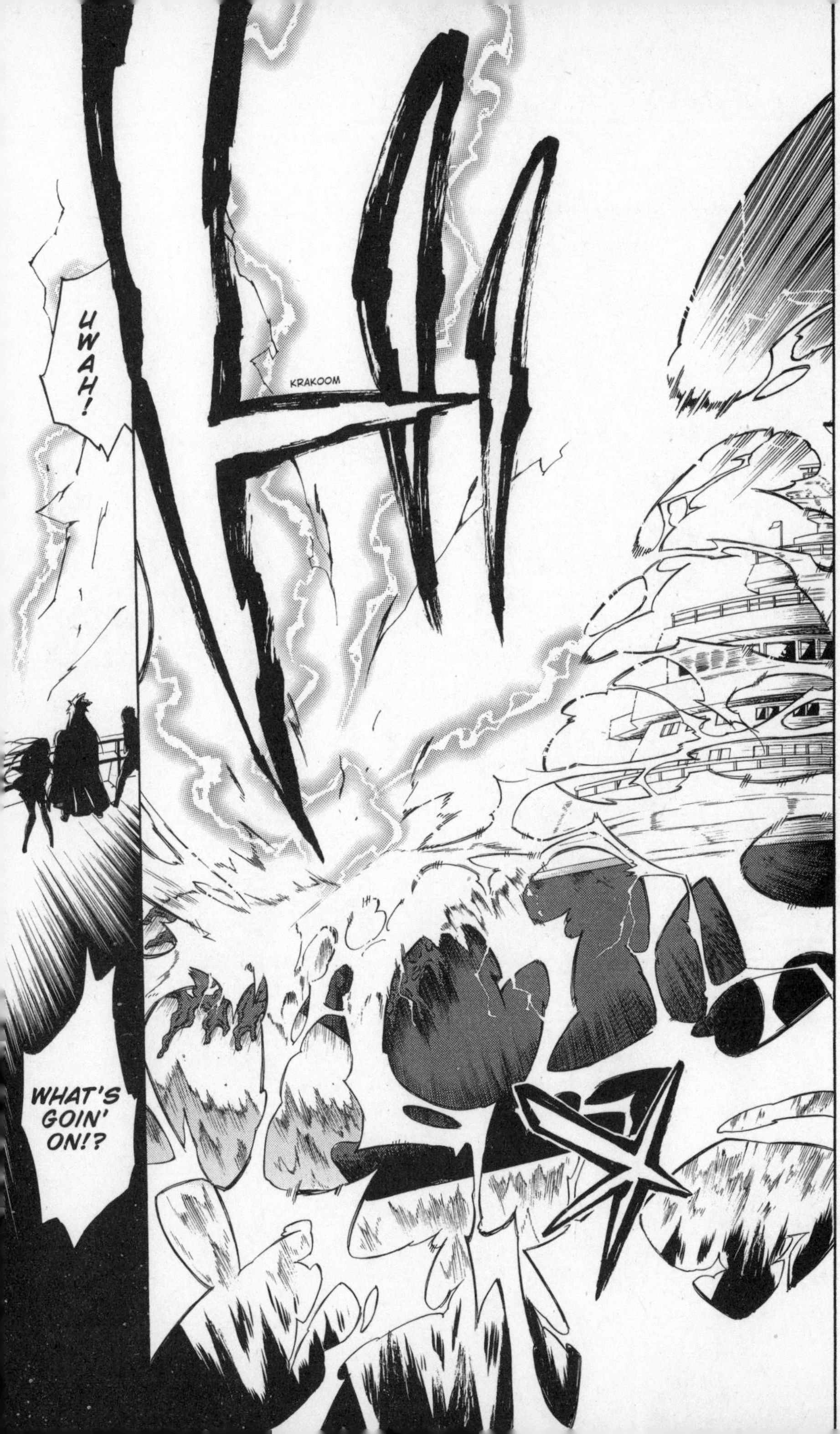
KRAKOOM
UWAH!
WHAT'S GOIN' ON!?

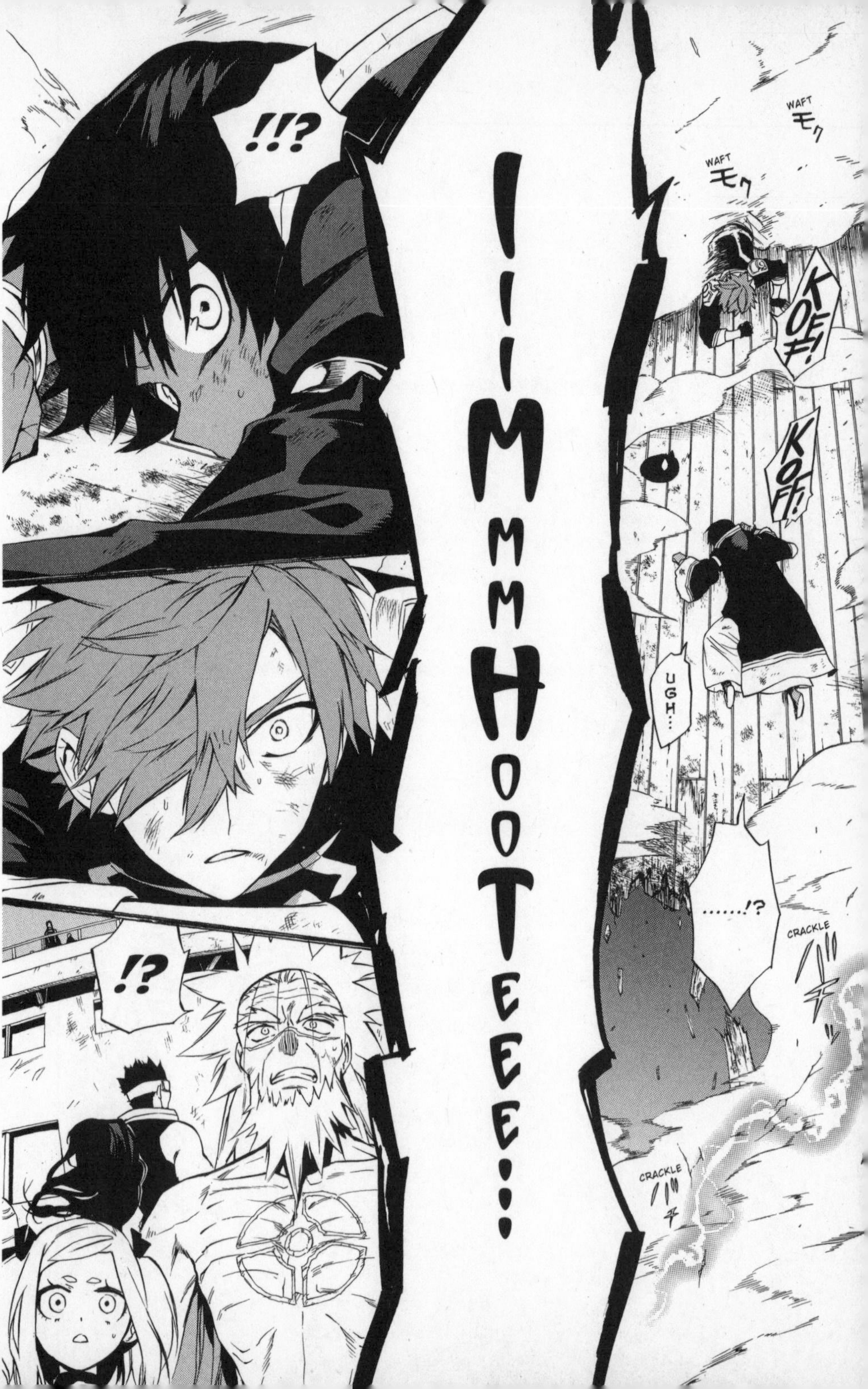
WAFT
WAFT
KOFF!
KOFF!
UGH...
......!?
CRACKLE
CRACKLE
IIIMMMHOOTEEE...
!!?
!?

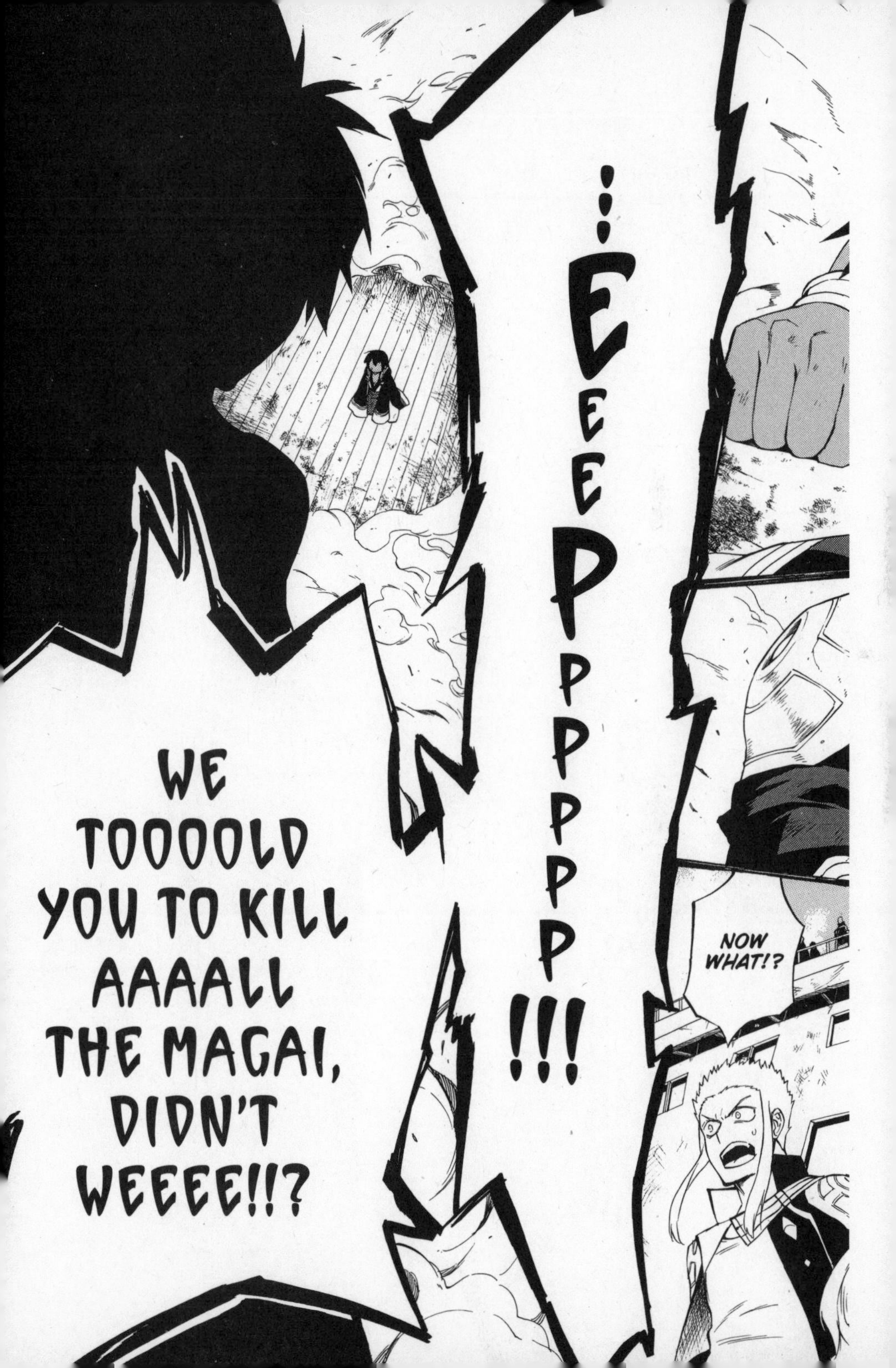
EEEPPPPP!!!
NOW WHAT!?
WE TOOOOLD YOU TO KILL AAAALL THE MAGAI, DIDN'T WEEEE!!?

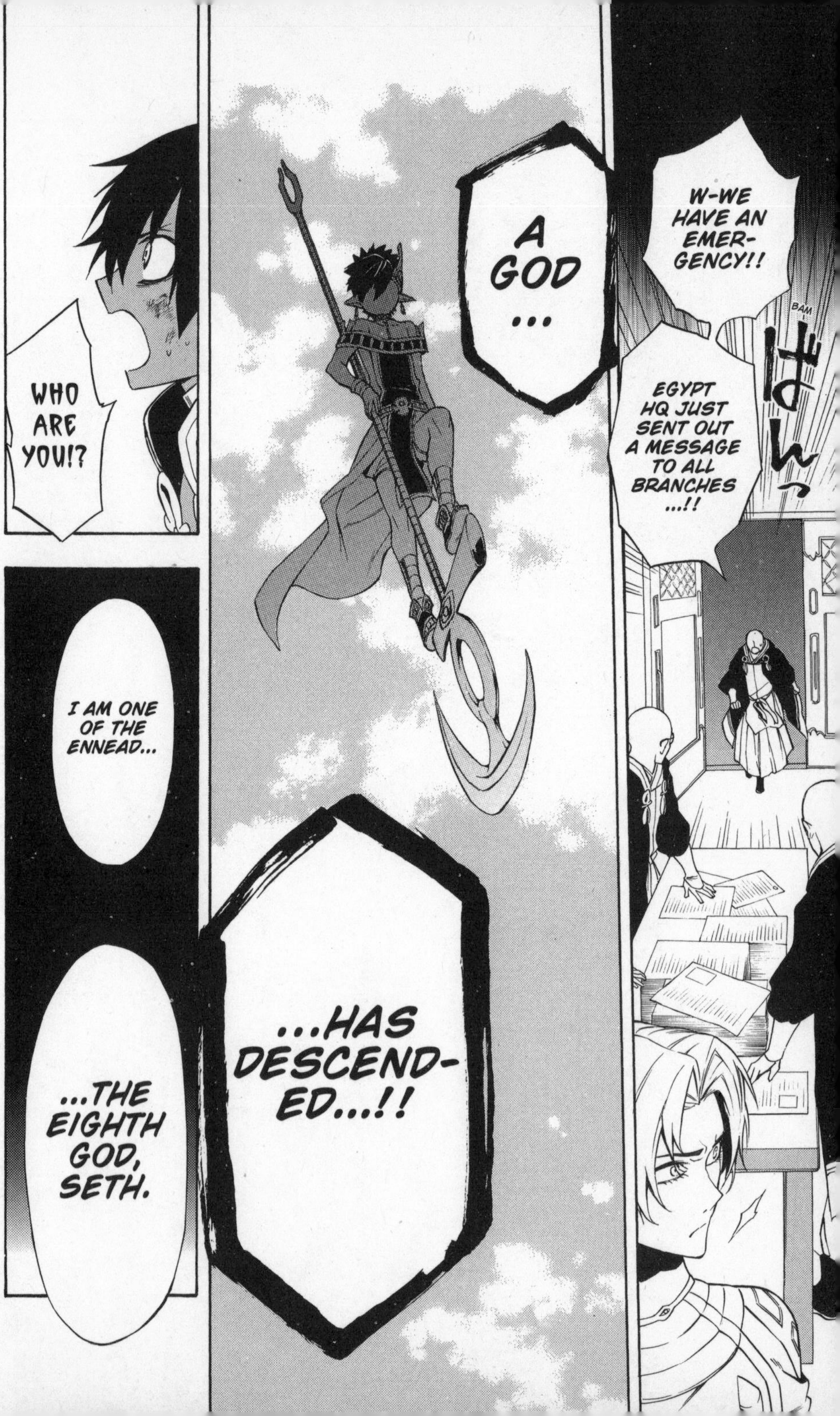
W-WE HAVE AN EMER-GENCY!!
BAM
ばん
EGYPT HQ JUST SENT OUT A MESSAGE TO ALL BRANCHES ...!!
A GOD ...
...HAS DESCEND-ED...!!
WHO ARE YOU!?
I AM ONE OF THE ENNEAD...
...THE EIGHTH GOD, SETH.

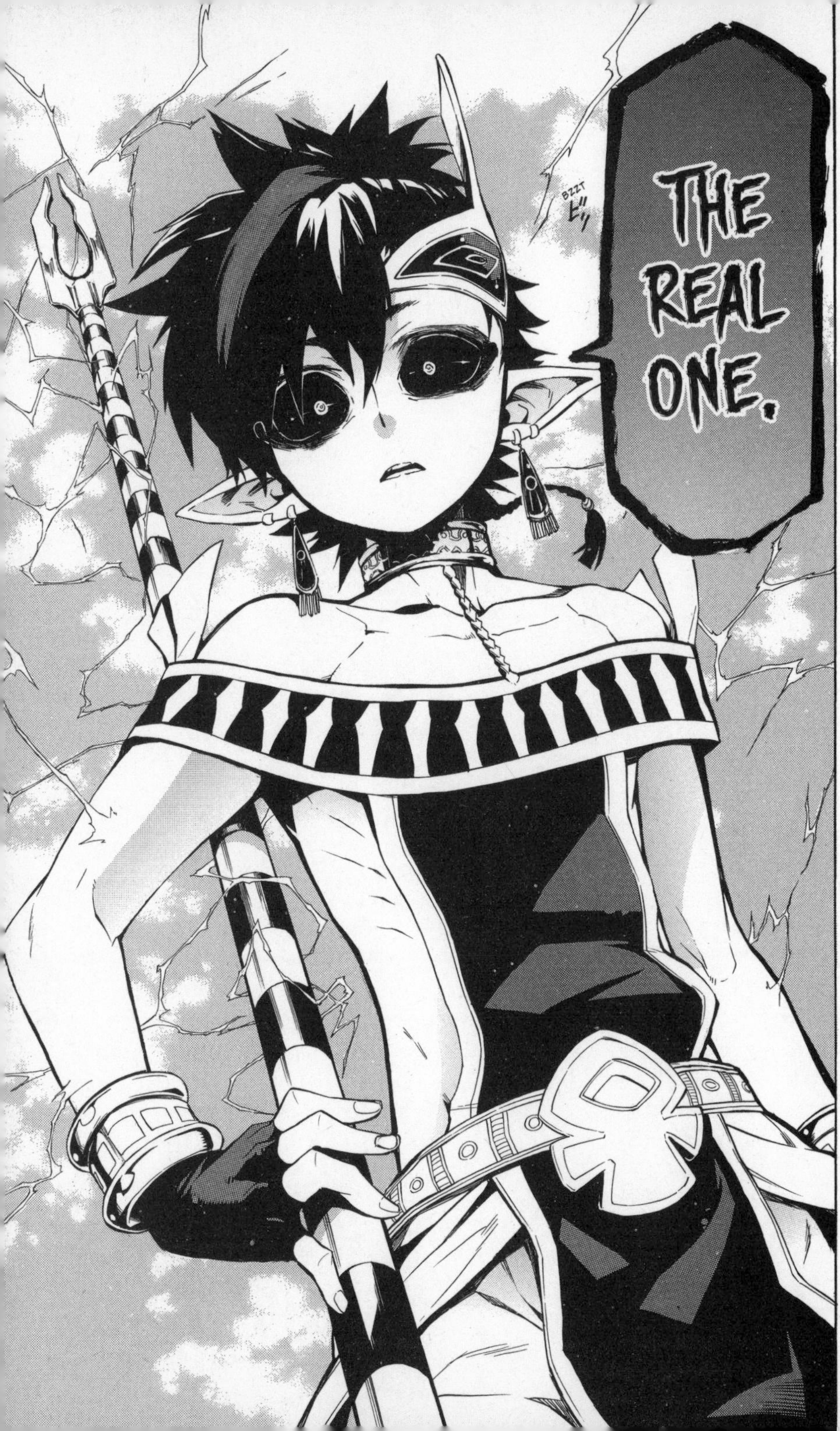
THE REAL ONE.
BZZT

Great Priest Imhotep

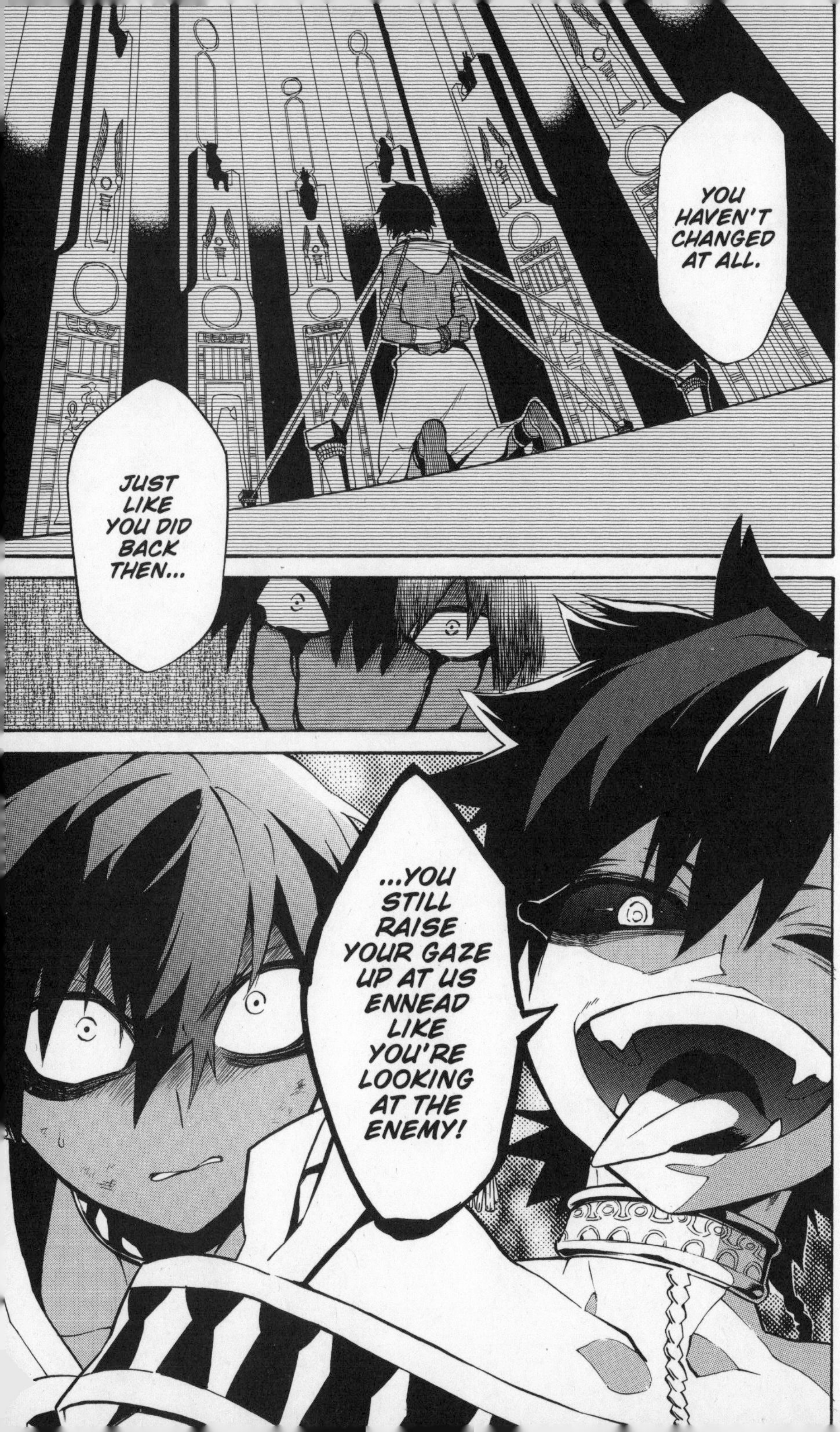
YOU HAVEN'T CHANGED AT ALL.
JUST LIKE YOU DID BACK THEN...
...YOU STILL RAISE YOUR GAZE UP AT US ENNEAD LIKE YOU'RE LOOKING AT THE ENEMY!

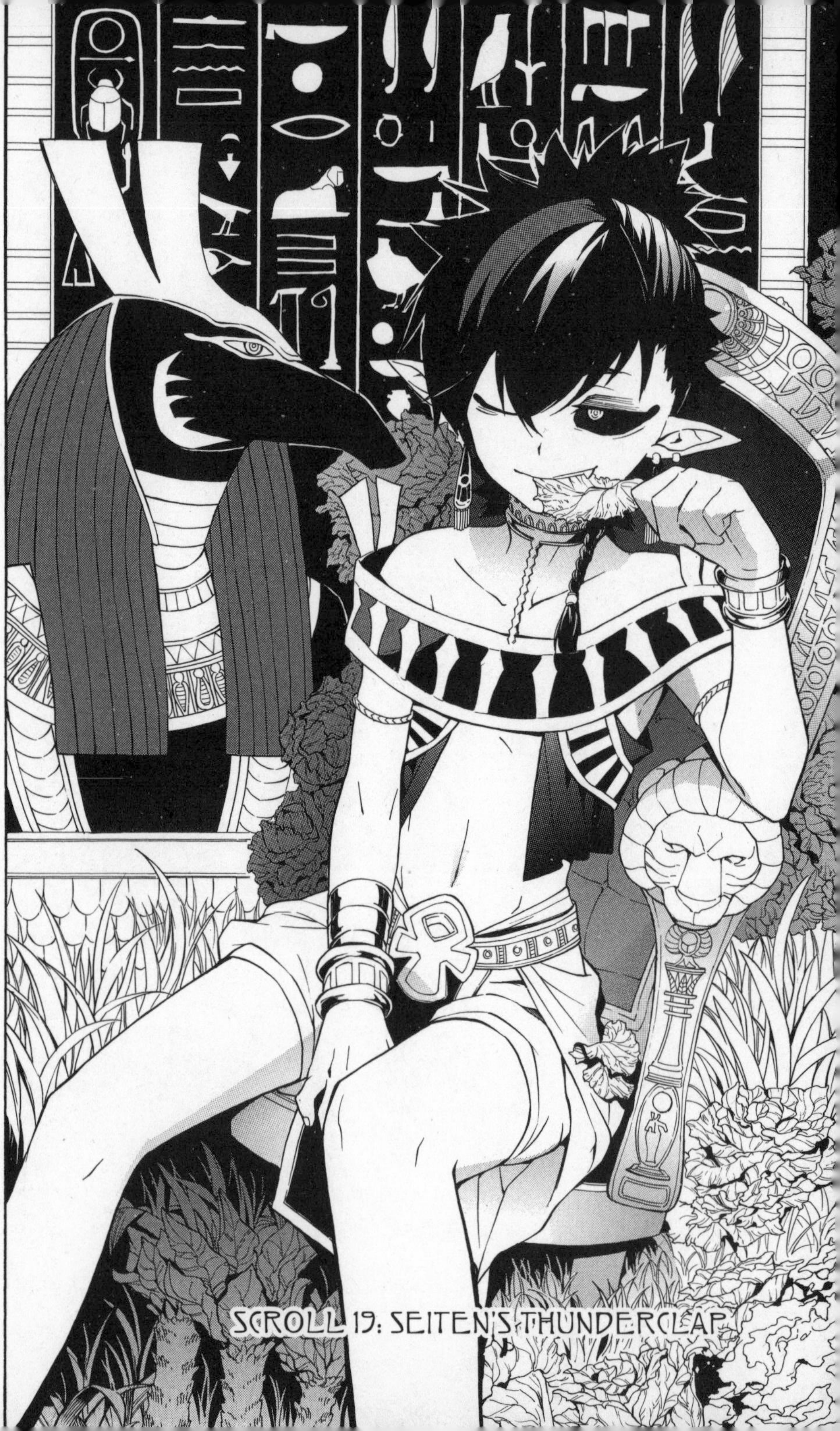
SCROLL 19: SEITEN'S THUNDERCLAP

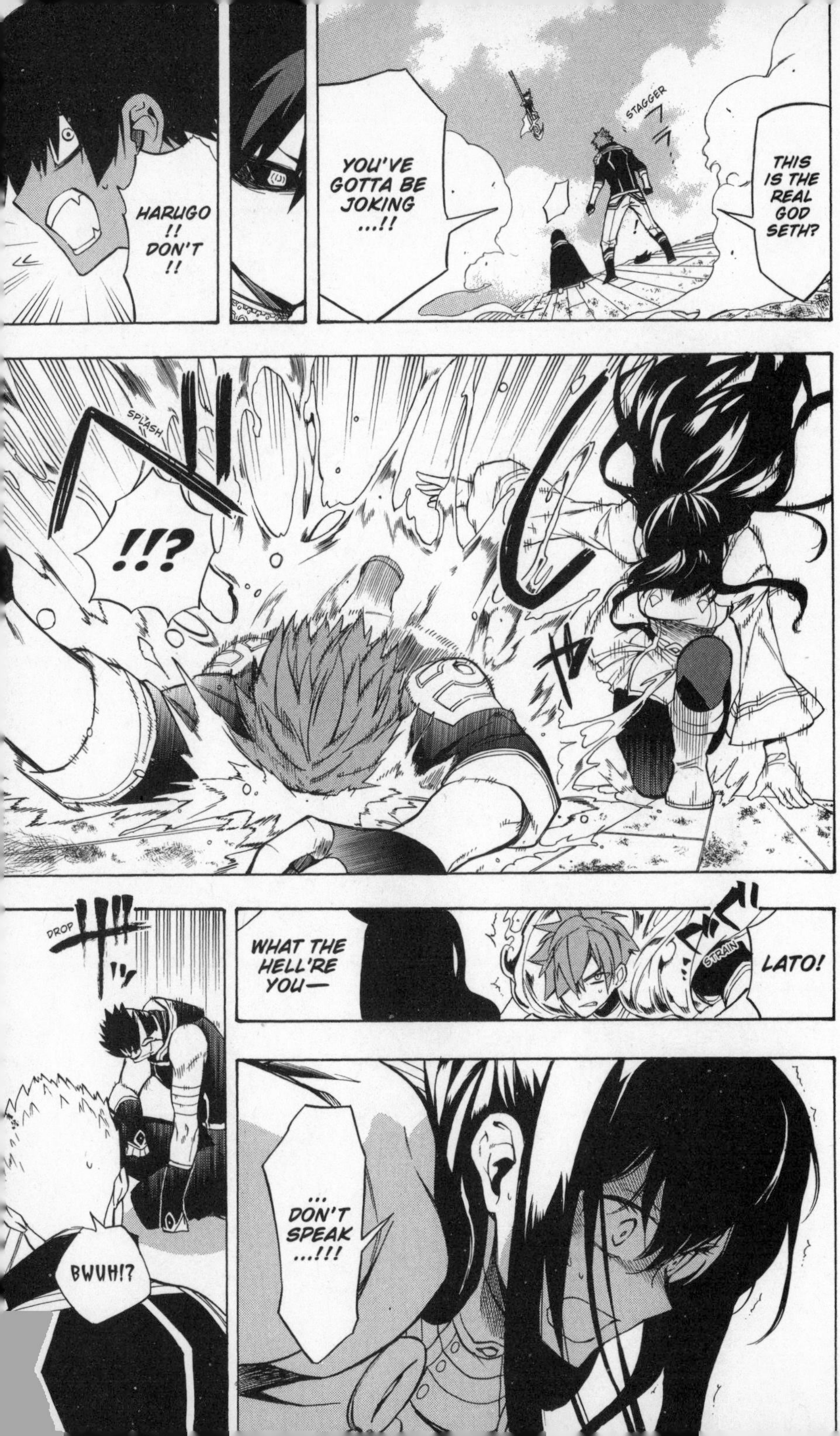
THIS IS THE REAL GOD SETH?
STAGGER
YOU'VE GOTTA BE JOKING ...!!
HARUGO!! DON'T!!
SPLASH
!!?
LATO!
STRAIN
WHAT THE HELL'RE YOU—
...DON'T SPEAK...!!!
DROP
BWUH!?

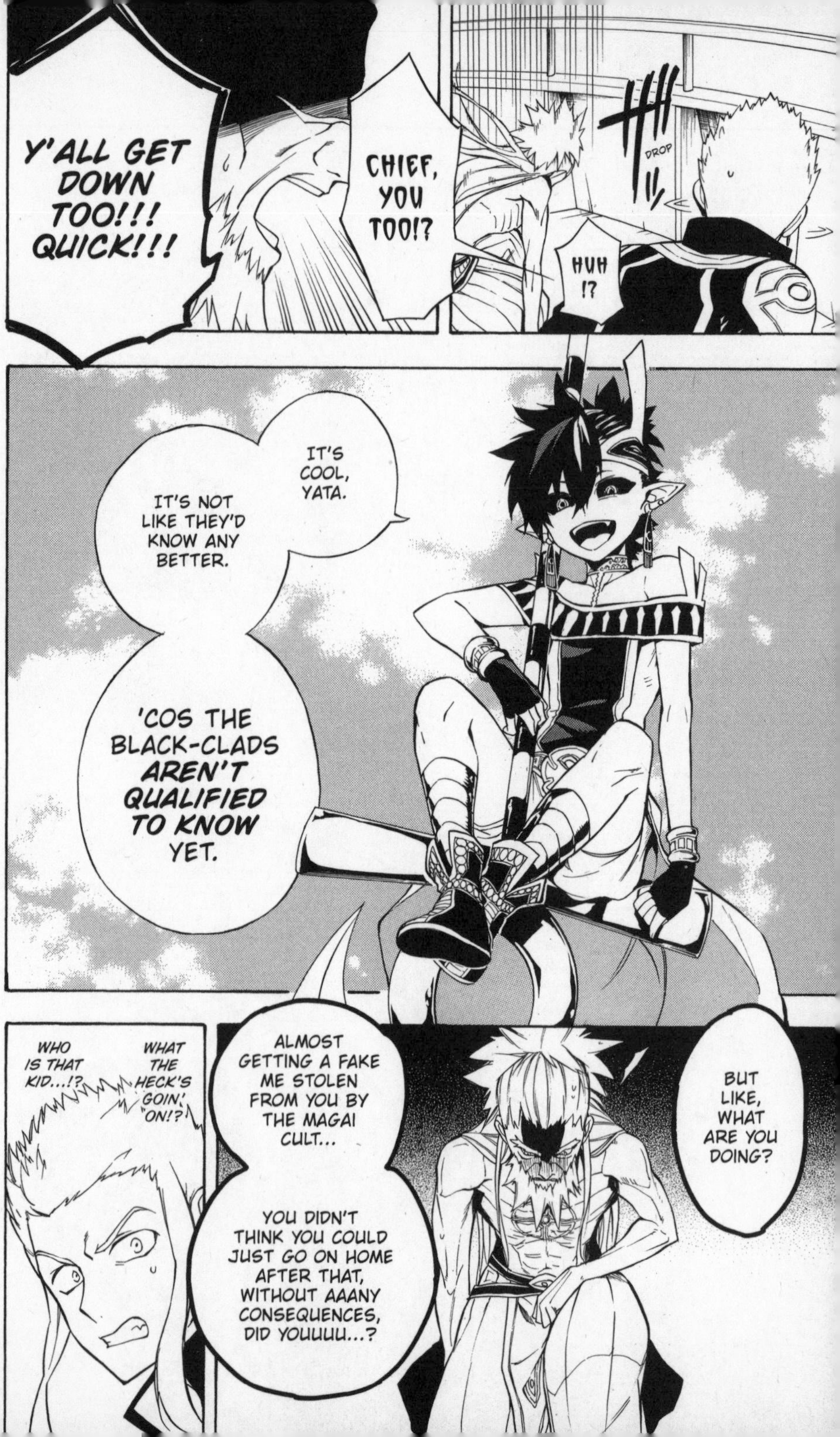
DROP
HUH!?
CHIEF, YOU TOO!?
Y'ALL GET DOWN TOO!!! QUICK!!!
IT'S COOL, YATA.
IT'S NOT LIKE THEY'D KNOW ANY BETTER.
'COS THE BLACK-CLADS AREN'T QUALIFIED TO KNOW YET.
BUT LIKE, WHAT ARE YOU DOING?
ALMOST GETTING A FAKE ME STOLEN FROM YOU BY THE MAGAI CULT...
YOU DIDN'T THINK YOU COULD JUST GO ON HOME AFTER THAT, WITHOUT AAAANY CONSEQUENCES, DID YOUUUU...?
WHAT THE HECK'S GOIN' ON!?
WHO IS THAT KID...!?

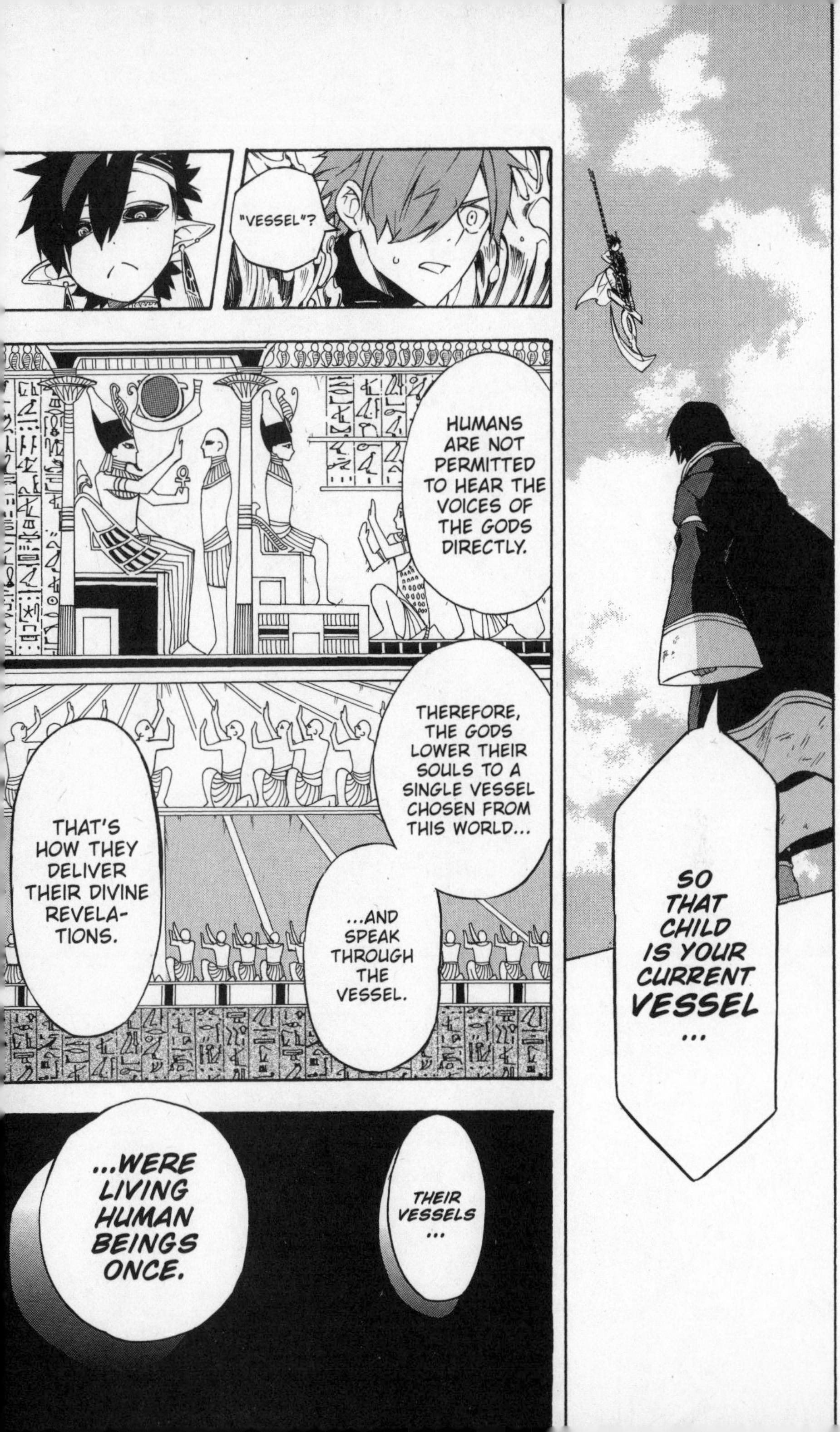
SO THAT CHILD IS YOUR CURRENT VESSEL...
"VESSEL"?
HUMANS ARE NOT PERMITTED TO HEAR THE VOICES OF THE GODS DIRECTLY.
THEREFORE, THE GODS LOWER THEIR SOULS TO A SINGLE VESSEL CHOSEN FROM THIS WORLD...
...AND SPEAK THROUGH THE VESSEL.
THAT'S HOW THEY DELIVER THEIR DIVINE REVELA-TIONS.
THEIR VESSELS...
...WERE LIVING HUMAN BEINGS ONCE.

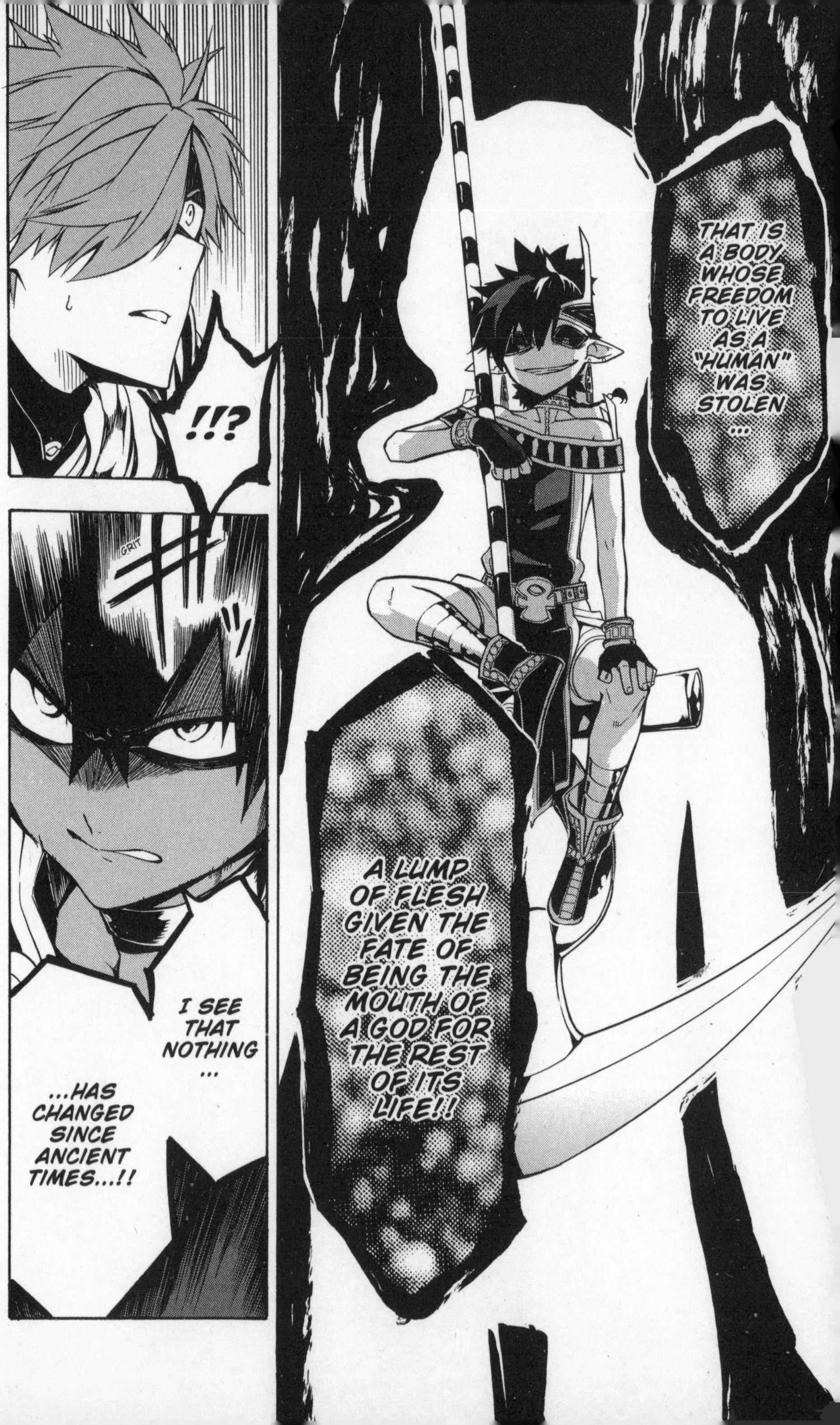

THAT IS A BODY WHOSE FREEDOM TO LIVE AS A "HUMAN" WAS STOLEN...
A LUMP OF FLESH GIVEN THE FATE OF BEING THE MOUTH OF A GOD FOR THE REST OF ITS LIFE!!
!!?
GRIT
I SEE THAT NOTHING...
...HAS CHANGED SINCE ANCIENT TIMES...!!

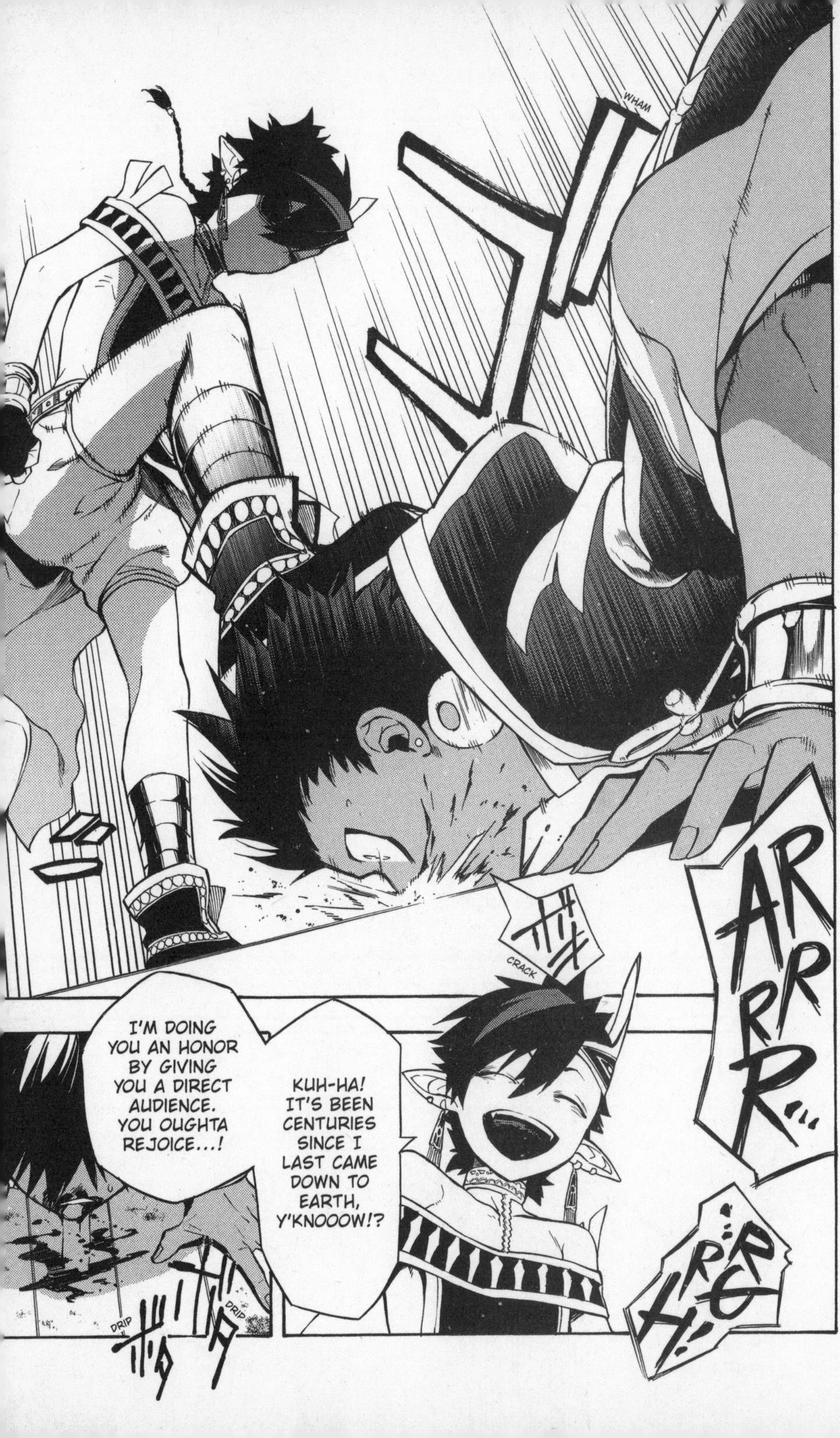
WHAM
ARRRRR...
CRACK
KUH-HA! IT'S BEEN CENTURIES SINCE I LAST CAME DOWN TO EARTH, Y'KNOOOW!?
I'M DOING YOU AN HONOR BY GIVING YOU A DIRECT AUDIENCE. YOU OUGHTA REJOICE...!
DRIP
DRIP

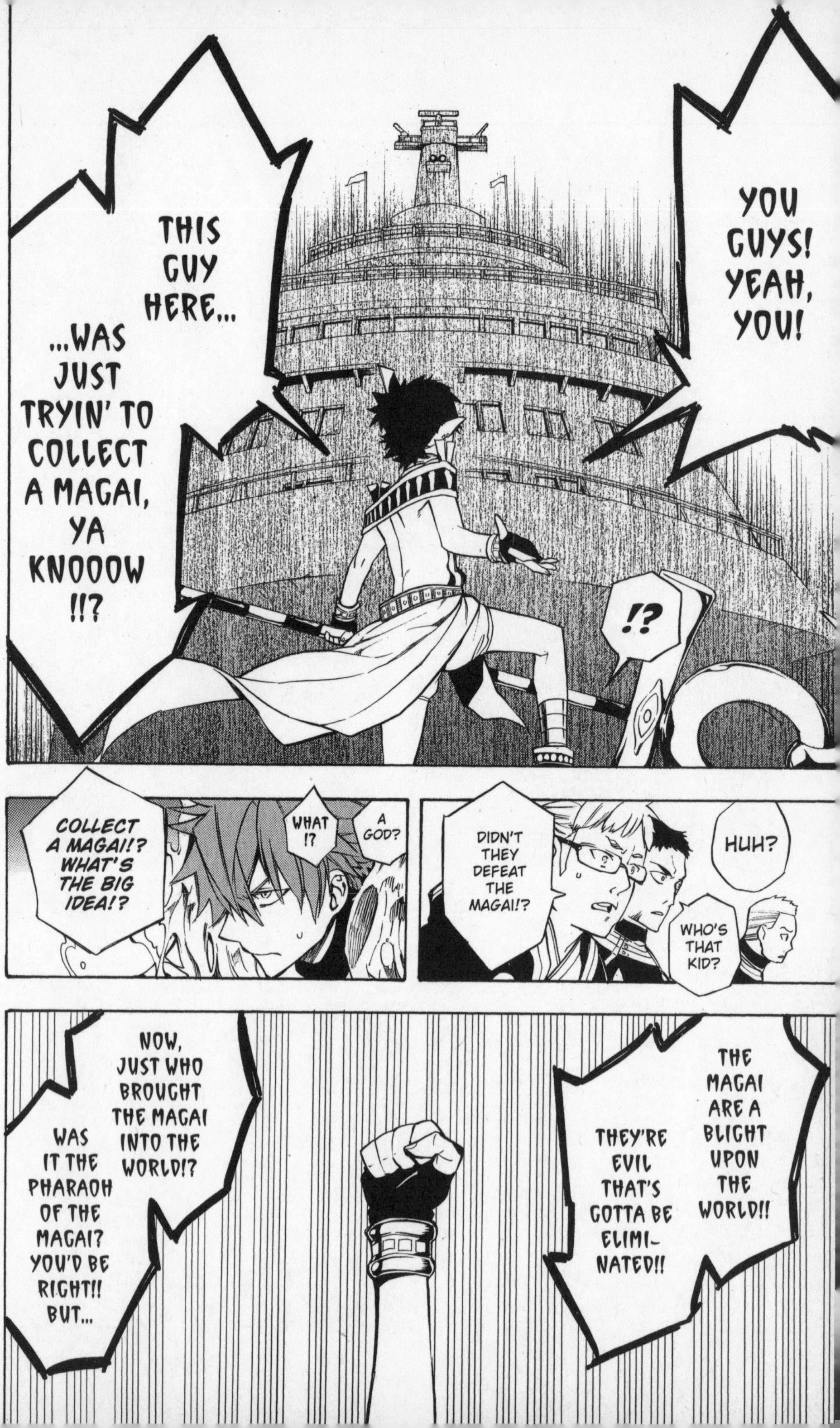
YOU GUYS! YEAH, YOU!
THIS GUY HERE...
...WAS JUST TRYIN' TO COLLECT A MAGAI, YA KNOOOW!!?
!?
HUH?
WHO'S THAT KID?
DIDN'T THEY DEFEAT THE MAGAI!?
A GOD?
WHAT!?
COLLECT A MAGAI!? WHAT'S THE BIG IDEA!?
THE MAGAI ARE A BLIGHT UPON THE WORLD!!
THEY'RE EVIL THAT'S GOTTA BE ELIMI-NATED!!
NOW, JUST WHO BROUGHT THE MAGAI INTO THE WORLD!?
WAS IT THE PHARAOH OF THE MAGAI? YOU'D BE RIGHT!! BUT...

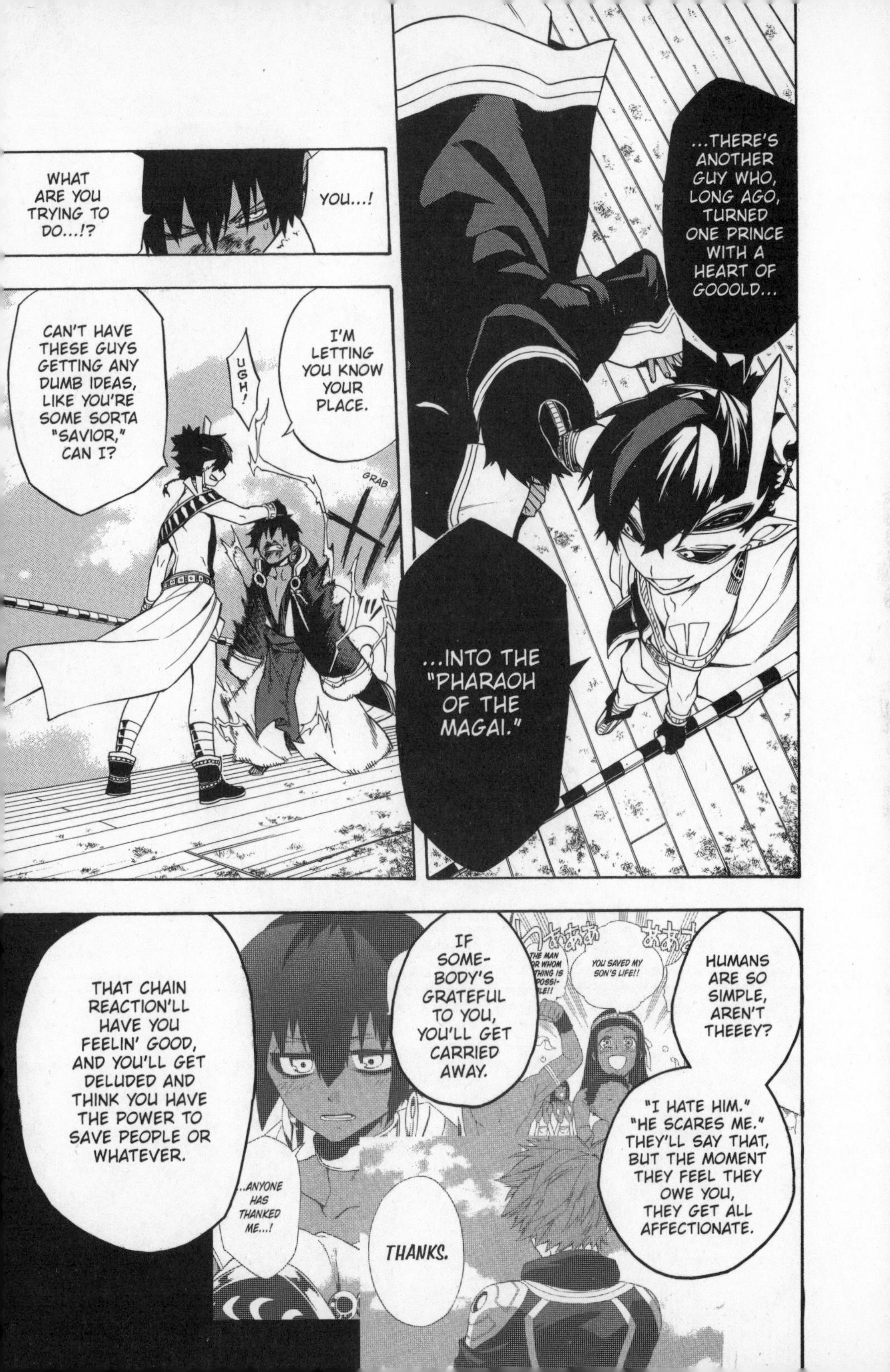
...THERE'S ANOTHER GUY WHO, LONG AGO, TURNED ONE PRINCE WITH A HEART OF GOOOLD...
...INTO THE "PHARAOH OF THE MAGAI."
YOU...!
WHAT ARE YOU TRYING TO DO...!?
I'M LETTING YOU KNOW YOUR PLACE.
UGH!
GRAB
CAN'T HAVE THESE GUYS GETTING ANY DUMB IDEAS, LIKE YOU'RE SOME SORTA "SAVIOR," CAN I?
HUMANS ARE SO SIMPLE, AREN'T THEEEY?
YOU SAVED MY SON'S LIFE!!
IF SOMEBODY'S GRATEFUL TO YOU, YOU'LL GET CARRIED AWAY.
"I HATE HIM." "HE SCARES ME." THEY'LL SAY THAT, BUT THE MOMENT THEY FEEL THEY OWE YOU, THEY GET ALL AFFECTIONATE.
THANKS.
...ANYONE HAS THANKED ME...!
THAT CHAIN REACTION'LL HAVE YOU FEELIN' GOOD, AND YOU'LL GET DELUDED AND THINK YOU HAVE THE POWER TO SAVE PEOPLE OR WHATEVER.

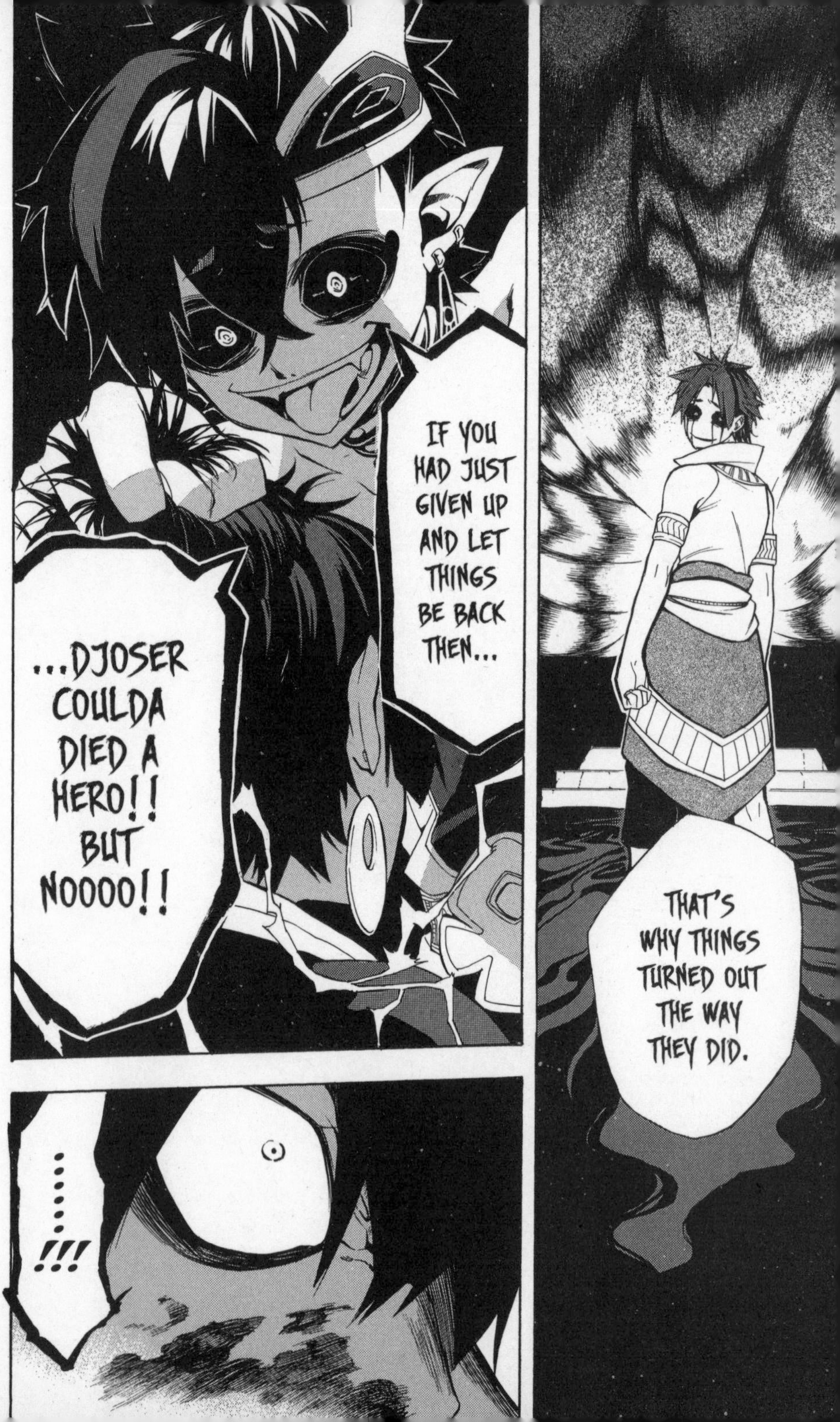
THAT'S WHY THINGS TURNED OUT THE WAY THEY DID.
IF YOU HAD JUST GIVEN UP AND LET THINGS BE BACK THEN...
...DJOSER COULDA DIED A HERO!! BUT NOOOO!!
......!!!

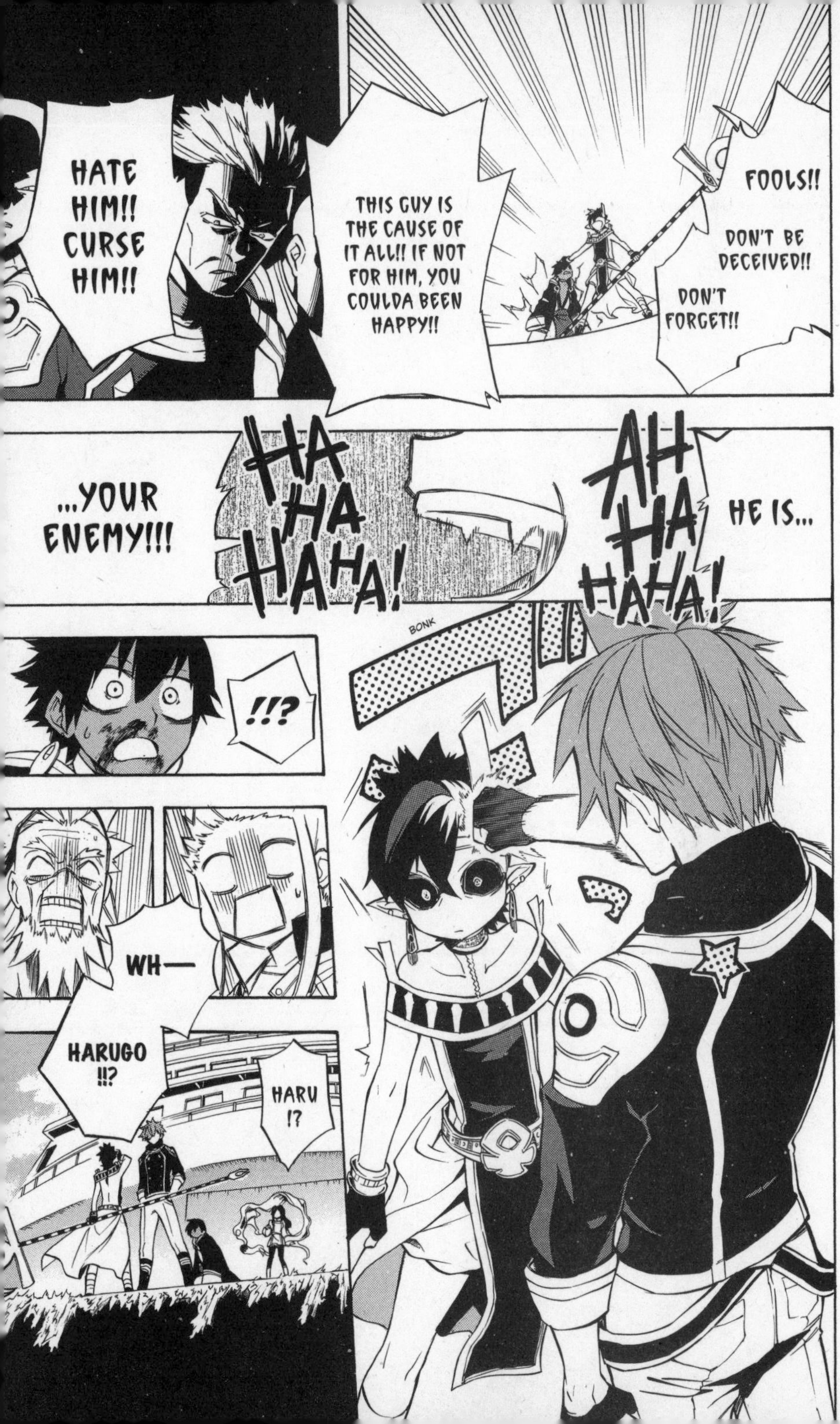

FOOLS!!
DON'T BE DECEIVED!!
DON'T FORGET!!
THIS GUY IS THE CAUSE OF IT ALL!! IF NOT FOR HIM, YOU COULDA BEEN HAPPY!!
HATE HIM!! CURSE HIM!!
HE IS...
AH HA HA HAHA!
HA HA HAHA!
...YOUR ENEMY!!!
BONK
!!?
WH—
HARUGO !!?
HARU !?

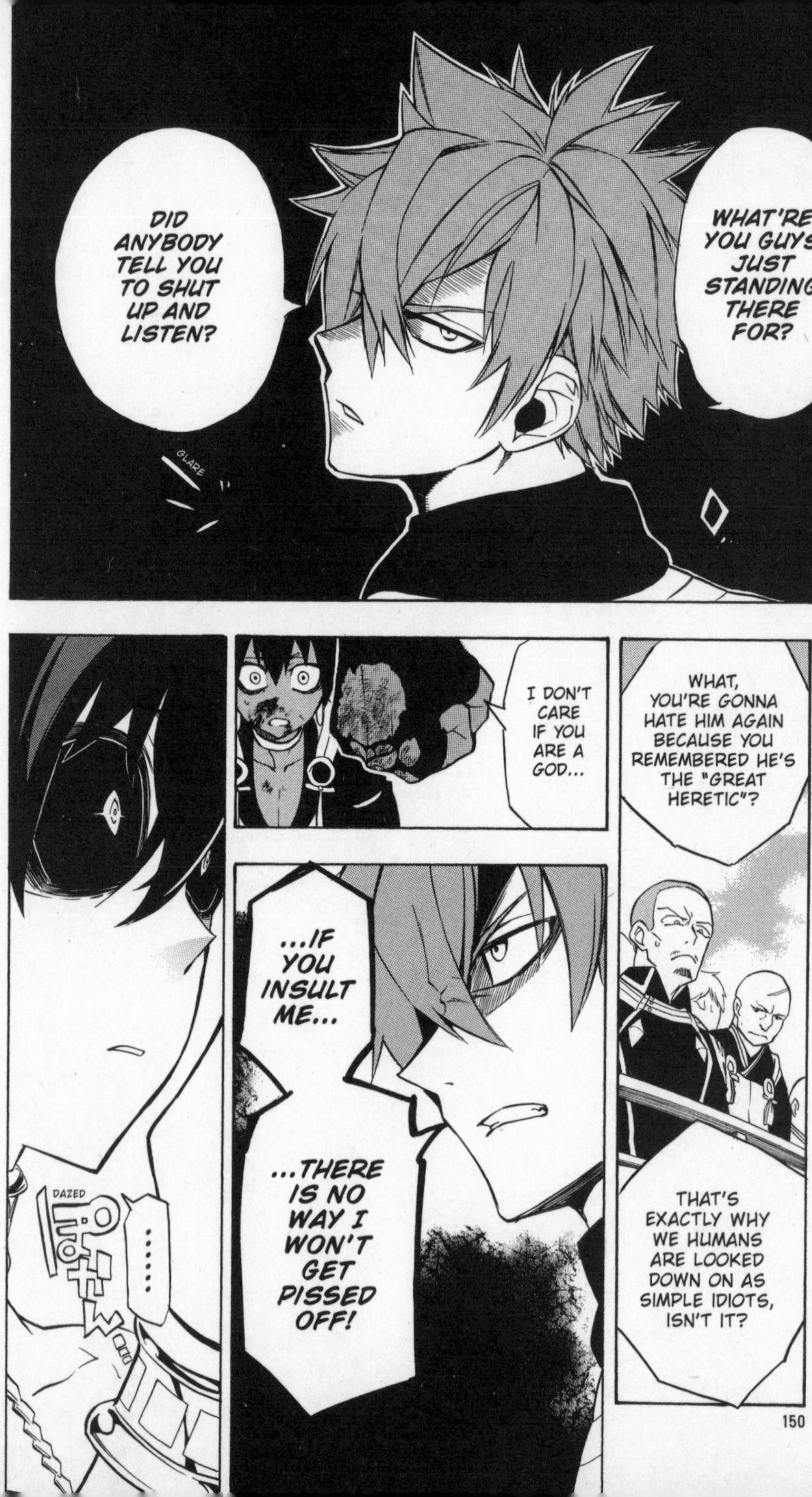
WHAT'RE YOU GUYS JUST STANDING THERE FOR?
DID ANYBODY TELL YOU TO SHUT UP AND LISTEN?
GLARE
WHAT, YOU'RE GONNA HATE HIM AGAIN BECAUSE YOU REMEMBERED HE'S THE "GREAT HERETIC"?
THAT'S EXACTLY WHY WE HUMANS ARE LOOKED DOWN ON AS SIMPLE IDIOTS, ISN'T IT?
I DON'T CARE IF YOU ARE A GOD...
...IF YOU INSULT ME...
...THERE IS NO WAY I WON'T GET PISSED OFF!
DAZED
......

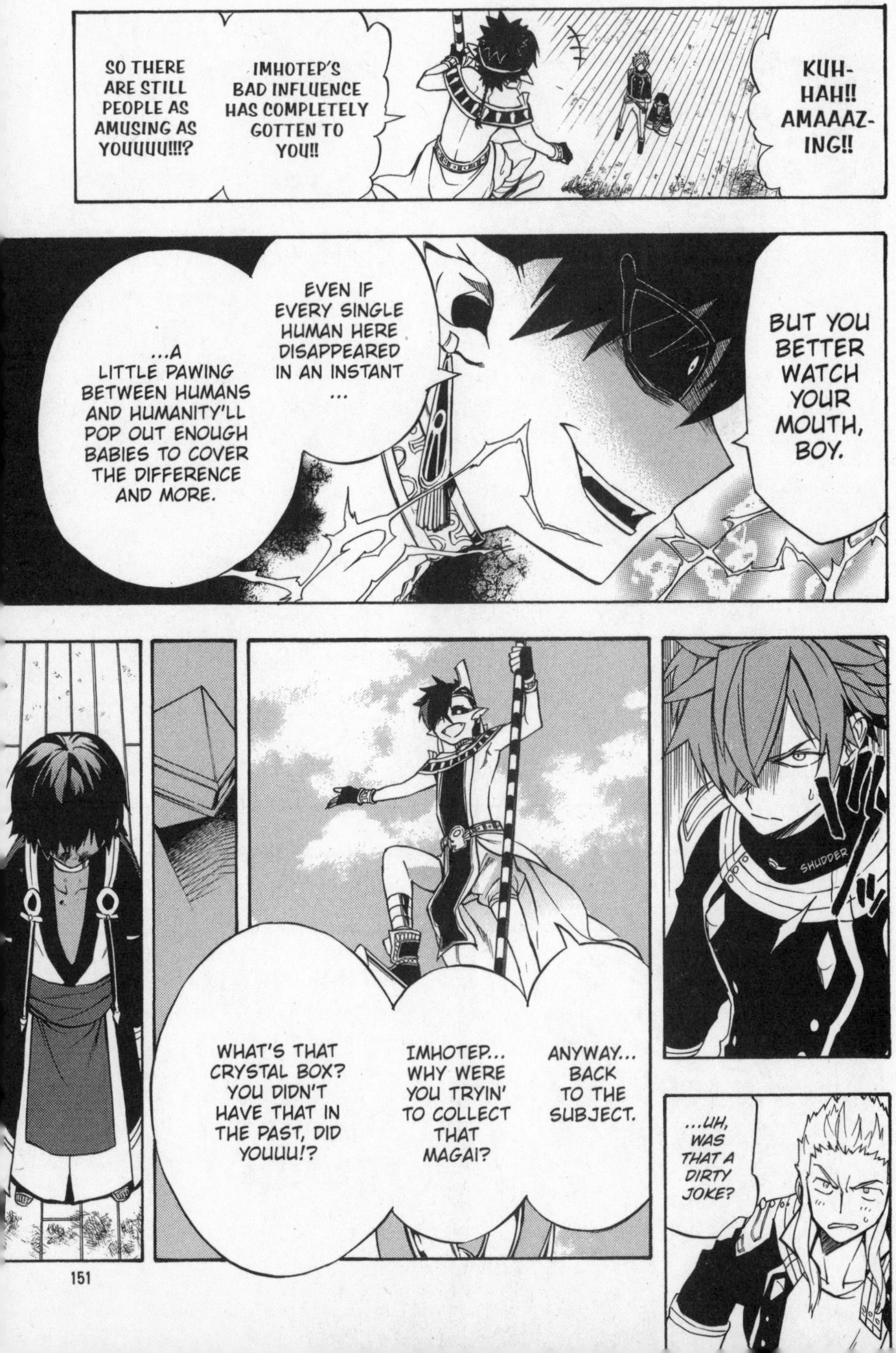
KUH-HAH!! AMAAAZ-ING!!
IMHOTEP'S BAD INFLUENCE HAS COMPLETELY GOTTEN TO YOU!!
SO THERE ARE STILL PEOPLE AS AMUSING AS YOUUUU!!!?
BUT YOU BETTER WATCH YOUR MOUTH, BOY.
EVEN IF EVERY SINGLE HUMAN HERE DISAPPEARED IN AN INSTANT...
...A LITTLE PAWING BETWEEN HUMANS AND HUMANITY'LL POP OUT ENOUGH BABIES TO COVER THE DIFFERENCE AND MORE.
SHUDDER
...UH, WAS THAT A DIRTY JOKE?
ANYWAY... BACK TO THE SUBJECT.
IMHOTEP... WHY WERE YOU TRYIN' TO COLLECT THAT MAGAI?
WHAT'S THAT CRYSTAL BOX? YOU DIDN'T HAVE THAT IN THE PAST, DID YOUUU!?

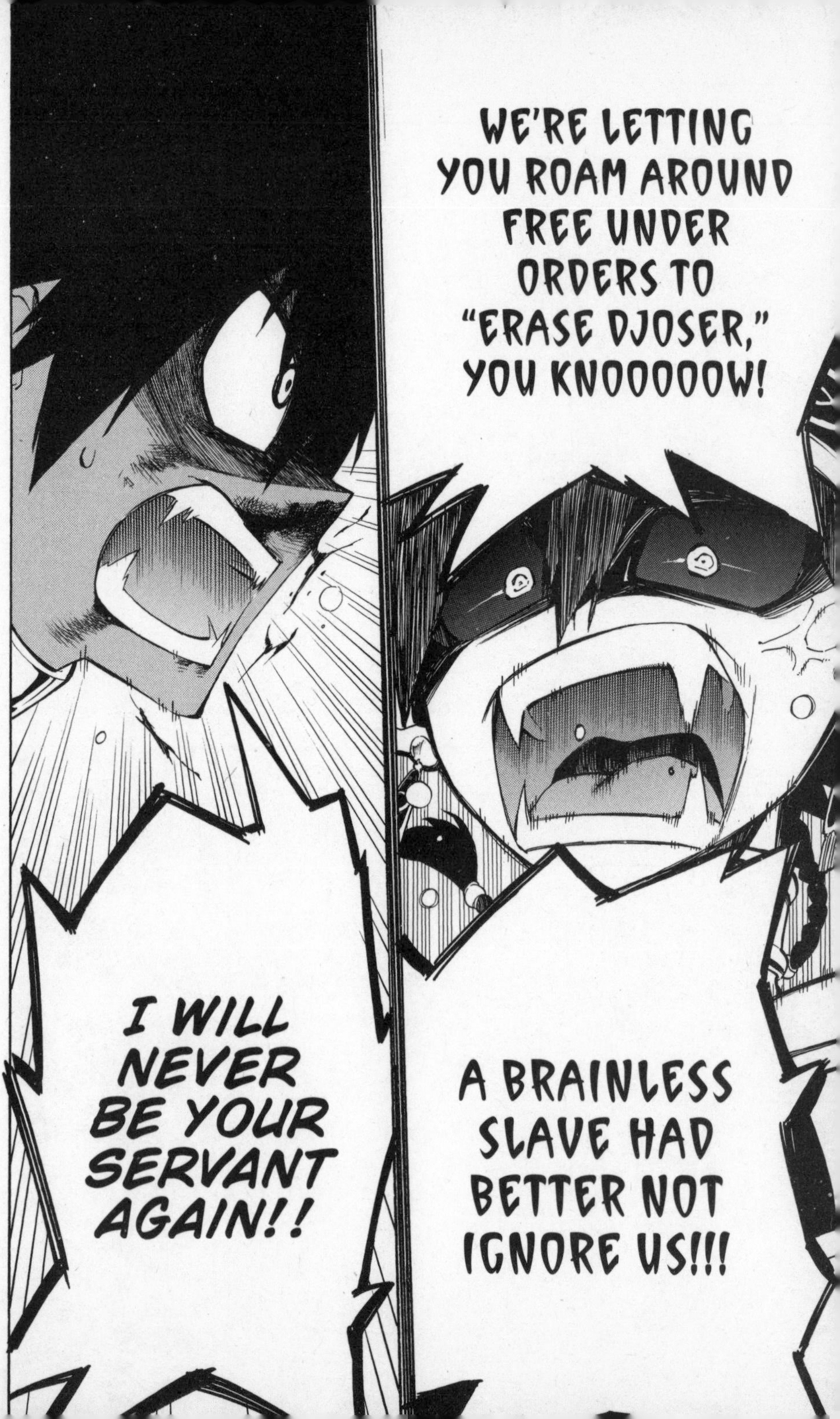
WE'RE LETTING YOU ROAM AROUND FREE UNDER ORDERS TO "ERASE DJOSER," YOU KNOOOOOW!
A BRAINLESS SLAVE HAD BETTER NOT IGNORE US!!!
I WILL NEVER BE YOUR SERVANT AGAIN!!

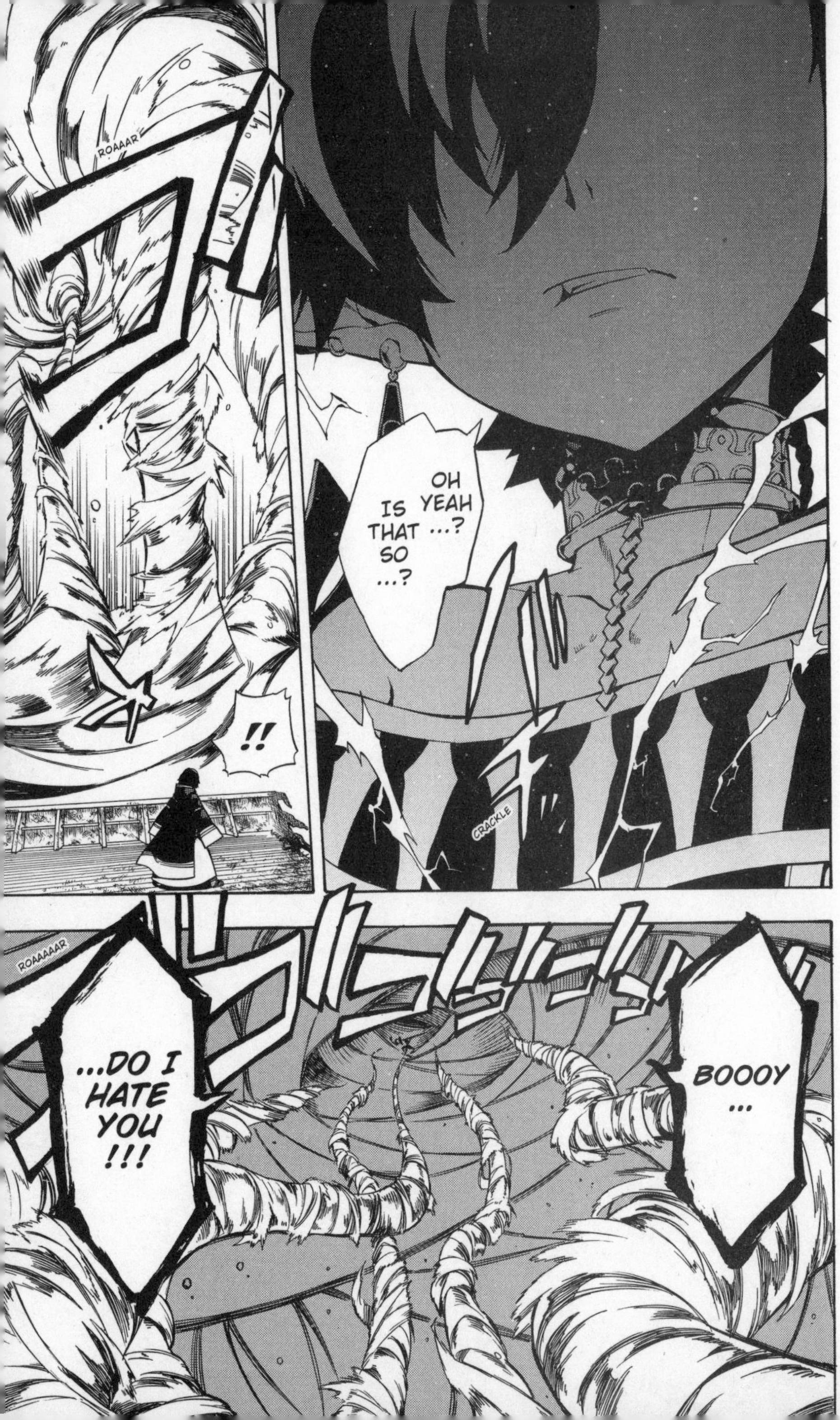
OH YEAH ...? IS THAT SO ...?
CRACKLE
ROAAAR
!!
BOOOY ...
...DO I HATE YOU !!!
ROAAAAAR

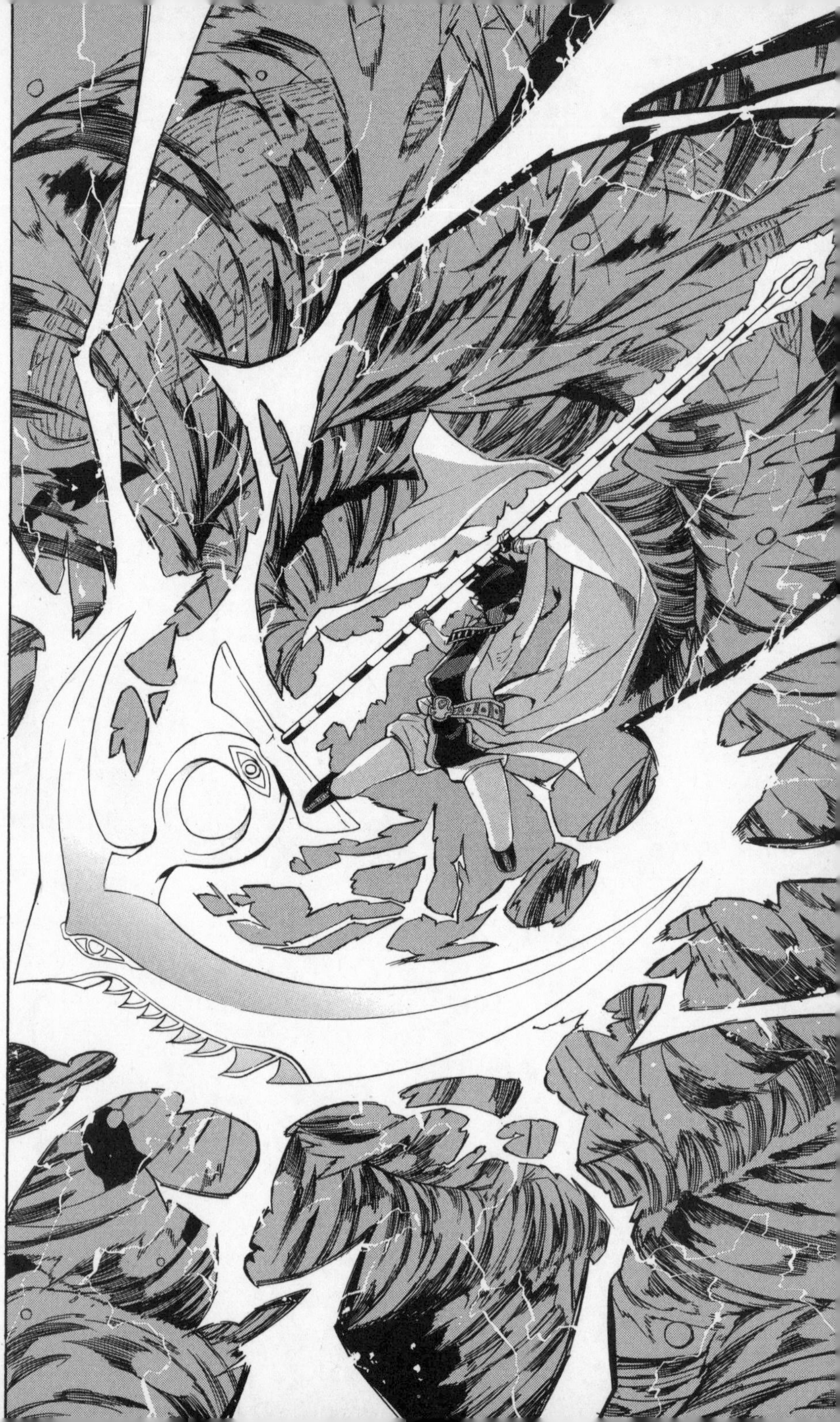

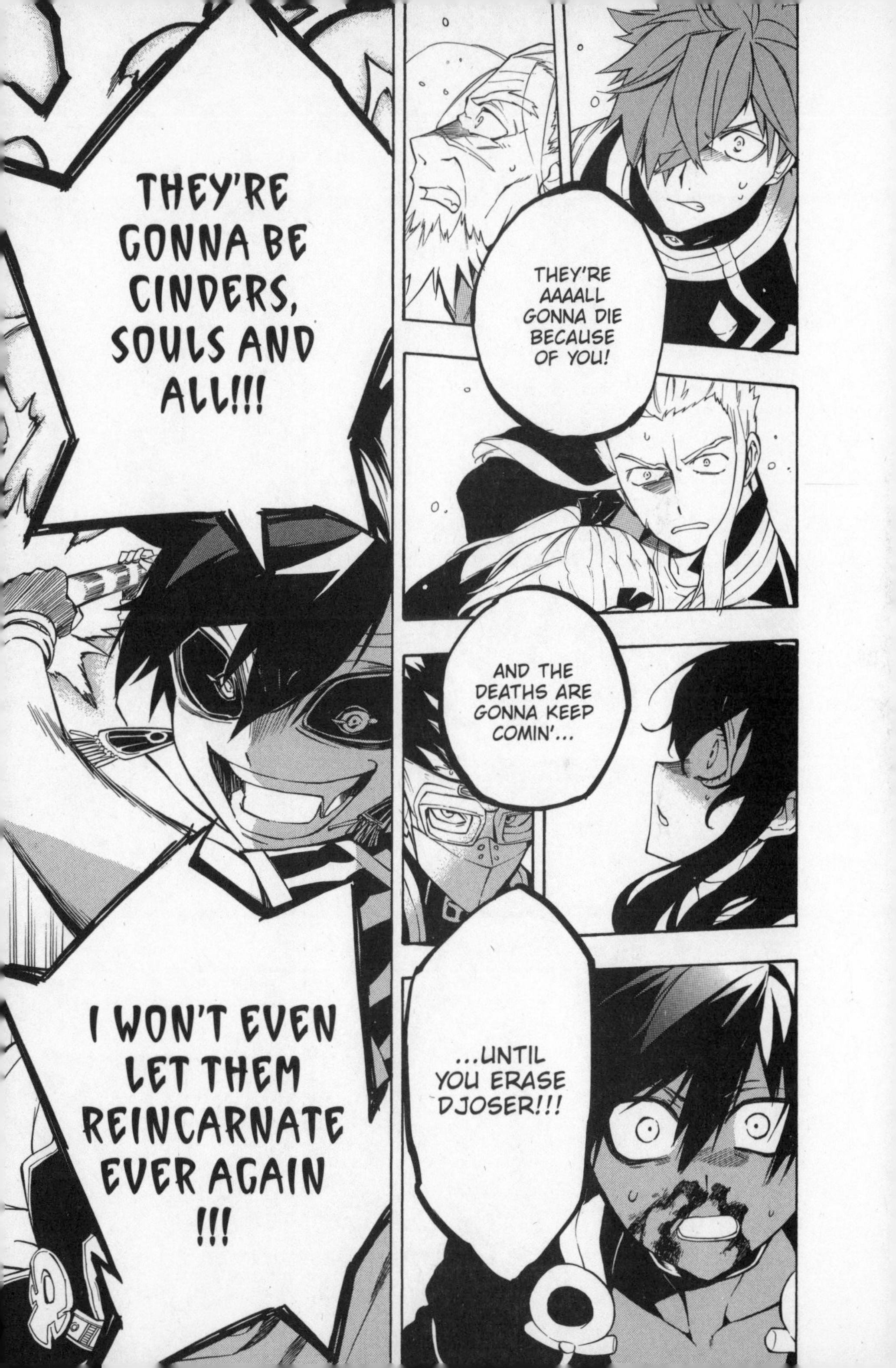
THEY'RE AAAALL GONNA DIE BECAUSE OF YOU!
AND THE DEATHS ARE GONNA KEEP COMIN'...
...UNTIL YOU ERASE DJOSER!!!
THEY'RE GONNA BE CINDERS, SOULS AND ALL!!!
I WON'T EVEN LET THEM REINCARNATE EVER AGAIN !!!

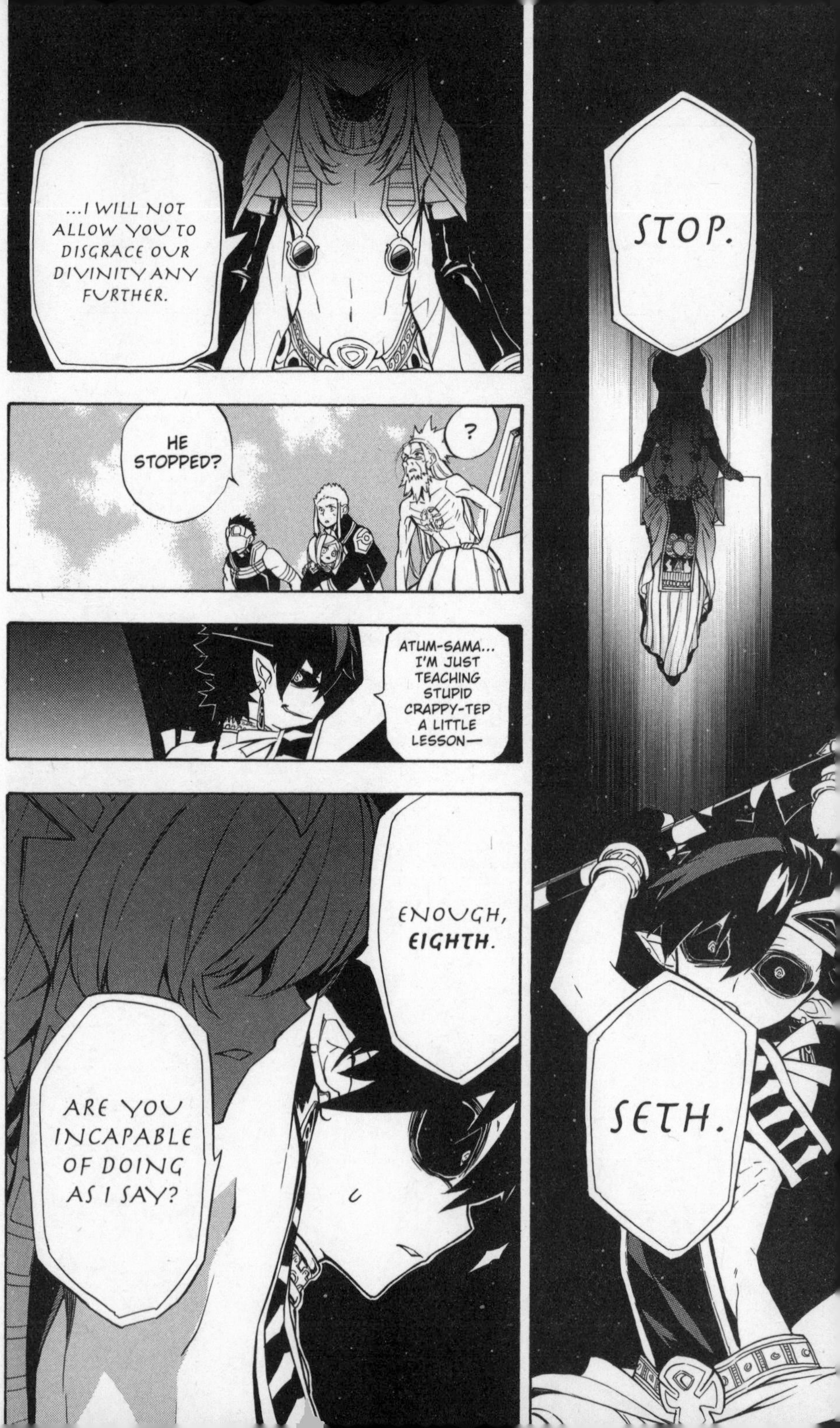
STOP.
SETH.
...I WILL NOT ALLOW YOU TO DISGRACE OUR DIVINITY ANY FURTHER.
HE STOPPED?
?
ATUM-SAMA... I'M JUST TEACHING STUPID CRAPPY-TEP A LITTLE LESSON—
ENOUGH, **EIGHTH**.
ARE YOU INCAPABLE OF DOING AS I SAY?

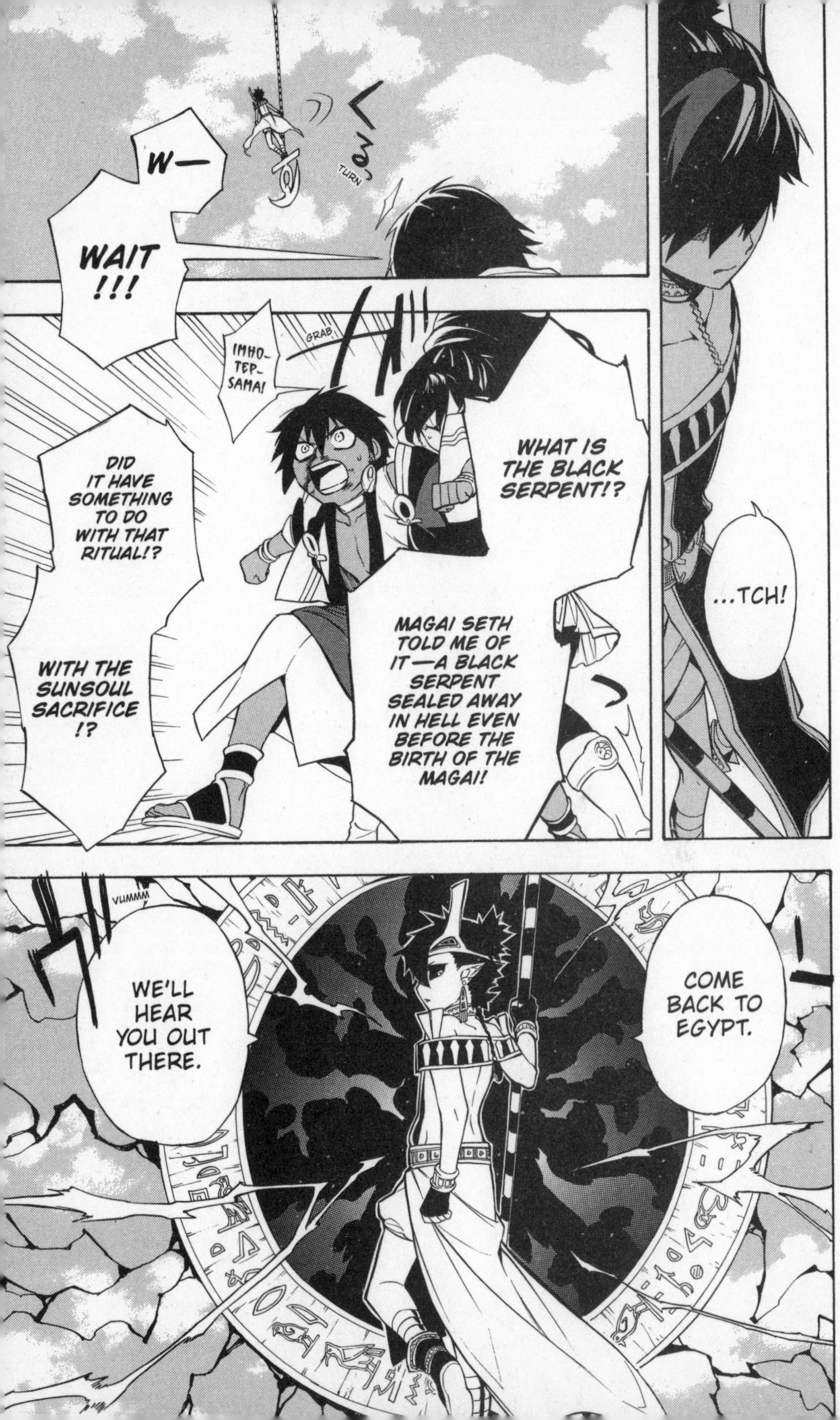

...TCH!
W—
くるっ
TURN
WAIT!!!
GRAB
WHAT IS THE BLACK SERPENT!?
IMHO-TEP-SAMA!
MAGAI SETH TOLD ME OF IT—A BLACK SERPENT SEALED AWAY IN HELL EVEN BEFORE THE BIRTH OF THE MAGAI!
DID IT HAVE SOMETHING TO DO WITH THAT RITUAL!?
WITH THE SUNSOUL SACRIFICE!?
COME BACK TO EGYPT.
VUMMM
WE'LL HEAR YOU OUT THERE.

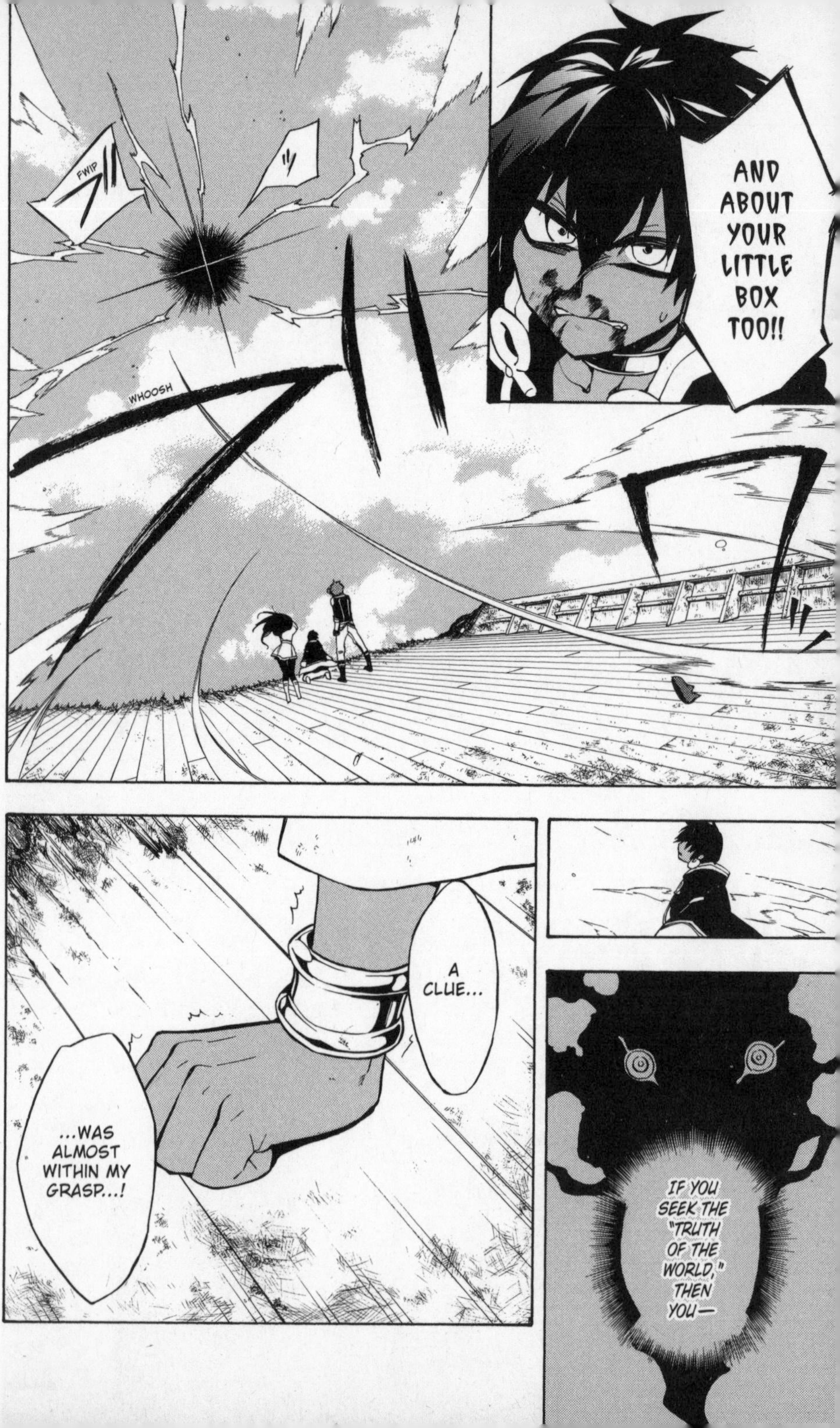
AND ABOUT YOUR LITTLE BOX TOO!!
FWIP
WHOOSH
IF YOU SEEK THE "TRUTH OF THE WORLD," THEN YOU—
A CLUE...
...WAS ALMOST WITHIN MY GRASP...!

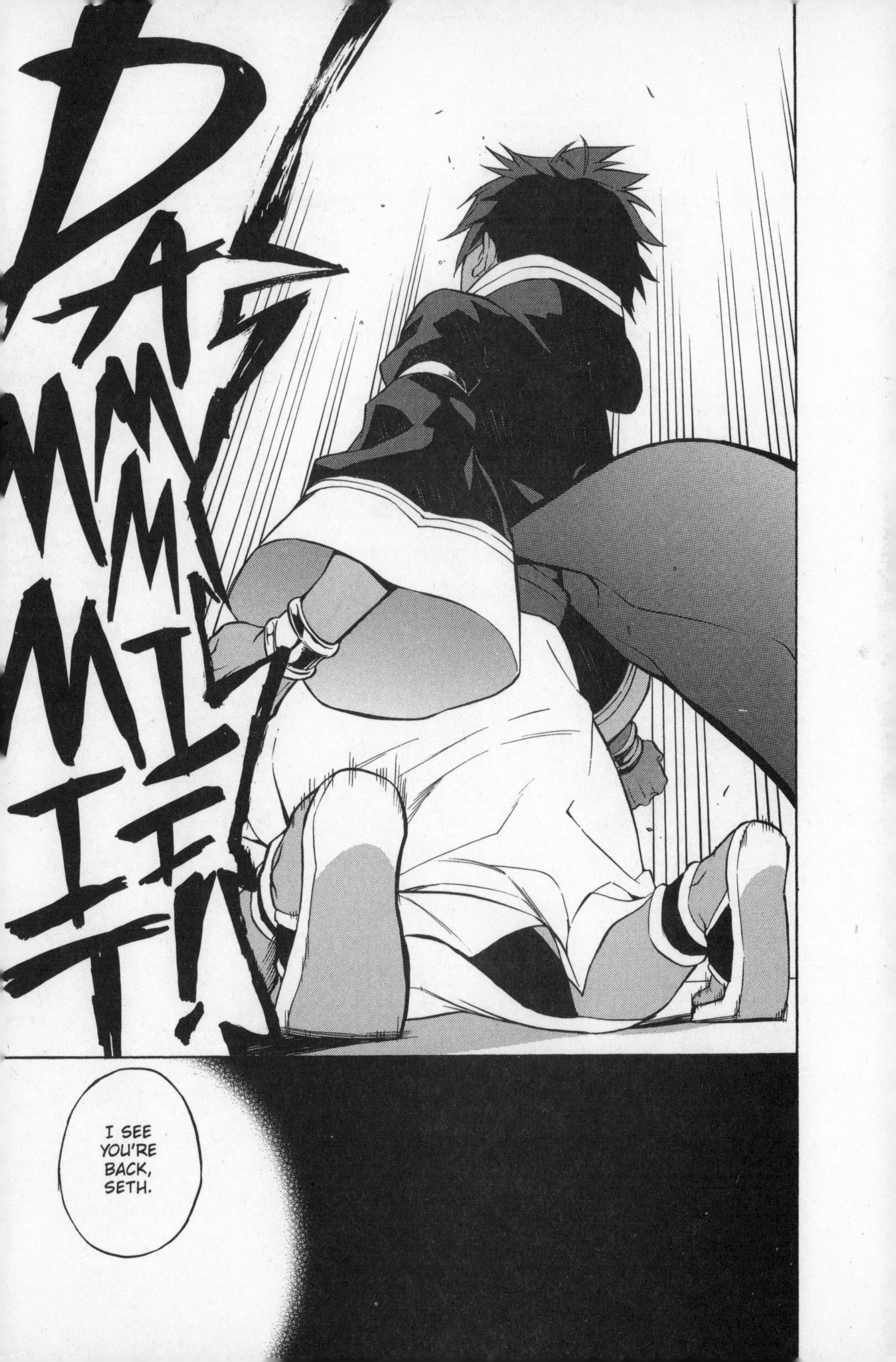
DAMMMMIIIIT!
I SEE YOU'RE BACK, SETH.

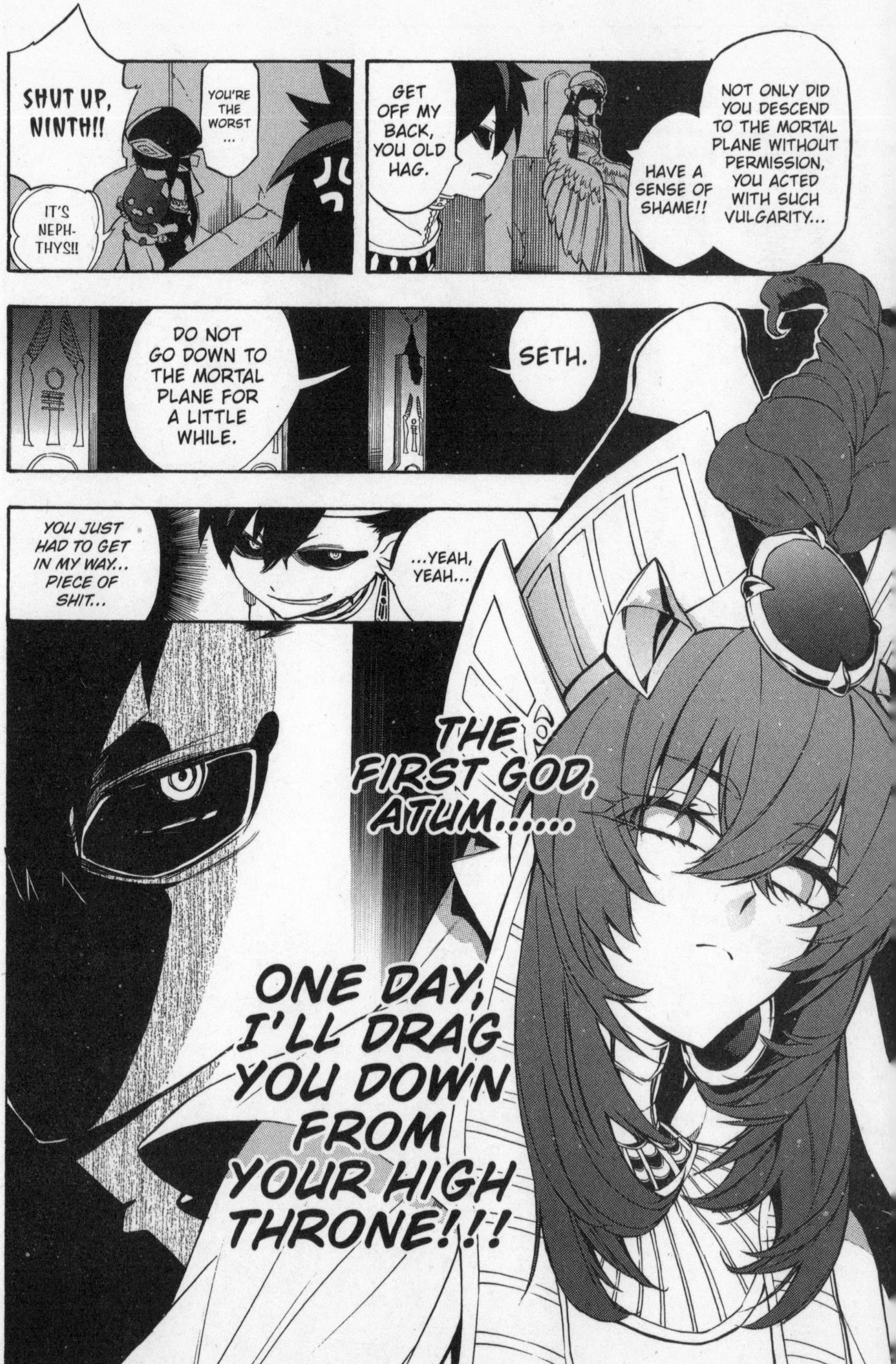
NOT ONLY DID YOU DESCEND TO THE MORTAL PLANE WITHOUT PERMISSION, YOU ACTED WITH SUCH VULGARITY...
HAVE A SENSE OF SHAME!!
GET OFF MY BACK, YOU OLD HAG.
YOU'RE THE WORST ...
SHUT UP, NINTH!!
IT'S NEPHTHYS!!
SETH.
DO NOT GO DOWN TO THE MORTAL PLANE FOR A LITTLE WHILE.
...YEAH, YEAH...
YOU JUST HAD TO GET IN MY WAY... PIECE OF SHIT...
THE FIRST GOD, ATUM......
ONE DAY, I'LL DRAG YOU DOWN FROM YOUR HIGH THRONE!!!

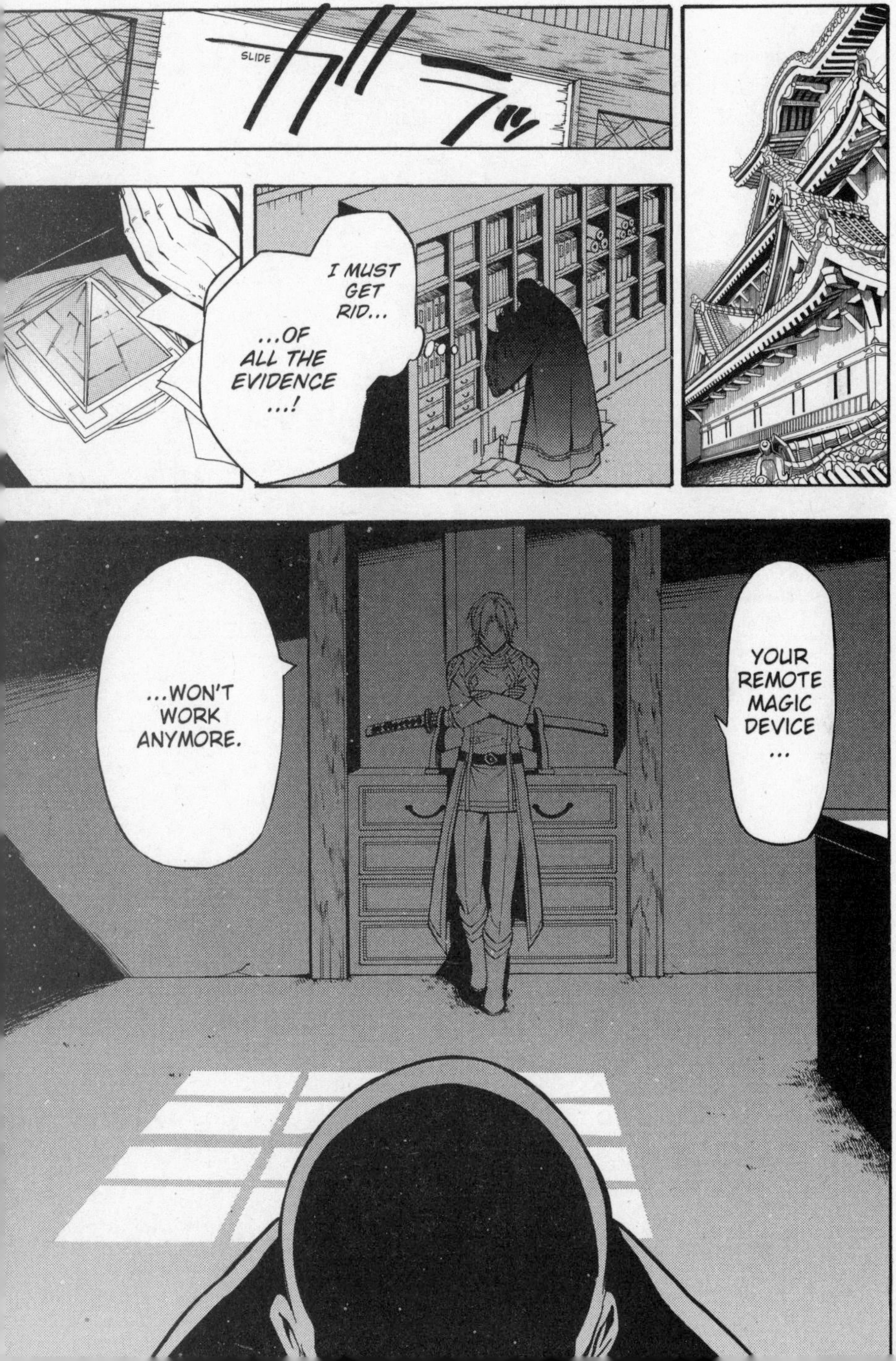
SLIDE
I MUST GET RID...
...OF ALL THE EVIDENCE ...!
YOUR REMOTE MAGIC DEVICE ...
...WON'T WORK ANYMORE.

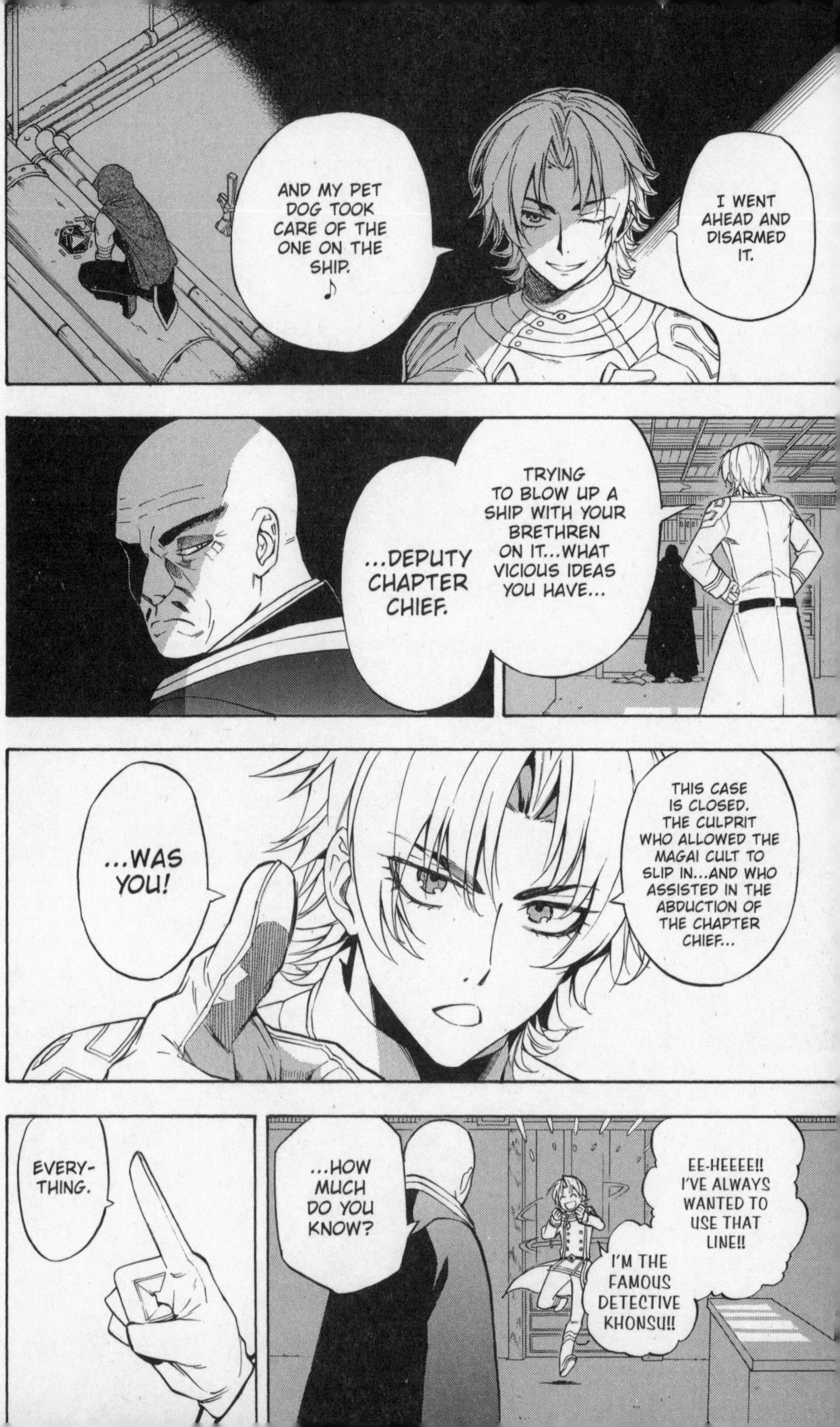
I WENT AHEAD AND DISARMED IT.
AND MY PET DOG TOOK CARE OF THE ONE ON THE SHIP. ♪
TRYING TO BLOW UP A SHIP WITH YOUR BRETHREN ON IT...WHAT VICIOUS IDEAS YOU HAVE...
...DEPUTY CHAPTER CHIEF.
THIS CASE IS CLOSED. THE CULPRIT WHO ALLOWED THE MAGAI CULT TO SLIP IN...AND WHO ASSISTED IN THE ABDUCTION OF THE CHAPTER CHIEF...
...WAS YOU!
EE-HEEEE!! I'VE ALWAYS WANTED TO USE THAT LINE!!
I'M THE FAMOUS DETECTIVE KHONSU!!
...HOW MUCH DO YOU KNOW?
EVERY-THING.

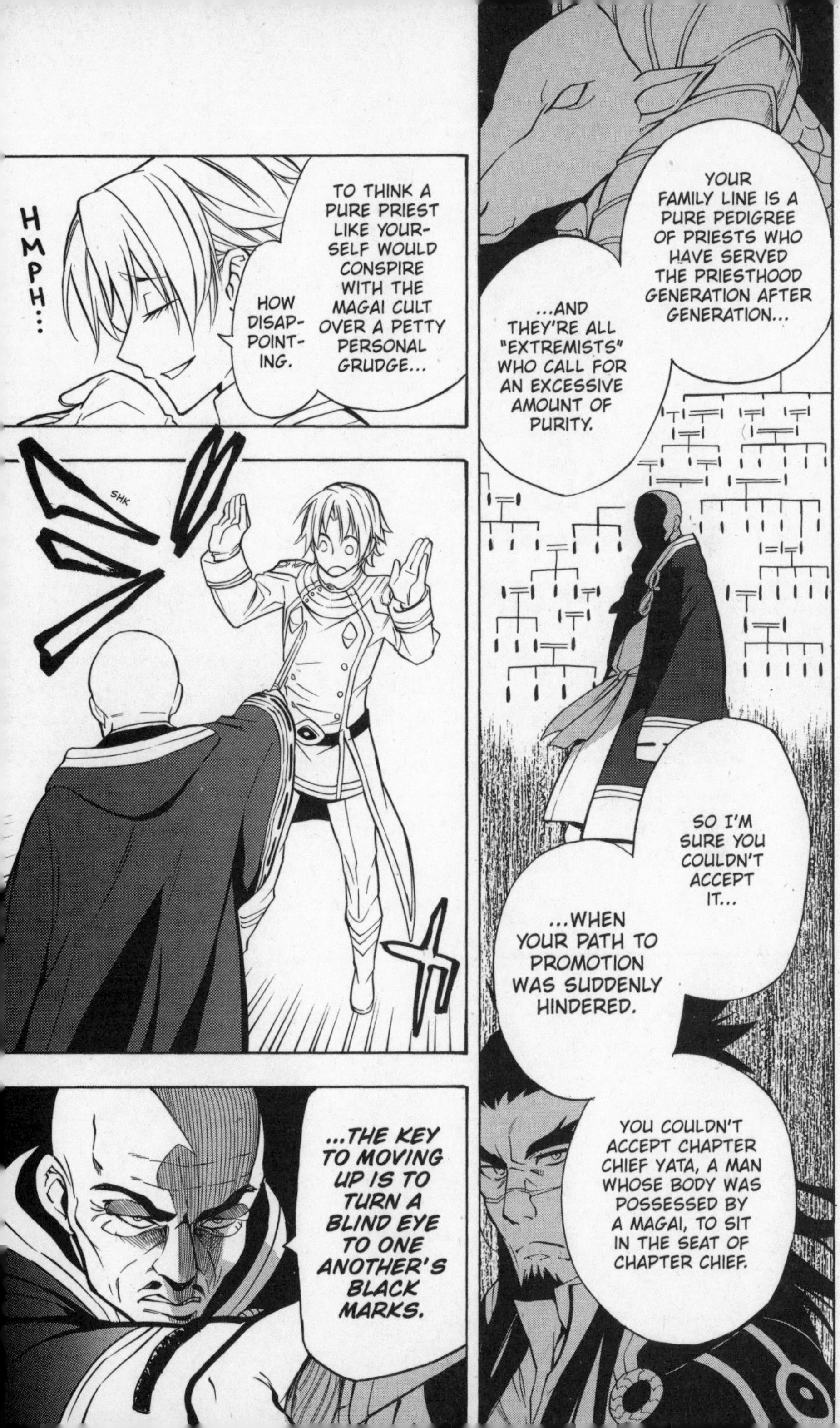
YOUR FAMILY LINE IS A PURE PEDIGREE OF PRIESTS WHO HAVE SERVED THE PRIESTHOOD GENERATION AFTER GENERATION...
...AND THEY'RE ALL "EXTREMISTS" WHO CALL FOR AN EXCESSIVE AMOUNT OF PURITY.
SO I'M SURE YOU COULDN'T ACCEPT IT...
...WHEN YOUR PATH TO PROMOTION WAS SUDDENLY HINDERED.
YOU COULDN'T ACCEPT CHAPTER CHIEF YATA, A MAN WHOSE BODY WAS POSSESSED BY A MAGAI, TO SIT IN THE SEAT OF CHAPTER CHIEF.
TO THINK A PURE PRIEST LIKE YOURSELF WOULD CONSPIRE WITH THE MAGAI CULT OVER A PETTY PERSONAL GRUDGE...
HOW DISAPPOINTING.
HMPH...
SHK
...THE KEY TO MOVING UP IS TO TURN A BLIND EYE TO ONE ANOTHER'S BLACK MARKS.

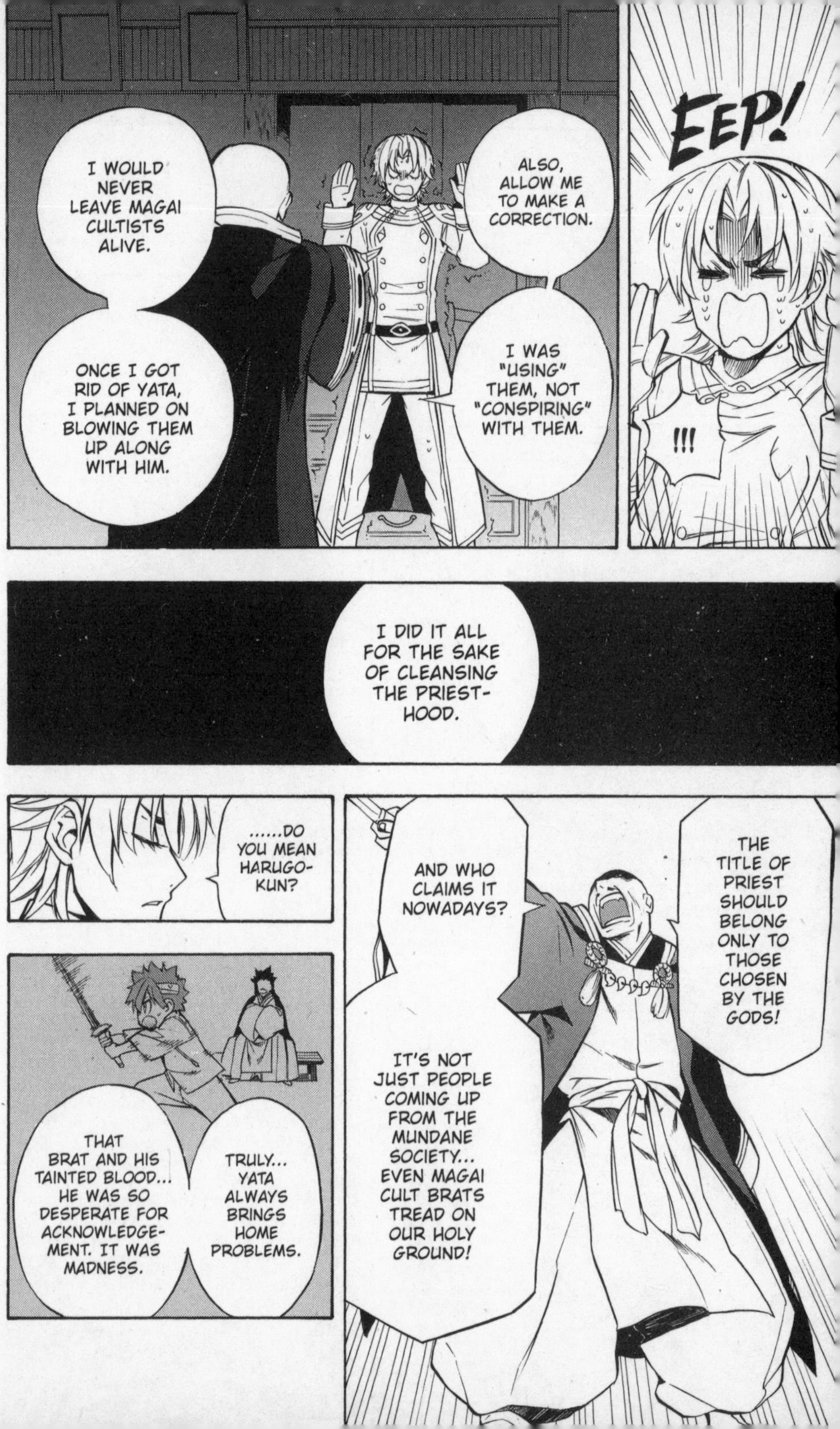
EEP!
!!!
ALSO, ALLOW ME TO MAKE A CORRECTION.
I WAS "USING" THEM, NOT "CONSPIRING" WITH THEM.
I WOULD NEVER LEAVE MAGAI CULTISTS ALIVE.
ONCE I GOT RID OF YATA, I PLANNED ON BLOWING THEM UP ALONG WITH HIM.
I DID IT ALL FOR THE SAKE OF CLEANSING THE PRIEST-HOOD.
THE TITLE OF PRIEST SHOULD BELONG ONLY TO THOSE CHOSEN BY THE GODS!
AND WHO CLAIMS IT NOWADAYS?
IT'S NOT JUST PEOPLE COMING UP FROM THE MUNDANE SOCIETY... EVEN MAGAI CULT BRATS TREAD ON OUR HOLY GROUND!
......DO YOU MEAN HARUGO-KUN?
TRULY... YATA ALWAYS BRINGS HOME PROBLEMS.
THAT BRAT AND HIS TAINTED BLOOD... HE WAS SO DESPERATE FOR ACKNOWLEDGE-MENT. IT WAS MADNESS.

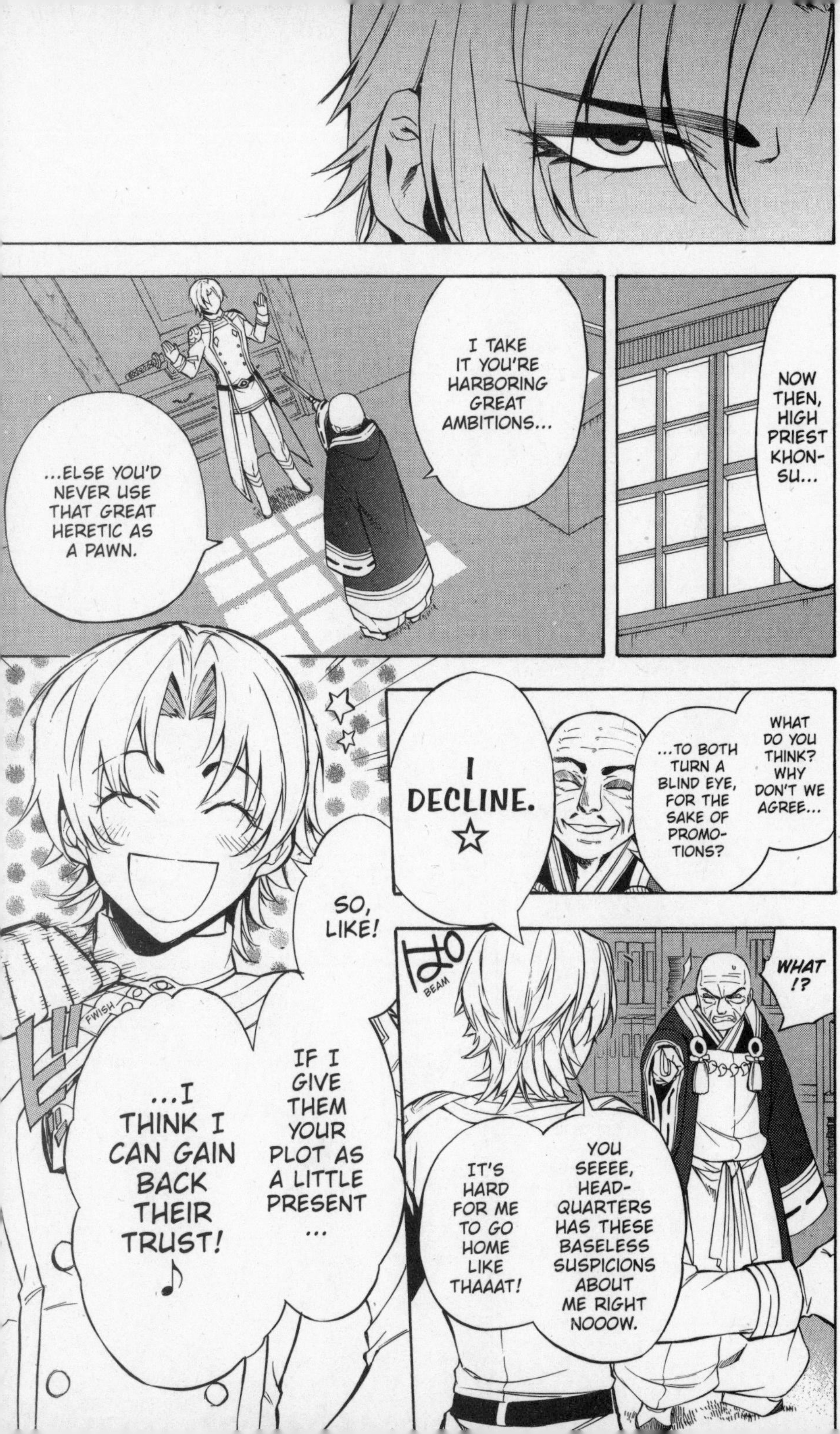
NOW THEN, HIGH PRIEST KHONSU...
I TAKE IT YOU'RE HARBORING GREAT AMBITIONS...
...ELSE YOU'D NEVER USE THAT GREAT HERETIC AS A PAWN.
WHAT DO YOU THINK? WHY DON'T WE AGREE...
...TO BOTH TURN A BLIND EYE, FOR THE SAKE OF PROMOTIONS?
I DECLINE. ☆
WHAT!?
BEAM
YOU SEEEE, HEADQUARTERS HAS THESE BASELESS SUSPICIONS ABOUT ME RIGHT NOOOW.
IT'S HARD FOR ME TO GO HOME LIKE THAAAT!
SO, LIKE!
FWISH
IF I GIVE THEM YOUR PLOT AS A LITTLE PRESENT...
...I THINK I CAN GAIN BACK THEIR TRUST! ♪

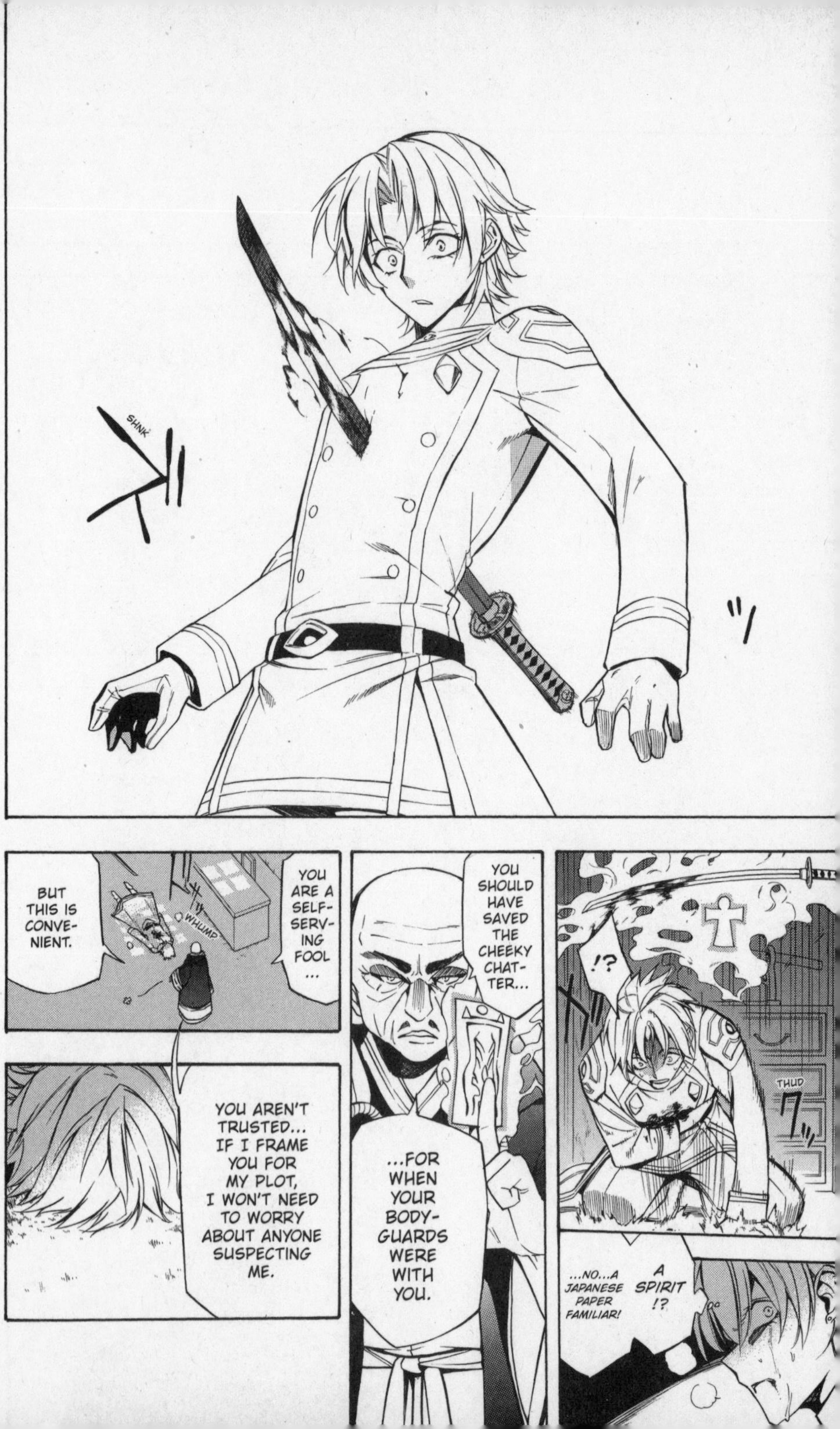
SHNK
!?
THUD
A SPIRIT !?
...NO...A JAPANESE PAPER FAMILIAR!
YOU SHOULD HAVE SAVED THE CHEEKY CHATTER...
...FOR WHEN YOUR BODY-GUARDS WERE WITH YOU.
YOU ARE A SELF-SERVING FOOL...
WHUMP
BUT THIS IS CONVENIENT.
YOU AREN'T TRUSTED... IF I FRAME YOU FOR MY PLOT, I WON'T NEED TO WORRY ABOUT ANYONE SUSPECTING ME.

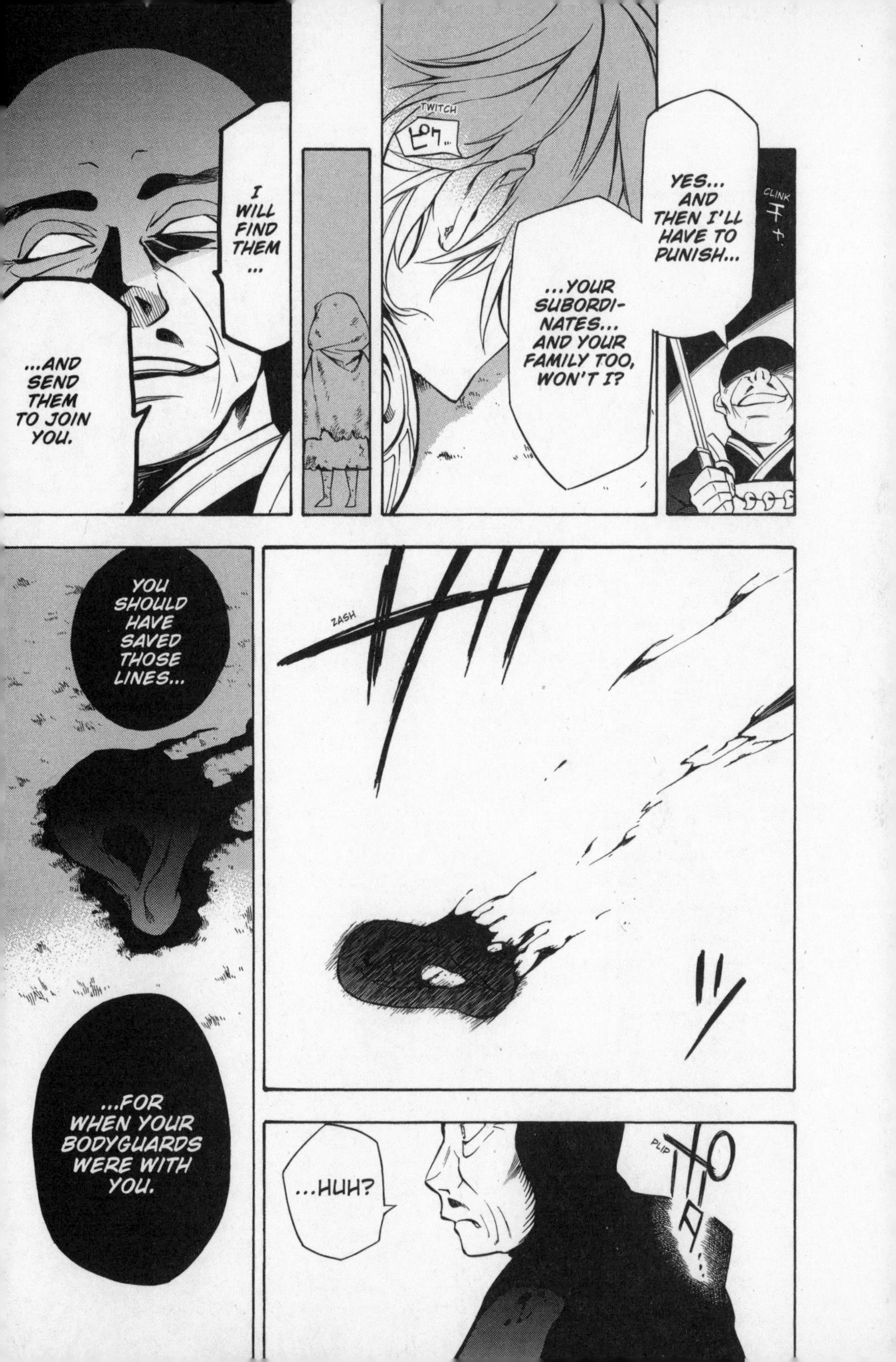
YES... AND THEN I'LL HAVE TO PUNISH...
CLINK
TWITCH
...YOUR SUBORDINATES... AND YOUR FAMILY TOO, WON'T I?
I WILL FIND THEM...
...AND SEND THEM TO JOIN YOU.
ZASH
...HUH?
PLIP
YOU SHOULD HAVE SAVED THOSE LINES...
...FOR WHEN YOUR BODYGUARDS WERE WITH YOU.

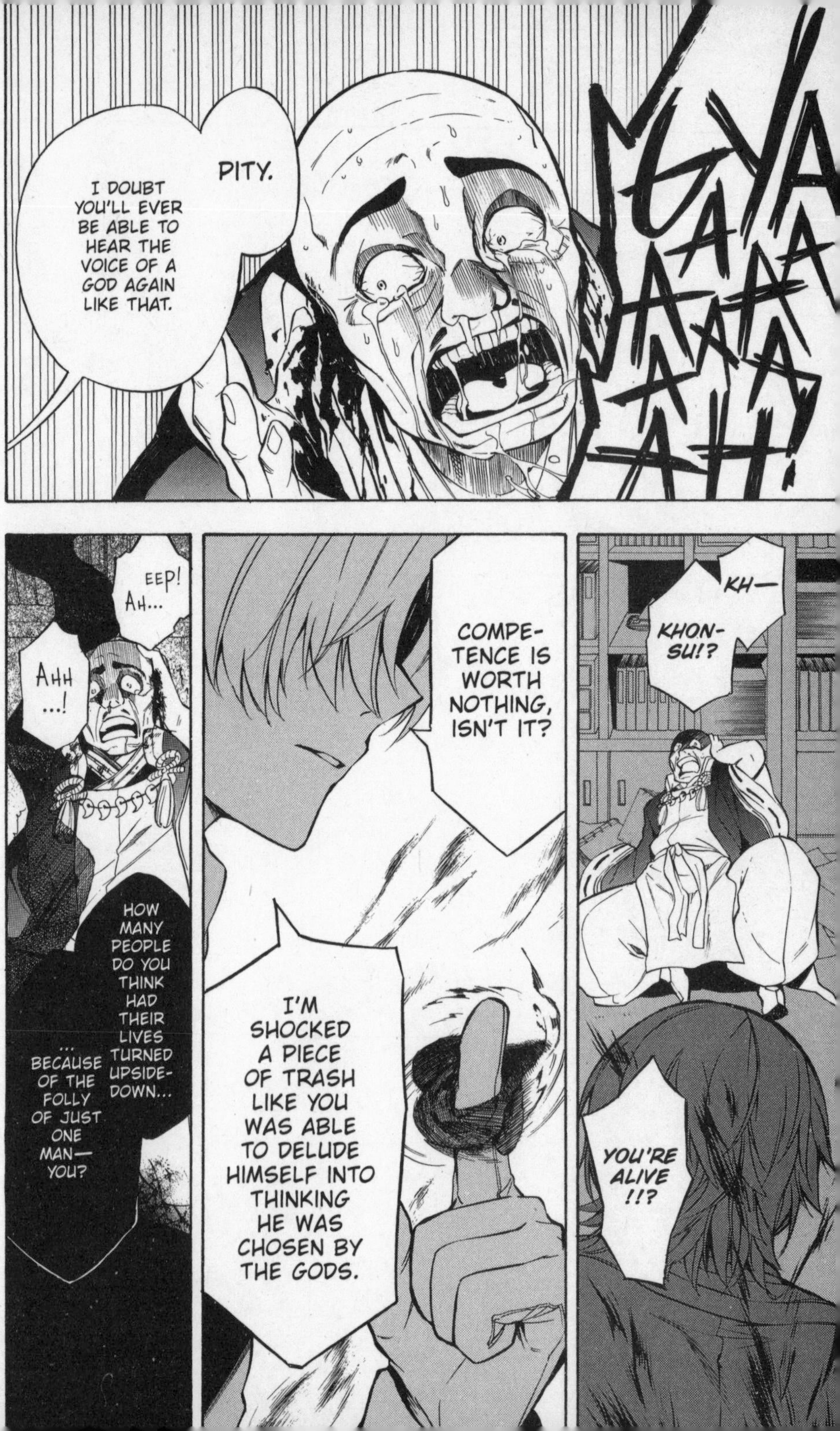
MGYAAAAAAAAAH!
PITY.
I DOUBT YOU'LL EVER BE ABLE TO HEAR THE VOICE OF A GOD AGAIN LIKE THAT.
KH— KHON-SU!?
YOU'RE ALIVE !!?
COMPE-TENCE IS WORTH NOTHING, ISN'T IT?
I'M SHOCKED A PIECE OF TRASH LIKE YOU WAS ABLE TO DELUDE HIMSELF INTO THINKING HE WAS CHOSEN BY THE GODS.
EEP! AH...
AHH ...!
HOW MANY PEOPLE DO YOU THINK HAD THEIR LIVES TURNED UPSIDE-DOWN...
...BECAUSE OF THE FOLLY OF JUST ONE MAN—YOU?

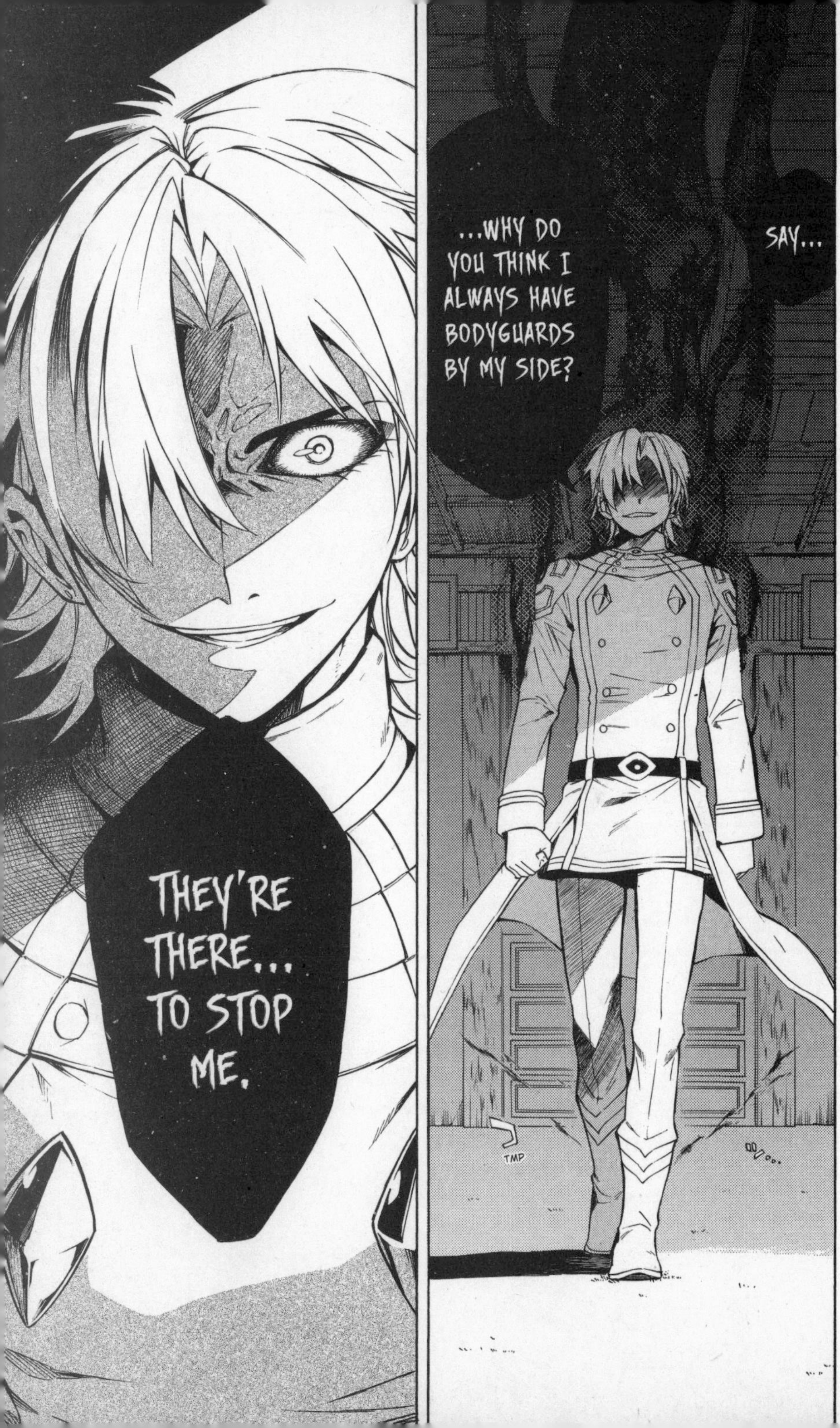
SAY...
...WHY DO YOU THINK I ALWAYS HAVE BODYGUARDS BY MY SIDE?
TMP
THEY'RE THERE... TO STOP ME.

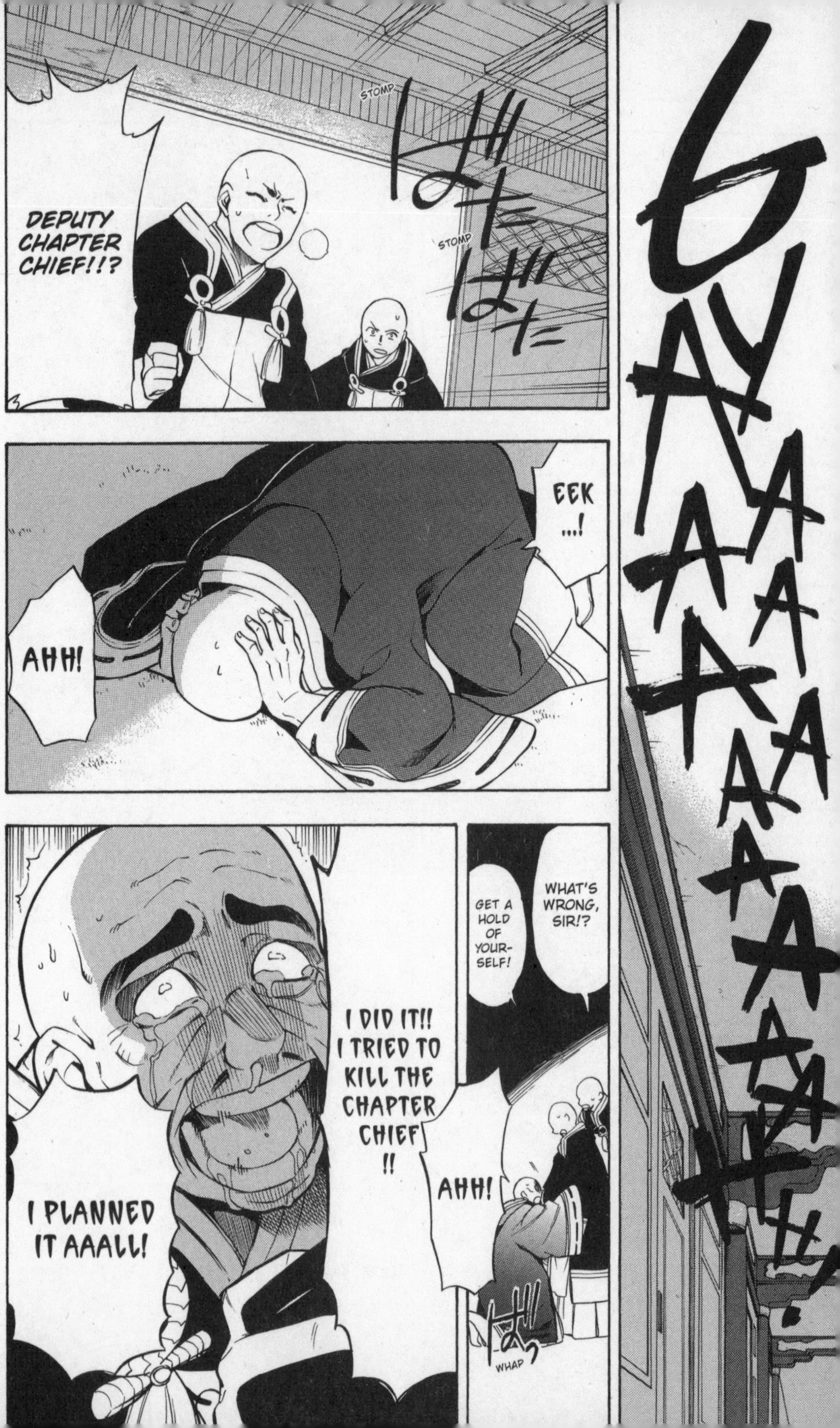
GYAAAAAAAAAAAAAAH!!
STOMP
ばた
STOMP
ばた
DEPUTY CHAPTER CHIEF!!?
EEK ...!
AHH!
WHAT'S WRONG, SIR!?
GET A HOLD OF YOURSELF!
AHH!
ばっ
WHAP
I DID IT!! I TRIED TO KILL THE CHAPTER CHIEF!!
I PLANNED IT AAALL!

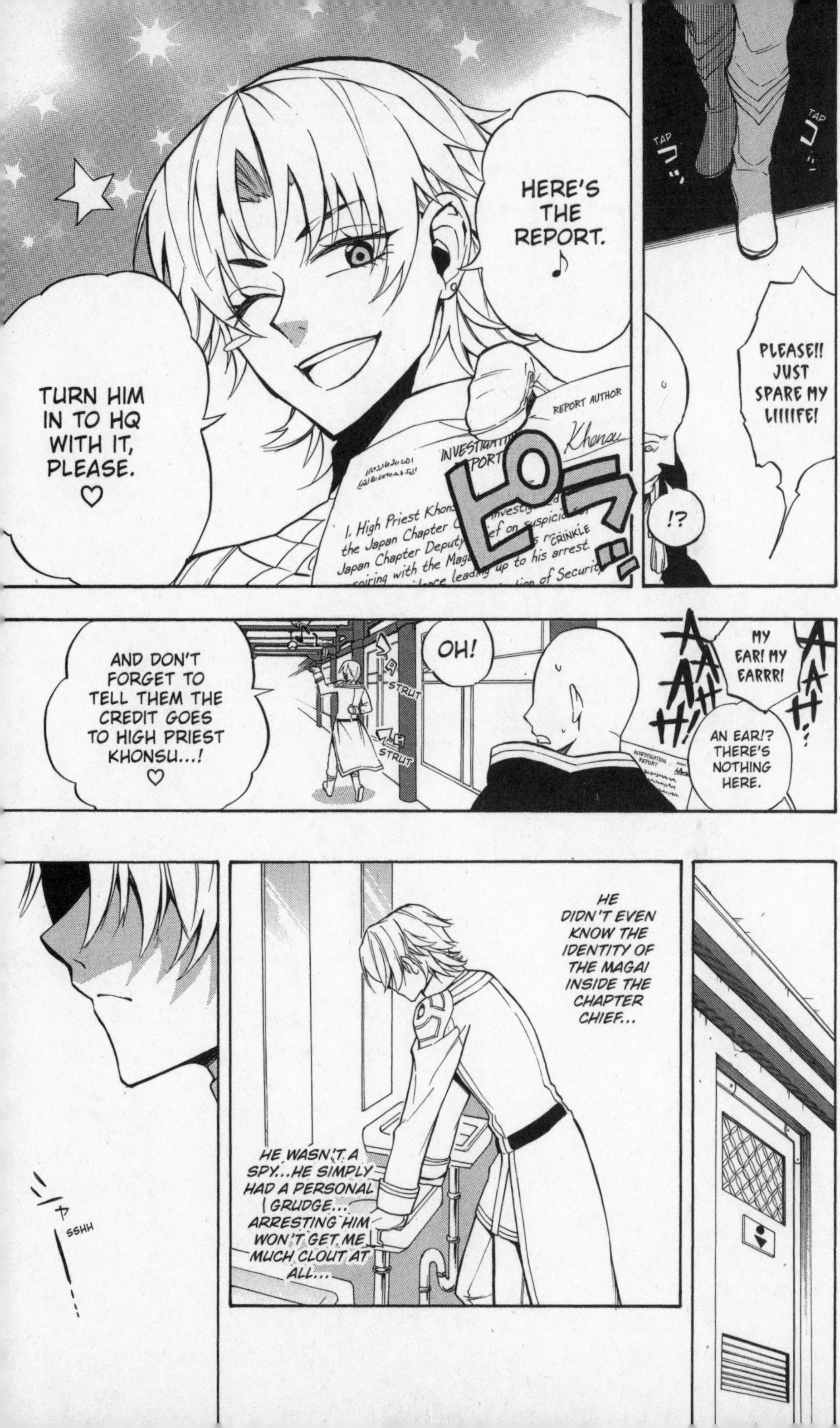
TAP
TAP
PLEASE!! JUST SPARE MY LIIIIFE!
!?
HERE'S THE REPORT. ♪
REPORT AUTHOR
Khonsu
INVESTIGATION REPORT
CRINKLE
TURN HIM IN TO HQ WITH IT, PLEASE. ♡
AAAH!
MY EAR! MY EARRR!
AN EAR!? THERE'S NOTHING HERE.
OH!
STRUT
STRUT
AND DON'T FORGET TO TELL THEM THE CREDIT GOES TO HIGH PRIEST KHONSU...! ♡
HE DIDN'T EVEN KNOW THE IDENTITY OF THE MAGAI INSIDE THE CHAPTER CHIEF...
HE WASN'T A SPY...HE SIMPLY HAD A PERSONAL GRUDGE... ARRESTING HIM WON'T GET ME MUCH CLOUT AT ALL...
SSHH

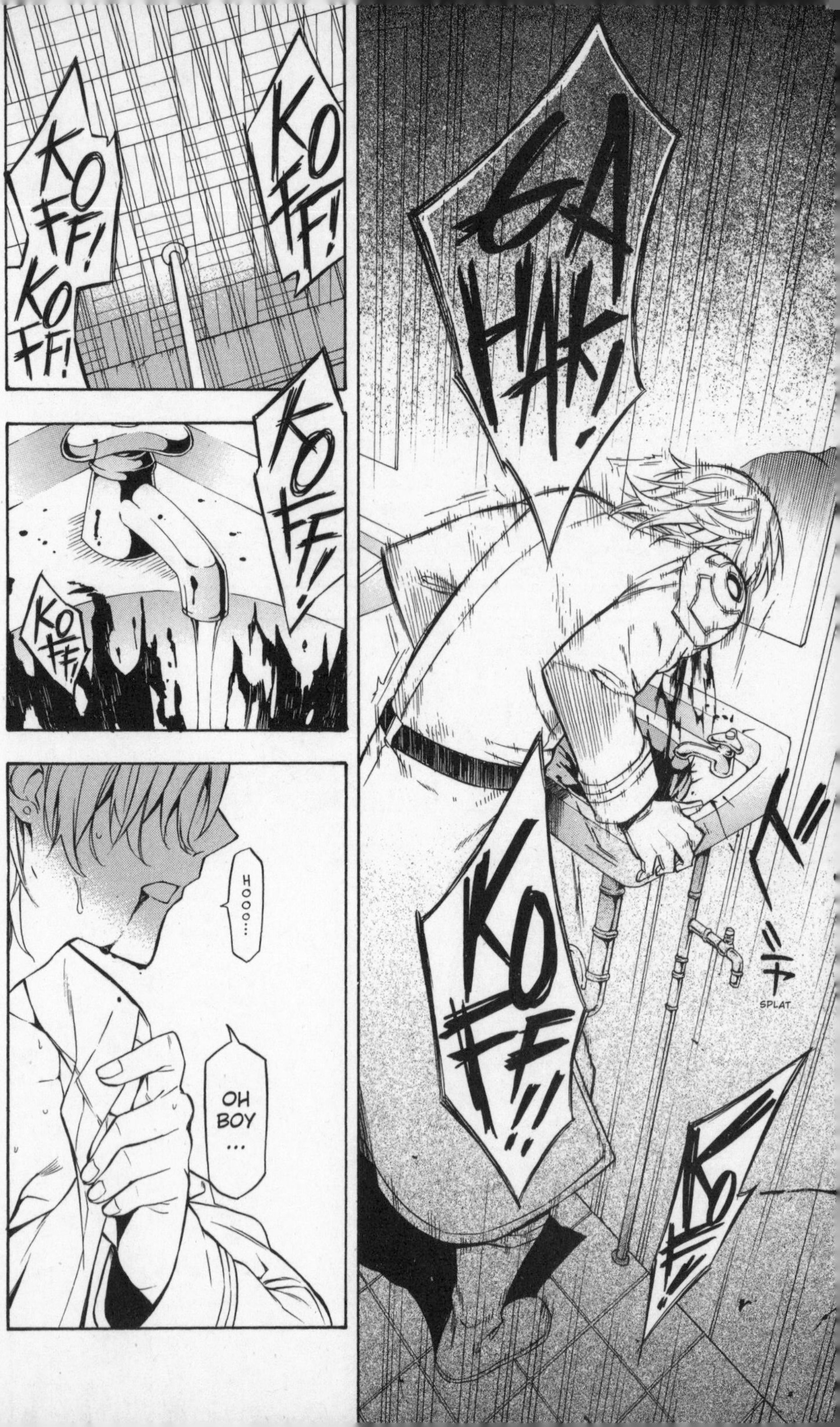
GAHAK!
KOFF!!
KOFF!
SPLAT
KOFF!
KOFF! KOFF!
KOFF!!
KOFF
HOOO...
OH BOY...

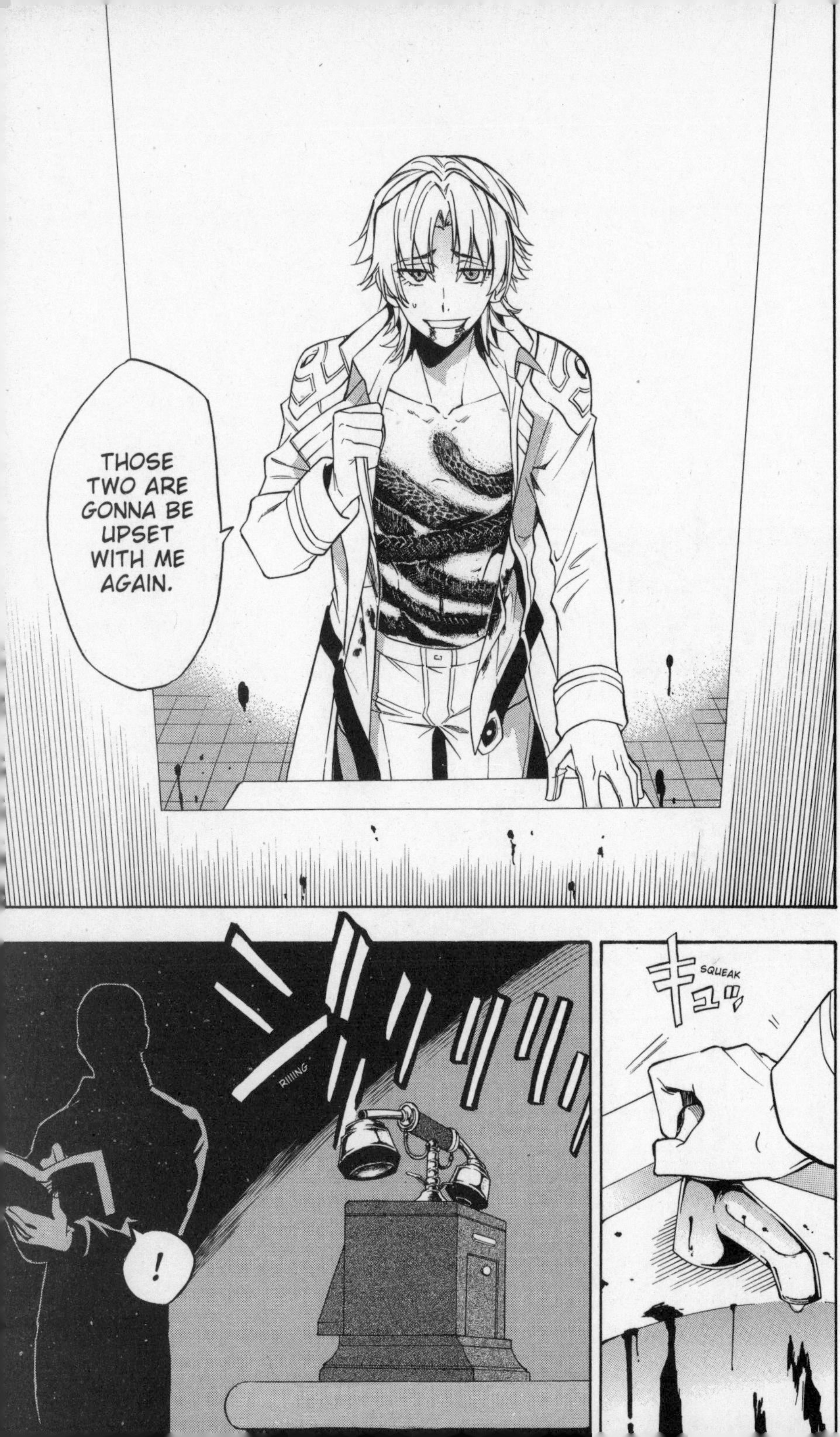
THOSE TWO ARE GONNA BE UPSET WITH ME AGAIN.
SQUEAK
RIIIING
!

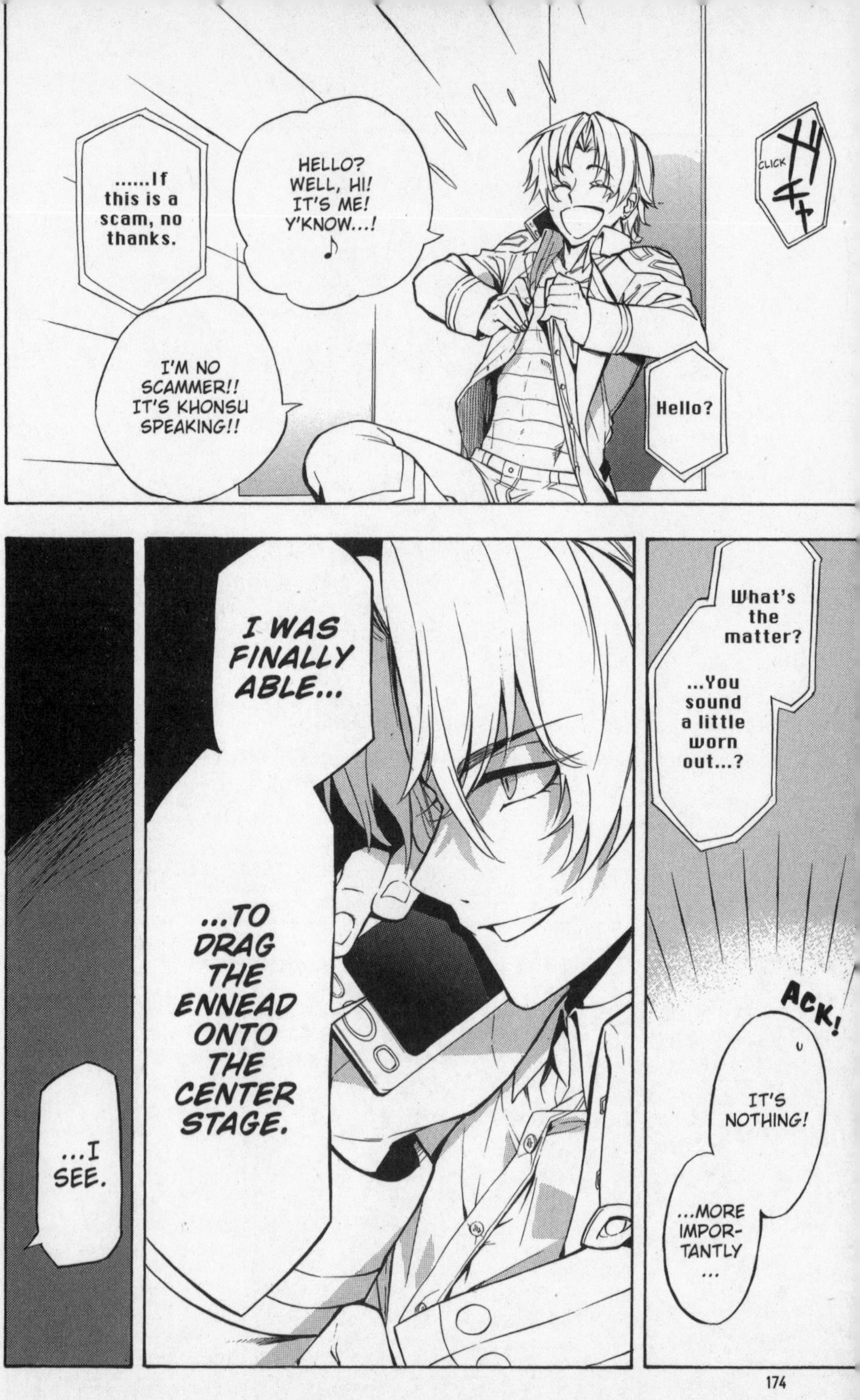
CLICK
Hello?
HELLO? WELL, HI! IT'S ME! Y'KNOW...! ♪
......If this is a scam, no thanks.
I'M NO SCAMMER!! IT'S KHONSU SPEAKING!!
What's the matter?
...You sound a little worn out...?
ACK!
IT'S NOTHING!
...MORE IMPORTANTLY...
I WAS FINALLY ABLE...
...TO DRAG THE ENNEAD ONTO THE CENTER STAGE.
...I SEE.

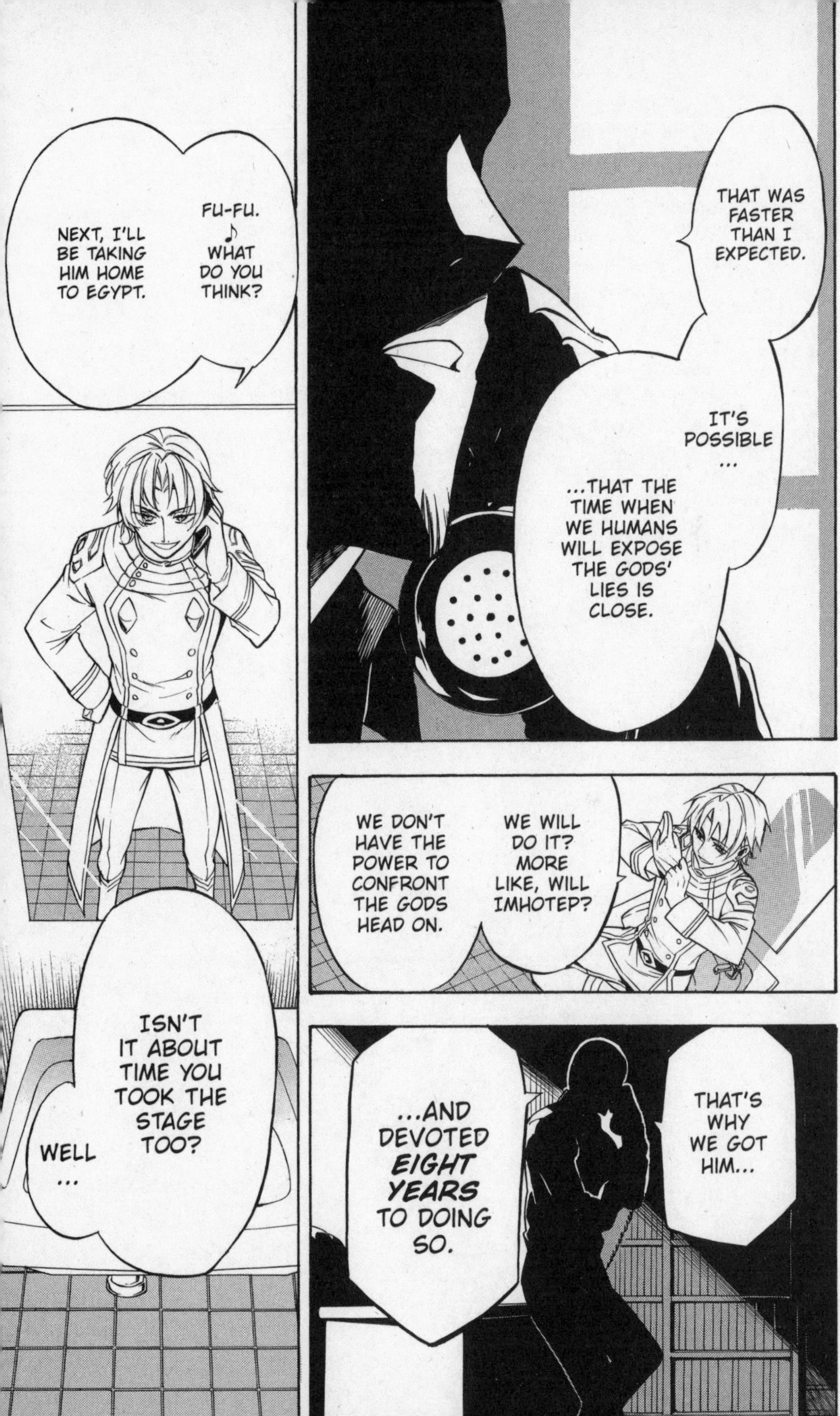
THAT WAS FASTER THAN I EXPECTED.
IT'S POSSIBLE...
...THAT THE TIME WHEN WE HUMANS WILL EXPOSE THE GODS' LIES IS CLOSE.
WE WILL DO IT? MORE LIKE, WILL IMHOTEP?
WE DON'T HAVE THE POWER TO CONFRONT THE GODS HEAD ON.
THAT'S WHY WE GOT HIM...
...AND DEVOTED EIGHT YEARS TO DOING SO.
FU-FU. ♪ WHAT DO YOU THINK?
NEXT, I'LL BE TAKING HIM HOME TO EGYPT.
ISN'T IT ABOUT TIME YOU TOOK THE STAGE TOO?
WELL...

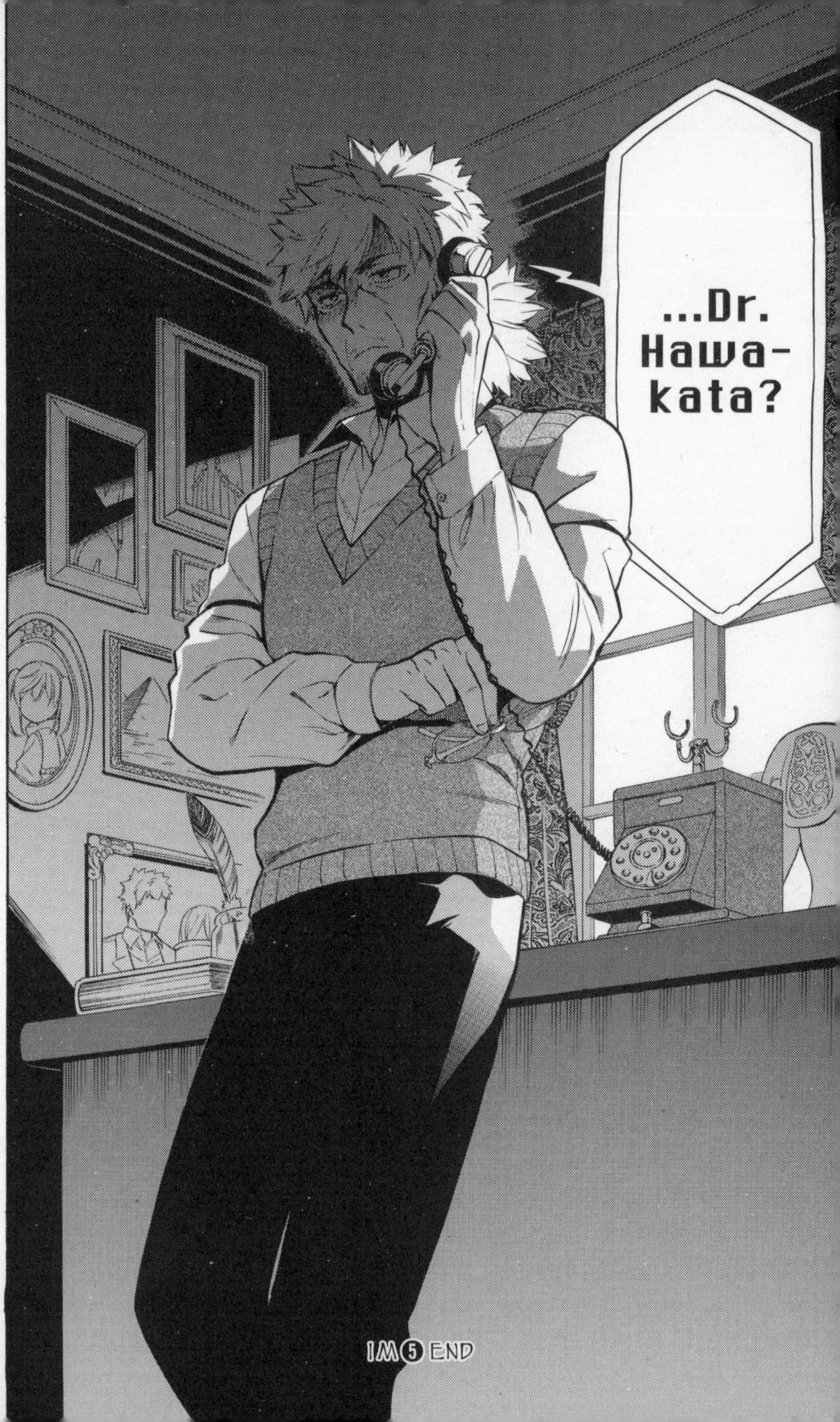
...Dr. Hawa-kata?
IM 5 END

EGYPTIAN MYTHOLOGY AS TOLD VIA PARODY:
"SETH'S WEAKPOINT"

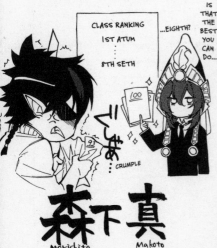

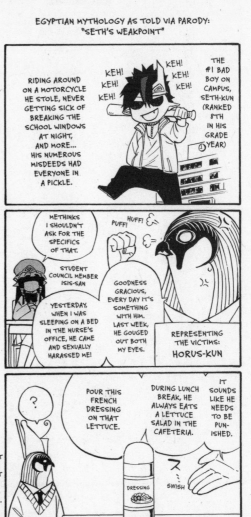

THE #1 BAD BOY ON CAMPUS, SETH-KUN (RANKED 8TH IN HIS GRADE YEAR)
KEH! KEH! KEH!
KEH! KEH! KEH!
RIDING AROUND ON A MOTORCYCLE HE STOLE, NEVER GETTING SICK OF BREAKING THE SCHOOL WINDOWS AT NIGHT, AND MORE... HIS NUMEROUS MISDEEDS HAD EVERYONE IN A PICKLE.
REPRESENTING THE VICTIMS: HORUS-KUN
HUFF!
PUFF!
GOODNESS GRACIOUS, EVERY DAY IT'S SOMETHING WITH HIM. LAST WEEK, HE GOUGED OUT BOTH MY EYES.
YESTERDAY, WHEN I WAS SLEEPING ON A BED IN THE NURSE'S OFFICE, HE CAME AND SEXUALLY HARASSED ME!
STUDENT COUNCIL MEMBER ISIS-SAN
METHINKS I SHOULDN'T ASK FOR THE SPECIFICS OF THAT.
IT SOUNDS LIKE HE NEEDS TO BE PUN-ISHED.
DURING LUNCH BREAK, HE ALWAYS EATS A LETTUCE SALAD IN THE CAFETERIA.
POUR THIS FRENCH DRESSING ON THAT LETTUCE.
SWISH
DRESSING
?
THEN CAME LUNCH...
AW YEAH, LUNCH TIME! ♪ HEY, LUNCH LADY, I'LL HAVE MY USUAL—
GYAAAAAAAAAAHHH!
SETH-KUN'S TRAUMA WAS TRIGGERED, AND HE MISSED SCHOOL FOR A WEEK.
WHAT KIND OF TRAUMA COULD YOU POSSIBLY GET FROM SALAD DRESSING ...?
WHAT'S GOIN' ON?

EXPLANATION

THE GODS SETH AND HORUS FOUGHT OVER THE THRONE. SETH MESSED WITH HORUS MANY TIMES, BUT THROUGH A PLAN OF THE GODDESS ISIS, HORUS'S SEED (REALLY, GUYS...?) WAS MIXED INTO SETH'S FAVORITE FOOD, LETTUCE, AND WHEN HE ATE IT WITHOUT REALIZING IT, HE WAS HUMILIATED.

Special Thanks

- Arisa Yukimiya
- Ui Kizuki
- Mai Kurozuki

SPECIAL HELP FROM:

- You Omura-sensei
- Makoto Kisaragi-san
- Luria-san
- Marimo Kanae-san
- Shinome-san

My editor,
Yuuichi Shimomura-sama

IS THAT THE BEST YOU CAN DO...
...EIGHTH?
CLASS RANKING
1ST ATUM
8TH SETH
100
93
CRUMPLE

森下真
Morishita Makoto

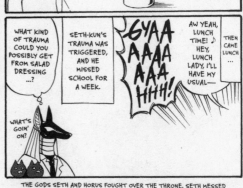

TRUE FEELINGS

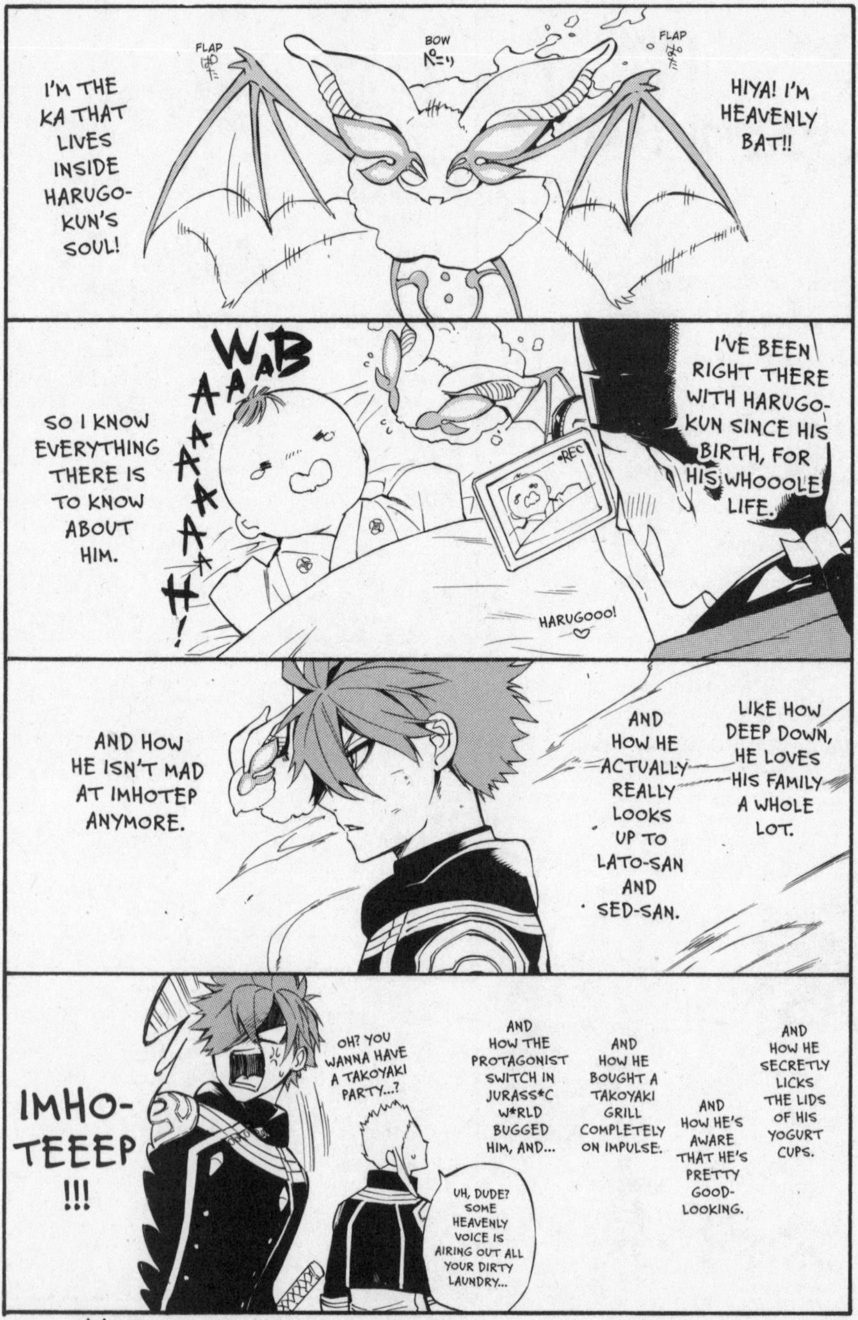

FLAP
HIYA! I'M HEAVENLY BAT!!
BOW
FLAP
I'M THE KA THAT LIVES INSIDE HARUGO-KUN'S SOUL!
I'VE BEEN RIGHT THERE WITH HARUGO-KUN SINCE HIS BIRTH, FOR HIS WHOOOLE LIFE.
•REC
WAAB
AAAAAAAH!
HARUGOOO!
SO I KNOW EVERYTHING THERE IS TO KNOW ABOUT HIM.
LIKE HOW DEEP DOWN, HE LOVES HIS FAMILY A WHOLE LOT.
AND HOW HE ACTUALLY REALLY LOOKS UP TO LATO-SAN AND SED-SAN.
AND HOW HE ISN'T MAD AT IMHOTEP ANYMORE.
AND HOW HE SECRETLY LICKS THE LIDS OF HIS YOGURT CUPS.
AND HOW HE'S AWARE THAT HE'S PRETTY GOOD-LOOKING.
AND HOW HE BOUGHT A TAKOYAKI GRILL COMPLETELY ON IMPULSE.
AND HOW THE PROTAGONIST SWITCH IN JURASS*C W*RLD BUGGED HIM, AND...
OH? YOU WANNA HAVE A TAKOYAKI PARTY...?
UH, DUDE? SOME HEAVENLY VOICE IS AIRING OUT ALL YOUR DIRTY LAUNDRY...
IMHO-TEEEP!!!

YOU MUST CEASE BLAMING ME FOR EVERYTHING.

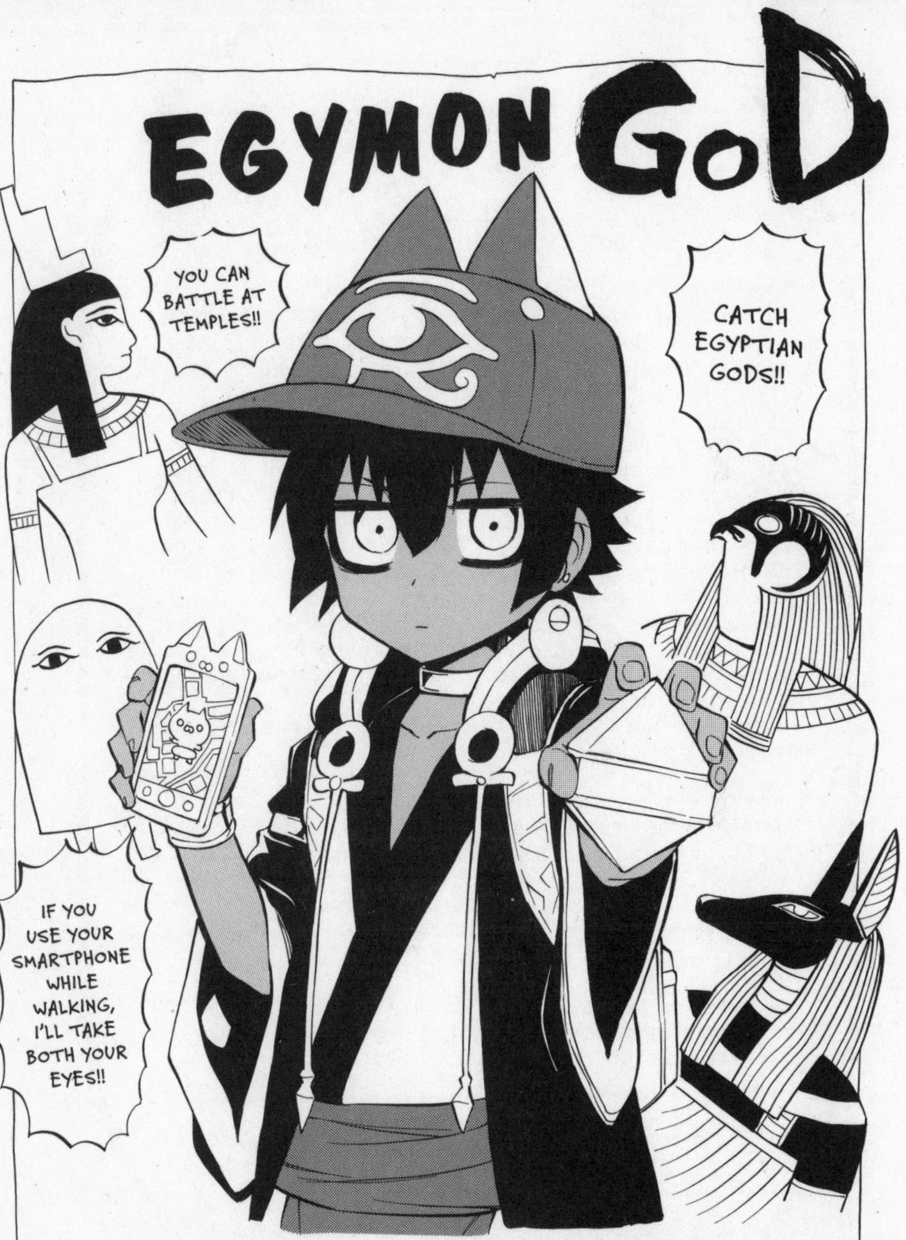
EGYMON GOD
YOU CAN BATTLE AT TEMPLES!!
CATCH EGYPTIAN GODS!!
IF YOU USE YOUR SMARTPHONE WHILE WALKING, I'LL TAKE BOTH YOUR EYES!!
COMING IN THE SUMMER OF 2016 BC!

I AM SO SORRY.

TRANSLATION NOTES

Common Honorifics

no honorific: Indicates familiarity or closeness; if used without permission or reason, addressing someone in this manner would constitute an insult.

-*san*: The Japanese equivalent of Mr./Mrs./Miss. If a situation calls for politeness, this is the fail-safe honorific.

-*sama*: Conveys great respect; may also indicate the social status of the speaker is lower than that of the addressee.

-*kun*: Used most often when referring to boys, this honorific indicates affection or familiarity. Occasionally used by older men among their peers, but it may also be used by anyone referring to a person of lower standing.

-*chan*: An affectionate honorific indicating familiarity used mostly in reference to girls; also used in reference to cute persons or animals of either gender.

-*sensei*: A respectful term for teachers, artists, or high-level professionals.

-*oniisan*, *nii-san*, *aniki*, etc.: A term of endearment meaning "big brother" that may be more widely used to address any young man who is like a brother, regardless of whether he is related or not.

-*oneesan*, *nee-san*, *aneki*, etc.: The female counterpart of the above, nee-san means "big sister."

Page 6

Moe (pronounced "mow-ey" with two syllables) refers to the feeling of affection and protectiveness one feels toward something cute, making "little sister *moe*" the experience of feeling like a protective big brother. While *moe* can be platonic, it is often mixed with attraction, which is why Lato and Inaba are..."not pleased" upon hearing Khonsu's opinion.

Page 166

A **Japanese paper familiar** is a spirit known as a *shikigami*. These spirits are kept in small objects, typically amulets or paper talismans, and can be summoned to do the bidding of *onmyoji*, who are traditional Japanese spiritualists.

Great Priest Imhotep

Akame ga KILL! ZERO

FULL SERIES AVAILABLE NOW!

THEY BELIEVED THAT EVERY TIME THEY TOOK A LIFE, THEY BROUGHT HAPPINESS TO ANOTHER...

Before becoming Night Raid's deadliest ally, Akame was a young girl bought by the Empire and raised as an assassin whose sole purpose was to slaughter everything in her path. Because that's what makes people happy... right? Discover Akame's shocking past in *Akame ga KILL! Zero*, the prequel to the hit series *Akame ga KILL!*

Yen Press

For more information, visit www.yenpress.com

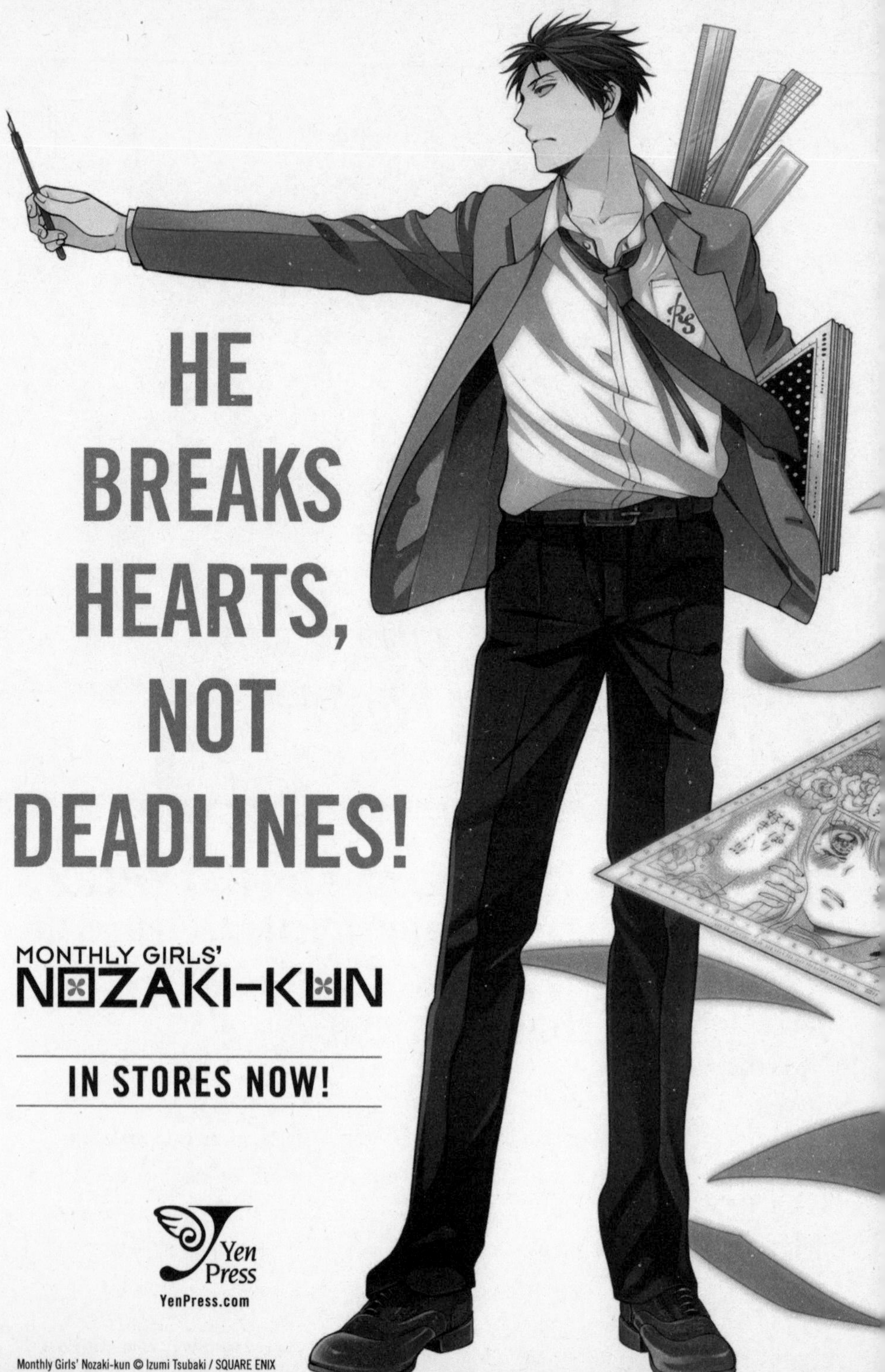
HE BREAKS HEARTS, NOT DEADLINES!
MONTHLY GIRLS' NOZAKI-KUN
IN STORES NOW!
Yen Press
YenPress.com
Monthly Girls' Nozaki-kun © Izumi Tsubaki / SQUARE ENIX

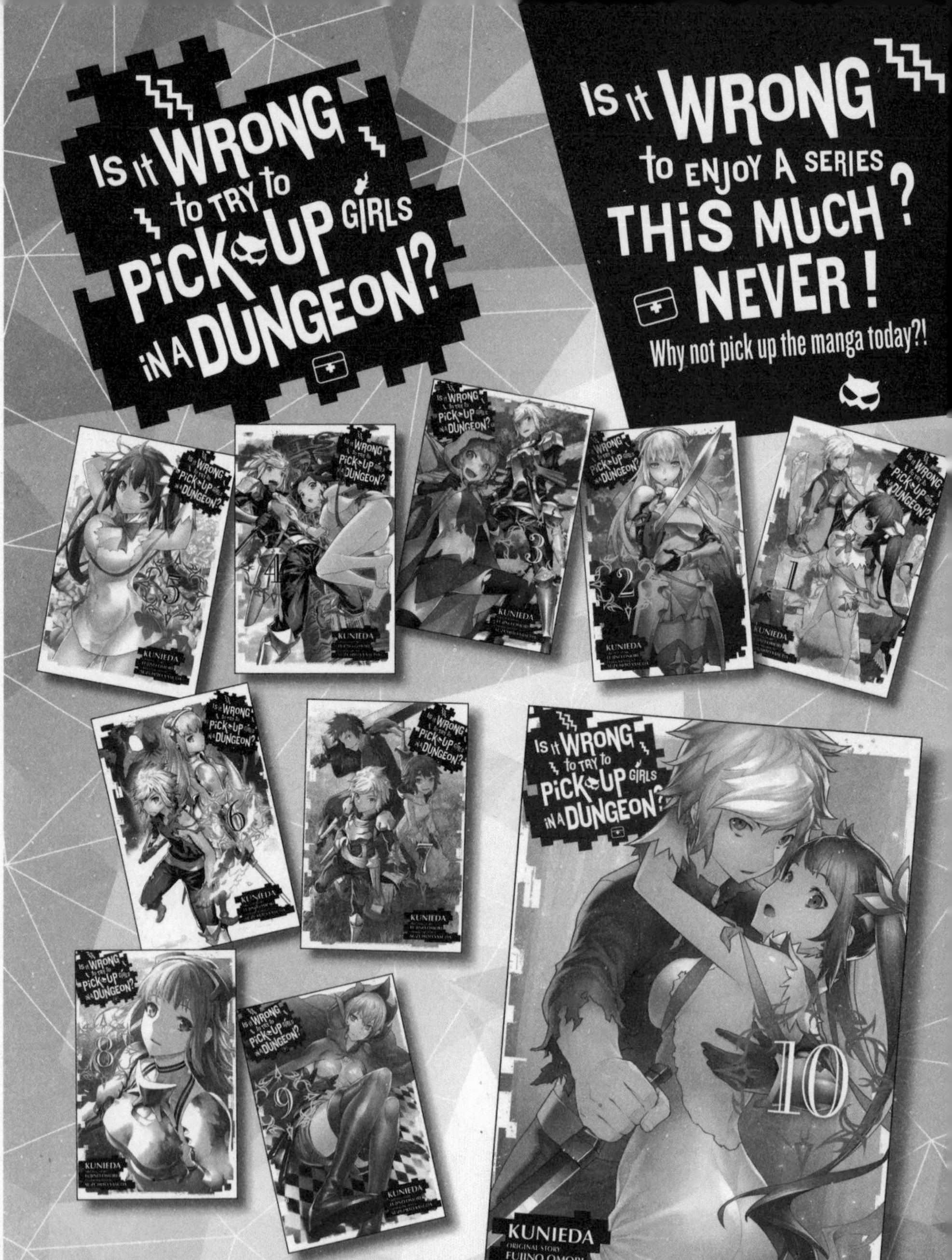

Is it WRONG to try to Pick-Up Girls in a Dungeon?
Is it WRONG to enjoy a series THIS MUCH? NEVER!
Why not pick up the manga today?!
10
KUNIEDA
ORIGINAL STORY
FUJINO OMORI
CHARACTER DESIGN
SUZUHITO YASUDA
IN STORES NOW!

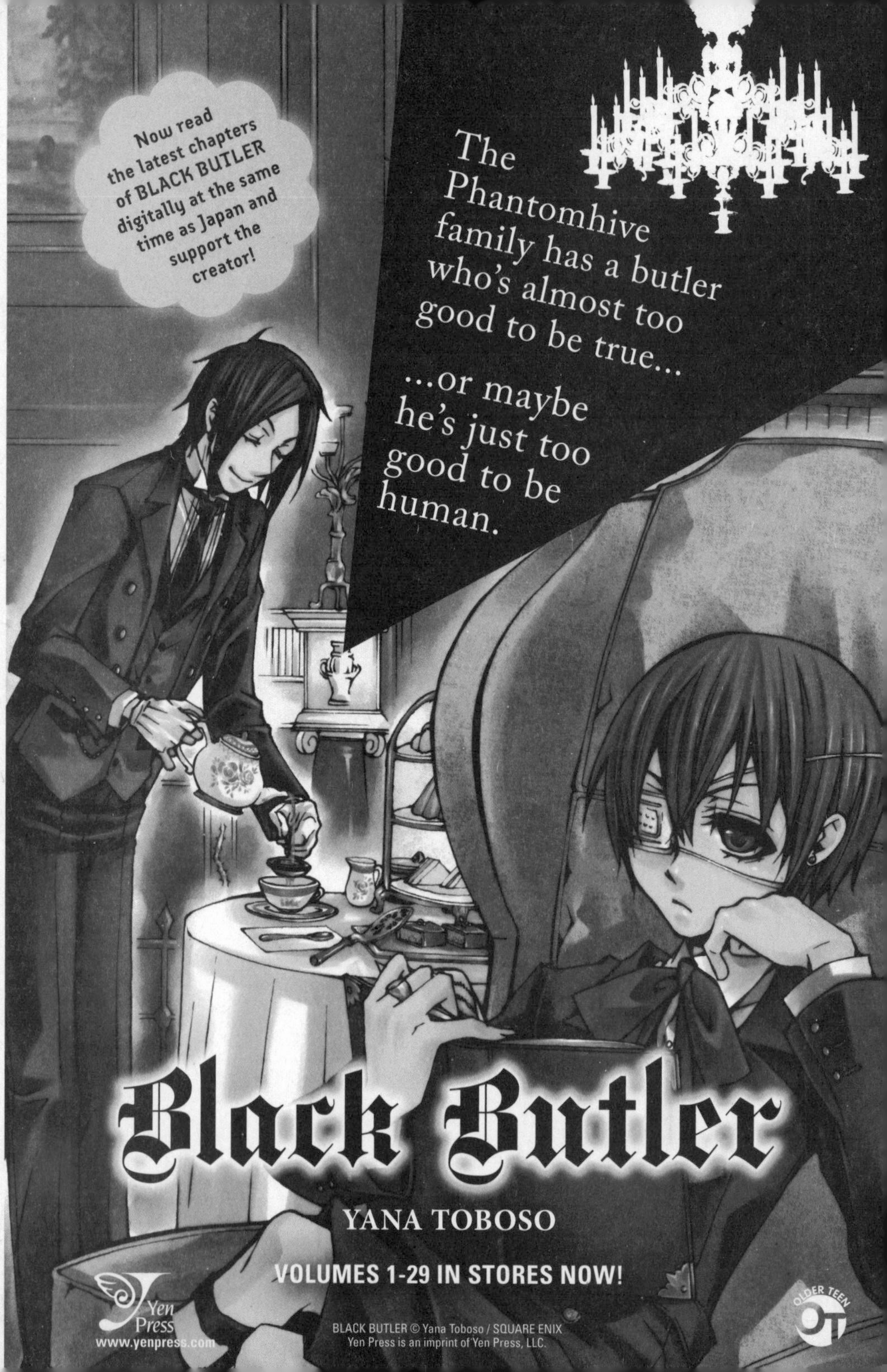
Now read the latest chapters of BLACK BUTLER digitally at the same time as Japan and support the creator!
The Phantomhive family has a butler who's almost too good to be true...
...or maybe he's just too good to be human.
Black Butler
YANA TOBOSO
VOLUMES 1-29 IN STORES NOW!
Yen Press
www.yenpress.com
BLACK BUTLER © Yana Toboso / SQUARE ENIX
Yen Press is an imprint of Yen Press, LLC.
OLDER TEEN
OT

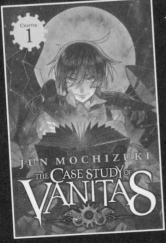

Great Priest Imhotep 5

by MAKOTO MORISHITA

Translation: Amanda Haley
Lettering: Rochelle Gancio

IM Vol. 5 ©2016 Makoto Morishita/SQUARE ENIX CO., LTD.
First published in Japan in 2016 by SQUARE ENIX CO., LTD. English translation rights
arranged with SQUARE ENIX CO., LTD. and Yen Press, LLC through Tuttle-Mori Agency, Inc.,
Tokyo.

English translation ©2018 by SQUARE ENIX CO., LTD.

Yen Press
150 West 30th Street, 19th Floor
New York, NY 10001

Visit us at yenpress.com ⚑ facebook.com/yenpress ⚑
twitter.com/yenpress ⚑ yenpress.tumblr.com ⚑
instagram.com/yenpress

First Yen Press Print Edition: October 2020
Originally published as an ebook in February 2018 by Yen Press.

Yen Press is an imprint of Yen Press, LLC.
The Yen Press name and logo are trademarks of Yen Press, LLC.

Library of Congress Control Number: 2019953326

ISBN: 978-1-9753-1146-9 (paperback)

10 9 8 7 6 5 4 3 2 1

WOR

Printed in the United States of America